FURNITURE RESTORATION

FURNITURE RESTORATION

STEP-BY-STEP TIPS *and* TECHNIQUES *for* PROFESSIONAL RESULTS

INA BROSSEAU MARX & ALLEN MARX

WATSON-GUPTILL PUBLICATIONS | NEW YORK

Senior Acquisitions Editor: Joy Aquilino
Development Editor: Christine Timmons
Editor: John A. Foster
Designer: Christopher Cannon, Eric Baker Design Associates
Production Manager: Alyn Evans

First published in 2007 by
Watson-Guptill Publications,
Nielsen Business Media, a division of The Nielsen Company
770 Broadway, New York, NY 10003
www.watsonguptill.com

Library of Congress Cataloging-in-Publication Data

Marx, Allen, 1922-
Marx, Ina Brosseau, 1929-
Furniture restoration : step-by-step techniques and tips for professional results / Allen Marx and Ina B. Marx.
p. cm.
ISBN-13: 978-0-8230-2070-6
ISBN-10: 0-8230-2070-3
1. Furniture—Repairing. 2. Furniture finishing. 3. Color decoration and ornament. 4. Gilding. I. Marx, Ina Brosseau, 1929- II. Title.
TT199.M375 2007
684.1'044—dc22

2006035694

Printed in Singapore

First printing, 2007
1 2 3 4 5 6 7 / 13 12 11 10 09 08 07

WE DEDICATE THIS BOOK TO Mitchell Jay Marx, our eldest son, whose infinite patience and unlimited accessibility were invaluable during the electronic preparation of this book

WE GRATEFULLY ACKNOWLEDGE those who spent countless hours in bringing this book to fruition:

Joy Aquilino, Senior Acquisitions Editor, who believed in our philosophy of restoration as shown in the courses we honed during our years of teaching, which she then expanded with patience, guidance, and an unerring eye.

Christine Timmons, Development Editor, who helped shape the book even further as a teaching tool by coming up with fresh perspectives during stimulating work sessions. John Foster, Editor, who meticulously and patiently tied all the various loose ends together in this book.

OUR GRATITUDE GOES ALSO TO THE FOLLOWING who have given graciously of their expertise: Michael W. Kramer, The Gilders Studio, for his knowledge of the chemistry of contemporary materials; Lark E. Mason, iGavel, Inc., for vetting the Asian lacquer objects we restored; Peter H. Miller, PHMiller Gallery, for his information and demonstrations of water gilding; Matthew J. Mosca, Artifects, Ltd., for adding to our knowledge of historic paint finishes; and Jonathan A. Preece, MPhil, for providing additional photographic resources.

LESS SPECIFIC, BUT JUST AS TANGIBLE, is the appreciation we have for: Students at The Finishing School, the Savannah College of Art and Design's Historic Preservation Department, and numerous other venues, who brought in objects with challenging problems that we could solve and photograph during restoration. Craftsmen of long ago, who, unknowingly, fostered our kinship with them since no one besides ourselves had ever seen their often-unusual constructions and tool marks we exposed briefly during restoration.

AND, LASTLY, WE WOULD BE REMISS if we didn't acknowledge the respect and admiration we gained for each other and for Robert Marx, our third son, during the years we worked and taught together, particularly when working with seemingly impossible-to-solve restoration problems. For three people with such different thought processes and traits to work together successfully was an unforgettable experience. The never-to-be-forgotten journey also included our other sons, Mitchell, Russell, and Eric, who gave of themselves graciously whenever they were needed.

PHOTOGRAPHIC CREDITS: All photographs, except those mentioned, were taken by Ina Brosseau Marx.

Contents

About Our Book

WE HAVE WRITTEN THIS BOOK for you whether you are:

→ would-be restorers who would like to know how to restore
→ amateur restorers who already restore
→ professional restorers who would like to augment their restoration skills
→ non-craftsmen who collect, curate, or appraise objects, and would like to guide restorers along the way.

No book can describe every type of damage that occurs on objects. Our goals are to acquaint you with problems we encountered and share with you the procedures and the guiding principle we used to solve them—which is whatever two hands have put together, your two hands can try to fix.

We will show you, on utilitarian pieces as well as on "grand" ones, how to:

→ repair broken elements and joints
→ renew damaged and missing edges
→ deal with beetle damage and warping
→ replace dimensional elements using molds and casts
→ restore surfaces of brownwood, painting, gilding, Asian lacquer, and veneers
→ discover, reconstruct, and inpaint damaged and missing design schemes
→ improve and care for the finishes on your surfaces.

The photographs of the problems we found—and the ways in which we solved them—are shown by the in-process photographs that we took while we were in the midst of restoring and during our classes at The Finishing School, Savannah College of Art and Design, and other venues.

Photographing to document a specific procedure during a restoration doesn't always allow for the best quality of lighting, background, or even focus. Although our documentation was valuable for teaching and lecturing, we never thought that a portion of our photographs would appear in a book. Bear in mind, though, that without these photographs—best quality or not—there would be no book.

This book is a joint venture between you and us. We've provided written and visual information for you as clearly as we can so that you may approach restoration with faith in your ability to use your head as well as your hands. The book is a "thinking" book as well as a "doing" book. We wish a book like this had been available to us during our career in restoration.

We hope this book will give you inspiration and confidence to undertake restorations of many different types of objects and, by so doing, join those of us who are, as Studs Terkel would say, "ordinary people doing extraordinary things."

INA BROSSEAU MARX & ALLEN MARX

Introduction

AS SOON AS ANY OBJECT IS MADE, natural and man-made elements such as light, moisture, pollution, and careless handling begin the process of deterioration. For hundreds of years, the fine arts and decorative arts, particularly furniture and objects made of wood, were cared and repaired by people referred to as restorers. But often, these restorers were limited in their knowledge and by the materials available to them at the time; in addition, they might had been required to place the desires of the object's owner over the best preservation techniques. This often resulted in overpainted surfaces and discarded portions of the object's original framework.

In the early twentieth century, museums began to use scientific methods and technology to care for and preserve their fine-art collections, and with this development the new field of art conservation was born. In time, the same technical approach was used for furniture and decorative arts, and now graduate programs in conservation for the fine and decorative arts exist at many institutions. These programs provide training in aesthetics, art history, studio arts, technology, and chemistry (to determine which materials will best restore an object).

In the early 1970s, an association of concerned conservators formed The American Institute for Conservation of Historic & Artistic Works (AIC) and put forth A Code of Ethics concerning the treatment of objects. Principles include:

→ Respect an object's integrity, meaning preserve as much as possible of its original "fabric," replacing missing areas and elements only where necessary. This was formulated in response to damage done to objects by restorers in past centuries.

→ Use tested materials for restoration that will slow the deterioration process (one of the goals of restoration) while doing no further damage. Conservators are aware that these new materials will undergo change over time—but at a rate that differs from that of the object's original materials.

→ Abide by the principal of retreatability. This means that since technology is constantly improving and restoration techniques that currently seem modern will certainly change in the future, an object should be restored in a way that can easily be reversed at a later date, if necessary. Retreating has a further implication of refraining from overtreating an object as well.

→ Stay current with the latest treatment methods and materials. As mentioned above, the field of conservation of fine and decorative objects is continually evolving, and new materials, technology, and innovative processes will develop as the field advances.

→ Document with photographs and written reports, the object's condition before treatment (termed condition before treatment, or CBT), during treatment (CDT), and after treatment (CAT).

We hope this book, which documents many of our restorations during our thirty-year career, will encourage you to realize that there are many processes available that will prolong the life of your furniture and objects. This is especially important in these days of heightened interest in antiques, since there are far more objects that need attention than there are conservators to treat them. You may even get the pleasure of seeing several of your restorations go up for auction, as we did.

For those of you beginning a new journey into the world of restoration, remember that the tools and techniques that may seem utterly strange to you now were just as unfamiliar at the outset to restorers before you, and they'll soon be a familiar part of your restoration world. For experienced restorers, we hope this book will provide you with renewed enthusiasm and perspectives for your work. And finally, for collectors, curators, appraisers, and all those involved in the decorative arts, we hope these pages will offer you new and exciting ways to relate to the objects in your world. ❧

DEFINING THE TERMS

The three terms most often used when discussing the care of furniture are conservator, restorer, and refinisher. Unfortunately, there are no exact definitions of conservator and restorer, because their roles and treatment procedures often overlap. The role of the refinisher is a bit more clearly defined, however. Below is a quick guide to help you navigate among the terms:

Conservators and restorers share many of the goals of stabilizing the condition of objects and preventing further deterioration. Both may use the same methods and materials, and follow the AIC principles concerning the restoration of objects. They may specialize in one or more types of objects and treatments, such as dealing with gilded frames, which entails structural and surface repair as well as gilding. Knowledge and experience are the important factors in each of these two categories of professionals, most of whom strive to continually improve their skills and expertise.

Refinishers rejuvenate existing surface finishes on wood, or apply new finishes after removing the damaged ones. They work mostly on wood surfaces that at one time had clear finishes without any opaque coating, such as paint, Asian lacquer, gesso, or gilding. They usually do not repair the structure on objects.

№ 1 ‖ Before You Restore

To be a restorer, it isn't necessary to be a cabinetmaker. In fact, there's a big difference between cabinetmaking, or constructing new objects meant for public view, and restoration, which integrates new materials into existing objects. Before undertaking the restoration of any object, determine what your restoration goals are. Do you want to restore the object as it was, using the necessary structural and surface procedures? Or, do you want to alter its appearance and/or change its function? Once you have a clearer idea of what you want to accomplish, you can begin to analyze what must be done to make the object structurally sound and aesthetically pleasing. Consider, also, whether a particular object is worth the time, energy, and money you may have to spend to restore it.

This detail of an Italian gilded side table (c. 1735) exhibits many of the tasks that face restorers: replacing missing carvings, reattaching broken-off pieces, stabilizing and recontouring surfaces, and gilding.

DETERMINING AN OBJECT'S VALUE

READING BETWEEN THE CATALOG'S LINES

Many major auction houses have beautiful catalogs of upcoming or past auctions of furniture and decorative objects, which are available for sale online or by phone. Whether you're able to attend the actual auction or not, studying these catalogs will help acquaint you with the elements of a particular style of furniture or decorative object and teach you what to look for when evaluating an individual object.

Understanding the Lingo

It's important to understand the lingo of these catalogs, which varies from one auction house to the next. Here are several important things to remember when reading a description of an object in any catalog:

- → A date included in the description indicates that the item is from a particular period and has had no major alteration or restoration.
- → The absence of a date in the description indicates that the item has had significant restoration or alteration.
- → Inclusion of the term style in the description indicates that the piece was made as a reproduction of an earlier period's style.

Before you've decided your restoration goals, there is a critical piece of information you may want to gather: What is the value of the object. We well remember, as newlyweds, cutting off the back of a chair to create a mirror frame, not realizing we had destroyed a mid-nineteenth century collector's item.

The value of an object is usually based on its rarity, age, condition (how close it is to its original state), and provenance or attribution (the record of its locale of origin and previous ownership). Fortunately or not, an object's value always fluctuates. That is to say, some of the above factors gain or lose value, as compared with others, depending on the whims of the marketplace. The timing of these changes is always unpredictable. Many auction houses will provide a free, verbal auction estimate (an off-the-cuff estimate of how much your object would bring at auction) provided you make an appointment with the appropriate department dealing with your particular object. They will charge for a written evaluation. On the other hand, if you want to pay for an even more in-depth estimate of your object's value based on different types of valuation, such as marketable cash value, fair market value, or replacement value, contact the Appraisers Association of American (AAA), the oldest nonprofit professional association of personal property appraisers in America (see Resources on page 268).

Appearances Can Be Deceiving

Another aspect governing value is the possibility that an object is not what it purports to be: It might be a later revival of an earlier period style, an honest reproduction, or a complete fake. Keep in mind that fakes of unadorned, clean-lined objects are more common than those featuring marquetry or heavy carving, for example, both of which take considerable time to produce.

In order to avoid being taken in by pieces that aren't genuine, it's a good idea to become knowledgeable about the physical and aesthetic elements of the objects that interest you. There are a number of ways to do this: attend previews of auctions, during which you can physically and visually examine objects; read auction catalogs (see Reading Between the Catalog's Lines at left); and visit museums and fine antique shops to learn about the attributes of a particular period's style and ornament. Train your eye to detect a mishmash of structure and ornament on objects that should, in fact, be true to one period. Over time, you'll begin to recognize pieces that aren't genuine and to also understand which restorations affect value and those that don't.

Does Restoration Affect an Object's Value?

It's no secret that much work is done in restoration shops affiliated with dealers of antiques in order to raise the value of damaged objects. This mirrors our own experience because every damaged antique that we restored—whether for private collectors, antique dealers, or museums—was worth much more after restoration than before, especially when accompanied by our photographic and written documentation. This was particularly true of a pair of early eighteenth-century torchères that we restored. When the surfaces of antiques such as these objects begin to fade, lift, and flake off as they age, damage to the object proceeds at a much faster pace than on a brownwood piece. And because of their fragile nature, these objects must be restored and preserved before the damage becomes too extensive.

This pair of early-eighteenth-century torchères (bottom) had an auction estimate of $20,000 to $30,000 dollars, which was much more than their value before restoration. The top photo shows their condition before we restored them.

Bottom photo courtesy of Sotheby's

ANALYZING OBJECTS FOR RESTORATION

To forestall any feeling of intimidation or of being overwhelmed by what you find that needs restoring, remember this: Other hands besides yours have already worked on your object, both constructing it and possibly repairing it. Many of the objects we've restored exhibited the imprint of other restorers before us, showing up often as incorrect repairs to an object's structure or surface—including obvious surface fills, ill-matched colors, or opaque finishes that had been coated over original art work. In the occasional case in which a previous restoration was acceptable (given the changes that age may have made in colors and textures), we left this work intact as part of the object's history. However, when the prior work was badly done, we had to—and you'll need to as well—remove these repairs before proceeding further with the restoration.

Diagnose Damage First

Begin by diagnosing the damage on your object, looking at it under a good light or in sunlight. Then use the Checklist of Possible Problems on page 16 to determine which structural, surface, and finish areas must be restored.

IS THE SURFACE ORIGINAL?

Another factor that will affect an object's value relates to what is actually being restored. On first perusal, it may seem obvious that the existing surface is what should be restored, as was the case with this toolbox on page 16 from a fire-fighting vehicle, painted in 1902, that we were restoring for a major museum's exhibition.

On closer inspection, the chipped-off paint on the upper far right revealed a prior coat of deep blue paint and a ¼-inch band of gold leaf, which was bordered in red. We found the same clues on the vehicle itself, and realized that an earlier decoration had been covered up at a later time. The restoration options from which to choose were: (1) remove the last coat to display the original coat, or (2) repair the last coat, completely covering up the original, painted layer. Happily, the museum curator was as excited as we were to have us restore the vehicle's original surface.

Above, the 1902 paint layer had covered up the original red, deep blue, and gold leaf decoration that was revealed in the chipped-off areas. A detail at top right of the restored vehicle exhibits the colors and decoration of the original layer. For more on the restoration of this toolbox and hose carriage, see also Abrading an Antique Toolbox on page 118 in Chapter 6, and Restoring Partially Visible, Overpainted Designs on page 256 in Chapter 10.

If test areas of an earlier layer reveal enough clues to permit correct restoration, the object's value appreciates because it is being returned to an earlier stage. Use the guidelines starting on page 256 in Chapter 10 to help you discover evidence of an earlier surface.

If the surface condition is so bad and a total reproduction is necessary, every effort should be made to document in photos and writing any original surface that may still exist—no matter how tattered the remains may be—as it will help maintain some of the object's value. See page 20 for more information about documentation.

MARX MAXIMS

When restoring an object, keep the following points in mind:

- → Many procedures will take longer than you think.
- → The unexpected happens more often than you expect.
- → Thinking "out-of-the-box" often produces creative solutions to problems.
- → Photograph! Photograph! Photograph (your work to document it)!
- → Remember when you're working, whatever two hands have put together, your two hands can try to fix.

CHECKLIST OF POSSIBLE PROBLEMS

Structure

- → One or more broken members (legs, arms, chair crests and so on)
- → Movement (wobble) in the joints
- → Broken dowels
- → Open miter joints in a frame or elsewhere
- → Split wood near hinges
- → Prior incorrect structural repair
- → Missing or damaged molding or trim
- → Warped wood

Surface

- → Gouges
- → Missing or damaged edges
- → Missing or damaged carved elements
- → Missing or damaged, slightly raised areas
- → Missing, damaged, or lifted Asian lacquer
- → Missing, damaged, or lifted veneer
- → Missing or damaged gilding
- → Missing or damaged color or design
- → Damage caused by insects or abuse

Finish

- → White rings
- → Black rings
- → Deteriorated finish coats
- → Unacceptable wood stains or color
- → Unacceptable wood finishes (too formal or informal)

PLOTTING A RESTORATION STRATEGY

Knowing your restoration goals will enable you to plan the order in which to do various procedures. Even though each restoration may involve unique structural and surface problems, the sequence of procedures usually follows the order listed below:

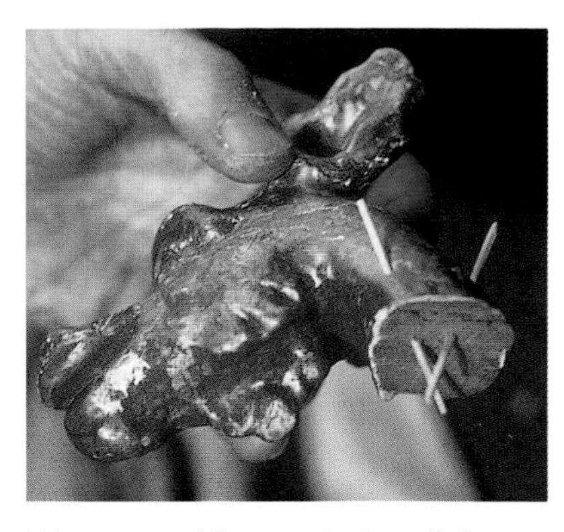

This was one of the many broken-off pieces that had to be rejoined to its original carving before we could proceed to any structural repair. See Tips for Open-Doweling on page 58 in Chapter 3.

Structure

If the object has a broken member, repairing this member is usually the first procedure. You can't successfully fix both a broken leg and joints at the same time, so start the same way the original maker did, putting each member of the structure in sound condition before assembling the whole structure.

The joints must be addressed next to make your object stable and safe. Often all the joints on older objects are loose. If so, dismantle the entire object, replace any broken dowels, repair any problem with joints, and reassemble the object. Then replace any damaged or missing moldings or trim.

Surface

Surface restoration allows you to do several procedures simultaneously, since they may appear on separate areas of the object and involve applications that need to dry before moving on to the next ones. For instance, you can glue and clamp one lifted area of veneer and, while that area is adhering, begin to fill surface gouges in other areas. While the filled areas are drying, you can make a mold from a duplicate carving, for example, for a dimensional detail that must be copied by creating a cast.

Damages on this drawer are being restored with a colored filler to bring the gouged areas up to the level of the surrounding surface. See Filling Surface Depressions and Abrasions on page 76 in Chapter 4.

Finishes

Color, design, and wood stains on a surface cannot be dealt with until any finishes coating them have been eliminated. Therefore, remove deteriorated finish coats and white rings before applying new color, design, and wood stains. Last of all, apply final finishes to enhance and protect the surfaces.

Developing Needed Skills

Another aspect of plotting a restoration strategy is taking into account the diverse skills that you will need to accomplish your restoration goals. One such important skill is manual dexterity, or the ability to work capably with your hands and tools (both existing tools and those you may need to invent to solve certain problems). If you haven't worked with your hands before, it certainly doesn't mean you can't. It's just another area to explore. Other useful skills relate to character and personality—and may be even more valuable to the restorer than manual dexterity—such as motivation to set goals and pursue them, desire to be a craftsman, patience to persevere, ability to organize procedures sequentially, and ingenuity to think up innovative, out-of-the-box solutions to problems. In your first attempts at uncomplicated restorations, you may be surprised—and pleased—to discover that these are qualities you may not have known you had.

The finish coat on the left had to be removed in order to restore the graining that was under it. See Removing Finish Coats on page 174 in Chapter 8.

Before starting to restore an object, you may find it helpful to create a similar sample surface on which to experiment the restoration processes you'll be using. This will allow you to test materials, which you then can apply on the least conspicuous area of the object—for instance, the under side of the object or on the back of a leg. Quash the tendency to try something new where it will be the first thing seen, for example, on the top of a table.

If, after analyzing the problems of a damaged piece and the possible solutions for restoring it, you discover that your abilities and temperament aren't suited to some of the processes required, have someone else who specializes in the processes perform all or part of the restoration. For instance, you may do all the structural work needed on an object, but have someone else attend to the surface.

WHEN IS IT TIME TO CALL IN A PROFESSIONAL?

The answer to this question involves clarifying what specific restoration you want a professional to do. If you want an object completely restored, the first thing to do is to find out the object's value. (See Determining an Object's Value on page 14.)

Getting Estimates for Restoration

Next, you need to get a cost estimate for restoring your piece from a professional restorer. When choosing a professional, try to find one who specializes in your type of object (for a referral, check with the AIC, included in Resources on page 268, or possibly with a local historical society). For instance, many professionals work only with brownwood objects (those exhibiting real wood on all surfaces with no added decorative painting, Asian lacquer, or gilding). If the object still has its original patina (a surface appearance grown beautiful with age), many brownwood restorers try not use abrasives or chemicals. But it's so rare that the original surface still exists on brownwood antiques that these restorers of real wood objects usually do structural repairs and then refinish the wood surfaces.

Finding Professional Help

Professionals who restore gilded objects can be found through referrals from the Society of Gilders (SOG) and the AIC, both of which are listed in Resources. As well, the guidance in Chapter 9 about restoring gilding on surfaces and behind glass will provide you with enough information to deal with professional gilders and/or possibly to do many of the restoration processes yourself.

Decorative surfaces coated with Asian lacquer or paint are restored by even fewer professionals than those servicing brownwood or gilded objects. This lack of knowledgeable professionals has resulted, nowadays, in many objects with Asian lacquer or painted finishes to be discarded. Restoring Asian lacquer today is particularly crucial since so much was destroyed when Mao Zedong Red Guards held sway in China in the 1960s.

This pair of nineteenth-century hinged chests on stands are the types of objects that can be restored with guidance found in this book.

Photo courtesy of Mallett

Many lacquer objects still in existence are usually in bad condition, although they may still be able to be restored. Chapter 4 deals with surface restoration, and will provide you with enough guidance to work with a professional restorer—or do much of the preparatory and remaining restoration on a lacquer or painted object yourself.

An Object's Value Is Key

In short, the answer to when it's time to call in a professional may be when your object is very valuable and you can find a qualified professional to restore it. On the other hand, if your object is not particularly valuable—and/or a professional restoration estimate exceeds its value—you may decide not to call in a professional but instead experiment with restoring the object yourself using the procedures in this book. You may also want to bear in mind that being a professional conservator or restorer doesn't necessarily ensure top-quality work (though referrals from the SOG and AIC are usually trustworthy). Some professionals may rush hastily through unseen, yet important, steps and processes because they may either be unfamiliar with the procedures or may feel they are too time-consuming—and, for a professional, time is money.

Conversely, if you decide to undertake the restoration, you'll probably not be concerned with watching the clock, since you're restoring for pleasure, not for financial gain. Yet, when the time comes—and it often does—that the quality of your work brings requests for restorations from others, remember this: Even though you charge a fee, your reputation is more important than your fee. Except when we restored private collections on-site and charged an hourly fee, we rarely billed clients for all the hours we actually spent working on their objects.

REVERSIBLE MATERIALS

All objects, particularly those constructed of wood (along with the materials coated over them), deteriorate as time goes by. One of the goals of restoration and conservation is to slow the deterioration process so that the object will last longer. Slowing the natural process entails using restoration materials that have been tested, are reliable, and will do no further damage to the object. Because these new materials will undergo change over time—but at a rate that differs from that of the object's original materials—they may need to be removed at a future date. For this reason all restoration materials should be reversible—that is, they should be able to be reversed, or removed, without damaging original areas of the object.

The current term for the reversibility of materials is *retreatability*—that is, the ability of materials to be removed and an area to be "retreated," possibly with materials, technology, and processes that were unavailable at the time of an earlier restoration. Retreating in relation to an area also has the added connotation of withdrawing from overtreating an object. The field of restoration of fine and decorative arts is in a constant state of flux; and new materials, technology, and innovative processes will continue to evolve as the field advances.

SAFETY

From the very beginning of our restoration and teaching careers, we had been concerned about the use of, and exposure to, harmful chemicals, especially those used by many conservators such as solvents like xylene, acetone, ethanol, and toluene. Studies have shown that in light of the various adverse effects of these substances on the body, special gloves, goggles, and respirators are recommended, as is refraining from eating, drinking, and smoking while working with these substances. Pregnant women should definitely avoid these substances as well as other toxic materials.

In our work and classes, we used liquids, pastes, and powders that met our safety and health concerns, and which were also reversible. These were mainly water- and alcohol-soluble paints, filling substances, glues, molding and casting materials, and most gilding supplies.

KEEP RECORDS OF YOUR TREATMENT HISTORY

As we mentioned in the Introduction, it is *extremely* important to document as much as possible the entire treatment history of your object with photographs and a written record of materials and processes you use. Photographic and written documentation entails keeping a complete record of all stages in the restoration process, from the first time you examine an object (CBT), throughout all procedures during treatment

CBT photo top left illustrates the table's condition when we acquired it. Note the lifting and tenting of the lacquer caused by the shrinkage of the unseasoned wood.

CDT#1 photo top right shows the process of cutting through the joint to separate the boards that make the table's base.

CDT#2 photo middle left documents the separation of the boards so that the textured lacquer boards could be set down.

CDT#3 photo middle right illustrates the sections from which the amber finish coating had been removed. Note the triangular bamboo dowel (one of two) that is projecting from the top of the separated board.

CAT photo bottom is a portion of the finished tabletop, complete with surface repair, design reconstruction, and finish coating.

(CDT), to the final results of your work after treatment (CAT). After completing a restoration, it's often difficult to remember what the damaged object first looked like; and CBT photos provide a good reminder for you (and your client).

Try to take the CDT photos of each area being treated from the same angle as the corresponding CBT photos, so that all treatments of the same area will be similarly recorded. Be aware, though, that in the throes of treating an object, it's often a nuisance to stop what you're doing to rearrange lights and to determine the correct angle for the photograph.

Although photographing may be time-consuming, it's nonetheless well worth the effort not only to document where and which treatment has been done but also to show clearly what is original to the object, compared to areas that have been restored. In our case, if we hadn't carefully documented our restorations photographically, there would be no before-and-after photographs in this book.

To give you an idea of photographic record-keeping, the photos above are a small sampling of the many stages we photographed during the restoration of a Chinese export tilt-top table (c. 1835).

A table 34 to 36 inches high—about countertop height—is great to work at while standing, but obviously requires a high chair, like a drafting chair, to work at it while seated.

ON TOOLS AND WORK SPACES

Many of the basic tools used in restoration can be found in your household: a hammer, a screwdriver, a pair of pliers, a portable drill, and a portable saber saw. For more complicated procedures, you'll need more sophisticated tools, which are easy to acquire. In fact, you may already have them in their toolbox: an X-ACTO knife; nail set and small hammer (such as a ball-peen hammer); mallet; various clamps; miter box; and backsaw. Basic tools and any additional ones you may need for specialized tasks will be shown and discussed in the relevant chapters throughout the book.

Your Work Setup

It would be wonderful if all of us who restore could have a completely outfitted workshop in a light-filled, airy space with good ventilation and enough room to set up photographic equipment. The reality is that all you really need is a worktable at the height that allows you to work comfortably while standing and sitting. Early in our restoration career, we used our kitchen and dining room tables, as well as any other table that would support our work.

If restoring becomes your passion, you'll put up with all sorts of inconveniences and make do, finding ways to surmount all the obstacles you encounter. In the end, you'll find that it's the object itself, not your tools or work space, that's important.

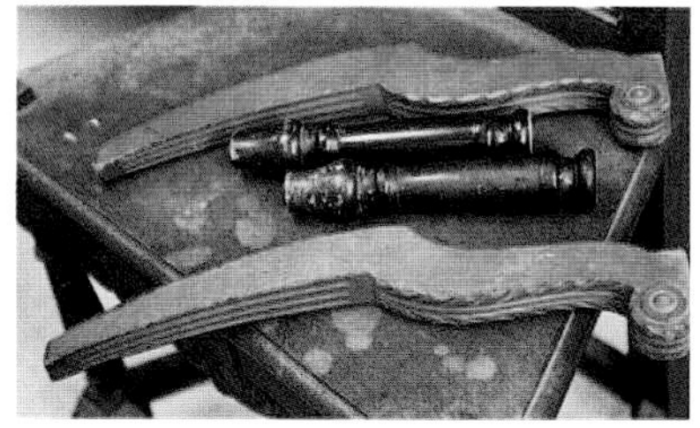

Recycling brought back to life this cast-off, one-armed chair (a 1920s version of a late-sixteenth-century piece) pictured at top. A damaged flea-market find yielded a pair of shaped legs and spindles above to serve as new, matched chair arms. Finished with toned copper leafing, the chair finally deserved the name it was given in the 1500s: a *caqueteuse* chair, from the French *caqueter* (to chatter or gossip), which ladies did while seated in chairs like this that were wide enough to accommodate the fashions of the day.

RECYCLE WOODEN OBJECTS TO PRACTICE YOUR SKILLS

As time goes by and modern technology develops more substitutes for wood, less and less real wood will be used for constructing furniture and other objects. For those of us who enjoy working with wood and want to preserve as many wooden objects as possible, the prospect of a dwindling supply makes us want to spring into rescue mode.

Castoffs Abound

Castoff wooden objects (most being mass-produced pieces made of perfectly good, solid, and often veneered woods, frequently covered by darkened coatings) are available in untold numbers in thrift shops, flea markets, and even set out on the curb for the taking. These castoffs also provide for those new to working with wood and restoration techniques a rich laboratory in which to develop and practice skills.

Refashioning Castoffs

Envision new objects that could be made from castoffs. We've created numerous one-of-a-kind furnishings from parts of other objects, among them: mirror frames fashioned from interesting chair backs; low benches from shortened side tables; planter bases from turnings cut down from tall legs, which were then connected; captain's beds from old-fashioned, high "buffets" made in the 1920s; and tables made from carved legs topped with contemporary tabletops. All of these transformations involved various procedures that are presented in this book.

We wrote this chapter to call attention to some of the concepts you might like to think about before undertaking any restoration project. By having an understanding of what your options are for restoring objects, you'll be more successful in your expectations and in the work that you do.

№ 2 ‖ Wood and Its Problems

WOOD IS BY FAR THE MOST COMMON material used for making furniture, frames, and many other decorative objects. And even if the surface of an object is completely covered with paint, Asian lacquer, or gilding, chances are that the structural base over which the surface coating was applied is wood. For this reason, understanding how to diagnose and restore damaged wooden objects requires first understanding the properties of wood, how it behaves under various circumstances, and how damage often occurs. The three main sources of damage to wood furniture and frames, each of which is addressed in this chapter, are: (1) moisture and its absence or excess in wood, (2) external factors like insects or careless handling, and (3) stress on the object's design and construction.

The extensive damage to the wood of this chair by powderpost beetles was exposed only after the top layer of wood that covered it was removed.

WHAT IS SEASONED WOOD?

Once a tree has been cut into boards, the boards must be dried, or "seasoned," to be used for woodworking. Seasoning involves putting the boards in a place where the air is drier than the wood in order to get rid of the excess moisture in the wood's cells. As the excess moisture is released into the drier air, the wood shrinks in width but not in length. For this reason, anyone who has ever bought lumber has found that a 1 by 8-inch board is usually really only about 7 5/8 inches wide.

Even more shrinkage can occur when objects in good condition (meaning those made of seasoned wood) are placed in very dry, overheated environments. Often these objects release additional moisture into the hot, dry air, and, in the process, develop many of the problems discussed in the first part of this chapter.

Conversely, after wood has been seasoned, the absorption of excess moisture from overly moist air can cause the wood cells to expand and warp or bulge up. If you have bought seasoned wood, only to have it warp after unknowingly storing it improperly, use the directions on page 29 to unwarp the wood.

Wood sometimes shrinks across its width, as it did in the detail of the reverse side of two of the eight panels on this late-nineteenth-century Chinese export screen, opening the panels and cracking the lacquer coating over them.

Trees are part of the plant kingdom, and are made up of wood tissue composed of cells. Throughout the life of a tree and even after it has been cut, wood cells absorb and release moisture in a process called *moisture exchange*. When cut wood is stored in a place where the air is dryer than the wood, it releases moisture into the air and its cells shrink. Conversely, if the wood is dryer than the air surrounding it, the wood absorbs moisture from the air and its cells expand. This natural process is ongoing, and the shrinkage and expansion of the wood cells can cause a variety of problems in wooden objects. For this reason, museums diligently control heat and humidity to preserve their collections.

Each species of tree—there are more than 100,000—has its own individual cell structure and reacts differently to moisture exchange, which is one of the reasons that experienced woodworkers are careful to select specific kinds of wood and seasoned cuts when constructing furniture (see What Is Seasoned Wood? at left). Yet all woods are subject to similar problems caused by moisture exchange, including the separation of joints, shrinkage of dowels, tent cleavage, and warping.

SHRINKAGE AND EXPANSION FROM MOISTURE EXCHANGE

The ongoing process of moisture exchange in wood causes two basic types of problems: shrinkage when the wood releases moisture into an overly dry environment and expansion when wood absorbs excess moisture from a wet environment.

Shrinkage in Wood Joints

Wood shrinks across a board's width but not in its length. Shrinkage of wood in an object indicates that the wood used in its construction was not properly, if at all, seasoned, or that the wood released moisture into an extremely dry environment after it was seasoned. In the detail of the late-nineteenth-century Chinese export screen at left, shrinkage from unseasoned wood is apparent in the 1/8-inch separation between two panels. On a large object like this screen, whose panels cannot be disconnected and repaired, the gap would be filled with filler paste and the lacquer repaired. See page 84 in Chapter 4 for information on repairing similar damage in objects that can be dismantled, and also page 40 in Chapter 3 for general information on dismantling objects.

Shrinkage in Miter Joints

Another type of shrinkage occurs in miter joints, which are formed from 45-degree-angled cuts of wood that are paired and joined at the corners of frames and moldings. When the wood in a mitered corner shrinks, it becomes narrower, causing the angles making up the miter to become more acute. As a result, the miter opens up on the inside corner, as shown in the photos on the opposite page.

Museum objects such as the frame below (original to the 1838 painting *The Love Letter* by Dutch artist Johannes Hendrik van West now in the Rijksmuseum Amsterdam), which shows the opening of the miter joint on the inside edge due to the wood's shrinkage, are usually left in this condition because repairing the frame would entail either cutting wood off both diagonal cuts or filling the gap and matching the gilding. Museums consider both practices unacceptable for objects in their collections. Frames of lesser value and importance can be repaired with the suggestions found under repairing miter joints in Chapter 3 on page 66.

Moisture exchange in wood presents particular problems for miter joints. When the wood in a miter joint shrinks, the angles of the cut wood making up the joint change, distorting the original miter and opening it up on its inside edges.

This detail, far left, is of the top left corner of the original frame of *The Love Letter,* and shows the opening of the miter joint on the inside edge due to the wood's shrinkage. At left is the entire frame.

Painting courtesy of Rijksmuseum
Photos taken by Hubert Baija

Shrinkage in Dowels

When a dowel (a thin, cylindrical wooden rod) connecting two parts of an object shrinks across its width and gets thinner, the joint is no longer held together tightly. Like other parts of a piece of furniture, dowels need to be made from properly seasoned wood. In the photo below, the separation of one joint of this mid-twentieth-century piano bench signals that the other joints have probably also loosened. See page 40 in Chapter 3 for information on repairing loosened joints.

Shrinkage in the dowels used in the joints on this mid-twentieth-century piano bench caused them to loosen and, when lightly tapped with a hammer (padded with the red cloth below it in the photo), came apart.

Tent cleavage is another type of damage resulting from the shrinkage of wood, which causes paint or any other coating applied on the wood to "tent" up and often flake off.

Shrinkage Causing "Tent Cleavage"

Another sign of shrinkage across the width of the wood is the lifting up, or "tenting," of paint and other applied coatings from the wood's surface along its length. The tentlike configuration of the lifted coating traps air underneath and is referred to as *tent cleavage*.

Lifted coatings are quite fragile and often break off, showing the wood underneath, as in the photo left. See page 85 in Chapter 4 for information on repairing tent cleavage.

Miter joints expand at the outer edges of a frame when they absorb moisture from the air.

Expansion in Miter Joints

Since there's a continuous exchange of moisture between wood and the environment, not only can wood release moisture into the surrounding air and shrink but it can also absorb moisture from the air and increase in width. As a result of the swelling from this absorption of moisture, the wood grain in frames opens up the outer corners, as shown in the photo at the left. Fortunately, this happens very rarely. For techniques on repairing miter joints that have opened up on the outside corner due to expansion or on the inside corner due to shrinkage, see page 66 in Chapter 3.

Expansion Causing Warping

Although expansion of wood causes fewer problems than shrinkage, warping, or the swelling of wood cells from excess moisture, is a common and particularly frustrating problem. When wood warps, it bulges outward from its original flat plane and is very time-consuming to repair.

Warping generally occurs when one side of a piece of wood is sealed with a coating and the other side is unsealed. This unsealed side absorbs moisture that expands the wood fibers, usually swelling them outward and causing the sealed side to curve inward. Warping is likelier to occur in pieces of wood that are freestanding, loosely attached, or attached on fewer than all edges. The photo below shows an example of warping in the veneer that was loose on the tabletop of an art nouveau round table (c. 1900).

On this round, art nouveau table, warping occurred in the veneer on the tabletop within a matter of hours after it became unglued. The warping occurred because the veneer had been finish-coated on its upper side, sealing that side, but was unsealed on its under side, allowing moisture to expand the wood fibers on this side.

UNWARPING WOOD

Understanding that warping occurs naturally as the cell structure of wood reacts to its environment offers up a solution to the problem: reverse the conditions that cause warping. That is to say, by removing moisture from the convex (outwardly bulging) side of the wood and adding it to the concave (inwardly cupping) side, you can equalize the moisture content on both sides and thereby flatten the wood. This works not only in theory but also in practice, but it takes far longer to unwarp wood than it took for the warping to originally occur. Because unwarping must be done gradually, it's a very time-consuming procedure. Be patient: Each unwarping process is unique, and the time each project will take cannot be predicted.

BUILDING A TOOLKIT: TOOLS FOR REPAIRING WARPED WOOD
In order to flatten warped wood using the general instructions on pages 29 to 31, you'll need to gather a few special tools that are shown in the photo above. From left, these tools include:

- → Glue syringe
- → Clamps, several sets
- → 1-inch-by-2-inch pieces of lumber
- → White vinegar (for removing old glue)
- → Cheesecloth
- → Palette knife
- → Paintbrush
- → #120 and #220 grit open-coat sanding paper
- → Lamp with a bulb (You could use another heat source, such as a portable heater or hair dryer as well.)
- → Kettle (a source of steam)
- → 2 flat boards

Photo courtesy of Connie Hougardy

The Keys to Unwarping

Heat, moisture, and pressure are the keys to unwarping wood, and if either heat or moisture cannot be absorbed into the wood cells, the flattening process will not be successful. Once the veneer, stain, paint, and glue have been eliminated from the wood, the unwarping process can begin. This process must be done gradually over a period of time and watched closely. The thinner the warped board and the more recent the warping, the shorter the unwarping process. Conversely, thick boards that have been warped for a long time may take many days to flatten and, in fact, may never get completely flat. Note that if you try to correct the warping too quickly, you risk splitting the wood. In short, keep this in mind: Wood must be coaxed to change its shape, not forced; the process must be gradual and can take many days.

Clamping Is Essential

To ensure that the flattening process proceeds gradually, you'll need some sort of clamping device to hold the wood. In addition to clamping the wood while unwarping it, you'll also need to clamp it tightly between boards immediately afterward, to prevent the wood's memory from returning and warping again. Only when you're ready to reinstall the flattened wood into the area that housed it originally should you take it out of the clamped boards.

To unwarp any flat wooden object that's warped—boards, panels, flat trays, lids, table drop-leaves, and shelves—use the general steps below (and see also Flattening Wood the Old-Fashioned Way on page 30. Also, on page 32 you'll also find a photo essay about unwarping a badly damaged fall-front of a seventeenth-century English secretary using the steps below.

STEP 1: REMOVE ANY COATINGS

Remove every bit of coating on both sides of the wood, whether paint, lacquer, veneer, or stain, so moisture can fully penetrate into the wood cells. Remove thin coatings, like paint, by scraping the surface with an X-ACTO knife, then abrading the surface to expose the raw wood with #220 grit open-coat sandpaper, being sure to sand with the grain of the wood. (See page 118 in Chapter 6 for information on abrading.)

FLATTENING WOOD THE OLD-FASHIONED WAY

Wood has, of course, warped for ages, and in earlier days folks used a very practical strategy for flattening it: They laid the warped wood on wet grass in strong sunlight, convex (outwardly bulging) side up, concave (inwardly cupping) side down. As the under side of the wood absorbed moisture from the grass, the upper side was heated by the sun. Little by little, the wood would relax and flatten out. These same principles of adding moisture to the concave side and extracting it from the convex side still underlie the current approach to flattening wood, as explained in the step-by-step directions for this procedure beginning on page 29.

STEP 2: REMOVE ANY VENEER

To remove veneer, try the following method first: Place a large sheet of heavy paper (an opened-out brown paper bag, for example) over the veneer and slide a dry household iron slowly over the paper. The heat of the iron will soften and re-liquefy old hide glue but not most modern industrial glues. Next, gently pry off the veneer by carefully inserting a palette knife between the veneer and the substrate. You may have to repeat the heating process more than once. (See page 171 in Chapter 8 for more information on removing veneers.)

To keep the newly removed veneer from warping before you replace it where it belongs, sandwich it between two rigid boards and clamp it together, or place heavy weights (heavy books often work) on top of the boards and the veneer.

If the above method does not work, try this: Insert white vinegar, warmed slightly on the stove, between the veneer and the substrate with a glue syringe or a brush to re-liquefy aged hide glue or yellow (aliphatic) glue. Then slowly pry up the veneer. When you've removed the veneer, place it in a clamp sandwich, as described above.

Although Asian lacquer usually cups slightly rather than warping, if you want to remove it, insert a palette knife between the lacquer and the substrate and gently pry off the lacquer little by little.

STEP 3: SAND AND CLEAN THE SURFACE

Once you've removed any veneer, sand the wood with a #220 grit open-coat sandpaper and wipe the surface with a wad of cheesecloth or a clean rag dampened with water and denatured alcohol to remove all traces of old glue and any other accretions that would prevent heat, moisture, or steam from penetrating the wood cells during the unwarping process.

STEP 4: GATHER CLAMPING SUPPLIES

Before beginning to unwarp the wood, have on hand the supplies required for a clamp sandwich (see A Clamp "Sandwich" opposite).

STEP 5: INFUSE MOISTURE AND CLAMP WOOD

Infuse moisture into the warped wood, using one of the following methods:

First method: Allow steam from a steaming kettle to play on both sides of the warped wood (wear protective oven mitts while doing this). Then make a clamp sandwich, as described in the box opposite, positioning the cupped side down. Adjust the clamps firmly enough to hold the wood under pressure but not so tightly that you split the wood. Then continue alternating the clamping and steaming procedure as described at the end of this step.

Second method: Dampen the concave (inwardly cupped) side of the warped wood thoroughly, then clamp as described above, with the concave side down. Arrange a heat source below the sandwich by resting each end of the sandwich on a chair (or other support) and placing a portable heater or a lamp (without a shade) under it. As an alternative, turn the clamp sandwich over, with the cupped side up, and place a gooseneck lamp or other heat source above it.

When you begin to see the wood dry out (it will get lighter and lighter in color as it loses moisture), add more moisture and heat, by either method described above. After doing this, add a bit more pressure by tightening the clamps slightly.

Keep alternating the steaming and gradual clamping process, repeating as many times as necessary until the wood has flattened as much as possible, given its thickness and the age of the original warping. This process of adding moisture and heat, and tightening the clamps gradually will prevent the wood from splitting.

STEP 6: PROTECT FLATTENED WOOD

Remove the clamps from the flattened wood, and place the wood between two covering boards immediately. Clamp the boards together tightly, and keep the unwarped wood clamped until you're ready to reposition it into its original housing.

STEP 7: REINSTALL WOOD IN OBJECT

If necessary, re-adhere any lifted or loose veneer neighboring the area housing the flattened wood. Remove the unwarped wood from between the two boards, replace it where it belongs, attaching it on all sides as it was originally housed.

A CLAMP "SANDWICH"

For repairing the fall-front of the seventeenth-century secretary on page 32, we devised a system of clamping that enabled us to straighten the wood gradually, then hold it in an interim state between wide boards until we could put it back where it belonged. For each of the two warped panels taken out of the secretary's hinged fall-front, we cut four 1-inch-by-2-inch pieces of lumber into 12-inch lengths. We encased the ends of each of the warped panels between two of these lengths, like a sandwich, as shown in the illustration below. To hold the "bread" of the sandwich in place and tighten it around the warped board to set in motion the flattening process, we used C-clamps, as shown in the illustration below. Alternatively, you could use bolts set into openings drilled in opposite ends of the 1-inch-by-2-inch pieces. Note that, if the warped wood is longer than 8 inches, you'll need to place an additional sandwich of 1-by-2s every 4 inches along the length of the warped wood.

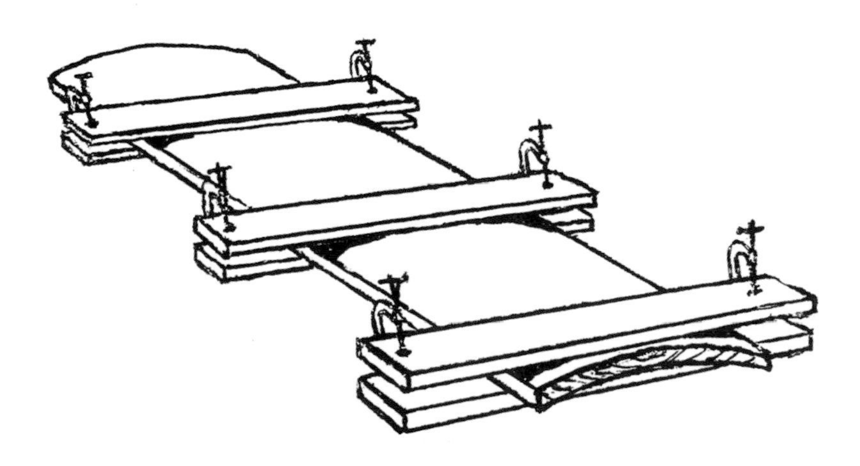

UNWARPING THE PANELS ON A SEVENTEENTH-CENTURY ENGLISH SECRETARY

This seventeenth-century English secretary suffered severe warping in the two central panels of its fall-front. In the photos right, the extent of the warping is apparent.

The fall-front was composed of walnut veneer covered with japanning, which is a coating of paint and shellac or varnish developed in the seventeenth-century Europe to mimic Asian lacquer.

After taking the panels out of the fall-front, we removed the stain on the inside, scraping the panels with an X-ACTO knife and sanding with #220 grit open-coat sandpaper to open the grain. Note that we sanded *with* the grain of the wood and changed sandpaper often.

Next we removed the walnut veneer and the japanning covering it from the outside of the panels with steam, warm vinegar, and a palette knife. Despite careful work, the veneer came off in many pieces. See Removing the Veneer on page 261 in Chapter 10. Next we steamed and clamped the panels, as described on page 29 and in A Clamp "Sandwich" on page 31. The unwarping process for both panels took several days, after which we kept them in between the clamped boards until we were ready to reinstall them in the secretary.

Meanwhile, we adhered the edges of lifted and loose veneer bordering the area where the panels were to be reinstalled (note the clamps, at the center back area of the photo, being used to secure the glued edges of the veneers to the substrate), a very important phase of this type of repair.

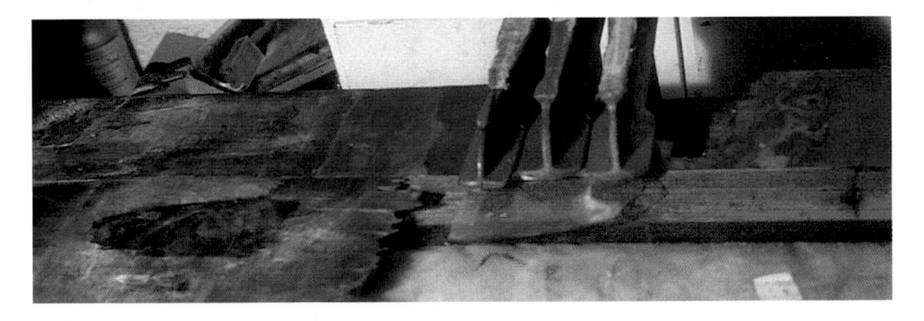

In the photo below left you can see the original stained panels on either side of the restored ones. Finally, below right, you'll find the completed restoration of the japanning on the repaired fall-front.

Bending Wood

The same elements—heat, moisture, and pressure—that are required to flatten warped wood may be used to bend straight-grain wood. For example, after a scarf break, the straight-grain molding around the edge of this nineteenth-century drum table unbent from its original steamed curve below left. With the drawer out of the table and the molding steamed, rebent, and glued in place, tape was applied from the inside the drawer opening to the under side of the table to create a strong "clamp" and hold the molding in place until it dried seen in the photo below right, from the under side of the table. The bottom photo is the restored section directly under the left side of the drawer opening.

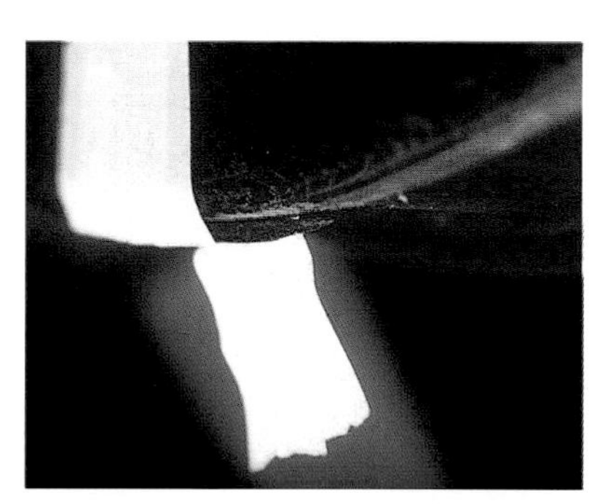

DAMAGE FROM EXTERNAL FACTORS

In addition to moisture exchange in cells, wooden objects can also suffer damage from external factors. Among the most common external agents causing damage are insects, carelessness and abuse, and the incorrect use of tools.

Damage from Powderpost Beetles

One common external source of damage to wood is an infestation of powderpost beetles, a disturbing condition usually termed *worm damage*. Larvae, hatched from eggs laid by adult beetles, burrow and

Right: Significant damage to furniture by powderpost beetles boring and tunneling into the wood can often remain long undetected, with only deceptively modest surface damage visible, as in this late-eighteenth-century English satinwood-grained chair.

Far right: This photo shows a close-up of the extensive damage, which had to be removed as the first step in repairing the chair's edge.

tunnel through the wood in search of the nutrients stored in the wood cells. This infestation can occur over a period of time, with the only indications of the problem the exit holes of the adult beetles and the frass (powdered wood) left around the holes. These holes are often pinpoint-size and indicate age by their color: Darker holes are old, due to the aging of the exposed wood, while lighter holes are newer and might indicate a current infestation, particularly if accompanied by frass. If you're concerned about a current infestation, place the object on a white sheet and observe it for several days to see if any frass appears around the object. If frass does appear, contact a museum expert or pest-control service for further guidance. Before doing that, however, you might also try a simple solution that some people with an infestation have reported having luck with: Spray an ordinary household-cleaning product into the holes several times to kill the larvae.

The insidious thing about beetle infestation is that the damage occurring beneath the surface as the larvae burrow parallel to it is often unseen and therefore unrecognized. The edge of the chair in the photo above left seemed to be all right when we examined it, except for apparently mild surface damage. But, as it turned out, this surface damage was deceptive: After further investigation, we discovered that the tunneling had removed a great deal of wood and that the damage was extensive and had to be cleaned out before the actual edge repairs could be made. See page 93 in Chapter 4 for information on repairing insect damage.

Damage from Abuse

We use the word *abuse* to refer to a wide range of external factors that can damage wood tissue, among them, accidents and careless handling of furniture; and unsupervised pets with a liking for chewing on wood (see the example at left of a chair arm severely damaged by the owner's dog). See page 76 in Chapter 4 for information on repairing such damage.

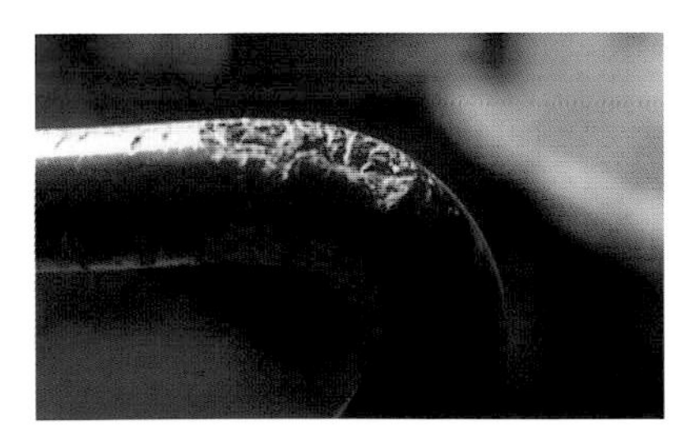

Pets can do damage that's much more immediately visible than that of powderpost beetles, as can be seen on the arm of this mid-twentieth-century chair that proved a favorite chewing spot for a family dog.

Damage from Incorrectly Using Supplies and Tools

A very common example of incorrectly using supplies and tools occurs when nails or screws are inserted carelessly into wood, often splitting the wood along the grain. The damage results from three possible factors:

1. Failure to predrill holes before inserting the screws or nails (since predrilling cuts through the grain, installed screws or nails push aside fewer cells and therefore risk less chance of splitting the wood).

2. Size of the screws or nails used compared to the predrilled holes (the width of the hole should be just slightly smaller than the width of the screw or nail to be inserted).

3. Placement of the screws or nails being inserted (if aligned in a row, there's more tendency toward splitting). Try to substitute hinges with staggered holes, which place less strain on the lengthwise grain of the wood. See page 70 in Chapter 3 for information on repairing a split caused by any of these problems.

Wood often splits when screws or nails are aligned when inserted, as they were in this hinge on a door from an early-nineteenth-century American secretary. The preventative solution to the problem is to stagger the insertion of screws or nails.

DAMAGE FROM STRESS ON DESIGN AND CONSTRUCTION

The parts of a piece of furniture that require the most strength and stability are its top surface, the sides of any case pieces (that is, square or rectangular frames that may or may not have shelves or drawers), drawer fronts, and—most important—legs. The wood that provides the necessary strength for these parts is sawn straight down the length of a tree and, in turn, displays the wood's straight grain along its entire length (see Strength in Wood on page 37).

Over the past several centuries, legs on furniture have often been designed with disregard for the inherent strength of the wood's straight grain. The double-curved cabriole leg of eighteenth-century France, for example, and the long, curved leg of the Regency and Federal periods in England and America, respectively, are designs that weakened the wood's straight grain by cutting curved shapes out of it. Subjecting such legs to stress generally causes them to split where the straight grain is weakest, namely, at the leg's sharpest curve.

For instance, the cabriole leg shown below on a reproduction eighteenth-century chair lasted in good condition for many years, during which the chair was lifted carefully whenever it was moved. But one day when it was dragged across the owner's carpeted floor, the rear right leg was put under stress and broke off at the natural straight grain above the foot, where the curve was the sharpest and the straight grain the weakest.

A curved cabriole leg, popular from the early to late eighteenth century (but so named in the late 1800s because of its resemblance to the leg of an animal in motion), was traditionally cut from a straight-grain piece of wood, as seen in the first photo. Therefore, where strength (straight grain) is needed the most—at the lower, sharper curves—there is very little to give support to the leg. As a result, cabriole legs often suffer splits when the weak lower curve is stressed, as in the second photo (the broken leg is resting on a book to prevent the chair from toppling over).

Scarf Breaks

In the photo of the upturned Regency-style drum table below, you can see that two of the legs have diagonal breaks similar to the break in the cabriole leg mentioned above. This very common diagonal break, often termed a *scarf break*, occurs along a curved leg's natural straight grain. For more information on how to repair scarf breaks, see page 70 in Chapter 3.

The vertical split in the leg of this nineteenth-century Chinese export garden stool above falls exactly along the straight grain, even though it seems to be diagonal to the leg.

On this upturned reproduction English Regency drum table at right, the split, or scarf break, occurred along the wood's natural grain at the base of two of the legs: one at the top right in the photo and the other (on the leg lying on the upended table) at the far left of the image. These two legs were shaped in a gradual curve that had been cut from the straight grain and, when stressed, split in the lower, weaker areas. (Note that the split in the center of the photo is not a scarf break. In this case, the break is along the same straight grain that's part of the table's straight-grain center column.)

The photo above left may make even clearer the likelihood of a diagonal break at the weakest point of a curved shape cut out of straight-grain wood. One of the curved legs of this nineteenth-century Chinese export lacquer wooden garden stool split along its straight grain where the curve was sharpest. Seeing the break in its correct vertical position emphasizes how curved legs (and other curved members cut out of straight grain) split apart when subjected to stress of one sort or another, and how understanding the properties of strength in wood will help you to repair this type of break successfully.

STRENGTH IN WOOD

All wood cells, whatever their size (which varies with the species of tree), are elongated and run down the length of the trunk, providing strength to the wood along its length. The terms *grain* and *grain direction* refer to this lengthwise arrangements of a tree's cells. When a board is cut from a tree log, the truest straight grain is produced when the log is "riven," or split down its natural lengthwise grain. Early furniture was solid and long-lasting because it was usually constructed of wood that was riven.

Wood Cuts and Strength

The cut of wood that provides the most strength and straightest grain to a board is quarter-sawn. In this case, the log is first cut lengthwise into four quadrants, each of which is then cut on the tree's radius from the log's outer circumference (the bark) into the tree's center (the pith) and down its trunk (the stem). The illustration right shows a quarter of a log and a board cut from it. The end grain of all quarter-sawn boards appears as parallel straight lines. Quarter-sawn wood shrinks and warps less than any other cut.

The strength of quarter-sawn wood is diminished wherever a curve is cut from it, as illustrated below left and middle. The sharper the curve is, the weaker the strength of the wood is in that area because very little straight grain remains there. The sharpest curved areas are the most vulnerable to breakage; if the curve is on a leg, it offers very little support to any object to which it's attached. The illustration on the far right shows that the more a leg can be cut in a gradual curve (where the center of the leg is made of mostly straight grain), the less chance there is for breakage.

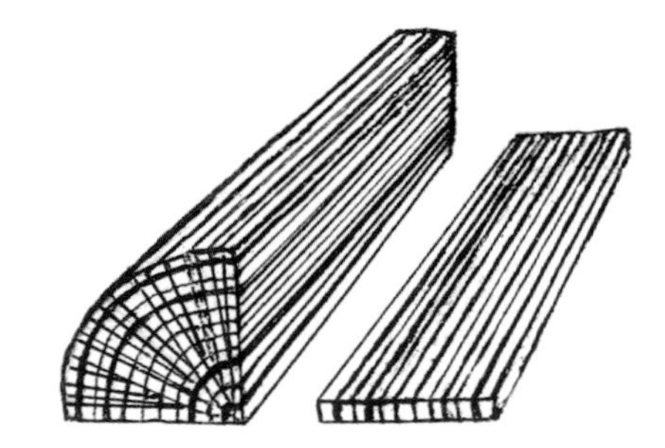

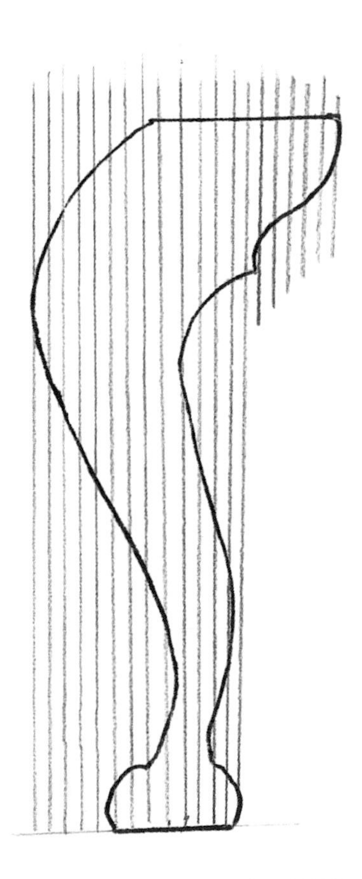

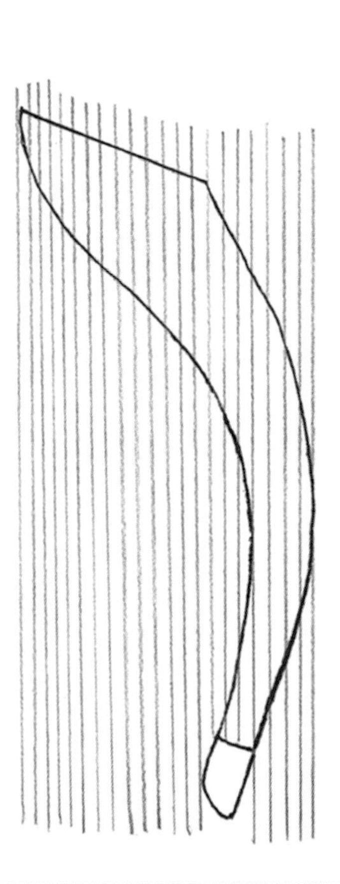

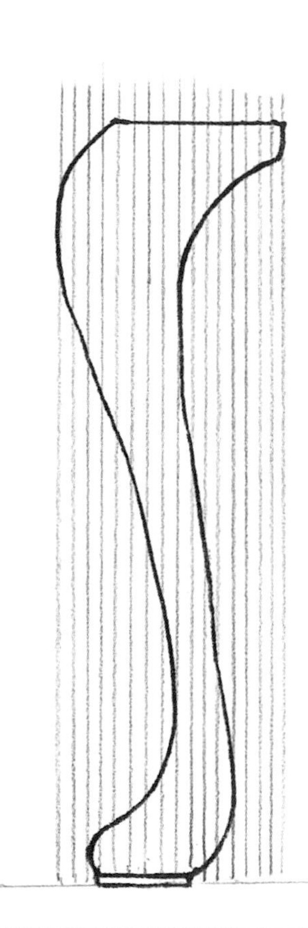

After reading the information in this chapter, you may have an "A-ha" moment upon realizing why a chair leg may have broken or why that drop leaf on your table warped. Be comforted, because once you understand the reasons why those—and other—problems occur, you'll be able to apply the solutions scattered throughout this book to remedy them.

№ 3 ‖ Repairing Structure

If the idea of repairing the joints on a frame or a piece of furniture seems intimidating, remember that all these joints were once put together—and possibly at some point later repaired—by other pairs of hands. By learning in this chapter how objects are constructed, how their joints are fastened, and how these joints can be stabilized, you'll also learn how to prevent future damage to your objects. (Throughout this book, we'll use the term *object* to refer to any piece constructed of wood.)

It may be helpful to keep in mind that, for the thousands of years that people have worked with wood, every object ever constructed of more than one piece of wood has had to be joined, or fastened together, in some way. Nowadays, joints connecting pieces of wood (called *members*) are constructed in one of two basic ways: (1) an extension of one member fits into an opening that's similarly shaped in the mating member; or (2) a separate element connects, or goes between, the two members of a joint. In addition to connecting two pieces of wood in the original construction, a joint can also refer to the repair of a broken member. In short, a joint connects two pieces of wood, wherever that join occurs.

This detail of an early-twentieth-century Chinese export cinnabar table is one of eight miter joints (each corner has two miters) that moved slightly, splitting the lacquer over all the joints.

JOINT PROBLEMS

The main problem with joining pieces of wood is the tendency of joints to become loose over time as an object (usually a piece of furniture) is used. The more an object is used and abused, or mishandled, the looser the joints can become. The best way to prevent joints from getting loose is to lift, not drag, furniture and refrain from tilting back on chairs. A periodic inspection of the underside of furniture will indicate whether any pieces of metal hardware (like corner braces) have screws that need tightening or replacing from the wide selection available in hardware stores and home-improvement centers.

The noise and movement that accompany loose joints signal that the best approach for repair is to dismantle the entire object and reglue all its joints rather than just addressing those that are currently squeaky and unsteady. (Note that there are products to swell wood fibers and provide a tighter fit at the joint, or you could push a wedge into a loose joint to tighten it; but these "fixes" are often temporary. You'll feel movement again as time goes by and will have only postponed the inevitable need to dismantle and reglue all the joints).

Although some objects with elaborate upholstery or complicated construction might be better off left alone and just handled with care (see When You Decide Not to Dismantle on page 44 later in this chapter), most objects with loose joints need to be dismantled and repaired because, if they're left unattended and receive abuse, they may fall apart after a while. For this reason, we'll begin this chapter by exploring how to dismantle a joined object. Then we'll address procedures for gluing and providing pressure to insure a good glue bond. And finally, we'll look at how joints are connected and how to repair miter joints and fractured members of joined objects.

DISMANTLING TAKES PREPARATION

Once you've decided to dismantle an object, there are a few preparatory steps. First, pick a work surface that's at a comfortable height for you (this may seem obvious, but we've seen many novice restorers working in tiring positions on work surfaces that are too low or even on the floor). Then follow the remaining preparatory steps:

STEP 1: PREPARE YOUR WORK SURFACE

Pad your work surface if you're going to turn the object upside-down to dismantle the joints. Use pieces of carpet or another heavy-duty material to protect the surface of both your object and the worktable itself. Then cover the padding with plastic drop cloths to prevent damage from spills.

STEP 2: PREPARE YOUR OBJECT

If your object is a wobbly chair or bench that's upholstered, you'll have to remove the upholstery in order to take the chair or bench apart. After turning the upholstered piece over on your worktable, pull out all the staples and upholstery tacks. (If your piece has elaborate upholstery that you're hesitant to remove, see When You Decide Not to Dismantle on page 44.)

STEP 3: REMOVE ANY SLIP SEATS

If your chair or bench has a slip seat (a thin, padded seat that's screwed in place from underneath through holes in the corner blocks), remove the slip seat by turning the piece over on your table and unscrewing the screws attaching it.

STEP 4: MARK EACH JOINT'S ADJACENT PARTS

Mark each adjacent part of a joint with the same number or letter, so you'll be able to match pieces that belong together when reassembling the object.

Using masking tape and a felt-tip pen to mark the various members of a joint you're dismantling will make it quicker and easier to reassemble the object.

STEP 5: TAKE NOTES AS YOU WORK

Analyze your object and take notes as you dismantle it, so you can see how it was put together and how to reassemble it.

To underscore the importance of marking joints and writing reassembly notes, look at the photo at right. Laid out on a table to greet us at a client's house, this pile of pieces belonging to an eighteenth-century commode had neither any marked joints nor any written assembly notes. It took hours to study all the pieces and finalize a plan for rejoining them, which was largely driven by deciding what to do with the small tambour door (visible at top right in the photo and shown in detail in on page 42). Had we attached the pieces in the wrong order, we could not have installed the tambour panel or the channels in which it slid.

It's invaluable to mark the parts of an object as you dismantle it and keep a record of its assembly. Deciphering the relationship of all the pieces in this unmarked pile from an eighteenth-century commode and figuring out the order for reassembly took a lot of time.

Once completed, the restored piece was very satisfying (note that the moveable front section pushes into the piece to close it).

Shown above is the restored commode, whose construction was ingenious. Among other intriguing features, the front legs on both the moveable commode section and the drawer housing it were designed as right triangles in profile. When the commode was pushed into the drawer to close it, the legs of both sections fit together to form a square.

WHAT IS A TAMBOUR?

Tambour panels and doors are used wherever flexibility is needed, as, for example, on the sliding top of a roll-top desk and for sliding panels. The closely set, ¾-inch-wide wooden strips that make up a tambour are usually adhered to a canvas backing to allow the tambour to slide in grooves positioned on two opposing edges. The photos right show the front and back of the tambour panel on the eighteenth-century commode.

A STRATEGY FOR DISMANTLING

Start by trying to discover what we call "subassemblies," or pieces that come apart and can be reassembled as a unit. After the various repairs are made on the subassemblies, these units can then be put back together to reconstruct the object. For instance, the sides of the bench below are each constructed of a pair of legs connected by an upper and lower crosspiece (called a *stretcher*), and each side can be considered a subassembly. The advantage of working with subassembly units is that you can concentrate on a few members at a time, instead of many. Just make sure as you work that you're correctly assembling the pieces making up each subassembly unit.

It's easier to dismantle an object and repair separate subassemblies than to repair all the joints at once. This bench was in the process of being dismantled (note the masking-tape IDs of each piece) and would be repaired, first, at the two end subassembly units, and then reconnected by the long stretcher (below the bench) and the long side pieces at top.

The Dismantling Process

To dismantle a wobbly object, it's possible that the only effort needed will be to gently tap around each joint in turn and to resist the urge to give a joint a single, hard blow. Do, however, resist that urge since too hard a blow can cause a break in that area or one nearby. Also be sure to use a rubber mallet (or a hammer with padding wrapped around it) along with a flat block of wood between the hammer and the joint in order to prevent damaging the object and to spread the force of the blows.

In most cases dismantling will proceed easily; but if you come across resistance, stop tapping. Look carefully for evidence of a nail or screw preventing the joint from coming apart.

Nails and screws that are below the surface present two problems: finding them and removing them. Look for filler material that may be covering a nail or screw set below the surface (it's usually a slightly different color and texture than the surrounding area). You'll probably have to cut away some of the surface with an X-ACTO knife to remove the recalcitrant nail or screw with a vise grip or pliers. If you can't remove a nail this way, try pushing it out the other end of the wood with a nail set and a hammer or mallet.

BUILDING A TOOLKIT: DISMANTLING TOOLS

In order to repair most joints, you'll need to dismantle the object. It's useful to gather the tools below (most of them are household tools) before starting to take your object apart, even though you may not need to use all of them.

- → Padding (like a remnant of heavy carpeting) and a plastic drop cloth for your worktable
- → Screwdriver
- → X-ACTO knife
- → Pliers
- → Masking tape and marking pen
- → Writing pad and pen
- → Mallet
- → Wood block
- → Nail set and a ball-peen hammer

When You Decide Not to Dismantle

In the case of an object with elaborate upholstery or complex construction, you may decide not to dismantle it. And if you find an older object impossible to take apart, it may be because a woodworker of an earlier century deliberately carved knoblike endings on stretchers and spindles, then inserted them into unseasoned wood so that, as the wood shrank and encased the knob endings, the construction would become permanent.

An alternative to dismantling such pieces is to reglue the joint by drilling an opening in an inconspicuous spot that will angle from one loose member of the joint into its adjoining member. Then insert glue with a glue syringe and turn the object upside down to allow gravity to cause the glue to seep down into the joint between both members. Keep handy a dampened piece of cheesecloth to wipe up the glue that doesn't obey gravity neatly but rather oozes out where it's not supposed to be. After the glue is in place, use a tourniquet to pull both members together (see pages 45 to 48 for instructions on making a tourniquet). To add strength to the glued joint, drill a hole from the exterior and insert a thin dowel after the glue has cured (see page 56 on open-doweling).

Cleaning Off Old Glue

After dismantling an object, you'll need to do one important thing before permanently reassembling it. Clean off all surfaces that are to be glued together. Removing the old glue is crucial because new glue will not bond well to it, and the resulting connection will be weak. To clean off the old glue, proceed as follows:

STEP 1: REMOVE OLD GLUE

Remove glue from all mortises (rectangular openings on one member of a joint), tenons (rectangular extensions on neighboring members that fit into the mortises), dowels (cylindrical wooden rods), and drilled openings for the dowels. Dried brown crusts covering parts to be cleaned are usually hide glue, one of several animal glues used for centuries. Apply warm water and white household vinegar with a brush or rag to dissolve hide glue. Although it doesn't dry out with brown crusts, modern yellow (aliphatic) glue can be similarly dissolved and cleaned off with vinegar.

STEP 2: REMOVE GLUE RESIDUE

Wipe off any glue residue with a slightly damp cloth. If there's still glue residue, lightly sand the area with #220 grit open-coat sandpaper or scrape it gently with an X-ACTO blade. The idea is to do as little damage as possible while removing all the old glue.

Glues have been used since the earliest times to join pieces of wood together to make a structure. In order to create a strong glue bond, some sort of pressure is needed to squeeze freshly applied glue into a very thin, even film until the connection sets and the adhesive can cure (harden all the way through). Once you've started gluing, it's crucial to be ready to apply pressure to the glue bond immediately.

PRESSURE IS KEY FOR A GOOD GLUE BOND

There are many ways to apply pressure to a glue bond. You can press glued parts together with your hands or use all kinds of devices—from simple things, like masking tape and wire brads, to slightly more complex tools, like various types of clamps, to something as complicated as a rope tourniquet. After you have evaluated the type of pressure that's best for your particular project, if you decide that applying a tourniquet is by far the best choice, you'll need to practice making one before using one on the object you want to restore.

BUILDING A TOOLKIT: TOURNIQUET TOOLS

To make a tourniquet for providing pressure to a newly glued joint so it can cure and form a good bond, you'll need the supplies below:

- → Good-quality heavy twine or rope
- → Scissors or a sharp knife
- → Aluminum foil
- → Newspaper
- → A long, thin implement like a pencil, screwdriver, or sturdy stick
- → Low-tack tape

The Time-Honored Tourniquet

One of the oldest and least expensive ways to provide pressure to a glued surface is to make a tourniquet with rope. You'll need a little patience to learn how to make a slipknot that's key to a tourniquet, but once you do, you'll find it invaluable not only for gluing but also for holding together many things in daily life (the tourniquet slipknot is the only knot we ever use to tie packages).

Using a tourniquet in a "dry-run" subassembly—that is, going through the stages of reassembling a subassembly unit without glue—is important in itself. It enables you to both gather all the materials needed for the later gluing process and also gain confidence in the assembly process without the fear that the glue might dry and your repair become permanent.

DRY RUN WITH A TOURNIQUET

Making a tourniquet involves a lot of little steps, but none of them is hard. Just proceed methodically through the directions below, and you'll be ready to try the real thing.

STEP 1: ASSEMBLE ONE SUBASSEMBLY UNIT

Begin by putting together the pieces that make up one subassembly unit.

STEP 2: CUT LENGTH OF ROPE

Cut a length of rope that will go around this subassembly unit two times, and add another 15 inches. On one end of the rope, you'll form a slipknot, which allows the rope to slip through it and be tightened as much as necessary to supply the pressure required while the glue cures.

STEP 3: PROTECT WOOD'S SURFACE

Because the pressure exerted by the tourniquet may be enough to mar the wood's surface, make protective pads for the wood by covering wads of folded newspaper with aluminum foil and lightly taping them to the wood with low-tack tape where the tourniquet will be placed. If you think the tape will leave a residue, it's not difficult to position the pads and keep in place with pressure from the rope alone.

STEP 4: BEGIN SLIPKNOT

Begin your slipknot by making a knot near one end of the rope, forming a loop that takes the rope on top of, under, and then through the opening.

STEP 5: CLOSE KNOT

Next, pull the end of the rope tightly to close the knot so that it looks like that in the photo. (Make sure your knot is close to one end of the rope.)

STEP 6: WIND ROPE AROUND SUBASSEMBLY

Wind the rope all the way around the pieces of wood that you're gluing, making sure that the rope is placed directly over the joints being connected.

STEP 7: WIND ROPE AROUND ITSELF

Place the end of the rope that you've just wound around the piece under the rope's other knotted end; then bring the rope's unknotted end back up and across in the direction from which it came.

STEP 8: MAKE LOOP

Loop the rope's knotted end over itself.

STEPS 9 AND 10: PULL KNOTTED END THROUGH LOOP AND TIGHTEN NEW SLIPKNOT

Bring the rope's knotted end up through the loop that just formed. This produces the loop through which the rope on the right can slide while being tightened. Continue pulling the rope's knotted end to tighten the new slipknot. Check to make sure that the slipknot is close to the first knot you made in Step 4, or it will not work.

STEP 11: PULL ROPE TIGHT

Tighten the rope by pulling it as tightly as you can back in the direction from which you brought it. Don't be concerned if it isn't as tight as you think it should be; the last part of the procedure will take care of that. Just be sure the knot you made at the end of the rope juts out of the "slip" section of the slipknot and serves as a "lock" to prevent the slipknot from opening up.

STEP 12: FORM ANOTHER LOOP

Before going back around the work, form another loop by bringing the rope up over, then under the length on the right, and pull it through the hole that forms.

STEP 13A: WIND ROPE BACK AROUND SUBASSEMBLY

Now wind the rope back under your work and around it, so it's almost back where you started making the slipknot.

STEP 13B: PLACE END BETWEEN TWO STRANDS

Then put this end of the rope between the two strands of rope to the right of the knot and pull tightly.

Step 4

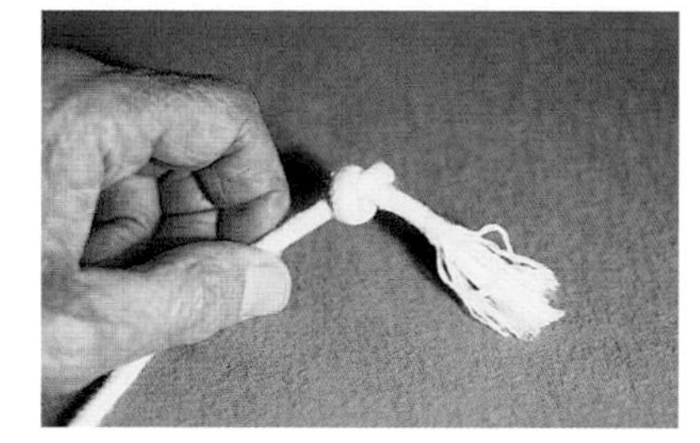

Step 5

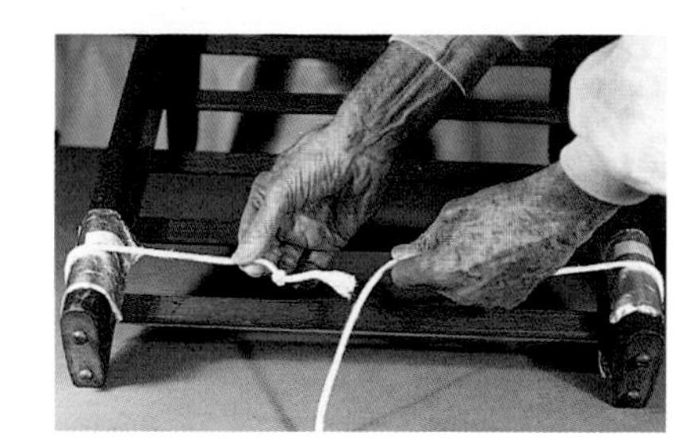

Step 6

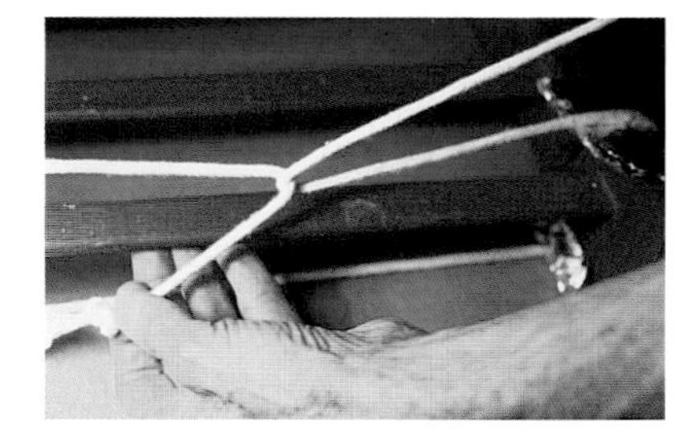

Step 7

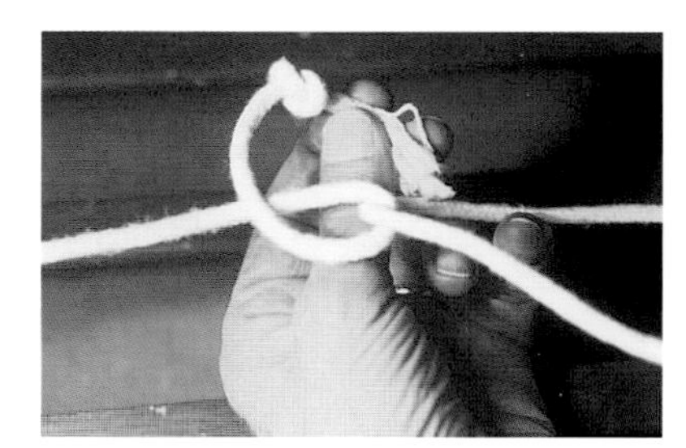

Step 8

Steps 9 and 10

Step 11

Step 12

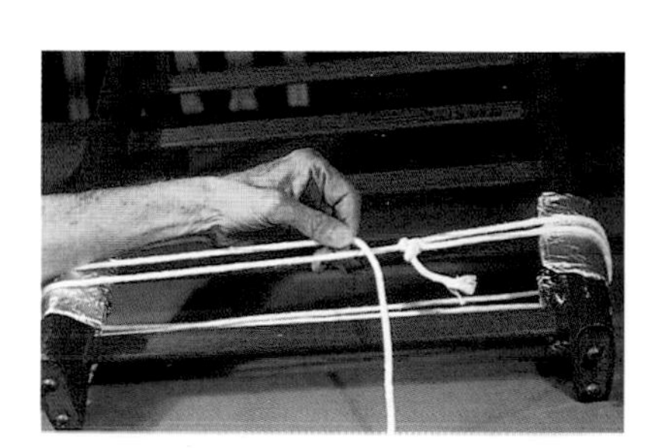

Step 13A

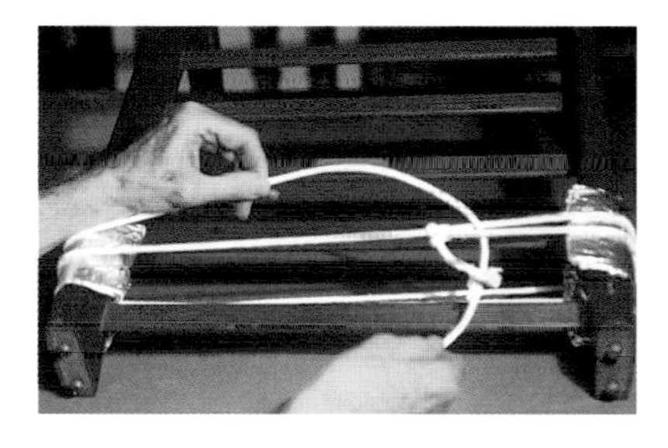

Step 13B

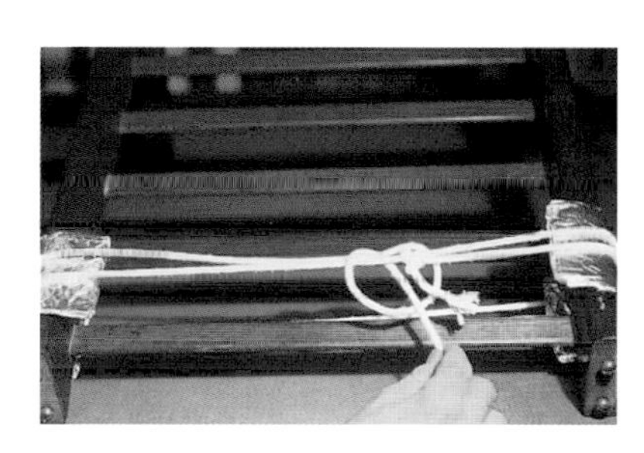

Step 14

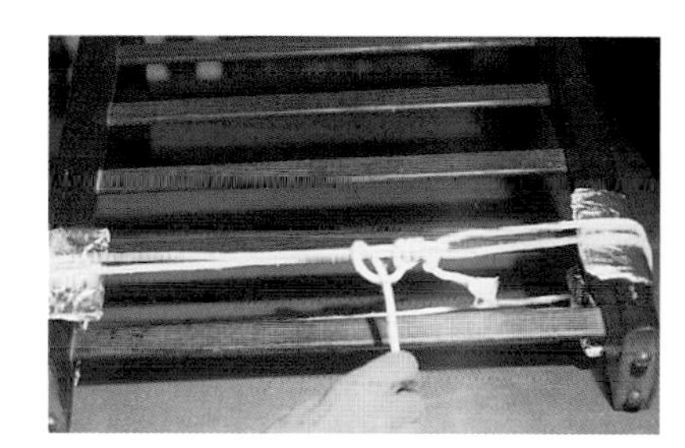

Step 15

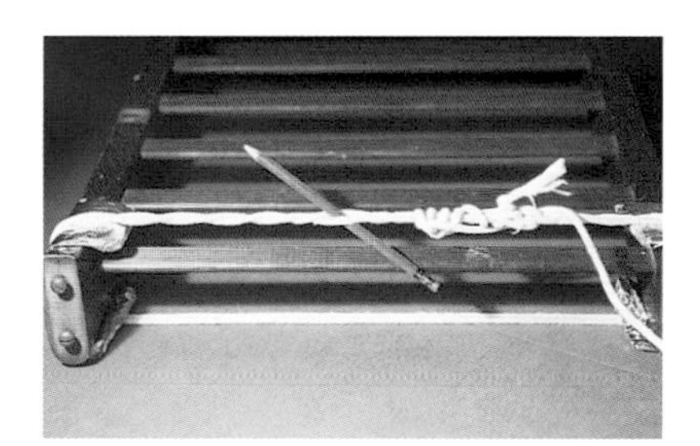

Step 16

STEP 14: MAKE NEW KNOT

Bring the same rope around to the other side of the knot, taking it up and over the two cords on the left. Then tuck it under the two ropes and pull it though the hole in the center of the loop.

STEP 15: MAKE SEVERAL SECURING LOOPS

This loop formation serves to secure the entire tourniquet before you twist in the implement that will tighten it in the next step. Repeat this step several times to make three or four securing loops.

STEP 16: TIGHTEN TOURNIQUET

Complete the tourniquet by pushing a long, thin implement like a pencil in between the two cords, and begin to twist it around several times. Once you've twisted the pencil as tightly as the rope will allow, anchor the pencil against the wood.

The photo to the right shows a chair we restored using a tourniquet, clamp, vice grip, and masking tape.

OTHER SOURCES OF PRESSURE FOR GLUING

Clamps are probably the most widely used of all the tools providing pressure for bonding glued surfaces. Available in a wide range of styles and sizes, clamps are operated by turning a handle (itself variously configured in a straight, T-bar, butterfly, or crank style) attached to a threaded bar that can be tightened or loosened as needed. Whatever their style, all clamps have a jaw depth that determines how far you can reach into the area that needs gluing and a length that determines the height available for clamping.

Clamp pressure should be distributed over an area wider than the head of the clamp to prevent the head from forming a depression in the wood. A flat, rigid cover of metal or plastic, called a *caul*, is helpful for keeping a depression from forming, as are the wrapped pads you made for your tourniquet dry run. Use one or the other with a clamp.

The photo below shows a variety of small, useful clamps, including a few unconventional clamps, like the artist's and automobile-pipe clamps, to remind you to keep your eyes open for any source that may yield clamps that serve your purposes. Look, for example, at medical-, auto-, and art-supply stores as well as the usual home-improvement centers and hardware stores. And also keep an eye out as you look through the photos in this chapter, where you'll see many different styles and sizes of clamps.

One particular type of clamp, called a *press screw*, is useful to know about. When we restored a very large, French art deco lacquer panel from the 1930s, we needed to devise a clamping system to reach much deeper into the surface from the edge than could be reached with the

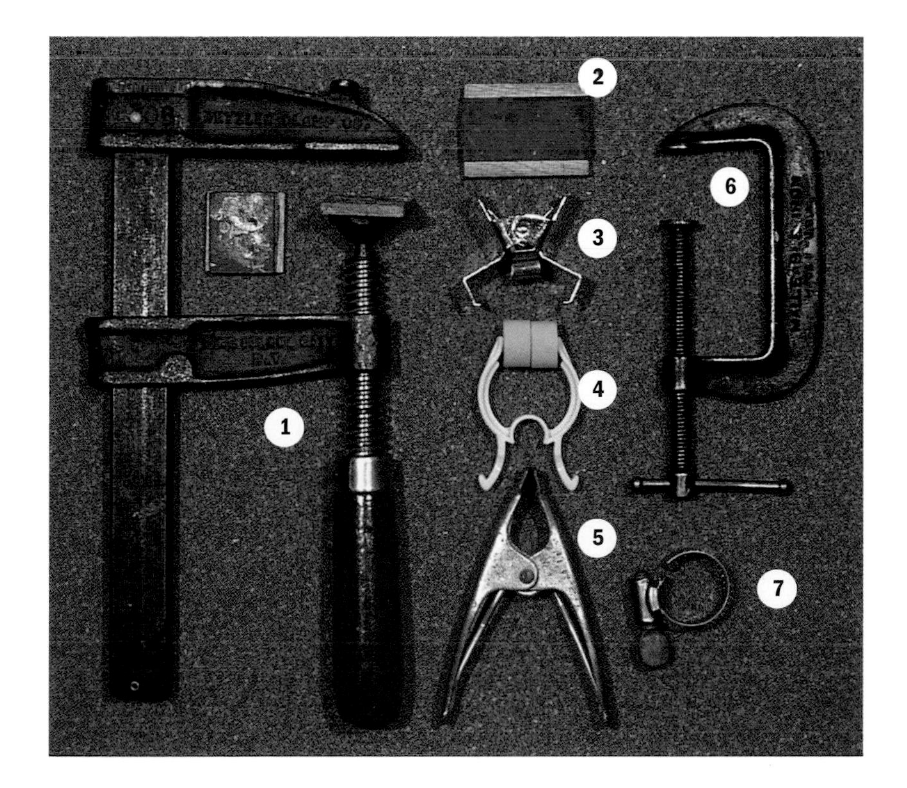

Useful clamps come in many sizes and styles, and from various sources: (1) Bar clamp with magnetic clamp pad; (2) magnetic clamp pad; (3) artist's clamp for canvases; (4) nose clamp from medical suppliers; (5) spring clamp; (6) C-clamp; (7) automobile pipe clamp.

In the veneer press we custom-made to restore a very large art deco panel, we used press screws (the three long, vertical threaded bars in the center) to supply clamping pressure 2 feet into the surface of the panel.

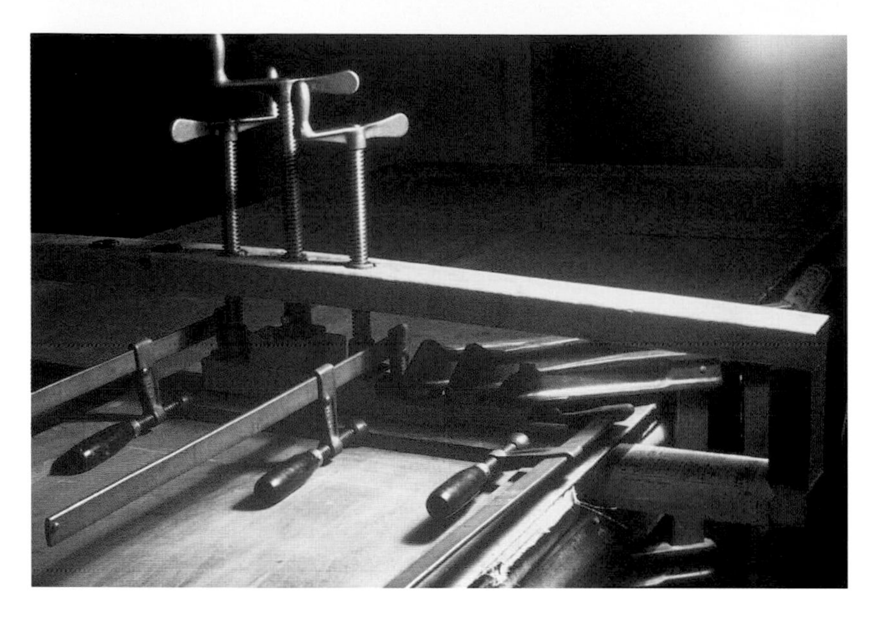

jaw depth of any existing clamp. We constructed what is known as a *veneer press* by making a 4-foot-by-6-inch frame from 2-inch-by-4-inch lumber, which was expansive enough to slide the 4-foot-wide panel through so that the lower section of the frame was underneath the panel. The press screws were inserted through the frame to provide clamping pressure to the panel. We used a variety of other clamps to supply pressure in the depth each could reach (see above). See Resources on page 268 for clamp sources.

Masking tape proved very useful for applying pressure to the glued joint re-attaching the arm on this Balinese wooden sculpture. As soon as the glued cured, a long dowel was inserted into the elbow joint to strengthen it.

Alternative Sources of Pressure

When a tourniquet or a clamp cannot be used to provide pressure for gluing, think of other alternatives. Masking tape is a very useful addition to your toolkit for holding oddly shaped pieces that need pressure and support while glue is curing, as you can see in the photo above.

Two tools that you may not think of to provide pressure are a bed of dry sand and your hands. They have solved occasional problems nicely for us over the years. For example, we used dry sand and our hands to join the many small pieces of the American lyre-shaped clock frame (c. 1835) below. After all the pieces had been attached and the glue had cured, we completed this repair with procedures explained on page 60 in this chapter).

To repair this American lyre-shaped frame (c. 1835), we first seated one large part of it in sand. Then we added and glued one piece of the broken frame at a time, holding each addition with hand pressure and allowing the glue to cure before adding the next piece.

GLUING GUIDELINES

Now that you've seen a range of tools and tactics for applying pressure to a glue bond—and you've resolved to gather tools for applying pressure before you start gluing—let's turn back to the subject of the actual gluing. It's important, first of all, to point out that the only glue we ever used for restoration is yellow glue, whose technical name is aliphatic (pronounced *a-le-FA-tik*) glue. This glue was developed in the 1950s (and made by only one company for 30 years) and was tinted yellow to differentiate it from white glues, which had been the most commonly used glues up to that time. Although both white and yellow glues are polyvinyl acetate (PVA) glues, the unique chemistry of yellow glue gives it extra qualities that have been valuable in our restoration of Asian lacquer and veneers: It relaxes both brittle and cupped substances, allowing them to be flattened out and then secured to their substrates. As well, yellow glue is reversible with heat and warm white vinegar. (See Resources on page 268 for one well-known source of yellow glue.)

Tips for Gluing

Getting a good glue bond requires more than just applying pressure to the bond. It requires understanding how glue behaves and what it will and will not do. With that in mind, here are some tips and guidelines for gluing:

BUILDING A TOOLKIT: TOOLS FOR GLUING AND REMOVING GLUE

Gather the tools below *before* you start gluing. As with some other procedures, you may not, in the end, use all the tools you've gathered.

→ Yellow (aliphatic) glue
→ Cheesecloth
→ Water in a low can
→ A glue brush (or an inexpensive brush with stiff bristles)
→ A glue syringe (its long, thin, straight or curved snout permits placing glue in out-of-the-way spots)
→ A palette knife or two, especially the offset type
→ White household vinegar
→ #220 grit open-coat sandpaper
→ X-ACTO knife
→ Thin, flat pieces of plastic, metal, or wood for a caul

→ As discussed earlier, new glue will not bond to old glue. Clean off all old glue, using #220 grit open-coat sandpaper and an X-ACTO knife. Then wipe the surface with a cloth dampened with warm white vinegar, and wipe again with a dry cloth.

→ Glue broken pieces together before too much time elapses, or the wood may shrink or expand.

→ Glue will not fill a space left by missing wood. It will only bond surfaces that fit tightly together. (See page 71 for information on epoxy putty, which can be used to fill a space left by missing wood.)

→ The larger the gluing area on both surfaces, the stronger the bond.

→ Pressure is needed to squeeze freshly applied glue into a thin, even coat.

→ If you're using clamps, also use cauls (rigid plastic, metal or wood panels of an appropriate size) under the clamps to spread the pressure over a larger area than the head of the clamp, which will prevent depressions from forming (see photos B, C, and D on page 87 for an example of a plastic caul under a clamp).

→ Prevent excess glue that has oozed out of a joint from bonding unintentionally to other surfaces by placing a layer of aluminum foil wherever this might happen.

→ Allow the glue to cure. This means hardening all the way through, not just on the top layer.

Steps to Gluing

The procedures for gluing and providing pressure to freshly applied glue are standard and apply across the board, regardless of the tool used to provide pressure. That tool will vary according to the size and shape of the object being glued, as you can see from the various examples of gluing procedures in this chapter. Because you practiced making a tourniquet earlier in this chapter (see pages 45 to 48), we'll use that tourniquet as the device for applying pressure while looking at the actual procedures for gluing an object back together.

After undoing the rope of your practice tourniquet and taking off the protective pads taped to the wood—and making sure that all the old glue has been removed from the joints—follow these steps below to glue your object back together.

STEP 1: GLUE ONE SUBASSEMBLY UNIT

Starting with one subassembly unit, insert glue into the cleaned-out mortises or dowel holes (see page 54 for more information about mortises, dowels, and other joint connectors). Insert the tenons or dowels into the proper openings, wipe away any glue that squeezes out with the damp cloth, and dry the area.

STEP 2: APPLY TOURNIQUET

Apply a tourniquet around the object as you did in your practice run. As more glue squeezes out, wipe it away, and dry the area.

STEP 3: LET UNIT DRY

Set the subassembly aside on a level surface to cure. Once the glue has hardened, take off the tourniquet and set the unit aside.

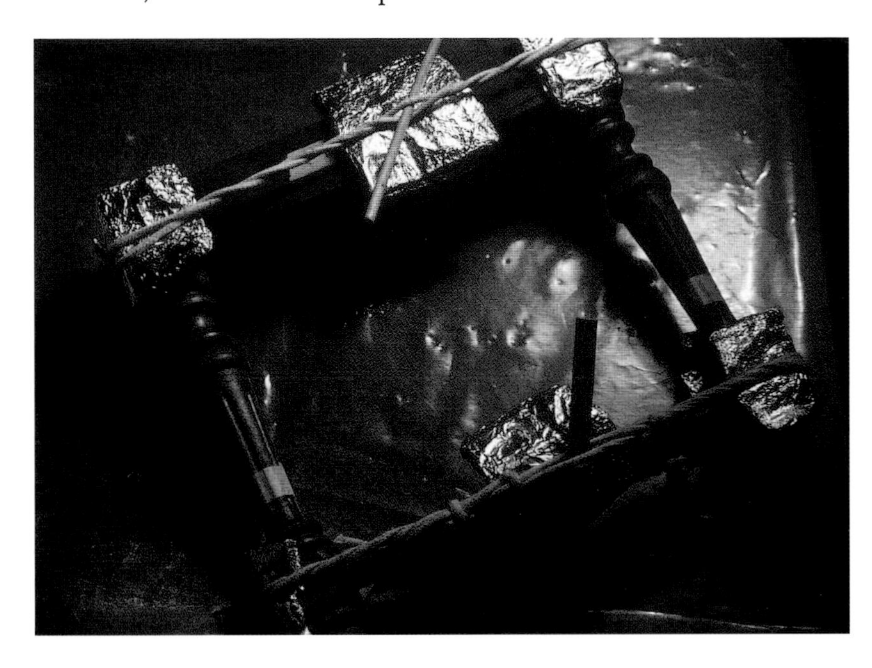

This is a subassembly of one side of a bench, with tourniquets applied directly over the joints being glued.

STEP 4: SIMILARLY TREAT OTHER SUBASSEMBLIES

Repeat Steps 1 to 3 with all other subassembly units.

STEP 5: JOIN SUBASSEMBLIES

Finally, apply glue wherever needed to join the subassembly units into the complete object. Then apply a tourniquet to the entire piece, and set it aside on a level surface to cure without distortion.

As the glue cured on the repaired joints, the bench was set aside on a level surface to prevent it from twisting out of shape.

On this mass-produced chair, all the spindles were inserted and had a tourniquet applied at the same time.

Be especially careful during your dry run and gluing procedures if your object has a series of spindles (lathe-turned members) or slats (horizontal strips across a chair back) that are attached between two opposite members. These spindles or slats must be attached all at once because, if just a few are glued in, you won't be able to insert the others. Therefore, glue and insert the bottom end of all the spindles or slats in the bottom mortises; then glue and insert all the top ends in the top mortises. Yellow glue allows enough time to apply glue in all the mortises, wipe away any glue that has oozed out, and place a tourniquet across each glued joint, as was done in the photo above.

JOINT CONNECTORS

When you dismantled your object, you were able to see that its joints were connected in one of two basic ways, both of which are hidden inside an object: either a *worked joint* or a *go-between joint*. A worked joint has one member shaped with an extension that fits into a correspondingly shaped opening in the joint's mating member. The most common worked joint is a mortise and tenon.

A go-between joint has a separate link that holds the joint together. The link can be variously shaped and is inserted into a compatibly shaped opening cut into each of the two pieces to be joined. Dowels, biscuits, and splines hidden within joints are examples of such links. For some restorations, you may have to innovate a link to solve a joining problem (see page 66 to look at the strategy we devised to connect and strengthen joints in one chair).

Other go-between connectors, for example, glue blocks, battens, corner braces, and hinges, are always applied to the outside of a joint.

Because modern technology is constantly being used to develop new woodworking products, it's a good idea to keep up with what's new to find out what may be useful to you.

Worked Joints: Mortises and Tenons

One of the earliest methods used in both the West and the Far East to strengthen the joint connecting two pieces of wood was mortise-and-tenon construction. A *tenon* is the extension cut on the end of one member of the joint and is usually rectangular in shape. A *mortise* is the opening on the adjoining member that mirrors the shape of the tenon and houses the tenon once the two members are joined. Basic mortise-and-tenon construction can be seen in the pieces of the small footstool below.

Far left: This dismantled, reproduction, eighteenth-century French footstool shows its mortise-and-tenon construction.

Left: The tenons have already been inserted into their mortises. One of the restored mortise-and-tenon joints is most clearly visible on the stool's far, inside corner.

The spindles on the left are parts of mass-produced joints. The dowels on the right are parts of go-between connectors.

Mass-produced worked joints were developed probably in the late nineteenth century to take advantage of machine lathe-turning. With this method, the ends of lathe-turned members—for example, spindles shown above—were given rounded extensions that were, in turn, inserted into matching round openings on the mating member.

Go-Between Connectors: Dowels

Dowels are cylindrical wooden rods used as go-between connectors and are the most common means of joining wood in industry today. Since the late nineteenth century, machines have made it profitable to produce dowels to fit into holes drilled with the same diameter. Dowels were widely used by the 1900s, first in inexpensive furniture and eventually in more costly pieces. Therefore, when you see multiple dowels of exactly the same length and width in an object, the dowels were probably mass-produced. By contrast, if you find dowels of slightly different sizes in an object, it indicates that the piece was probably individually handcrafted rather than mass-produced.

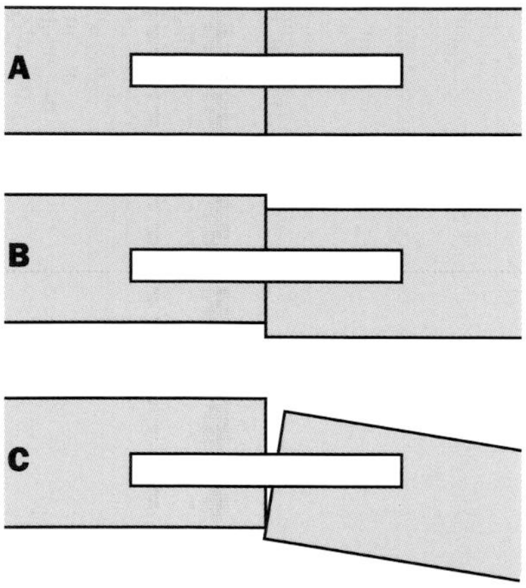

A

B

C

Drilling the holes for blind-doweling (which joins parts invisibly on the interior of a joint's two members) calls for great care to make the holes match up exactly (A). If the holes are drilled unevenly (B) or off-angle (C), the members will not join properly.

BLIND-DOWELING VS. OPEN-DOWELING

Dowels are glued into holes drilled into the two opposing sections of a joint, thereby connecting the sections. The drilling process is termed *blind-doweling* if the two mating holes are hidden within the interior of the object. If the drilling is done from the outside of the object into its interior, the process is called *open-doweling*, and only one hole is drilled (starting on the exterior surface) for each dowel that's inserted.

Doing your own blind-doweling in adjoining members of a joint calls for great care when drilling the dowel holes, or the pieces will not join correctly. As you can see in the drawing at left, Part A shows opposing holes drilled correctly, allowing the two parts of the joint to align properly. Parts B and C show incorrect drilling: Part B displays holes drilled unevenly, with the one on the right drilled too high; and Part C illustrates off-angle drilling (the hole on the right was drilled at an angle instead of parallel to the edges of the wood, producing an off-angle joint).

For our restorations, we preferred open-doweling to blind-doweling for many reasons: The process is easier, quicker, and more accurate than blind-doweling. It's done after the glue has cured on a joint repair, adding strength to the joint. Filling in the holes drilled on the surface (always in places that aren't readily visible) is a small price to pay for the clear advantages of open-doweling. See page 76 in Chapter 4 for information on filling holes.

COMMERCIAL AND NONCOMMERCIAL DOWELS

There are two types of dowels discussed in this chapter: commercial (made primarily to connect two pieces of wood) and noncommercial (made for purposes other than connecting pieces of wood).

Sold in hardware and home-improvement stores in bags or individually, commercial dowels are short wooden rods similar to the dowels used in the woodworking industry to join wood. These rods are variously labeled dowels, dowel pins, spiral-cut dowels, and fluted dowels. The spiral and fluted indentations on these dowels prevent the joint connection from being glue-starved, and allow excess glue to ooze out. In our restorations, we used commercial dowels, whatever their name and configuration, only to replace broken or missing dowels for mass-produced objects.

By contrast with commercial dowels, noncommercial dowels are cylindrical wooden rods of any width and length that are intended for a variety of non-woodworking purposes—for example, round wooden toothpicks, wooden manicure sticks, and long, thin wooden poles. These noncommercial dowels can be customized to solve the problems of strengthening a joint for which a commercial dowel is too wide, too short, or otherwise unsuitable.

Photo courtesy of Connie Hougardy

BUILDING A TOOLKIT: DOWELING TOOLS

Most of the tools below are available in hardware stores and home-improvement centers.

1. A drill (portable electric or battery-operated)
2. Dowel centers
3. Manicure sticks
4. Commercial dowels
5. Clamps
6. An awl or ice pick
7. A drill gauge (a flat metal plate with graduated holes cut out to indicate differing sizes of drill bits)
8. A variety of drill bits
9. Several grits of open-coat sandpaper, ranging from #80 to #220
10. A saw with fine teeth (a hacksaw or a Japanese hand saw)
11. A ball-peen hammer
12. A nail set
13. A long drill bit

Doweling Tips

When working with dowels, both commercial and noncommercial, you'll find these tips helpful:

→ Dowels are cut from straight-grain wood, which means that they may shrink in width but never in length.

→ When cutting dowels to length initially, err on the side of making them too long rather than too short (you can adjust the length later).

→ When inserting dowels into dowel openings, they should be 1/8 inch shorter than the length of the combined holes you're drilling. If a dowel is too long, it may not allow the joint to close tightly.

→ A dowel's width should be slightly less than one-third the width of the wood being joined. Dowels that are too wide may split the wood surrounding them when they're inserted.

→ Noncommercial dowels should be "kerfed," or scored, with an X-ACTO knife along their entire length to allow excess glue to ooze out.

→ Chamfer (cut or bevel at an angle) the inserting end of a dowel to prevent it from splintering when being driven into an opening.

→ Put a "stop collar" on your bit with a piece of masking tape to prevent drilling the dowel hole deeper than you intend.

TIPS FOR OPEN-DOWELING

Below are some tips for open-doweling:

→ When open-doweling, examine your glued and cured repair for the most inconspicuous area—usually the underside of the joint repair—on which to begin drilling. Make sure your dowel stick is long enough to go through all the adhered joints—whether only one or several joined pieces. Test the angle of your drill by "sighting" it from both sides and the front to make sure the drill bit places the opening where it's needed. Insert a dowel into the drilled opening that's longer than the opening (we often inserted the whole uncut stick, which showed immediately whether the drilling angle going through the repair was correct). Then mark the dowel with a sharp pencil where it exits the opening, and cut the dowel ⅛ inch shorter than the pencil mark. Fill small openings on the surface from open-doweling, with guidance from Chapter 4.

→ Open-doweling across a scarf break must always be angled perpendicular to the break. As well, always use a minimum of two dowels across a scarf break (see the discussion of repairing scarf breaks on page 70).

TIPS FOR BLIND-DOWELING

Below are some tips for blind-doweling:

→ When blind-doweling, mark the correct place to drill an opening in an opposing member of a joint with a tool called a *dowel center* (see Building a Toolkit: Doweling Tools on page 57). This small, round metal device (sold in pairs in four sizes: ¼ inch, 5⁄16 inch, ⅜ inch, and ½ inch) has a sharp-pointed tip that's inserted into the drilled opening on one side of a joint, and, when the two members of the joint are pressed together, makes a mark on the opposing side of the joint to note the correct location for the other drilled opening. To turn the small dot made by the dowel center into a pilot hole (which prevents the drill bit from skittering around), deepen the mark made by the dowel center with an awl or an ice pick.

→ Choose the correct size of drill bit for the dowel you want to insert. Drill bits are available for wood or metal. Metal-twist drill bits (which we used on wood) are available in various small widths, while spade bits for wood are available from ¼ inch to wider widths for drilling large openings.

→ Use a minimum of two dowels in most joints to prevent pivoting. Don't position the dowels too close to one another or too near each end.

Replacing Broken Commercial Dowels

If a dowel breaks or is missing from a joint, you'll need to replace it if you want to restore the joint to its original state. Replacing broken dowels is time-consuming and requires patience to perform many separate tasks involved, but it's not very difficult. Of course, you can saw off any broken dowel, glue the mating parts together, and, after the glue has cured, do open-doweling, as described in the open-doweling tips on page 58.

You'll need commercial dowels to replace the broken or missing ones in your object. To match the size of the existing dowel with commercial dowels, remove an existing full or partial dowel. To do this, keep twisting the dowel to loosen it. Also try adding a little warm vinegar around the dowel's base to see if that will break the glue bond. The dowel will usually release rather easily because it has either shrunk and/or the old glue has dried out. If you can't remove the broken dowel, follow the directions below.

If you find that you can't match the exact size of the dowel(s) you want to replace, buy dowels that are a bit larger, and reduce their size this way: Insert the commercial dowel into the chuck of your drill, and place the dowel on a metal file. As the drill turns the dowel, the file will abrade it, reducing its width.

To reduce the width of a commercial kerfed dowel, we positioned the dowel in a drill and used a metal file to narrow the dowel as the drill turned. Then we kerfed (scored) the dowel again with an X-ACTO knife.

You can also reduce the dowel's width by holding a strip of #80 sandpaper tightly around the dowel to abrade it as the drill turns. Keep testing the dowel's size by periodically trying to insert it into the joint opening. You want it to slide in the opening leaving very little room for glue to surround it to make a bond, but the dowel shouldn't be too loose.

MEASURING THE DOWEL LENGTH NEEDED

To find out how long to cut your replacement dowel, insert one end of the replacement dowel in one existing opening and make a mark with a pen or pencil even with the end of the joint opening. Remove the dowel from the opening, and put the other end in the opening opposite it. Again mark the point on the dowel where it exits the hole.

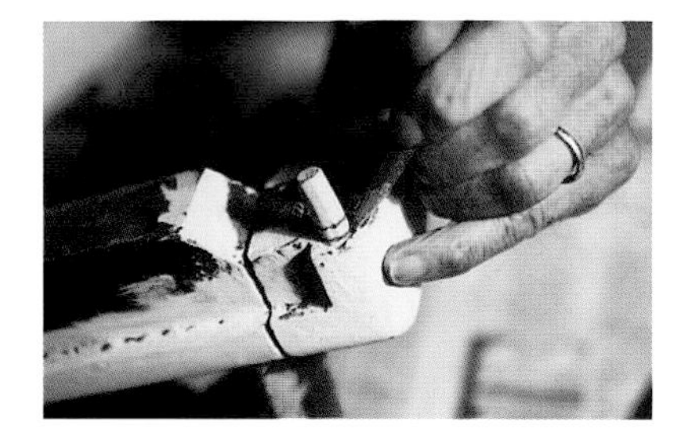

To determine how long to cut a replacement dowel, insert one end into one of the two dowel openings and pencil-mark where the dowel exits the hole. Place the other end into the opposing hole and mark where it exits. Add the two marked lengths, and cut the dowel ⅛ inch shorter to clear the opening and allow the joint to close tightly.

Adding together both marked lengths will give you the total, exact length of the two openings in which the dowel will be placed. Cut the replacement dowel ⅛ inch shorter than the full exact length, so the dowel won't prevent the joint from closing tightly.

WHEN YOU CAN'T REMOVE A DOWEL

If you have one empty dowel opening but the mating dowel opening houses a dowel that cannot be removed, saw that dowel off level with the surrounding area. Sand the sawed-off area smooth with grades of

The hole made by the dowel center (in the sawed-off dowel at top) merely shows where to place the point of the drill bit. Use an awl to make a deeper pilot hole to "seat" the drill bit and keep it from skittering around when you start drilling.

To drill a dowel hole, sight the drill position from all angles—front, sides, and top—to ensure that it will make a completely vertical hole.

sandpaper ranging from a coarse grit (#80) to a finer one (#220). This surface must be level before you proceed to the next step of using a dowel center to mark the remaining dowel's center point.

WORKING WITH A DOWEL CENTER

Choose the dowel center that fits best into the empty opening of the mating joint (test the dowel centers by placing them one at a time into the opening to find the correct size). Slip the correct dowel center into the opening opposite the area you've sawn. Press both wooden members of the joint together tightly. The metal point on the dowel center will put a sharp indentation (which can be made larger with an ice pick, awl, or an X-ACTO blade to serve as a pilot hole) in the center of the sawed-off dowel. The photo top left shows both the metal dowel center in the open lower hole and the mark of the dowel center on the upper area where the dowel has been sawed off. To create an opening for the new dowel, seat the drill in the pilot hole and drill straight down vertically (we're using a spade drill bit in the photo below left.

After injecting glue in both openings, insert the new dowel, connect the two halves of the joint, clamp the joint, and allow it to set for 30 minutes or longer. Wipe off any glue that oozes out.

If both mating ends are blocked with broken dowels, saw both dowels off level with the surrounding wood, and sand the wood smooth, as explained above. Then drill both holes open again with a drill bit of the correct size, and proceed as explained above. Alternately you can drill two holes elsewhere if need be, or, as suggested in Doweling Tips on pages 57 to 58, glue, clamp, and open-dowel the joint rather than blind-doweling it.

Noncommericial Dowels

We taught blind-doweling to our students because once in a while they brought furniture into class that needed replacement of commercial dowels. But we did open-doweling procedures exclusively in our own restoration work where it was appropriate.

The open-doweling sequence of repair we developed was, first, to reconnect all separate pieces with adhesives and let them cure, and then to insert thin dowels through all the adhered joints to strengthen them. This procedure required dowels that were longer and thinner than the commercially available dowels. Below is a variety of noncommercial dowels that we put to use in open-doweling.

ROUND WOODEN TOOTHPICKS

Round wooden toothpicks proved just what we needed to restore an American, lyre-shaped clock frame (c. 1835) on page 51. This frame had been made from one piece of wood, which meant that its top and bottom sections had no strength and consequently, over time, had broken apart. We found this out after removing the burlap glued to the back of the frame to keep the split pieces together. Because the wood was thin and delicate, we needed very thin, strong dowels with which to do open-doweling.

Far left: The adhesive (probably hide glue) on this nineteenth-century American lyre-shaped clock frame had failed. Our planned repair involved regluing the broken pieces, then open-doweling the repaired joints to strengthen them.

Left: We did a dry run of the open-doweling, inserting the wooden-toothpick dowels at angles to double-check the positioning of the drilled holes. The dowels were shortened before gluing them in.

After gluing together all the pieces that had split apart, as shown above left, and allowing the glue to cure, we drilled openings with a very thin drill bit and inserted the straight, center part of round wooden toothpicks as dowels. Installing the toothpicks in crossed-over angles (after the photo was taken, the full toothpicks used to check the angle of the drilled holes were cut down to their center sections) on both the upper and lower sections of the frame contributed extra strength.

MANICURE STICKS

The noncommercial dowels that we found endlessly useful were manicure sticks (which we refer to just as *sticks*, a term we'll use from now on in this chapter). Available wherever nail-grooming supplies are sold, sticks are made of maple, a strong hardwood, and are cut on the straight grain, making them very strong and stable. Their width and length were perfect for the type of joint restoration we had innovated: providing extra strength to glued and cured joints of all types by using open-doweling, something we could not have accomplished with shorter, wider commercial dowels.

We began using sticks after noticing that many of the mid-nineteenth-century Chinese export objects that we were restoring contained thin bamboo dowels, which were triangular in cross-section. Manicure sticks seemed a good substitute.

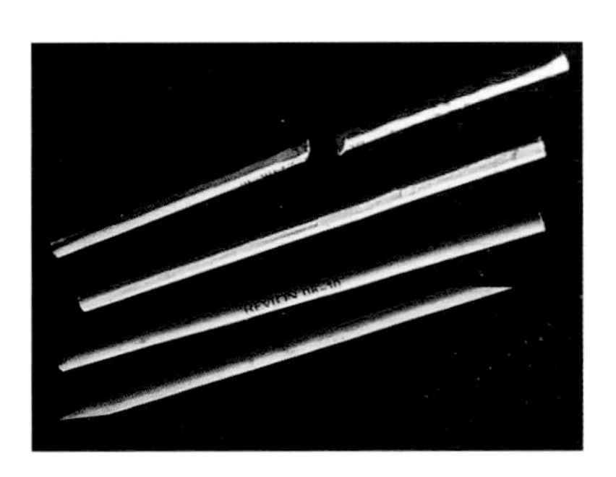

Far left: Notice the two dowels in the middle of this Chinese export tilt-top table. They're the original, triangular-cut bamboo connectors similar to many we found on Chinese export objects we restored that gave us the idea to use thin, long manicure sticks for our restorations.

Left: Manicure sticks make great narrow dowels, and we often cut them in half, like the top stick, since this is a handy, workable size. The second stick from the top was flattened a bit to allow excess glue to escape.

One of the many restorations in which we used sticks and open-doweling included repairing the crest rails (the top horizontal pieces) on a set of ten chairs. Typical of our open-doweling procedure, we first glued the joint and allowed the glue to cure. Then, before we began drilling the dowel hole, we made a pilot hole with the tip of an X-ACTO blade, so the drill would enter the pilot hole cleanly and not skitter around. The top left photo on page 62 shows that we made a "stop collar" on the drill bit with masking tape to mark the depth at which we needed to stop drilling the hole.

Right: To strengthen the glued and cured joints on the crest rails of a set of ten chairs, we open-doweled the joints with manicure sticks. To drill a dowel hole of the correct depth, we made a "stop collar" with masking tape on the drill bit to indicate when to stop drilling.

Far right: With a small, folding Japanese saw, it was quick and easy to shorten the stick to the correct length.

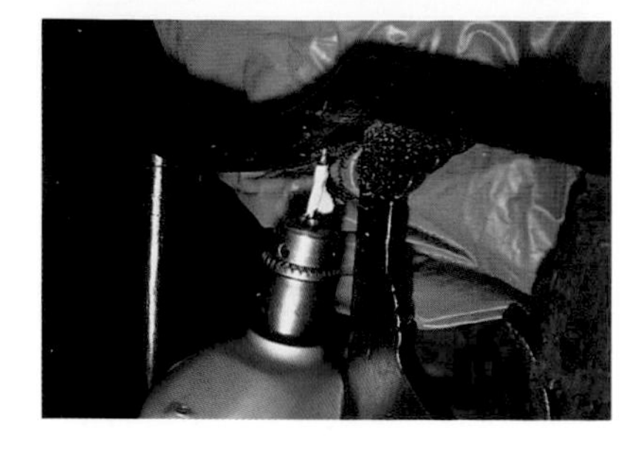

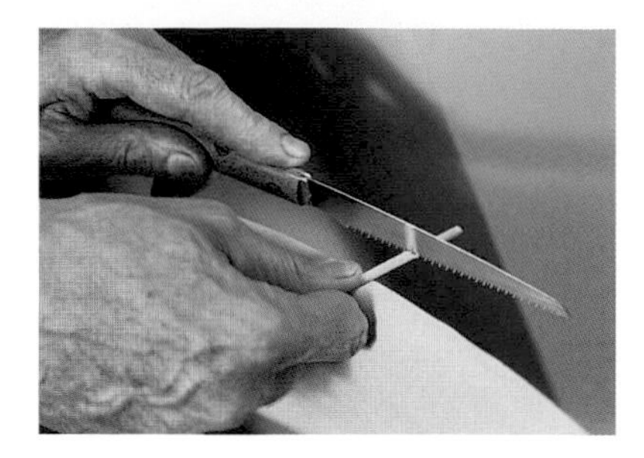

Next we inserted a stick into each dowel hole and pencil-marked where the stick exited the opening. Then we cut the stick ⅛ inch shorter than that pencil mark.

We injected yellow glue into the opening with a glue syringe, then inserted the shortened stick and drove it all the way in with a nail set and mallet.

LONG HARDWOOD POLES

In addition to using manicure sticks for open-doweling in most restorations, once in a while we needed much longer dowels to impart strength. Home-improvement centers, hardware stores, and some craft stores sell hardwood poles that are up to 4 feet in length and range in width from ¼ inch to 1 inch. We used the long drill bit shown on page 57 to drill long openings from the exterior to deep within the interior, going across the joint to add extra strength to an object.

The photo at bottom left shows a long hardwood pole before it was pencil-marked at the exit hole to indicate where it had to be cut. The pole was open-doweled from the flat underside of the carving and crossed through the horizontal line of the joint (about 10 inches). It was used to strengthen the joint where a heavy carving, one of a pair cut off a high buffet from the 1920s, was being connected to a tabletop. At bottom right is one of the two legs that was doweled.

At right, a long hardwood pole is being used to strengthen the joint where a heavy carving, one of a pair cut off a high buffet from the 1920s, was being connected to a contemporary tabletop. The completed restoration is shown at far right.

OTHER GO-BETWEEN CONNECTORS

Although dowels are by far the most commonly used go-between connectors, there are other options, particularly for strengthening existing joints. The choice of connectors depends entirely on the specific joint that needs strengthening (for instance, there are special connectors—glue blocks or corner braces—for strengthening two pieces of wood that connect at a right angle). Given that your project will have its own set of variables, the basic information below will nonetheless get you started with choosing the best option for connectors for the task at hand. Thereafter, your hardware store or home-improvement center can help you assemble the supplies we've outlined below and may even be able to point out new products to consider for your project.

Biscuits

Developed in the 1950s in Switzerland, biscuits are an example of combining an age-old procedure (inserting a connector inside a joint) with a new tool (a saw with a specially shaped blade) to produce a new product. Available in three slightly different sizes (see the photo at right), biscuits are made from wood fibers that are meant to expand with glue, producing a stronger bond than a smaller connector like a dowel offers because they provide a larger surface to be glued (remember that the more gluing surface, the stronger the bond). Biscuits are particularly useful in miter joints.

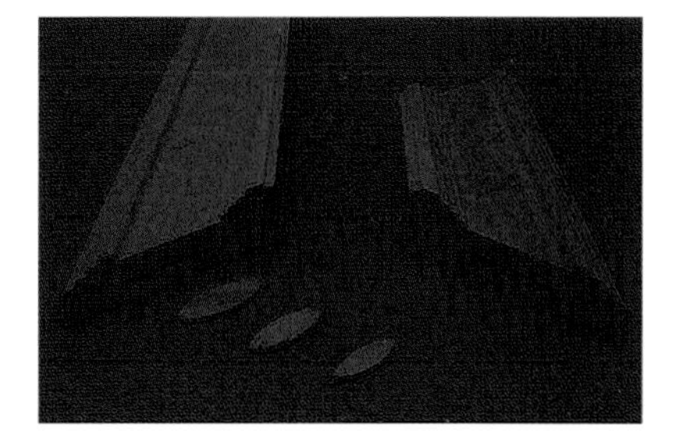

A biscuit is a wood-fiber connector (available in several sizes) that swells once glue is applied and creates a strong joint.

Splines

Splines are a much older connector than biscuits. They're cut on straight grain and, like biscuits, are especially useful in miter joints, since the miter's weak end-grain-to-end-grain joint structure is strengthened considerably by the spline's straight grain. Because splines are so much thinner than biscuits (which expand), they can be inserted in wood of less depth.

It's best to glue and clamp the joint together, and, after it has cured, make a saw cut (or kerf) into both members at the joint (see the photo at right). After the spline has been adhered, any excess wood can be cut off. Alternately, after the joint has been adhered and cured, you can chisel out of the back an opening the shape of the spline running across the joint, then glue in the spline.

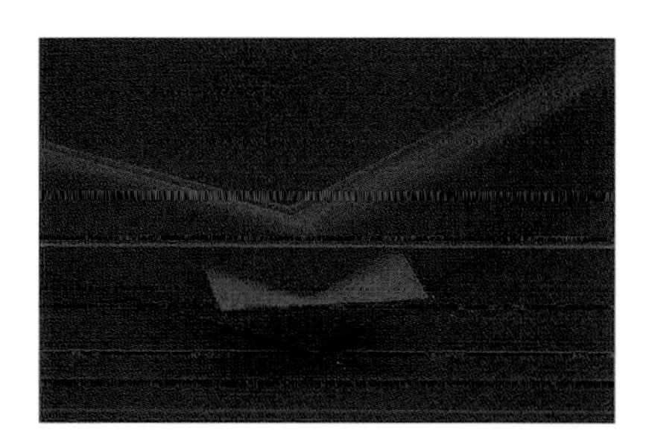

This hardwood spline has been inserted with glue into the saw kerf (scores) in a miter joint, before being trimmed flush with the frame.

Photos courtesy of P.H. Miller Studio 8 Gallery

Hinges

Hinges are connectors of a special sort: They allow movement of both parts of a joint.

When purchasing hinges for new work, choose those with screw holes arranged in an alternating pattern rather than aligned in a single row, as they were on many older hinges. This straight alignment of screws often causes the wood to split along the grain line, as discussed on page 35 in Chapter 2 and seen in the photo at top of page 35.

In this case, the wood that had split could be reconnected easily because it fit so tightly and was repaired soon after it was noticed.

Right: To repair the split in this hinged panel, caused by the original hinge having screw holes aligned in a row, we injected glue into the split, allowed it to cure, and then drilled angled holes for manicure-stick dowels to be inserted to strengthen the repaired joint.

Below: The split was barely noticeable after it was grained.

To repair the split, we removed the hinge, inserted glue into it with a thin palette knife, then clamped the door from side to side across the width of the wood to provide pressure for the glue the length of the split. The glue was allowed to cure, after which we open-doweled the repair for strength. The photo at top shows the open-doweling sequence of the repair, and the photo above the completed repair.

Glue Blocks

Glue blocks are usually rectangular joint strengtheners, which are cut on the straight grain and used in multiples to reinforce joints set at right angles. In the photo top, opposite page, numerous glue blocks set very close to one another reinforce the joint of the serpentine tabletop and fretwork apron on the underside of this eighteenth-century English Chippendale tea table. Straighter joints don't require as many glue blocks.

Glue blocks can be cut small or large, according to the needs of the object being repaired. For instance, we've cut glue blocks as small as 1/4 inch by 1/4 inch by 1/2 inch and as large as 1 1/4 inches by 1 1/4 inches by 3 inches. When using glue blocks, be sure to fit them tightly against both parts of the joint after applying glue, and then clamp them in place until the glue cures.

The serpentine-curved sides of this eighteenth-century Chippendale tabletop (upside-down on our padded worktable) required many more glue blocks than would be needed for joints on straight sides.

Battens

Cut along the straight grain, battens serve to strengthen wood joints—often those that join long pieces of wood to one another. They're also especially useful to put on the underside of a freshly un-warped piece of wood that's attached on only one edge, as, for example, the drop leaf of a table would be.

Because battens are positioned on the underside or back of a structure, they are visible, as you can see in the photo below right. To use a batten, glue it on the underside or back of the wood being supported; and, if the wood is thick enough, also screw the batten into the wood.

The reverse side of this French Régence mirror frame (c. 1715) appears to have had battens installed when the frame was constructed.

Corner Braces

In prehistoric times, right-angled formations of tree branches often served as wooden "connectors" after being lashed to the two members of a right-angled joint (see the photo below left). Today's right-angled, metal corner braces are a vast improvement on their precursor and are available in all sizes. The photo below right shows an older, hand-forged version of a corner brace.

We've seen many corner braces used to strengthen already-glued joints on the underside of tables and even in the corners of right-angled seat frames. However, refrain from gluing the corner braces in place and then inserting screws in the holes, which defeats the purpose of the screws, which are supposed to be removable.

Far left: This recreation of a prehistoric raft in the Kon-Tiki Museum outside of Oslo, Norway, shows perhaps the earliest known corner-brace "connector" for a right-angled joint: a right-angled tree branch lashed to the L-shaped joint of the mast and a horizontal member under it.

Left: The corner joint of this eighteenth-century Chinese table is strengthened by a hand-forged, metal corner brace, which is old but not original to the table.

To repair the broken tenons that were originally cut off-angle on a late-nineteenth-century Italian chair with curved sides, we hit upon using wooden Venetian-blind slats, which we steamed and bent around a coffee can.

Bending straight-grain go-betweens (the light-colored wood in the curved sides) solved the problem of providing a strong connecting link between the members of the joints.

Innovated Go-Betweens

Occasionally you may find that none of the commercially available go-between connectors is quite what you need to repair an object. That was certainly the case when we restored a late-nineteenth-century Italian chair with curved sides that had originally been joined with mortise-and-tenon construction. The original mortises and tenons had split apart because, in order to accommodate the chair's curved sides, the maker had cut the mortises and tenons on a curve rather than on the straight grain. This meant the grain in the joint was off-angle and weak.

To replace the original, curved tenons, we innovated a variation on a go-between link: We bent wooden Venetian-blind slats as go-betweens to join and strengthen the chair joints. We did this by sanding the paint off of the slats, then wetting, heating, and clamping them to a coffee can to bend them into a curve (see the photo top left). We inserted the bent slats into the long, curved mortises that were original to the chair. The photo below left shows the back and curved-slat replacements inserted into the curved mortises of the partly reassembled chair.

MITER JOINTS

A miter joint is constructed of two pieces of wood, each cut diagonally to join to the other piece and produce the overall angle of the joint. In other words, a 90-degree right-angle joint, like that on the corner of a frame, for example, is formed from two pieces cut at opposing 45-degree angles. Miters can be composed of many different angles, but the most common miter is 90 degrees.

The diagonal ends of a miter are end-grain wood, which, when joined together, produce one of the weakest joint connections possible. Miter joints on frames need strong support, using one of the several connectors mentioned above (dowels, biscuits, or splines).

Repairing Miter Joints on Frames

Most of the time when the pieces of wood making up a frame shrink or expand, they do so more or less equally. But if there's a noticeable difference in width among the pieces of a frame (some narrowed from shrinkage, others widened from expansion), the frame is better left as is. We caution you not to try to disassemble any frame with miter openings, thinking that you can reassemble the existing pieces: Unfortunately, you'll end up with four pieces that don't make a frame.

Be aware that the dimensions on frames that have shrunk or expanded will be different from what they were originally. Frames that have shrunk have larger inside dimensions, which means that any glass in the frame may have to be replaced. Frames that have expanded will have larger outside dimensions.

Assuming that all four miter corners have opened equally because of shrinkage or expansion, the main way to repair such damaged miter joints on frames is filling the open joints (see pages 26 and 28 for more information on wood shrinkage and expansion). If the wood in the miter has shrunk, you'll be working with the frame's inside corners; if the wood has expanded, you'll work with the outside corners. All four miter joints will need similar filling treatment.

Adding suitable material, like epoxy putty, to fill out the inside or outside corner of the miter returns the miter to its true, original angle, which is usually 90 degrees. The amount of epoxy putty required varies with the extent of the corner's shrinkage or expansion. To determine how much needs to be added to the miter to fill out the angle, start by using a protractor to draw the center line of your miter angle (for example, 45-degree line for a 90-degree square corner) on a piece of paper. Then align the actual center line of the miter with the drawn line, and the difference between the miter and drawn line equals the amount needed to fill out the miter.

Fill the gap with epoxy putty, using the drawn line as a guide for cutting the sharp right angles in the epoxy putty with an X-ACTO knife on the inside and outside corners and for scoring a sharp line to simulate the corner's 45-degree miter line (assuming you're dealing with a 90-degree miter). When all the added material has cured, match the surrounding surface (gilding or paint, including using graining to match real wood).

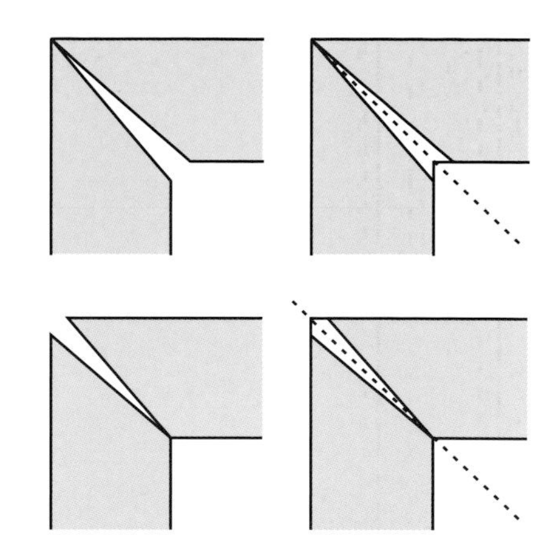

When wooden frame members shrink, the miters open up on the inside corners (top). When wooden frame members expand, the miter joints open up on the outside corners (above). To repair either type of damage on all four corners, you need to fill the corners with epoxy putty to rebuild and close the miters, a process that will slightly change the overall size of the object.

AN ORNAMENT AS AN ALTERNATIVE

As an alternative to the strategy discussed above—or in addition to it—you could place ornaments at the corners to cover the miter damage or repairs. A wide variety of wood and plaster ornamental shapes are available in stores, or you could customize the repair by making a mold and cast of your own corner ornament (see Chapter 5 for information

This detail of an early-twentieth-century Chinese export cinnabar table is one of eight miter joints (each corner has two miters) that moved slightly, splitting the lacquer over all the joints.

on making molds and casts). For example, we used casts from a madeleine-cookie pan mold to ornament inside-corner miter repairs, as shown on page 97 in Chapter 5.

Repairing Miter Joints

Whether large or small, all miter joints have the potential for opening up because of the weak end-grain construction at the joint's diagonal edges. This potential for damage is especially true for tables that don't have stretchers to prevent the legs from splaying out and the miter joints from getting even slightly loose. On tables that are coated with, for example, lacquer, paint, or gesso and gold leaf, even the slightest movement of the miter joint can cause cracks, as happened in the early-twentieth-century Chinese cinnabar lacquer table in the photo on page 67.

To repair this table, we built an understructure to stabilize the joints and eliminate the possibility of further movement. Starting at the understructure and going through the corner joints, we open-doweled

At right, our repair involved building an understructure to stabilize the table and its joints, and then open-doweling through the understructure and into the joints to strengthen them. In this shot of our dry-run repair, we drilled deeply enough to pass through the 1-inch-by-4-inch wood pieces (that we prepainted to match the underside of the table), and into each corner leg. Below is a detail of one of the corners of the restored table.

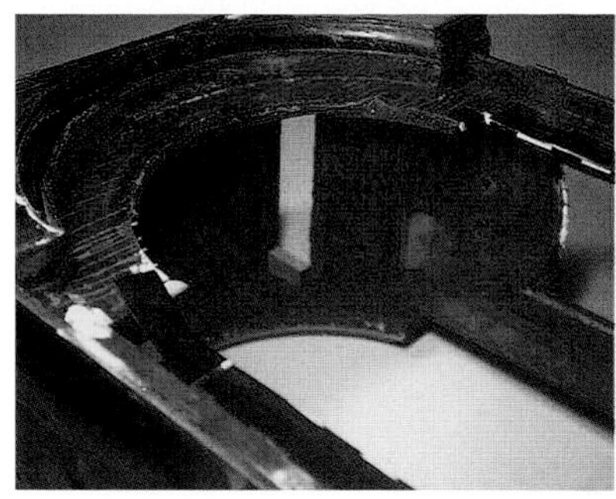

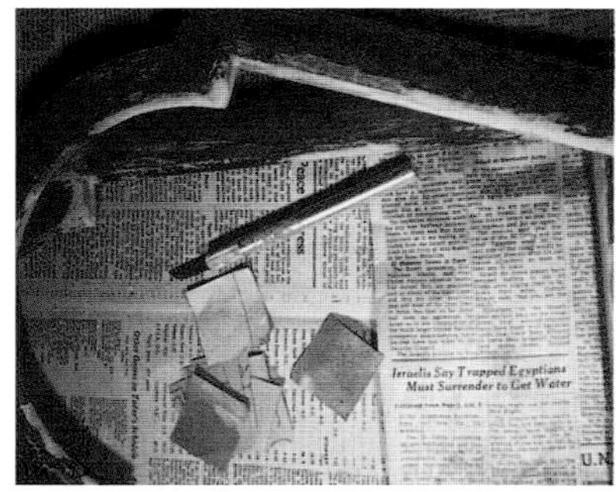

these joints to further strengthen them. The angles at which the sticks were inserted can be seen in the photo of the dry run before they were shortened and glued. After the joints were stabilized, we restored the surfaces to complete the restoration. (Also see pages 110 to 111 in Chapter 5 for further information on restoring this table.)

REPAIRING THIN MITERED MOLDINGS

Thin moldings are often attached to objects to provide a softer ending to a sharply cut edge. When the outer contour of an object has right angles, the moldings must be mitered to accommodate the change in direction. One example of this is shown on the bracket clock case above made by Henton Brown of London, c. 1740, destined for the Turkish market. The change of direction at each corner required a miter joint.

To repair the missing moldings on this piece, we cut very thin quarter-round moldings just the right size. Then we replaced the missing section of curved molding with a piece of quarter-round molding dampened to make it flexible enough to bend around the arc.

If you're working with thin moldings, be aware that you can strengthen them. You can do this by tapping thin, small wire brads (another "connector") below the surface with a ball-peen hammer and a nail set after gluing the molding in place.

To replace the small, missing, mitered moldings on this eighteenth-century English bracket-clock case, we used low-tack black electrical tape to provide pressure while the glue was curing. The tape was strong enough to hold the molding in place but not so strong that it damaged any existing paint. At above middle the missing moldings are shown replaced. At bottom is a close-up of the restored moldings on the inner arched frame. Finally, at top left is a brachet clock of the same style and period of our restoration project.

Top left photo courtesy of Mallett

REPAIRING FRACTURED MEMBERS

Repairing fractured members of an object is different from the problem of connecting joints. Joint ends are fashioned to fit tightly against each other: Fractured members can split along a straight grain, or they can break in such a way that part of the wood is damaged or destroyed. When the break is a clean one—for instance, along a grain line—and is caught early enough, there will likely be no change in dimension because of shrinkage or expansion. The repair merely entails fitting the parts together after gluing, clamping them until they cure, and then open-doweling exactly perpendicular to the split. This is the approach used for repairing scarf breaks, which split cleanly along the straight grain.

Repairing Scarf Breaks

Scarf breaks occur on wooden members that were not originally cut along the straight grain. These breaks split the wood from one edge obliquely (at an angle) across to the other edge, as seen below. They're common occurrences that you'll need to repair, whether you're dealing with a broken member that's still attached to the object or one that's broken off (and which you need to repair before reassembling the object). In either case, once you've repaired the scarf break by gluing, clamping, and allowing the glue to cure, you should strengthen the repair by open-doweling the site of the break from underneath the member. There are two important rules to remember when doing this repair: (1) the angle of the doweling must be perpendicular to the diagonal scarf break; and (2) a minimum of two dowels must be used to prevent pivoting.

At the top of the next page is an example showing both kinds of scarf-break repairs: repairing a broken member that's still attached to an object and repairing a member that has broken off or been taken off an object. In this case, the object is the reproduction English Regency drum table you saw on page 36 in Chapter 2. Upturned, in the top right photo on the opposite page for repair, the table had three areas where splits

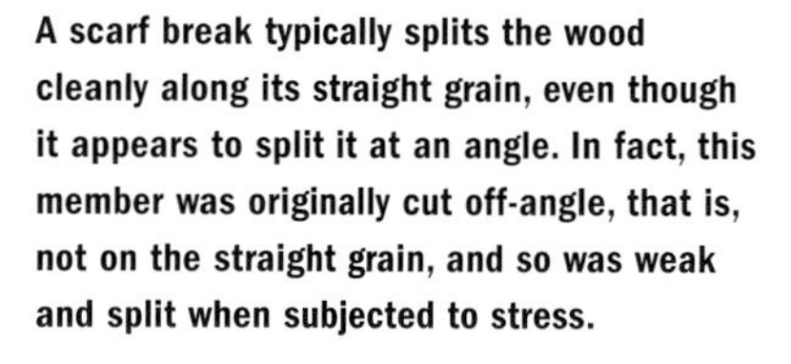

A scarf break typically splits the wood cleanly along its straight grain, even though it appears to split it at an angle. In fact, this member was originally cut off-angle, that is, not on the straight grain, and so was weak and split when subjected to stress.

On this reproduction nineteenth-century English Regency drum table, note the scarf breaks along the natural straight grain on the upper right leg in the photo top right and on the broken-off leg lying on the underside of the table, which also has a scarf break at its foot. At bottom right, the legs have been repaired but not yet in-painted. At top left is a classic early-nineteenth-century English Regency drum table, which is very similar to the one we restored.

occurred: on the central column of the base, which, when it broke, took one leg along with it; on the split end of the leg that broke off; and on the leg on the right in the photo.

The chronology of repair involved first gluing, clamping, and curing the broken-off end back on the leg that had split off the column base. Next, the whole leg was reattached to the base. Then the right leg was repaired the same way. And finally all three repairs were strengthened with open-doweling done perpendicular to each joined area.

Repairing Fractured Members with Epoxy Putty

Unfortunately, not all fractures occur along grain lines and produce neat breaks with all the pieces intact. Beetle damage, careless handling, bad previous repairs, and stresses are just a few of the causes for breaks that are not pristine. In such cases, the ends of the break are often damaged, and the fit of the broken pieces is not tight enough to use glue for the repair since glue cannot fill a gap or replace missing wood. For breaks like these, a different material is required, and the one that we found works best to fill gaps and bond messy breaks is a two-part epoxy putty. Epoxies may not be a preferred material in conservation, but they're often used (the choice is between using a little epoxy to save an entire object or not intervening at all and allowing the object to further disintegrate).

After mixing the resin and hardener that make up the putty (see Mixing Epoxy Putty on page 73, you must use it within a relatively short time, unless you put it in water, which prevents it from drying out while you're working with it. Even though the epoxy putty is very strong, open-doweling provides extra reinforcement.

The right end of the late-nineteenth-century Japanese dressing stand on the next page, for example, had been repaired previously with dowels that were too short and an adhesive that was too thick. As a result, it eventually fell apart. To repair the stool, we applied epoxy putty to both edges of the wood to be joined, making sure to fill in the gaps that remained because of wood that was missing. When the epoxy putty had cured thoroughly, we drilled openings for the dowels so that they would pass through all three pieces that had been joined together. Note the ¼-inch sections of epoxy putty that were needed to fill the gaps.

Because epoxy putty can both bond pieces together and fill in gaps of missing wood, it was the adhesive/filler needed to reattach this volute curl that had split off a late-nineteenth-century Japanese low dressing stand.

We applied the mixed epoxy putty to both edges of the wood to be joined, making sure to fill in the gaps that remained because of missing wood.

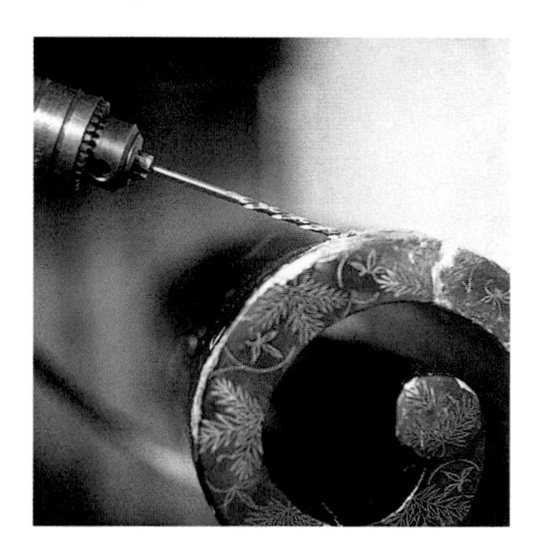

Right: When the epoxy putty had set thoroughly, we drilled openings for the dowels so that they would pass through all three pieces that had been joined together. Note the two ¼-inch sections of epoxy putty (the white areas in the curve of the curl) needed to fill the gaps.

Far right: We open-doweled all three pieces of the stand to strengthen the joint. By inserting uncut manicure sticks, we could verify the correct angles of the openings. After marking the sticks at the exit holes, we cut them ⅛ inch shorter, and inserted them with a nail set and a ball-peen hammer.

Top left: This is the completed restoration of the Japanese dressing stand. The volute curl on the left was used as a model to repair the curl on the right.

Top right: This Kangxi period (1662–1722) dressing stand, an earlier version of the one we restored, had an auction estimate of $7,000–$9,000.

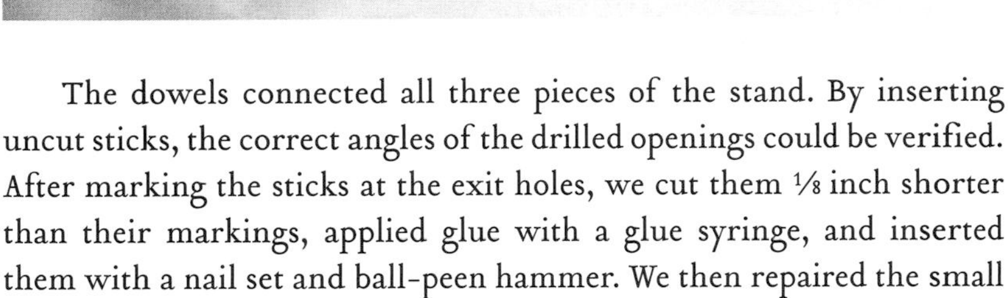

The dowels connected all three pieces of the stand. By inserting uncut sticks, the correct angles of the drilled openings could be verified. After marking the sticks at the exit holes, we cut them ⅛ inch shorter than their markings, applied glue with a glue syringe, and inserted them with a nail set and ball-peen hammer. We then repaired the small holes in the lacquer as outlined in Chapter 4.

At top is a view of the restored dressing stand. The volute curl on the left was used as a model for the repaired volute curl on the right.

MIXING EPOXY PUTTY

Epoxy putty is composed of a resin and hardener, both differently colored, that need to be mixed together thoroughly until the putty is a uniform color throughout. To mix epoxy putty, follow the directions on your product's label (usually these products direct you to mix equal parts of both components). You may want to wear disposable gloves from a pharmacy or craft store if your skin is sensitive and since you may be exposed to this putty over a long time. Generally speaking, however, the mixing and molding processes go quickly. In either case, keep wetting your hands or gloves slightly, which will both help you mix the epoxy putty and mold it into place.

The photo at right shows mixing together the two parts making up the epoxy: the resin (in this brand of epoxy, the brown material) and the hardener (the beige material). To mix the epoxy, first form a ball of the same size of each of the components. Then, roll the ball into a rod. Next twist the rods together, and work the twisted rods to mix the materials thoroughly. Once the color is the same throughout, the epoxy is fully mixed.

We've presented so many varied structural problems and the solutions for repairing them in this chapter that you'll probably be able to diagnose and restore similar joint dilemmas of your own with confidence.

№ 4 ‖ Restoring Surfaces

THE TERM *surface restoration* covers a lot of ground. It refers to repairing all sorts of surface problems—everything from a finish that's chipped or abraded to a broken or missing edge, an area destroyed by insects, or brittle paint that has raised up from or broken off the surface. Regardless of the specifics, all surface restoration deals with either repairing the surface itself—the gilding, lacquer, paint, and so on—and/or repairing the substrate, or base, on which the original surface layer was applied. This chapter addresses restoring substrates, surfaces, and simple, low-relief contours.

If you're working with an object missing one or more full or partial carvings with complex contours, turn to Chapter 5 for detailed information on making molds and casts. For information on restoring color, graining, or gilding on a surface, see Chapters 6, 7, and 9, respectively. If you need to restore missing painted or gilded decoration and are unsure of how to even begin researching and rebuilding the design, look at Chapter 10 on recreating missing surface designs. And if you want information on applying a final finish (a clear finish like shellac or varnish), head for Chapter 8.

The figures pictured here, engaged in traditional pursuits, are on a detail from a late-eighteenth-century Chinese three-fold lacquer screen.

Photo courtesy of Mallett

FILLING SURFACE DEPRESSIONS AND ABRASIONS

BUILDING A TOOLKIT: SURFACE-RESTORATION TOOLS
Surface repair tools and supplies, available in arts-, crafts-, sculpture-supply, and hardware stores, include, from the left, the following:

- → Pigments for coloring filler materials
- → Filler paste
- → Flat palette knife
- → #120 and #220 grit open-coat sandpaper
- → Dental probing tools
- → Magnification
- → X-ACTO knife
- → Varied paintbrushes
- → Flexible, offset palette knife
- → Cheesecloth and water

Photo courtesy of Connie Hougardy

If the surface of an object is gouged, chipped, or abraded, the damaged areas need to be filled, or built up, to restore both the substrate and surface to its original state. The key material for making these repairs is a commonly available, ready-mixed, viscous paste or gel generally referred to as modeling, or filler, paste. Throughout this book we'll use the term *filler paste* or *filler* to refer to this material.

Filler paste can be used to solve problems on top of and beneath a surface, and it creates strong grounds for any gilding or inpainting, including graining and design reconstruction, needed to complete a restoration. Available in stores selling art, craft, and sculpture supplies as well as from suppliers of conservation and restoration materials (see Resources on page 268), filler paste fulfills many requirements for surface restoration: It's water-based and mixes well with other water-based materials; it adheres well to surfaces and accepts other materials over it; it cures solid to permit shaping and smoothing; and it's dimensionally stable and reversible, if need be, in the future.

Working with Filler Paste

The main goal in filling a lost area is to restore it to the level of the original surface surrounding it. You'll need some patience while filling an area, but you can fill one or more lost areas at a time. Each loss is independent of the others. Below are the general steps involved in filling lost or damaged areas.

STEP 1: CLEAN THE SURFACE

Remove all loose materials from the damaged surface. Do not try to remove any material that's adhered tightly, which can actually be helpful since it provides some tooth, or roughened surface, on which to attach the new filling material.

STEP 2: CLEAN AND DRY ADJACENT AREAS

Keep a wad of cheesecloth dampened with water handy to wipe away any filler paste that may get on an adjacent area. After wiping the area with damp cheesecloth, wipe it again with dry cheesecloth. Try to avoid using tape to mask adjacent areas. If you must do so, see Tapes and Taping on page 153. Be careful about using tape to mask an area—as we've experienced, tape can mar a surface, which takes time and effort to correct.

STEP 3: APPLY FILLER PASTE

Using a flat, rigid palette knife, apply a small amount of filler paste, as is, to one area of loss. While this area is drying, begin to fill another damaged area if there are several. As each newly filled area dries solid to the touch, add more filler paste, if needed, to build the repaired area up to the level of the surrounding surface. If you're using a material that shrinks or cracks as it dries, fill the fissures with more filler paste.

Repeat this step until you've filled each damaged area flush with the surface level surrounding it. Some damaged areas may be deeper than others and need more material added, one layer at a time.

STEP 4: SAND FILLED AREAS

Next, "sand" the filled repairs smooth with a small wad of slightly dampened cheesecloth. After the smoothed surface has dried thoroughly, sand it with #220 grit open-coat sandpaper (open-coat refers to the fact that, unlike many sandpapers, you can brush this sandpaper off and reuse it). Then wipe the surface again with a small wad of slightly dampened cheesecloth.

Use a rigid, flat palette knife to push the filler paste into crevices and depressions of the surface you're repairing.

STEP 5: TEST SMOOTHNESS OF REPAIR

Now test the shape and smoothness of your repair by running your finger over the filled and surrounding areas while looking away. Your fingertips are much more sensitive than your eyes in detecting low or high areas. Then further sand or refill any repair needing more attention before proceeding to the next step. Each time you refill an area, smooth it and retest the evenness of its surface; then repeat the process yet again, if necessary.

Testing the smoothness of a repair with your fingertips is the most crucial step in surface restoration since painting or gilding over a poorly repaired surface will, in fact, highlight the poor repair. Aim for as seamless a repair as possible at this stage. The completed restoration will reward your patience, time, and effort.

STEP 6: CLEAN REPAIRED SURFACE

Once you've completed the repair, check the surface for any stray bits of filler paste elsewhere on the object, and gently wipe them clean with a slightly dampened wad of cheesecloth. Then wipe them again with dry cheesecloth.

Filler paste is excellent not only for filling damaged or abraded surfaces but also for building up very fine, damaged, or missing low-relief designs on a surface. On the nineteenth-century wooden clock dial in the photos below, we used filler paste to first repair the damaged flat surface and then to build up the slightly raised design on top of it.

Coloring Filler Paste

Filler paste can be colored easily to produce a filler that matches the color of a surface. Use water-based colorants, such as gouache and acrylic tube colors or powdered pigments, all of which can be found in art-supply stores. (For detailed information on mixing colors, see Mixing and Matching Colors on page 129 in Chapter 6).

The face of this early-nineteenth-century American wooden clock dial was both abraded and partially missing elements of its thin, raised ornamentation. Filler paste served to remedy both problems before final inpainting and gilding completed the restoration.

Film canisters are handy containers for saving colored filler mixtures. Put a dab of the filler on the lid and body of the canister to easily identify the mixed color it contains.

Coloring filling materials offers several advantages: It saves a step since the colored filler provides a base coat color on which to do any artwork. As well, the color is an integral part of the filler so that, as the filler is sanded down, the color remains. The colored filler also stays workable longer than uncolored filler, allowing more time to complete a repair, especially when the filler is saved in a film canister.

OPTIONS FOR MATCHING COLOR

With regard to deciding which color to match on the object you're restoring, there are two basic choices: You can match the opaque color on the original surface, particularly if it will be the color on which you'll restore artwork. Or, you can match the color found beneath any glazes (sheer layers of color), graining (painted simulation of wood), gilding, or other decorative painting. You'll often be able to find the needed color on a slightly worn area on the object. If you have trouble finding the color, try using magnification to examine the surface.

In the photos at opposite, right, you'll find an example of using colored filler paste under graining to restore one of a pair of early-nineteenth-century, rosewood-grained Baltimore card tables. We matched the color of the filler paste to the real mahogany showing in the lost areas of graining (see photo A on the opposite page). Because we had to add graining over the damaged surface areas we would fill, we finished those filled areas slightly lower than the final surface level in order to accommodate the additional layers of graining that would be applied. To mix colorant into the filler paste, follow the steps below:

STEP 1: MIX PIGMENT AND FILLER PASTE

Mix the colorant and filler paste on a plastic lid or any suitable flat palette. Use a flexible palette knife to mix a small amount of pigment into a glob of filler paste. The amount of paste will depend on the number and size of lost areas needing to be filled. It's better to mix more rather than too little colored paste since trying to match a colored filler can be quite frustrating and time-consuming. Any excess can be saved in tightly closed film canisters and has a long shelf life.

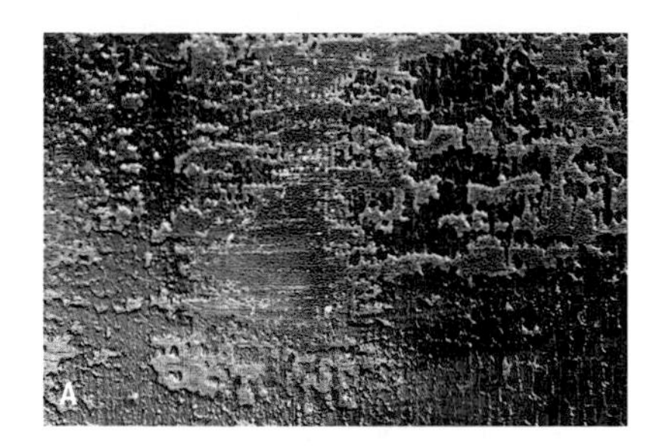

On this early-nineteenth-century, rosewood-grained Baltimore card table (one of a pair), filler was colored to match the real mahogany visible where the graining was missing (A). After the colored paste was applied (B) and smoothed, the first stages of graining were inpainted (C). The final graining and gilding were then added to complete the restoration (D).

STEP 2: ADJUST COLOR AS NEEDED

To adjust the color, gradually add small amounts of pigment into the wet filler paste, and mix the two parts thoroughly with each addition. Since, as described in Tips for Color Mixing on pages 130 to 131 in Chapter 6, water-based paint mixtures change color and get dull as the water dries out of them, it's important to mix the colors while your filler-paste mixture is still wet.

Note that if this is your first attempt at matching colors, don't be discouraged if it takes longer than you expect. As you gain more experience with mixing colors, the process will become less intimidating and shorter.

Filling Surfaces on Asian Lacquer

For restoring Asian lacquer, we generally use the same tools, materials, and processes as those you've just read about, with one exception: Before filling a lost area of lacquer, the lifted lacquer surrounding the void must be secured. For this extra preparatory step, you'll need a few additional supplies: yellow glue (technically called "aliphatic glue"), clamps (that may be small, medium, or very large like those in chapter 3), and cauls (thin pieces of rigid plastic) (see photo C on page 87, which shows a caul held in place by a magnetic clamp pad).

This late-eighteenth-century lacquer-on-ceramic vase, one of a pair, shown after we restored it, is profusely decorated with inlays of mother-of-pearl and metal elements. See page 265 in Chapter 10 to view stages in the restoration.

WHAT IS ASIAN LACQUER?

Lacquer is a natural substance tapped from trees just like rubber and maple syrup. In the Far East there are several species of trees that yield lacquer, but Chinese lacquer comes from a sumac tree called *Rhus Vernicefera* and dubbed the "lacquer tree." Lacquer had been used as a coating on functional and decorative objects for ages, dating back as far as, by some accounts, 5000 B.C. Always applied over a ground (see Grounds for Asian Lacquer on page 83), lacquer is prized for its durability (it's impervious to heat, water, insects, and almost everything else—except, of course, abuse) and also for its brilliant, soft sheen once cured.

Asian vs. European Lacquer

The term Asian lacquer refers to objects coated with authentic lacquer and produced in the Far East, specifically China, Korea, and Japan. The term *European lacquer* denotes objects coated with paint, shellac, or varnish to try to duplicate the unmatchable brilliance of a real lacquer surface. This chapter addresses only repairs on Asian lacquer. European lacquer (termed *vernis Martin* in France and *japanning* in English-speaking countries) is repaired like any other painted, shellacked, or varnished surface (see Chapters 6, 7, 8, and 10).

Domestic and Export Objects

Before the nineteenth century, Asian lacquer objects were made only for the domestic use of emperors, scholars, and wealthy merchants. These objects were painstakingly produced with only the finest materials, and the lacquer effectively became integral to and protective of its wooden substrate. As a result, these early Asian lacquer objects rarely exhibit problems caused by the shrinkage of their wooden substrate. By contrast, however, the lacquer objects that began to be produced in the nineteenth century for export were often made of unseasoned wood with knots. When this wood reacted badly to changes in temperature and humidity, it shrank, causing the joints to open and the lacquer, in turn, to split and also lift off the wood and tent. Other problems common to export objects include cracking, missing areas, delamination, damaged edges, and blistering of the lacquer.

Above: Note the lifted lacquer at the bottom of the photo, in contrast to the lacquer at the top, which has relaxed and been adhered to its ground with clamp pressure after having had yellow glue inserted beneath it.

Above right: After regluing the loose lacquer to its ground, apply cauls and then clamps.

We happily discovered by accident that the chemistry of yellow glue softens and relaxes brittle, cupped lacquer, as you can see in the photo at above left. We also found that by placing cauls—we generally use 1/16-inch-thick pieces of clear plastic—on top of the surface after gluing the brittle lacquer and before clamping it to dry, we could see any glue that squeezed out when pressure was exerted by the clamps (see Gluing like a Pro on page 82). On the next page are the steps to follow when you need to adhere lifted lacquer to a substrate.

STEP 1: CLEAN THE SURFACE

Gently lift the loose lacquer with a palette knife or similar tool, and brush away any loose material on the substrate with a dry paintbrush.

The first step in restoring Asian lacquer is to clean beneath any loose lacquer, lifting it up with a palette knife and gently brushing or scraping away any debris.

STEP 2: INSERT YELLOW GLUE

Use a very thin, flexible, offset palette knife to insert a thin layer of yellow glue as far as you can under the lacquer, as in the photograph below. When you apply pressure with a clamp in Step 4, any excess glue will be forced out (see also Gluing like a Pro on page 82).

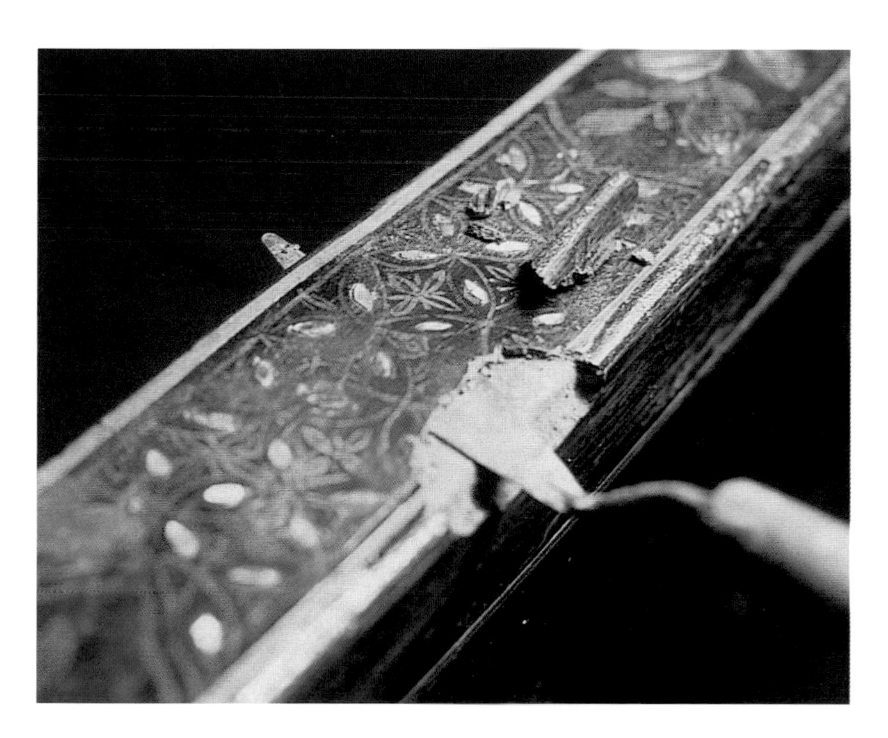

Use a thin palette knife to insert yellow glue beneath loose pieces of lacquer to relax the lacquer and, in turn, re-adhere the pieces to their ground.

STEP 3: COVER GLUED AREA WITH A CAUL

Place a clear plastic caul over the area that has been glued.

GLUING LIKE A PRO

To create a good bond between two surfaces, glue must be spread as a thin, even film between the two surfaces. Excess glue inserted between two surfaces will squeeze out as pressure is applied from clamping tools. If glue does not squeeze out, it may be because either not enough glue has been applied and the bond is "glue-starved," or, alternately, the pressure from the clamps is not tight enough to force the glue out.

STEP 4: APPLY AND TIGHTEN CLAMPS

Apply and tighten one or more clamps over the caul to apply pressure to the bond and squeeze out any excess glue. The photo on page 80 shows many clamps being used, each exerting pressure on a separate area of the lifted lacquer being adhered. Because a glued area must cure before each clamp holding it can be removed and used elsewhere, it's a good idea to own a supply of clamps. Besides, moving and repositioning the clamps and cauls takes a lot of time, not to mention the energy required to lift clamps like these that can each weigh many pounds.

STEP 5: REMOVE CAUL

You should be able to see excess glue that has squeezed out under the plastic caul, at which point it's time to remove the clamp(s) and the caul to clean off the surface.

STEP 6: CLEAN EXCESS GLUE

Using a dampened wad of cheesecloth, clean off every surface with excess wet glue on it, that is, the underside of the caul and the top surface of the lacquer. Then wipe these surfaces with dry cheesecloth.

STEP 7: REPLACE CAUL AND LET DRY

Replace the caul and clamp(s), and tighten the clamp(s).

This process is very time-consuming but absolutely crucial for successfully adhering loose or cupped lacquer to its ground. And making sure that all the lacquer on an object is stabilized is mandatory before moving on to filling voids on the surface. After adhering all the lacquer on this screen, we applied colored filler paste (mixed with black and burnt-umber gouache) to the lost area, as you can see in the photos at bottom.

Notice the difference how rough the dried colored filler was before it was abraded (right) with #220 grit open-coat sandpaper and dry #400 grit silicone carbide paper, and after (far right).

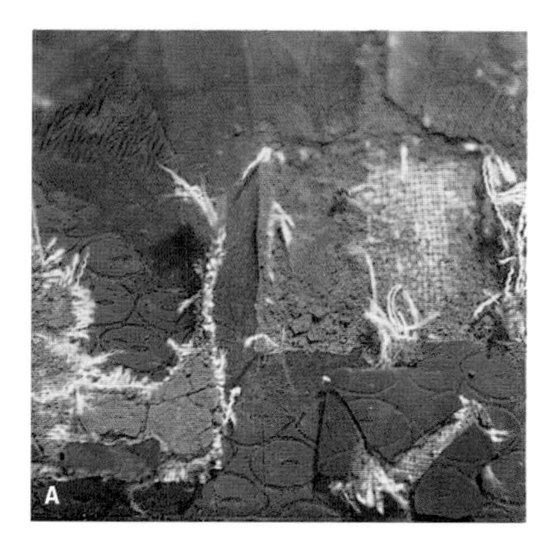

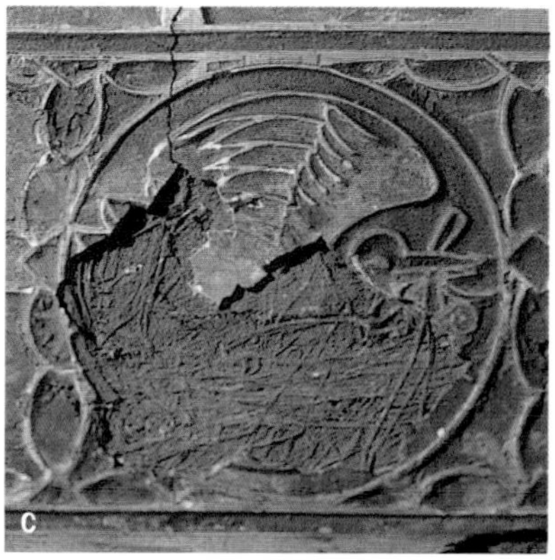

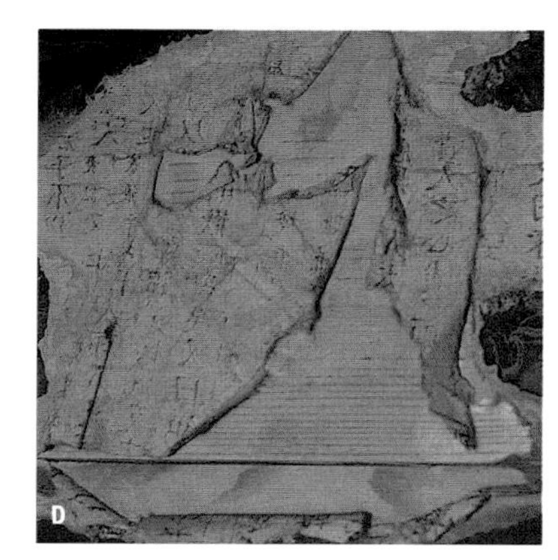

GROUNDS FOR ASIAN LACQUER

In a lacquer object, the coatings of lacquer are applied over the object's substrate, which is usually wood. The first layers applied over the substrate are made of varied substances mixed in with lower grades of lacquer. The materials used for this "ground" vary widely and can include everything from clay, ashes, grasses, and woven fabrics to dried pig's blood and ground animal horns. The type and quality of ground materials, as well as the wood on which they're coated, often serve to date and locate the origin of the object since they differ from region to region. Unfortunately, wood and ground coats are not visible after a lacquer object has been restored. At left is a small gallery of lacquered objects on a variety of grounds, in which we can only describe the most obvious substances.

The ground of clay, powdered material, and fabric indicated that this was an eighteenth-century domestic Chinese, incised lacquer table (A). This nineteenth-century Chinese export garden stool had a ground of coarse clay mixed with thick grasses (B). A late-nineteenth-century Chinese export screen had a ground of grasses mixed with clay scooped from the river banks of the region (C). The only ground we uncovered on this late-nineteenth-century Chinese export tabletop was composed of several layers of Chinese paper (D). The ground on this mid-nineteenth-century Chinese export cabinet door was thick clay mixed with ashes (E).

DISMANTLE LACQUER OBJECTS BEFORE REPAIRING SURFACE

When joints on a lacquer object separate due to the shrinkage of unseasoned wood, the separation causes the lacquer coating to split and lift (see A and B, showing one of a set of four early-nineteenth-century Chinese export nesting tables). Restoring the object in the most stable, aesthetic way calls, first, for entirely separating the joints to dismantle the object. If the split portion is connected to a base (as on a tabletop), first detach the split portion from its base and then separate the object at the joint (C). Next, re-adhere the lifted lacquer along the edge of each separate joint (D), and rejoin the pieces (E). You'll also need to fill any gaps with filler paste, inpainting missing parts of any design, and, where necessary, reconnect the joined pieces to any bases (F). The restoration was the largest of the set of four tables, similar, as you can see, to the quartet of Chinese export nesting table (G), photo © Christie's Images Ltd. 2006).

A

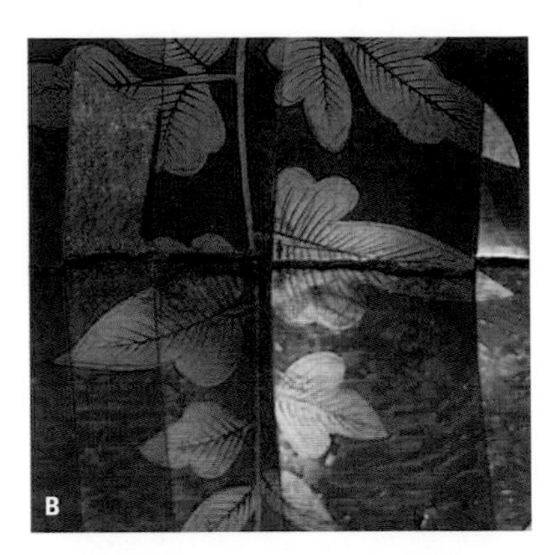
B

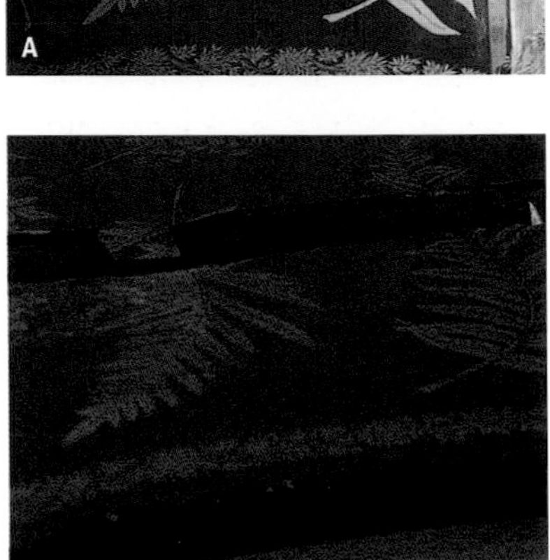
C

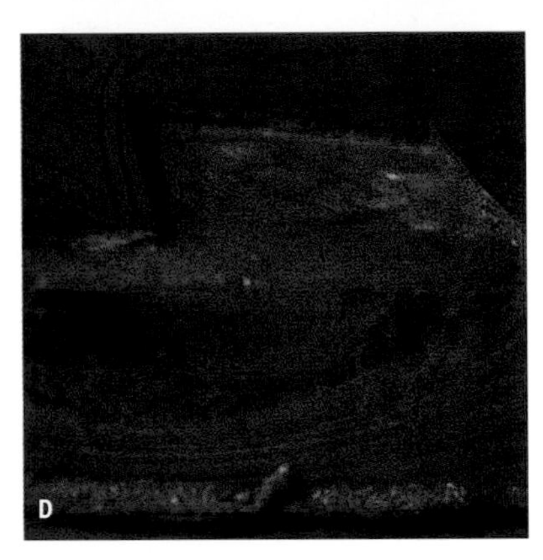
D

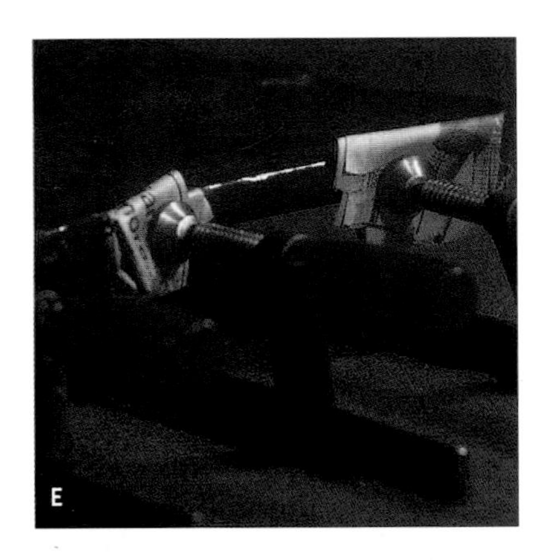
E

F

G

REPAIRING TENT CLEAVAGE

As explained in Chapter 2, when wood dries out and shrinks across its width—as unseasoned wood does over time—any paint, Asian lacquer, or clear finish coating over the wood will not shrink with it but instead lift up in tentlike fashion, trapping air underneath along the length of the grain. This phenomenon is called *tent cleavage*. Regardless of a design's orientation, wood will shrink only across its width, as you can see in the photo top right. And often on a damaged surface, tent cleavage and lost areas of paint, lacquer, or the finish coating go hand in hand (below right). To simultaneously remedy an area of tent cleavage and repair the lost areas of paint associated with it, follow the procedures below:

Wood shrinks across its width, and any design painted on the wood, regardless of the design's orientation, will lift and delaminate when the wood shrinks, producing what's called tent cleavage and often a total loss of paint in the tented areas.

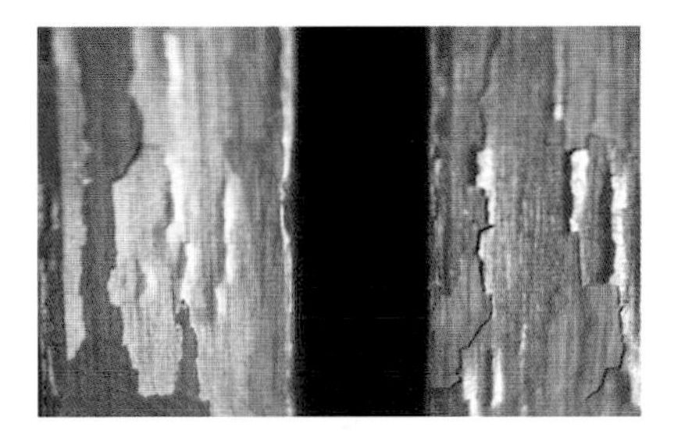

Areas of tent cleavage (see raised-up surface at right on the painted lathe) are often accompanied by much paint loss (as at left).

STEP 1: REMOVE TENTED AREAS

Remove the tented areas, cutting them away with a sharp X-ACTO blade and gently scraping off any raised or loose, brittle paint. We have at times used melted wax to readhere tented areas.

STEP 2: CLEAN SURFACE

Sweep away all loose material, leaving only paint that's securely attached to the ground.

STEP 3: MIX GOUACHE/FILLER PASTE

For inpainting, prepare a gouache/filler-paste mixture that matches the color of the area abutting each paint loss. Thin down the mixture with very little water, so it can be brushed on with an artist's brush, as shown below. You may have to add more gouache and/or apply several layers to match the color and depth of the surrounding paint layer. This thinned-down gouache/modeling-paste mixture can be used both for repairing tent cleavage problems and also for simple, shallow paint losses, like those in below middle and right.

At left, a door from a nineteenth-century Chinese export cabinet suffered tent cleavage and missing areas of paint. After the tent cleavage was repaired, gouache and filler paste were matched to the areas to be inpainted, and the mixture was applied with an artist's script-liner brush, which is long, thin, and flexible.

Above, the edges of this leg sustained enough abrasion to lose paint. The losses were replaced with a thinned-down mixture of gouache and filler paste used as paint.

Repairing Tent Cleavage on Asian Lacquers

Tent cleavage on Asian lacquer behaves differently from tent cleavage on painted surfaces. Because lacquer (even that on Chinese export products) is so sturdy, the tented portion remains strong and can be treated with the procedures below to restore the surface:

STEP 1: ASSESS SIZE OF TENTED AREA

Determine the length of the tent cleavage. Photo A on the opposite page shows a tented area of about 2 inches.

STEP 2: DRILL INTO APEX OF TENTED AREA

Use a drill with a fine bit to carefully drill directly into the apex, or uppermost part, of the tented lacquer. The number of holes you'll need to drill depends on how extensive the tenting is. Try to drill a hole every 1 inch or so.

STEP 3: INSERT YELLOW GLUE

Using a glue syringe, insert yellow glue into all the drilled holes, which will soon soften and relax the brittle lacquer enough to allow it to bond to the wood underneath.

STEP 4: APPLY CAUL TO TENTED AREA

Place a piece of transparent plastic, approximately 4 inches square and 1⁄16 inch thick, over the area of tent cleavage as a caul. The size of the caul will vary according to the length of the tent cleavage you're repairing (see photo B on the opposite page).

STEP 5: ADD WOOD OVER CAUL FOR EXTRA PRESSURE

Place the clamp over the caul so that the head of the clamp is positioned directly over the area being glued. If you want extra clamp pressure, place a piece of wood under the clamp's head before tightening the clamp.

Photo C on the opposite page shows a type of clamp pad available in hardware or home-improvement stores with a magnetized slab embedded in it, so it clings to the head of a clamp. If you can't find this type of wood pad, it's easy to make with 1⁄4-inch slabs of wood and magnetized strips sold in crafts and hardware stores. Assemble and use the magnetic clamp pad, as shown in the photo.

STEP 6: CLEAN EXCESS GLUE

Remove the caul and clamp immediately in order to clean all the surfaces of excess glue. Then replace the caul and clamp, and tighten the clamp.

STEP 7: FILL AND INPAINT REPAIRED AREA

After flattening the tented area (E on the opposite page), fill the voids with colored filler paste and inpaint as needed to complete the missing design. Photo F on the opposite page is the completed restoration.

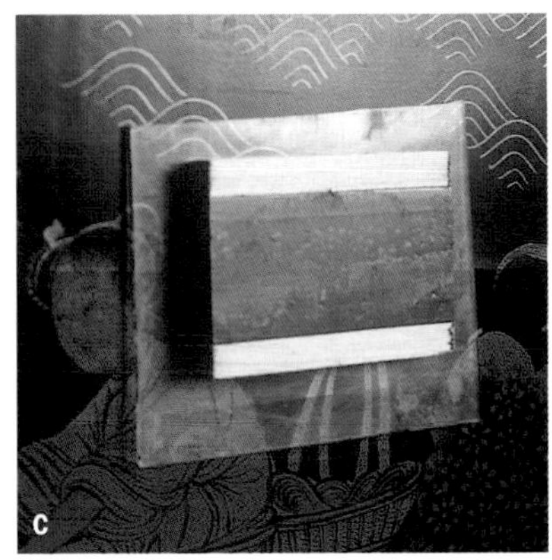

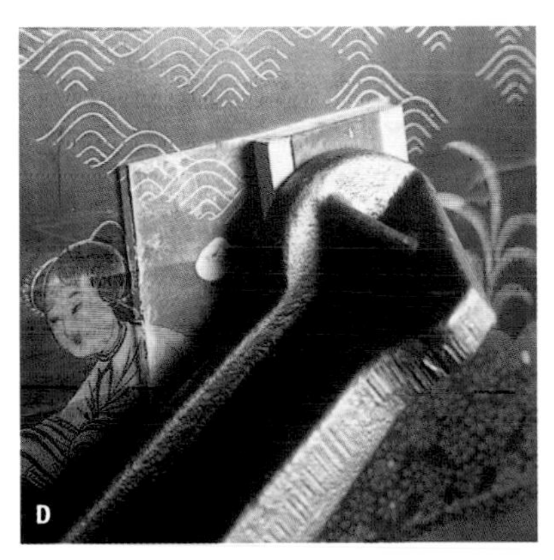

This nineteenth-century eight-panel Chinese export lacquer screen had numerous areas of damage from tent cleavage (see the buckled horizontal area in the middle), and we had to find a way to insert adhesive under each tented area (A). Using a fine bit, we drilled directly into the apex of the tent in two places and used a glue syringe to insert yellow glue into the openings. After the glue had relaxed the tented lacquer, we placed a caul over the lacquer (B). Then we placed a wooden pad with a magnetized inset (to attach to the head of the clamp) over the caul (C). When we applied a clamp and tightened it, the excess glue was forced out (see the round white shape peeking out on the left of the caul (D). After unclamping and cleaning the repair, we reapplied the caul and clamp and let the glue set. After each tented area had flattened (E), we filled the holes with colored filler paste and inpainted as needed to complete the restoration (F).

REPAIRING EDGES

ADDING TO YOUR TOOLKIT: REPAIRING EDGES

In addition to the tools already listed in Building a Toolkit: Surface-Restoration Tools on page 76 you'll need a few other tools for rebuilding damaged edges. Available at hardware and home-improvement stores, these tools include, from top to bottom:

→ Ball-peen or other small hammer
→ Fine-tipped nail set
→ #18 or #20 x 3/4-inch or 5/8-inch wire brads (or other small, thin nails or escutcheon pins the same size)
→ Epoxy putty

Objects whose edges have been damaged can be repaired easily using the tools and materials shown at left. The basic process is a simple one that involves first tapping wire brads (or other small nails) into the missing area 3/8 inch or more below the final desired surface level to build an "armature" and then beginning to cover the armature and rebuild the void with epoxy putty, another type of filling material made by mixing together a resin and catalyst, or hardener (see Step 3 below). Because epoxy putty dries very hard, it would take considerable time and energy to sand and shape it, once dry, to the exact edge contour needed. Therefore, the easy alternative is to create an anchoring bed of epoxy putty over the armature and, once the epoxy dries, top it with a layer of filler paste that can be sanded and shaped easily. To make this type of edge, proceed as follows:

STEP 1: CLEAN AREA

Wipe and brush the damaged area clean of anything unstable, such as wood or paint fragments.

STEP 2: INSERT WIRE BRADS FOR ARMATURE

Use a ball-peen or other small hammer and a nail set to tap in wire brads (or other small nails) as close together as you can without damaging the substrate. Be sure to set the armature at least 3/8 inch or more below the surface of the final contoured edge (see the left end of the photo below). This will allow room to build up epoxy putty over the armature and, as well, add an overcoat of filler paste.

STEP 3: MIX EPOXY PUTTY

To mix the epoxy putty, follow the directions in Mixing Epoxy Putty on page 73 in Chapter 3.

STEP 4: MOLD ARMATURE

Use your (gloved) fingers to mold the epoxy putty around the armature, covering it completely but leaving 1/8 inch on all sides (see the right end of the photo below) so that you can add a second layer of filler paste on top of the putty after it has cured. If you have extra epoxy putty left

At left on this practice molding, the wire-brad armature can be seen in the void. A similar armature filling the void at right has been covered by a base layer of epoxy putty, left 1/8 inch lower than the surrounding areas in order to accommodate a final layer of filler paste that will get shaped and smoothed.

over, place it in a container filled with water covering the putty (we use an old cat-food tin and don't bother covering it, though you could cover it with a plastic-can cover from the grocery store). The putty will stay flexible and usable stored like this (you may need it for other repairs later in the same session) but will harden left in the open air.

STEP 5: ALLOW EPOXY PUTTY TO CURE
Allow the applied epoxy putty to cure totally overnight.

STEP 6: MIX AND USE DESIRED COLORANTS
If you want to take advantage of the benefits of mixing colorants into your filler paste, refer to the instructions in Coloring Filler Paste on pages 77 to 79. After thoroughly mixing colorant into the filler paste, scoop the colored filler paste into a film canister (or another container that can be closed tightly), dab a bit of the mixture on the cap and side of the container to identify the color, and close the container tightly.

STEP 7: APPLY FILLER PASTE
Using a palette knife, apply the (colored) filler paste over the cured epoxy putty. Cover the top and any sides that are visible.

STEP 8: BLEND REPAIR AND SURROUNDING AREAS
Use your fingers and shaping tools to blend the repair into surrounding areas. Add or remove filler paste as required.

STEP 9: CLEAN SURFACE
Wipe away any filler paste that gets on adjacent surfaces, using a slightly dampened wad of cheesecloth.

STEP 10: SHAPE AND BLEND SURFACE
As the filler paste dries, continue to shape and blend it, using the slightly dampened wad of cheesecloth as a gentle shaping tool.

STEP 11: LET SURFACE DRY
Allow the filler paste to cure thoroughly. Once the paste is dry, sand it lightly with #220 grit open-coat sandpaper, and wipe the surface with the dampened cheesecloth. Again let dry.

STEP 12: CHECK SURFACE
As mentioned before, let your fingertips feel the sanded areas to determine where you may need to add or sand down the filler paste.

STEP 13: COMPLETE SURFACE FINISHES
Finally, refer to the appropriate chapters for information on inpainting, gilding, or clear wood finishes.

The great majority of edge repairs are uncomplicated, though time-consuming, even though the initial damage may look extensive. On the wooden arm of a chair chewed away by a pet, one of our students used the simple repairs above to restore the arm visually to its original state, as you can see in the photos at the top of page 90.

On this badly damaged chair arm, installing wire brads was the first step in rebuilding the contoured edge. After a base coat of epoxy putty was applied over the brads and allowed to dry, a layer of colored filler paste was added, cured, etched in, and filled with burnt-umber gouache/filler paste to simulate pores of wood. At top right is pictured a pair of eighteenth century chairs exhibiting arms of a similar shape.

Photo top right courtesy of Mallett

In fact, wire brads and filler can be used to restore any edge shape, as seen on the edge of the klismos-type leg of this nineteenth-century chair before the final graining was done (below left). In the case of an edge repair made near the tip of a chair foot, be careful to end the rebuilt edge just slightly above the floor to prevent chipping (below right).

Broken-off corners on mitered joints are another problem that can be solved with edge-repair pins and filler. On the base of the japanned English fall-front secretary (c. 1680) at left on the opposite page, the mitered corners (also chewed by a pet) had an armature inserted into each separate section of the miter. Epoxy putty was separately molded over each section, before filler paste was applied. After the filler paste was applied and before it had completely hardened, the edge of a flat palette knife was pressed into it to mark the miter joint. Note: Whenever you repair an area that must simulate a joint, scratch or press an incision at the joint line (at right on the opposite page). The flat piece of lathe (a thin, narrow strip of wood) was added along the front edge to strengthen the edge even more.

The wirebrad/epoxy-putty/filler-paste trio serves as a useful repair for various shapes, including the klismos-type leg on a nineteenth-century chair. Note that when repairing the foot on a leg, you need to end the repair slightly above the floor to prevent chipping when the piece is moved.

Broken corners are another problem that's easily solved with wire brads, epoxy putty, and filler paste. The mitered joint was repaired while still connected, but the joint line was emphasized.

Repairing Edges on Asian Lacquer

Although repairing edges on Asian lacquer objects involves essentially the same process and tools and materials as those discussed already, the one thing that sets this procedure apart is the absolute necessity of getting rid of all loose, unstable surface materials before beginning the repair. Dried-out clay, grasses, and fabric on the lacquer's ground pose a particular problem if not removed (see also Grounds for Asian Lacquer on page 83). The rather typical, late-nineteenth-century Chinese export garden stool in photo A on page 92 is shown before cutting away all unwanted clay and grasses. Photo B shows an area cleaned off, after which brads were inserted. This particular restoration was done early in our career, when we were applying epoxy putty over brads for the first time. As you can see in photo C, after the material hardened, we realized our mistake: overfilling the areas of loss, which took us three days of sanding to correct in order to reduce the epoxy to the right level. That experience taught us to always make sure that the uppermost layer in a repair with brads was made of a material that was easy to shape and sand, like filler paste. Fortunately for us, this stool, seen when the repair was complete in photo D, was modest in size.

WHICH SURFACE-REPAIR STRATEGY TO CHOOSE?

If you're wondering how to determine when to apply and shape filler paste and when to use epoxy putty over an armature of wire brads, here are some guidelines:

→ When you need a layer of filler on an area that doesn't require internal support, use filler paste.

→ When strength is needed, especially on an edge, use epoxy putty over an armature of wire brads, and cover that base with filler paste.

→ And, finally, if you need to replace carved contours or multiple units of the same shape, consider using the materials and procedures detailed in Chapter 5 on making molds and casts.

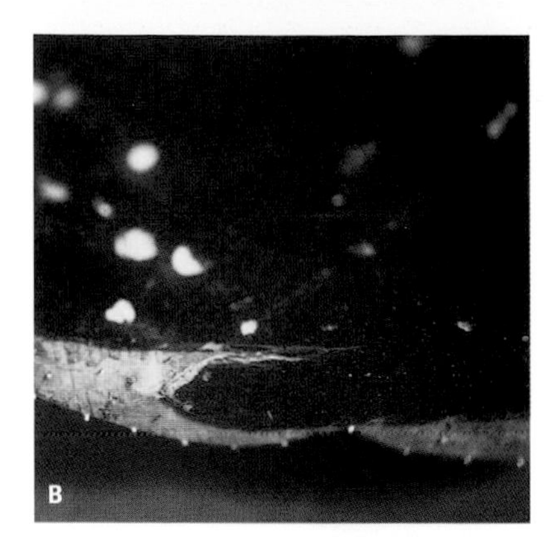

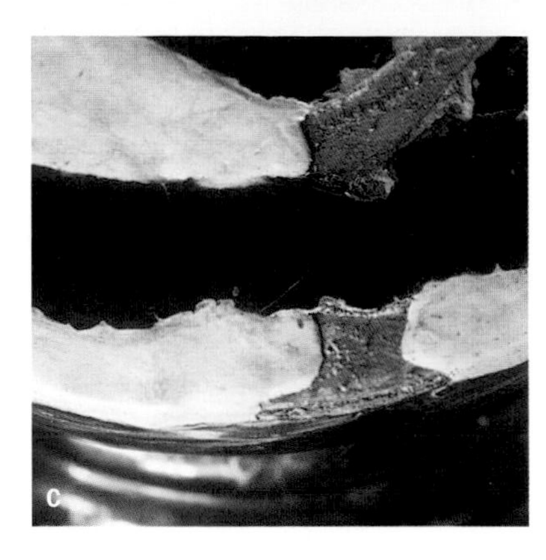

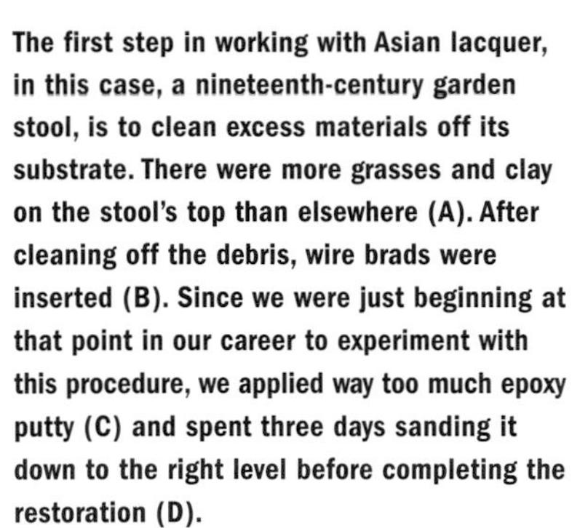

The first step in working with Asian lacquer, in this case, a nineteenth-century garden stool, is to clean excess materials off its substrate. There were more grasses and clay on the stool's top than elsewhere (A). After cleaning off the debris, wire brads were inserted (B). Since we were just beginning at that point in our career to experiment with this procedure, we applied way too much epoxy putty (C) and spent three days sanding it down to the right level before completing the restoration (D).

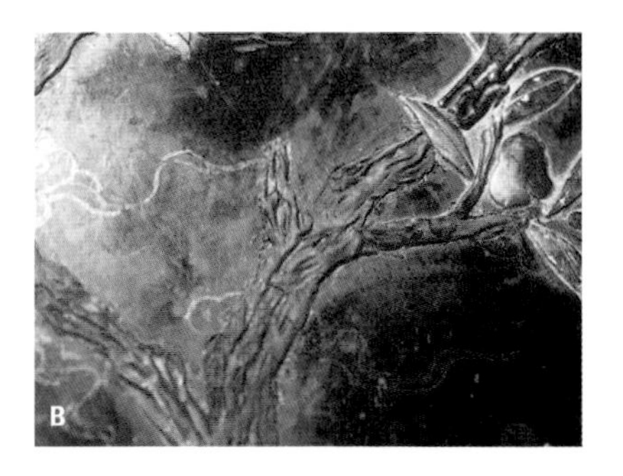

Wanting to match missing ornamentation to the area on the lower left, we used a wire cutter to shorten the height of the wire brads we installed (A). After coloring filler paste, we applied several layers (B), letting each one dry before adding the next, then blended in the repair with the original tree branch (C).

ANOTHER USE FOR AN ARMATURE

In addition to building an armature over which to fill a deep void on the object's surface, an armature can be used along with filler paste and epoxy putty to lend strength as you restore built-up, textured surface ornamentation. In the example above at of a nineteenth-century Chinese export table, the brads and filler materials added height to the replacement section of a tree branch.

REPAIRING BEETLE DAMAGE

At one end of the edge-repair spectrum are simple repairs like those that you've just seen; and at the other end are the most extensive, complicated—and gut-wrenching—edge repairs we've ever made. These latter repairs were made on a set of six late-eighteenth-century English satinwood-grained chairs. While examining the chairs in our client's house, we took careful notes on the many problems present but didn't spend enough time testing the surface for hidden powderpost beetle damage (hereafter referred to as "beetle" damage). This turned out to be a big mistake! We urge you to benefit from the important lesson we learned from this restoration: Be sure not to rush your initial investigation and assessment of a damaged object. The photos at right document the edge repair of the beetle damage on one of these chairs.

As our work on the first chair progressed, the edge of the seat, which, at first, had seemed to need only a simple surface repair (A), disintegrated more and more (B). What worried us—as you might guess—was that if the tunneling extended into the wood where the seat caning was attached, the caning would become disconnected. This would mean losing the original caning and having to replace it with new hand-caning. Fortunately, to our great relief, the damage ended without disturbing the caning.

After removing every bit of frass (powdered wood left by the beetles) and brittle, beetle-eaten wood, we were ready to begin installing brads as armatures (C). As in the step-by-step directions previously, we applied epoxy putty over veneer-pin armatures for strength and durability, making sure it remained at least 1/8 inch below the surface of the final contour. Finally, after the epoxy putty had cured, we topped it with gouache-colored filler paste, which we then grained to mimic satinwood and complete the restoration (D).

Restoring surfaces encompasses some of the most satisfying processes in restoration, worked usually on small areas on which you can devote as much or as little time at any one sitting as you like. Using the best craftsmanship you can muster in each of these sittings will reward you with real pleasure in your work and, in the end, a beautifully restored surface of which you can be quite proud.

Restoring surfaces is one of the best introductions to the restoration of objects, as the areas that need restoration are usually small, the procedures provide instant gratification, and the end results are sources of great satisfaction. ❧

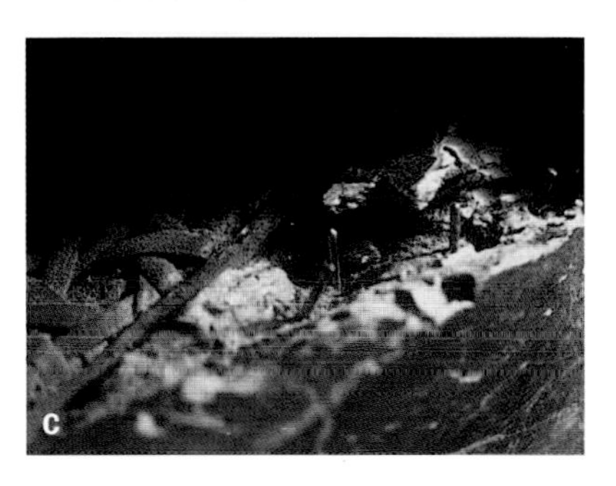

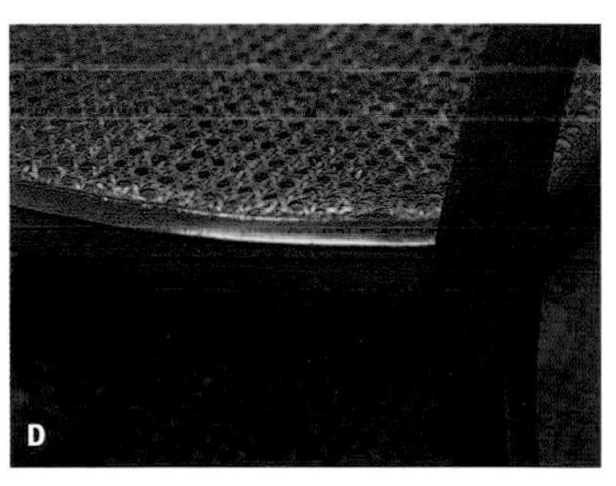

On first examination, the damage on this late-eighteenth-century English chair seemed to require a simple surface repair. However, as we worked, we found that beetle-tunneling had destroyed almost the entire edge (A, B). After thoroughly cleaning the damaged edge, we installed nails as an armature (C) for the epoxy putty and a final filler-paste overcoat. Photo D shows the restored area of this chair.

Nº 5 || Making Molds and Casts

MANY READERS, FACED WITH A MISSING OR broken part on an intricately carved or contoured surface, might assume that they need to be an expert hand-carver to restore the piece. But we restored many an object like this without knowing how to hand-carve, and you don't need to know how to, either. Instead you can make use of the mold-making and casting procedures that we turned to regularly over the years to restore all sorts of missing or damaged dimensional elements.

Mold-making and casting are processes that go hand in hand. Making a mold of a dimensional element you want to copy gives you a negative impression of that element. In turn, filling that mold with casting material, letting it dry, and removing it from the mold gives you an exact copy, or positive impression, of the original element.

To repair the missing leg of this American federal window bench (c. 1810), a mold of the missing portion from the other paw foot was made.

You can make a mold on any vertical, horizontal, or curved surface, regardless of the type of object you're working with. And you can even reinforce the inside of a cast with an armature to make it stronger and more durable than the missing or damaged original. Inserting an armature does not change the cast object's outer contour at all, and reinforcing a cast in this way is especially useful when replacing elements that are constantly exposed to abuse, such as the carved corners of a table.

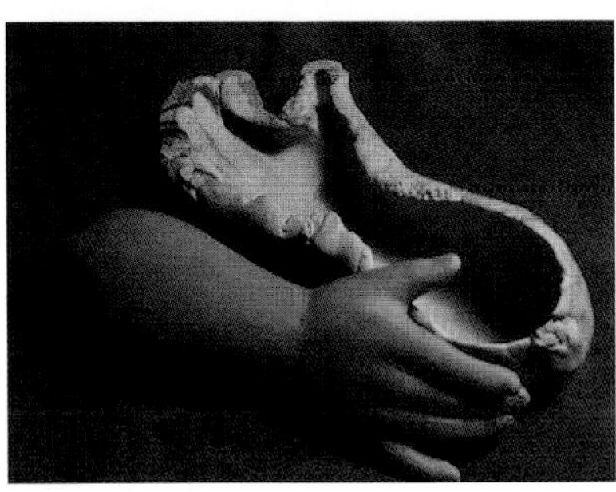

Molds and casts can be made of objects that vary widely in size, from the dime-size acorn ornament, whose casts amply decorated a nineteenth-century grand piano, to the relatively large, 9-inch-long forearm missing from a satyr on an eighteenth-century gilded Italian side table.

FINDING THE SHAPE TO MOLD

Mold-making and casting are particularly appropriate for restoration because casts are made of materials that can be removed at a later date, if necessary. As with all restorations, we urge you to keep photographic and written records of the restoration process, including documenting the location of all replacements and repairs.

Over the years, we made molds and casts to restore innumerable objects, from everyday pieces to antiques, ranging from the seventeenth to twentieth centuries. The size of the elements that we molded and cast varied, too, from the diminutive, ½-inch acorn mold (see top left) that produced casts to replace two dozen missing decorative acorns on a nineteenth-century Steinway grand piano, to the 9-inch forearm (at left) missing from a satyr on an ornately carved, Italian, gilded side table (c. 1735), whose restoration is described in detail on page 227 in Chapter 9.

Making molds and casts takes patience and a little time, but it isn't difficult. Before you can make a mold, however, you need to find a shaped area or element on your object—or on another object—with the design contours you want to copy.

After deciding what you want to replace with a cast, the next step is to find an intact duplicate of the missing or damaged shape to mold. Sometimes locating that shape takes no time at all. At other times, you'll need to do a bit of detective work.

If you have to search a little to find a duplicate of the missing or damaged element, start by placing the object on a work surface high enough to examine it easily. Don't be disappointed if you can't find the shape you need immediately. Often it may turn up where you least expect it. If it's impossible to move your object, you'll have to examine it *in situ* (where it is), which may involve a little contortion on your part, but just think of it as good exercise.

In a Pinch, Look for Mirror-Image Shapes

If a thorough search of your object fails to turn up a duplicate to make a mold of, look next for a reverse, or mirror, image of the shape you need, which you can adjust after casting it, if necessary. For example, in the case of the French Régence mirror frame (c. 1715) at top left on the opposite page, the original petal carving on the upper left corner of the frame had separated at mid-joint and vanished. Even though the undamaged carving on the upper right corner was a mirror image of the damaged upper left corner, we made a mold of it and then cast the missing petals to repair the left corner of the frame, adjusting the petals with minor reshaping using an X-ACTO knife.

Don't be discouraged by the prospect of repairing an intricately carved surface like that on the early eighteenth-century gilded frame at above left. Making a mold of an intact mirror image of the damaged or missing element enables you to cast a replacement easily. Here, the frame's top right corner (middle) provided the reverse image for the mold and subsequent cast, and, with several adjustments to the petal forms, a first-rate repair ready for gilding (right).

In the case of the satyr missing an arm on the table on page 227 in Chapter 9, we needed an existing right forearm from the satyr on the left corner of the table from which to mold and cast the forearm—it wouldn't do to have a satyr with two left forearms!—and fortunately we were in luck. But had the damaged satyr been much less conspicuously placed on the table and our only option had been to make a cast of a left forearm, we could have turned the left-hand cast over before it was totally cured (making the thumb then face in the right direction) and recarved it a bit to make use of it.

Finding Moldable Shapes Elsewhere

If you can't find a duplicate on the original of the element you need to replace—or a reverse image that you can adjust—look for a similar shape elsewhere. You might find it in a completely unrelated—and maybe unexpected—object: The madeleine pan (for making small cookies), for example, in the photo at below right, offered a perfect, ready-made mold to make the casts we needed for the restoration of a small frame shown below left.

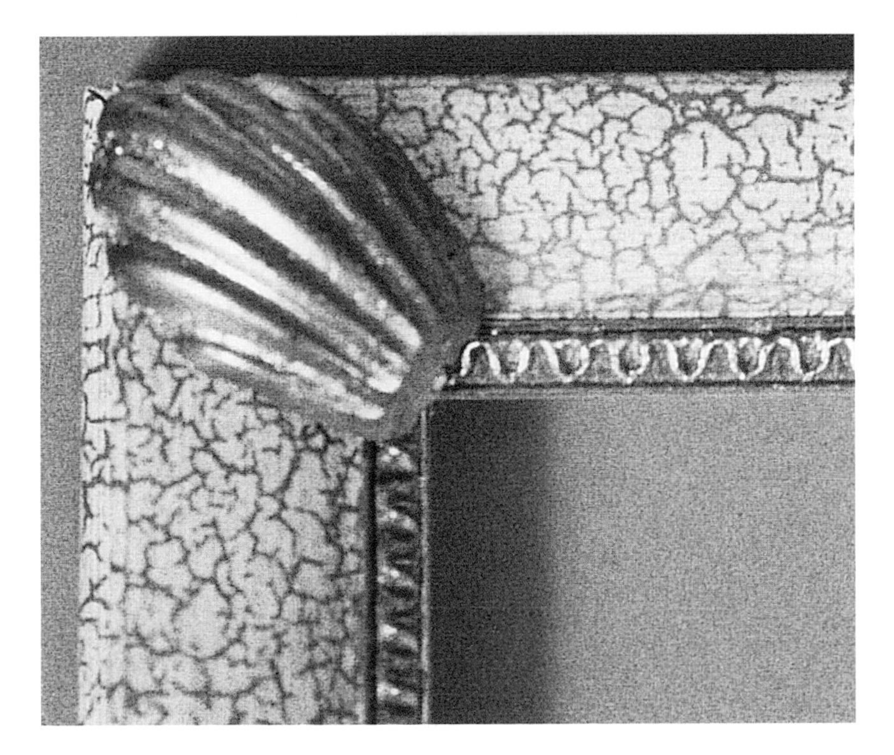

Above: If you can't find an intact shape on your object to mold and cast, look elsewhere. Here, a madeleine-cookie pan provided the perfect mold to cast shells for a restoration. One shell cast dries in the mold, while others at right have been covered with copper, silver, or gold leaf.

Left: The cast shown here, one of four, proved just what was needed to cover the corner miters on a frame that had opened due to shrinkage.

BUILDING A TOOLKIT: MOLD-MAKING TOOLS

In addition to the other tools listed below, you'll need one of the two basic types of mold-making materials discussed in text, either flexible or inflexible. Your choice may differ with each restoration.

- → Mold-making material, either flexible or inflexible
- → Filler paste
- → Palette knife
- → #220 grit open-coat sandpaper
- → Small cheesecloth squares
- → Talcum powder or rottenstone (finely ground limestone)

Molds made from flexible mold-making materials easily flex to release their cast, to reproduce complex, undercut surfaces well, and can be reused numerous times.

MOLD-MAKING MATERIALS

Mold-making materials fall into two broad categories: flexible and inflexible materials. New versions of both types of molding materials are being developed all the time, so it's a good idea to stay current with these developments to find the products that will best serve your specific needs.

Flexible Mold-Making Materials

Choose flexible mold-making materials when the object you're copying has many undercuts (hollow areas beneath an overhang), as, for example, in the intricate casts in the photo at below left (shown with their blue-green molds). A flexible mold can be opened out to release a heavily carved cast in perfect condition, then spring back into shape and be reused, if needed. Because flexible mold-making materials are very durable, many casts can be made from a single mold. And most flexible materials enable high-quality reproduction of all the details on the original object, as you can see in the photo.

There are two basic types of flexible mold-making materials: (1) putty-based materials, and (2) liquid-based materials. The putty-based materials, called "silicone-impression materials" (and generically known as polisiloxicane materials), are composed of two parts, a putty and a catalyst (hardener), with the catalyst either another putty or a liquid in a tube. By contrast, the liquid-based materials are made either from a different type of two-part silicone material or from a one-part latex-rubber material.

PUTTY-BASED MATERIALS

We favor putty-based (silicone-impression) materials over the liquid materials for several reasons: (1) we prefer handling solid rather than liquid materials; (2) once mixed, the putty mass can be applied to any plane of an object—a flat horizontal or vertical surface, whether on top or underneath, or a curved surface; (3) it cures more rapidly; and (4) it reproduces extremely meticulous detail.

Unlike most liquid mold-making materials, flexible putty-based materials can be applied to a vertical surface, as this was to the carved molding of a frame on a wall. The mold (at top) produced an excellent cast of the intricately carved original (at bottom).

Although putty-based, silicone-impression materials may seem more expensive than other types of mold-making materials (their price reflects the fact that they're packaged in large quantities), they have a long shelf life and can be used for numerous restorations. You can find this material in stores catering to sculptors and restorers; and, since this nontoxic material is used in dentistry, your dentist may also be able to direct you to other sources of supply. The green, white, and pink silicone-impression materials shown in this chapter are those we used over many years and reflect the formulas of various manufacturers of sculptural and dental materials. (On page 100, you'll find detailed information about mixing putty-based silicone-impression materials and making a mold with them.)

LIQUID-BASED MATERIALS

Liquid-based, two-part, silicone-impression materials and one-part, latex-rubber mold-making materials are useful when time isn't a factor and also when you need to make a large-scale mold, for example, of the entire side of a frame (a valuable advantage for frame-makers). You can buy these products from suppliers of arts, crafts, and sculpture materials, and on pages 102 to 103, you'll find detailed information about mixing and making a mold with them.

Inflexible Mold-Making Materials

Inflexible mold-making materials can be used when the area being molded has no undercuts and if the mold can be lifted straight off the object without becoming distorted in the removal process. Some inflexible materials may, in fact, be slightly flexible, but most do not open out and then spring back to their original shape. As well, inflexible materials usually produce molds with less sharply defined details than those made with flexible mold-making materials.

Arts-and-crafts stores stock a wide range of inflexible mold-making materials, from liquids and powders made into liquids (like plaster of paris) to solids (including many varieties of claylike products). You could even use children's clay in an emergency—we did once on a very simple but important carving and were careful after taking the impression of the object to lift it straight off the surface and immediately place the mold in the freezer to keep the warmth of our hands from distorting the clay. As a general rule, however, inflexible materials aren't used much by restorers. For information on how to work with these materials, see Using Inflexible Mold-Making Materials above right.

Before You Make a Mold

The process of making a mold is simple and takes very little time (unless you're using liquid materials, which must be brushed on or poured, layer by layer, as described in Working with Liquid Mold-Making Materials on pages 102 to 103). In a nutshell, the process involves mixing your selected mold-making material, pressing it firmly onto the surface of the object or area you're molding, and removing it after it has cured.

It's important to bear in mind, though, that a good cast can come only from a good mold. This means that you should strive to make a

USING INFLEXIBLE MOLD-MAKING MATERIALS

Inflexible mold-making materials are generally used for molding an object with a surface that's lightly carved but has no undercuts. There are two basic types of inflexible mold-making materials—powders, like plaster of paris, which must be mixed with water, and clay or claylike material, which requires no mixing. Each inflexible mold-making material has its own directions, which need to be followed carefully to get a good mold.

Preparations for Use

In the case of a powder/water mixture, you'll have to allow the mixed material to thicken enough to be spooned out and hold its shape before applying it to make a mold. By contrast, clay and claylike materials are ready to use out of the package and are simply pressed over an object to make a mold.

Depending on the label's instructions, the mold should be air-dried, baked, or placed in a freezer to harden until you're ready to make a cast. Because the curing time on these materials varies widely, compare the label directions when deciding on a product. Keep in mind, too, that, unlike clay materials, powder/water mixtures require both mixing and clean-up. Whatever product you choose, study your object before making the mold to locate the carved areas and depressions where you'll need to press most firmly to produce a good mold.

mold that's nearly as perfect a negative image of your object as you can make it. The tips offered by the pair of steps below will help you get the best mold possible:

STEP 1: REPAIR SURFACE TO BE MOLDED

Before mixing the materials for your mold, repair any surface defects on the area you're going to copy, using the information and techniques in Chapter 4. It's far better to repair a single surface—the one to be molded—than to repeatedly repair the surface of each cast produced by a mold of the original, imperfect surface, as we did at the beginning of our molding activity.

STEP 2: PREPARE ANY MATTE SURFACE

Before making a mold from a matte antique surface, sprinkle the surface with either a bit of talcum powder if the piece is light-colored or rottenstone (finely ground limestone) if it's a darker shade. This will help preserve any matte or dusty patina on the original surface.

WORKING WITH MOLD-MAKING MATERIALS

Although you can measure out ahead of time the two parts making up a silicone-impression material above, (the putty at left and catalyst at right), don't mix them until immediately before making your mold because they'll begin to harden rapidly. To mix them, roll the balls into rods, twist the rods together, and knead the "braid" until the color is uniform.

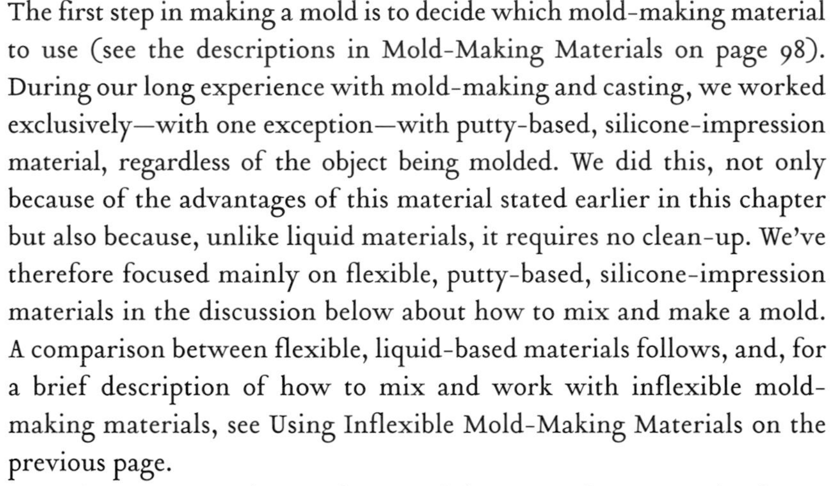

The first step in making a mold is to decide which mold-making material to use (see the descriptions in Mold-Making Materials on page 98). During our long experience with mold-making and casting, we worked exclusively—with one exception—with putty-based, silicone-impression material, regardless of the object being molded. We did this, not only because of the advantages of this material stated earlier in this chapter but also because, unlike liquid materials, it requires no clean-up. We've therefore focused mainly on flexible, putty-based, silicone-impression materials in the discussion below about how to mix and make a mold. A comparison between flexible, liquid-based materials follows, and, for a brief description of how to mix and work with inflexible mold-making materials, see Using Inflexible Mold-Making Materials on the previous page.

Whatever your choice of material, be sure to have enough of it on hand to form a good, strong mold. Making a strong mold includes adding extra material on the edges to build them up substantially and protect them from the added wear of being released from the original object and, later, the cured cast.

Working with Silicone-Impression Materials

To find out how much putty and catalyst either of the two-part, putty-based, silicone-impression materials described above will need to make a strong mold, measure the unmixed putty on an object as follows before adding the catalyst: If your material uses one part putty to one part putty-like hardener, cover the area to be molded with the putty alone, then remove the putty and measure out an equal amount of putty-like hardener. Roll each component into a ball, but do not mix the balls together until you're ready to make your mold.

Mixing Silicone-Impression Materials

To mix silicone-impression material made of a putty and a liquid catalyst, follow the product label's directions to determine the ratio of drops of catalyst to putty (measured out in a scoop, which comes with the putty). To figure out how much putty is needed for each object, record the number of scoops of putty that will provide dense coverage of the object, again covering the object with the putty alone, as explained previously (we wrote down each scoop as we took it out of the container). Once you've determined the number of unmixed scoops needed, remove all this unmixed putty from the object and figure out how many drops of liquid catalyst to mix with this putty. Do this by multiplying the specified number of drops of catalyst per scoop (as noted on the label directions) times the number of scoops measured when covering the object. For example, if seven drops of catalyst are needed for one scoop and four scoops are required to cover the object, mix 28 drops of catalyst into the putty just before you're ready to make the mold.

Making a Silicone-Impression Mold

Before starting the steps below, study your object so that you're aware of every depression, undercut, and detail. Once you've mixed the silicone putty with either its putty or liquid catalyst, the materials will begin to set hard within minutes; and knowing beforehand where to press your fingers into a hollow will produce a better mold.

STEP 1: MIX SILICONE PUTTY

To mix one part putty with one part putty-like hardener, form each part into ball and then each ball into a long, thin "rod." Twist the two rods together, and knead the resulting "braid" until they blend into one homogeneous color, as shown in the similar mixing process on page 73 in Chapter 3.

If you're using the putty/liquid-catalyst material, mix the predetermined amount of drops of catalyst into the putty immediately before making the mold.

STEP 2: SMOOTH INSIDE OF MOLD

Before pressing the prepared silicone putty mixture over the object, quickly smooth what will be the inside of the mold with your fingers. This ensures that the cast's exterior will be free of imperfections. Don't fret, though, if, after making your mold, you see some creases or dents in it. The casts from these molds will have the reverse problem—outward lines and bumps—which can be filled or sanded off easily. Remember that if you're going to make many casts from a mold, it will take a lot less time in the end to make your mold as nearly perfect inside as possible, but you'll need to work quickly.

STEP 3: PRESS PUTTY AROUND OBJECT

Once your mold is ready, press the molding material carefully, firmly, and quickly around the object so that it touches all parts of the surface, as shown in photo A on page 102. Leave the material on until it cures hard (within minutes), and then spread the mold open carefully to remove it.

Knowing beforehand that the silicone-impression molding material had to be pressed firmly around each talon on this hand-carved box lid in order to get a good, thin, round mold insured that the cast would be just right (A). Pictured in photo B are the molds from which the talon casts were made and the installed casts.

In photo B above, note the "shoulders" on two of the molds extending beyond the talons that were molded. Except in rare circumstances (as in the case of the tiny talon being molded in photo A, whose "shoulder-less" mold is shown at the top in photo B), molds should be made somewhat larger than the immediate area being molded in order to produce a solid-edged, shouldered mold.

MOLDING AN AREA WITHIN A CARVED SECTION

If you're replacing a damaged or missing segment within a carved section, mold a larger area from a duplicate part that extends beyond the damaged or missing area (and beyond the usual shoulder) so that the cast produced can be cut and interlocked within the existing carvings, like a jigsaw puzzle. This entails studying the original, intact carving from which you plan to make the mold and comparing it to the place where you'll install the cast to insure that the cast is larger. You'll find that making a sketch of each of the areas (you don't have to be an artist to do this) will help you decide where to enlarge the mold so that your cast can be cut to blend seamlessly with the surrounding area. You'll find an example of interlocking a cast and an existing carving shown in photos C and D on page 111.

MOLDING AND CASTING—A CASE IN POINT

The value of using silicone-impression material for making molds of intricate carvings is illustrated clearly in our restoration of a missing foot on the octagonal Chinese export lacquer tea caddy (c. 1850) on the opposite page. Tea caddies were a very popular export from China, particularly in the mid nineteenth century (the word "caddy," a corruption of the mid-sixteenth-century term *catty*, from the Malaysian *kati,* referred to a weight equal to 1 to 1½ pounds, or the amount of tea leaves contained in the caddy). Most caddies were rectangular, or less commonly octagonal, with shaped lids and dragon-headed feet, like this piece.

At some point, one of the caddy's feet was replaced by a lump of unknown material, probably applied to keep the piece level (A). To restore the missing foot, we made a mold and, in turn, a cast of each of the foot's two parts (which were assembled to appear as one carving) from one of the other dragon-headed feet in good condition (B). Photos C and D show the restored foot and caddy.

Working with Liquid Mold-Making Materials

Liquid mold-making materials are useful for molding large objects that are not intricately carved. Frame-makers, in particular, often find these liquid products beneficial.

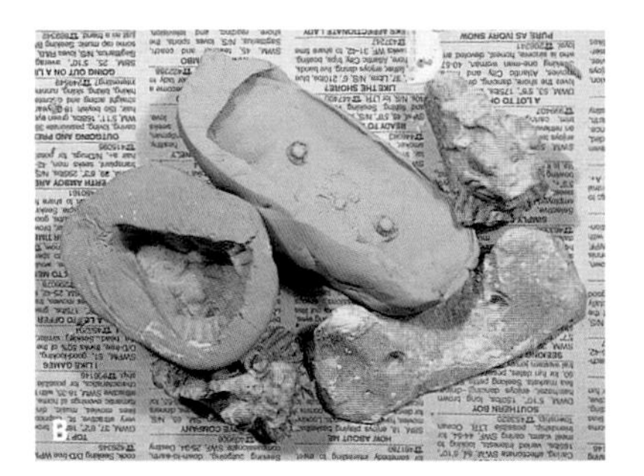

To restore the missing dragon-headed foot on this nineteenth-century Chinese export tea caddy, replaced with a lump of unidentified material (A), we made molds of one of the other intact, two-part feet. Photo B shows two dragonhead casts from the deep mold, and a double-curved cast of the foot's backing from the shallow mold. When the two casts were joined, they appeared to be one carving (C). Photo D shows the foot in place of the restored caddy.

Long the only liquid mold-making material in use, one-part liquid latex rubber is natural rubber from the rubber tree (*Hevea brasiliensis*), suspended in a water-and-ammonia base. Resembling rich milk (hence the name *latex,* from the Latin *lactic* meaning "milk"), liquid latex rubber is used unmixed, directly from the container. A more recently developed two-part silicone liquid mold-making material is composed of a liquid resin and a liquid catalyst, and requires mixing.

Both liquid mold-making materials can be brushed or poured on, one layer at a time. The first layers are the most important because they capture the object's detail. The many additional layers (the number depends on the object being molded) provide strength and solidity to the mold. Drying and total curing time depend on the humidity and temperature of the environment in which the mold is being made.

By looking at a comparison of these two liquid mold-making products, you'll understand why we recommend the liquid silicone material: Because the silicone material uses a catalyst to harden, its curing time is very predictable; it has a natural ability to release from an object; and it has no shrinkage or odor. By contrast, liquid latex rubber dries by dehydration, making its drying time very unpredictable; it may need a release agent applied to the object being molded; and it has a 12 percent shrinkage rate and a "fishy" odor. Instructions for using each product vary and need to be followed carefully to produce a good mold.

MAKING A CAST

BUILDING A TOOLKIT: CASTING TOOLS

In addition to the other supplies noted below, choose one of the several types of casting materials listed. Your choice may differ from one casting project to the next.

- → Casting material: Commercial powder to be mixed with water OR two-part epoxy putty
- → Powdered pigments and water-soluble colorants
- → Clay
- → X-ACTO knife
- → #220 grit open-coat sandpaper
- → Yellow glue
- → Palette knife
- → Small cheesecloth squares and a small can of water

Casts used for restorations can merge imperceptibly with an original object, particularly if you've followed our recommendation about interlocking the cast with the existing carvings, as outlined on page 101. After a cast is installed, it can be colored, textured, and finished to match an original surface.

Casting Materials

A cast can be created from any material that can be pressed or poured into a mold, allowed to harden into the mold's shape, and then released from it. The ideal casting material is nontoxic, simple to mix, easily shaped with an X-ACTO knife and sandpaper, able to have an armature inserted, and also adheres to surfaces and accepts paints and gilding materials over it.

OUR PREFERENCE: "ROCK-HARD WATER PUTTY"

We found that an inexpensive, dry, powdered putty, referred to on the product label as "rock-hard water putty," (see the Resources on page 268) fit the bill and worked very well for the casts we made over the years. Sold in home-improvement centers and in hardware and paint stores, this powder mixes easily with water (in a ratio of three parts powder to one part water) and pours readily, or can be scooped, into a mold. While still uncured, it accepts armatures that will strengthen the cast and can be colored with water-soluble colorants and powdered pigments. It adheres well to surfaces and can be cut, sawn, filled, and drilled, as needed. And, finally, it accepts all types of coatings (like paints, gesso, and gilding) over it once the cast has cured. In the photos below, we had to cast a brass boss to complete the restoration of this early-nineteenth-century rosewood-grained card table shown in its condition before treatment at left, and after at below right.

Rock-hard water putty was used to mold the missing brass boss for this card table. After the cast was made, it was gilded and patinated.

Steps to Making a Cast

Making a cast is pretty straightforward. It involves a few preliminary steps to prepare the mold, gather armature supplies if they're to be used, mix the casting material, pour or press it into the cast, let it cure, and remove it from the mold. Included in the steps below are several tips that will help you get the best possible casting results from your molds:

STEP 1: POSITION THE MOLD CORRECTLY

Set the mold on the work surface, shoring it up, if necessary, with clay, or place it in a bed of sand to insure that the open area of the mold is level.

STEP 2: CLOSE ENDS OF OPEN MOLD

If the mold is open on both ends (we call this a "trough mold"), close the ends with clay (or a similar material) to prevent any liquid casting material from flowing out (see the photo at right), in which one end has yet to be closed.

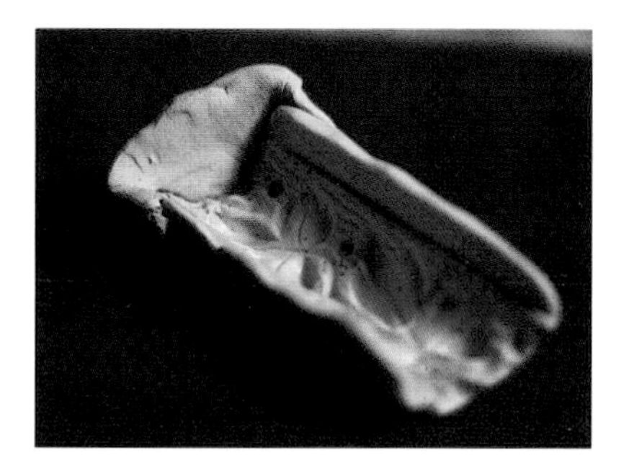

If your mold is a "trough mold," or open at one or both ends, close the end(s) with clay to keep the casting material from flowing out.

STEP 3: MIX CASTING MATERIAL

Mix the casting material according to the directions on the label.

STEP 4: ADD COLORANTS TO CASTING MATERIAL

Water-based colorants or dry, powdered pigments can be added to the casting material to provide a good base color for the color matching you'll do later.

STEP 5: FILL THE MOLD WITH CASTING MATERIAL

Fill the mold with any casting material up to, but not above, the top. The reasons for this are threefold:

1. When the cast dries and the water evaporates, the cast will shrink very slightly.

2. Pouring just to the top allows enough room for the glue layer needed to join the cast to the object.

3. It saves the time and effort of having to sand or cut away excess casting material that has bulged over the top of the mold (which actually will be the bottom of the cast when removed from the mold).

STEP 6: LET CAST CURE

Casts (especially those with complicated carvings) should be allowed to cure until very dry so that they don't break apart when taken out of the mold.

STEP 7: REMOVE CAST FROM MOLD

When removing a cast from a mold, turn the mold upside down and spread it apart as much as possible, which will allow the cast to drop out.

We recommend making many casts from your mold. This enables you not only to experiment with cutting and fitting options but also to have enough casts on which to practice—and get good at—color-matching the cast to the existing surfaces of wood, paint, gilding, or Asian lacquer. Having enough casts on which to experiment with gilding and patinas

You may need to make several casts from a mold to restore an object. Making multiple casts enables practicing color-matching, gilding, graining, and so on, in order to best match the original. At top left are the molds and "raw" casts of bosses (round ornaments), which were then gilded and patinated, to restore a late-eighteenth-century English sideboard (top right).

(top left) enabled us to match the original bosses (raised ornamentation attached separately to a surface) more easily on the late-eighteenth-century English sideboard above (see Patination for Leaf on page 216 in Chapter 9 for guidance on creating patinas).

Strengthening a Cast

Some casts are formed from enough casting material to be quite strong, but other casts can be delicate and need strengthening in order not to break apart. We were quite successful over the years with inserting metal and mesh materials as internal supports for thin, fragile casts.

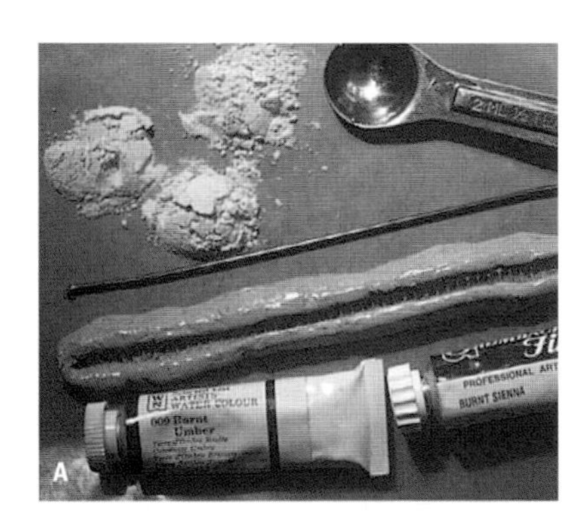

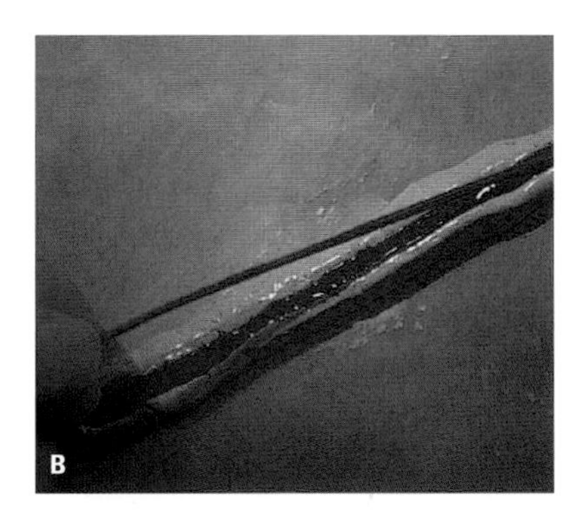

Casting material can be strengthened with an armature and colored with gouache paints. Photo A shows preparations for restoring spiral moldings on a nineteenth-century tea caddy: three parts powdered casting material measured out (top left), gouache colors (bottom), a green mold ready for casting material (center), and a cut wire for an armature. We added the wire to the colored, wet casting material to strengthen it (B). Before installing the cast, we glued down the lifted veneer on the caddy's top (C). Photo D shows the completed restoration of the moldings.

To add strength to a fragile cast, insert one or more stiff wires (even pieces cut from a wire coat hanger) into not-yet-hardened casting material. If the material is too liquid, the wire or other armature will sink to the bottom of the mold (which will be the top of the cast). The photos at the bottom of the opposite page show preparing and strengthening a cast with a piece of wire coat hanger to restore the delicate, spiral moldings on a nineteenth-century tea caddy. After the lifted veneer was adhered, the casts were matched to the existing moldings and then installed to complete the restoration.

To strengthen a delicate, wafer-thin cast, wait a few minutes after pouring the cast, then embed a piece of cheesecloth within the wet casting material, and allow it to dry. The photo at top right shows the back of a cast embedded with cheesecloth. Photo C on page 109 exhibits the same cast installed into a screen.

When working with a shallow cast, it's a good idea to store it in its mold until you're ready to install it to prevent damaging it. This is particularly true when the cast is curved and has had cheesecloth embedded within it, as was the case with the cast in the photo at above right.

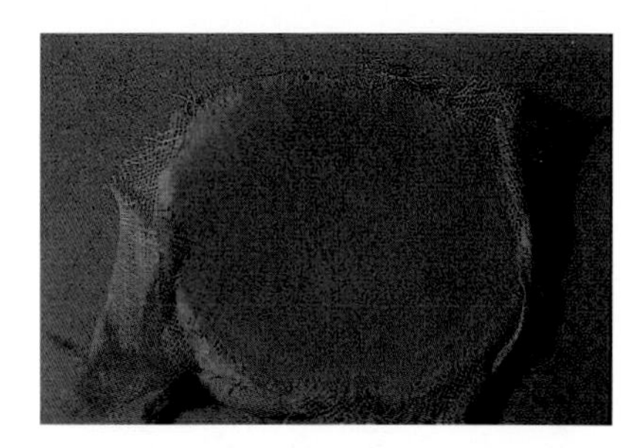

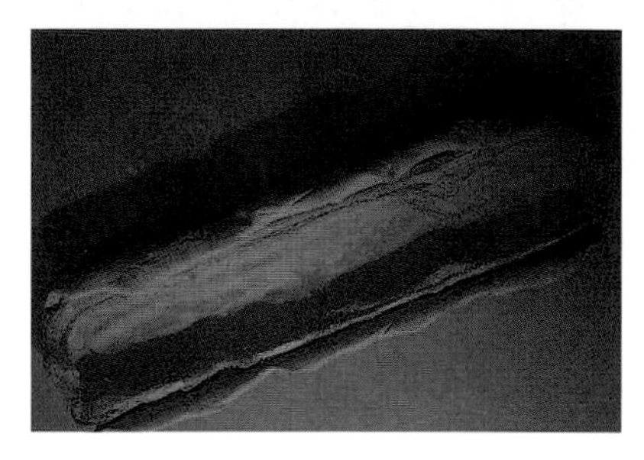

To stabilize and strengthen thin, delicate casts, embed cheesecloth into the coating material of the flat or curved cast a few minutes after pouring.

STEPS FOR INSTALLING CASTS

Installing a cast culminates the mold-making and casting process. In this stage, you'll see that all your attention to detail from the very beginning has been worth it. The following guidelines will get you started on this last phase of the mold-making and casting process.

Before Installing a Cast

To ensure that the process of installing your cast goes smoothly, you'll need to take care of a few preliminary tasks, which are outlined below:

STEP 1: SECURE LOOSE OR LIFTED SURROUNDING AREAS

To secure loose or lifted areas abutting the open space where you'll insert the cast, use a palette knife to slip glue between the substrate and the loose/lifted areas; then clamp the area, as explained in detail in Filling Surfaces on Asian Lacquer, starting on page 79 in Chapter 4.

STEP 2: CLEAN AREA TO RECEIVE CAST

Scrape or sand away any bits of glue, gesso, or epoxy remaining in the area where you'll insert the cast as seen below.

For a cast to fit evenly and securely, the "bed" on which it will sit must be completely smooth.

Doing a dry-run installation helps you test the height, angle, and alignment of the cast.

Photo courtesy of Sydney Miller

STEP 3: ROUGH UP AREA IF CAST IS FLAT-BACKED

Rough up (with #120 grit sandpaper) or crosshatch (with an X-ACTO blade) any bed where a flat-backed cast will be attached to provide "tooth" to the gluing surface.

STEP 4: TEST CAST'S FIT

To test whether the cast you've made fits the area where it will be installed, do a dry run without glue and set it into position.

STEP 5: ADJUST CAST AS NEEDED

Make any changes that Step 3 proves necessary. If the cast is too low, add filler paste to raise it. If it's too high, shave the excess off the flat base of the cast with an X-ACTO knife or reduce it by sanding with #220 grit open-coat sandpaper. It may need just sanding off a whisker of material to compensate for the tiny height that will be added by the glue.

STEP 6: TEST FOR HEIGHT DISCREPANCIES

Before adhering the cast, run your fingertips over the area where it meets the surrounding areas. Look away, or close your eyes, while doing this. Your touch will expose more height discrepancies between the two pieces than your eyes will see.

Steps to Installing a Cast

After you've tested the fit of the cast as explained above, installing the cast should not be difficult if you follow the guidelines below:

STEP 1: APPLY GLUE AND ADHERE CAST

Place a thin, even layer of yellow glue on both the cast and the surface that will receive it. Let the glue set for a few seconds; then adhere the cast to the surface, pressing it very firmly in place. Continue pressing the cast in place with hand pressure for a few minutes to give the glue a chance to bond. Wipe away excess glue with a wad of damp cheesecloth until the surface is clear; then dry the area. If the surface of the cast is not too convoluted, apply a clamp over a pad wrapped with aluminum foil (see Replacing Missing Extensions on page 110).

STEP 2: CHECK CAST'S POSITION

As the glue cures during the next few minutes, check the position to make sure it's aligned correctly from all angles and make any alignment adjustments necessary.

STEP 3: CLEAN EXCESS GLUE

Remove any adhesive that oozes out with a slightly dampened cloth.

Installation is the one phase of restoring missing or damaged dimensional elements that requires more judgment and skill than other phases. As well as making aesthetic judgments about installing a cast, you'll also need to make practical decisions about integrating the cast into the original surface. Even if you've made decisions about this during the initial analysis of your object and have planned an installation strategy, stay flexible in case you find that you need to change plans.

INSTALLING A CAST ON A CHINESE EXPORT SCREEN

We had planned to retain all fragments of the original lacquer on the early-twentieth-century Chinese export screen, a detail of which is seen in photo A below. Circular forms, known as roundels, appeared every 8 inches around the entire border of this four-panel, 8-foot-wide-by-6-foot-high screen, with every fourth roundel repeating the same motif. But, on investigation of the one roundel that was severely damaged (B), we discovered that the joint under the roundel had opened, splitting the lacquer. Therefore, we had to change our strategy, remove the entire roundel, and expose the underlying damaged joint in order to repair it.

After repairing the joint, we proceeded with replacing the roundel (refer to Chapter 3 for instruction on how to repair joints). Photo C shows the very thin cast, which had cheesecloth embedded in it for stability. After trimming the cast with scissors, shaving off a bit of the cast on the underside, we adhered the roundel with glue, pressing it in and wiping off excess glue that oozed out.

Examining one of the similar roundels under magnification revealed the order in which the original colors had been applied, giving us the chronology for the inpainting we would do on the installed cast. You can see in photo D the roundel before final "aging" to match the surrounding areas.

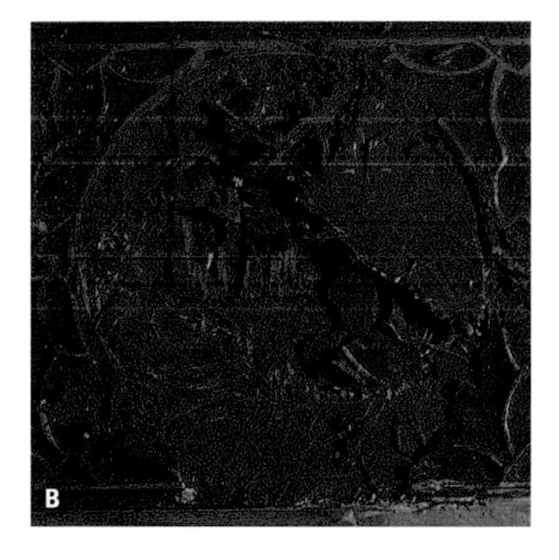

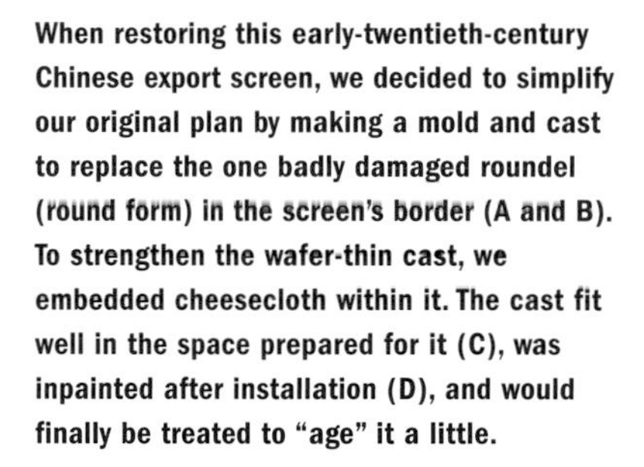

When restoring this early-twentieth-century Chinese export screen, we decided to simplify our original plan by making a mold and cast to replace the one badly damaged roundel (round form) in the screen's border (A and B). To strengthen the wafer-thin cast, we embedded cheesecloth within it. The cast fit well in the space prepared for it (C), was inpainted after installation (D), and would finally be treated to "age" it a little.

Photos courtesy of Sydney Miller

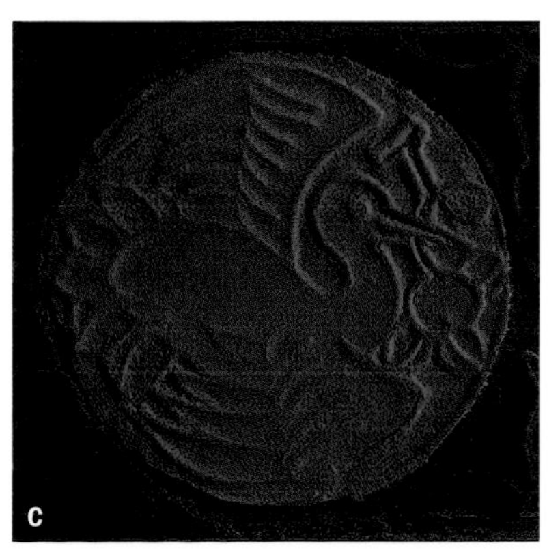

REPLACING MISSING EXTENSIONS

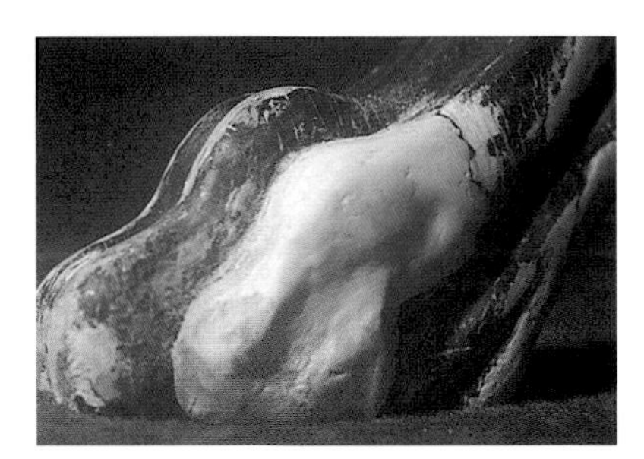

For centuries, woodworkers have glued sections of wood together to extend the wood's width and produce a larger piece to hand-carve or turn on a lathe. Over time, many of these additions have become loose or were lost entirely, but mold-making and casting can provide replacements to solve this very common problem. The telltale signs of this damage are flat, raw, or overpainted joints where carving should appear. To verify that there are pieces of wood missing, compare the areas in question to similar ones in good condition elsewhere on the object.

Among other pieces that came to us with this problem was a particularly fine, American federal window bench (c. 1810). The carved portion on the paw foot on the inside right leg was missing, and the end of the remaining joint had been over-painted black to cover the raw wood where the extra section of wood had originally been joined (see the photo at top left).

To repair this piece, we made a mold of the missing portion from the other paw foot. We used a powder/water casting material, allowed it to cure, and then glued and clamped it onto the missing area (middle left). (Note the cotton batting encased in aluminum foil, used instead of a more rigid caul to conform to the carvings on the cast being clamped.) At bottom left the glued cast awaits inpainting to match the *verte antique* (antique green) coloring popular in the early nineteenth century. The restored paw foot is shown in the photo above. In Chapters 9 and 10, you'll find detailed information on the other procedures we used to complete the restoration of this bench.

INSTALLING A CAST ON A CHINESE LOW TABLE

In the case of a restoration of a mid-nineteenth-century Chinese low table carved from many layers of cinnabar lacquer, shown on the opposite page, we again had judgment decisions to make: which portion of a cast to use and how much free-hand surface restoration to do. Photo A shows the corner of one of the table's four legs, all of which had similar damage.

After making a mold, we made casts from epoxy putty, so the corners would be strong at the roundest curve, where future damage could occur. Photo B shows two of the many casts made for the table. Some casts were used in their entire length, while others were shortened to fit into spaces like shown in photo C. This photo also shows the free-hand detailing with an X-ACTO knife using filler-paste surface-restoration materials to marry the cast to the surrounding lacquer. Photos D and E show one of the restored corners.

On the border of the same table, we again used mold-making and casting to repair the damaged ornamentation. But in this case, we had first begun treating the restoration as a regular edge repair (see page 91 in Chapter 4), as you can see from the two wire brads in photo F. In this same photo, you can see the mold we made of the Greek Key design element after deciding part-way through the one edge repair that making molds and casts for the many damaged areas would produce better, far quicker results. Remaining flexible enough to rethink the repair strategy on this piece rewarded us both in terms of time spent and the excellent results we obtained.

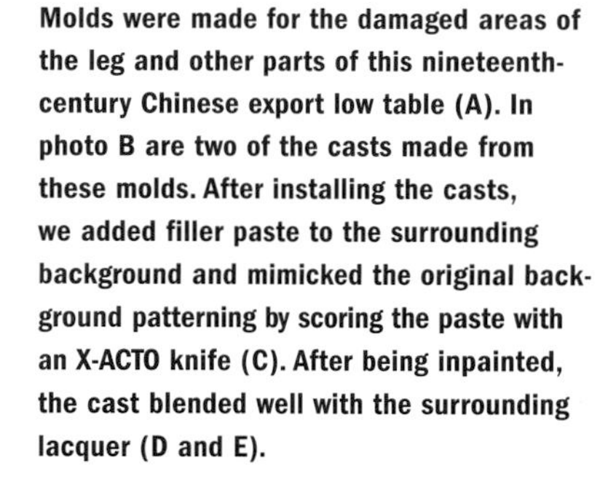

Molds were made for the damaged areas of the leg and other parts of this nineteenth-century Chinese export low table (A). In photo B are two of the casts made from these molds. After installing the casts, we added filler paste to the surrounding background and mimicked the original background patterning by scoring the paste with an X-ACTO knife (C). After being inpainted, the cast blended well with the surrounding lacquer (D and E).

Another repair on the same table shown at F reinforces the need to remain flexible throughout a restoration project. Originally we planned to treat the table's Greek Key edge motif as a surface repair (see the wire brads in the upper-left center motif). But, because of the number of damaged motifs, we decided instead to restore with molds and casts, which quickly yielded excellent, uniform results.

Installing Selected Elements of a Cast

Occasionally we've come across pieces with damaged areas containing elements that were left intact. Such was the case with the badly damaged middle portions of a pair of early-eighteenth-century English torchères (tall stands for holding candelabra), shown in the photos on the opposite page. As you can see at the top right in photo A, some of the ornamentation on the piece remained intact. Therefore, we decided to repair the piece by making molds and casts to fill the missing area, but didn't want to remove the remaining original elements just to be able to use the entire cast. Taking a clue from the damage on the piece, we decided to selectively use areas of the cast for the repair. We cut the needed raised design elements out of the cast, adhered them in the correct positions on the torchères, and then did free-hand surface-repair treatments with filler paste (see Chapter 4) to complete the restoration.

We had made the cast with epoxy putty because the design motifs and background were shallow, but cutting the motifs out of the cast turned out to be time-consuming. In retrospect, it would have been better had we cut them out of the cast before it had completely hardened or, alternatively, had we used the powder/water material we generally used, which is much easier to cut even though it's quite hard after curing.

After applying all the design elements to both torchères, we matched the background texture in the repaired area, first smoothing on a thin layer of filler paste, then reproducing the texture by pressing a nail set with the right diameter into the still-malleable paste. Finally, to complete duplicating the surface pattern, we used the tip of an ice pick to impress a dot in the circular pattern left by the nail set (photo B). Photo C shows one of the completed sections of the restoration; and photo D displays the restored torchères in front of a late-eighteenth-century, Adam-period, inlaid-marble fireplace, a fitting setting in which to pay tribute to the impressive role of mold-making and casting in restoration. You may have already realized that these torchères are the same pair that we had an auction estimate of $20,000 to $30,000 after our restoration (photo E), as noted on page 15 in Chapter 1.

While reading this chapter, it's possible that you have already thought of objects in your possession with damaged or missing pieces of carving that could be restored by mold-making and casting. Imagine the pleasure and comments you'll get after you restore them.

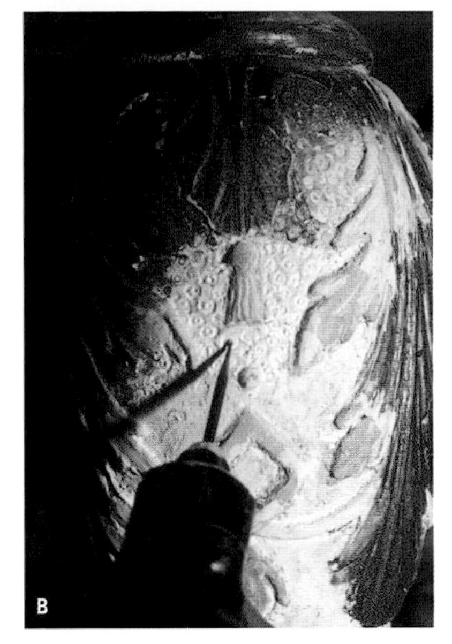

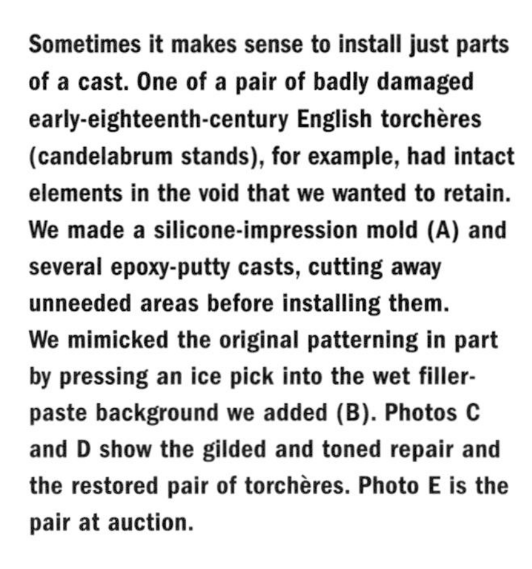

Sometimes it makes sense to install just parts of a cast. One of a pair of badly damaged early-eighteenth-century English torchères (candelabrum stands), for example, had intact elements in the void that we wanted to retain. We made a silicone-impression mold (A) and several epoxy-putty casts, cutting away unneeded areas before installing them. We mimicked the original patterning in part by pressing an ice pick into the wet filler-paste background we added (B). Photos C and D show the gilded and toned repair and the restored pair of torchères. Photo E is the pair at auction.

Photo E courtesy of Sotheby's

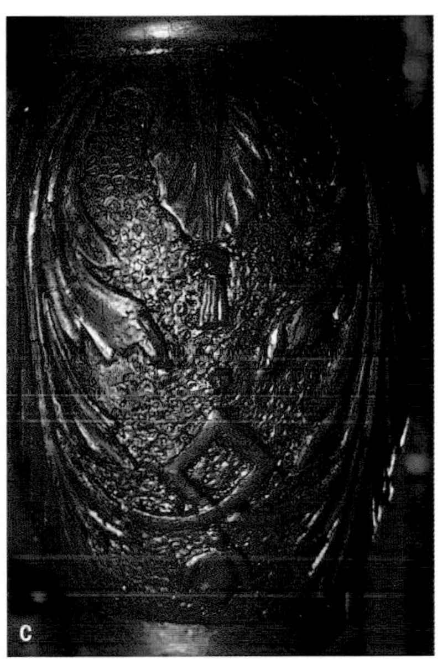

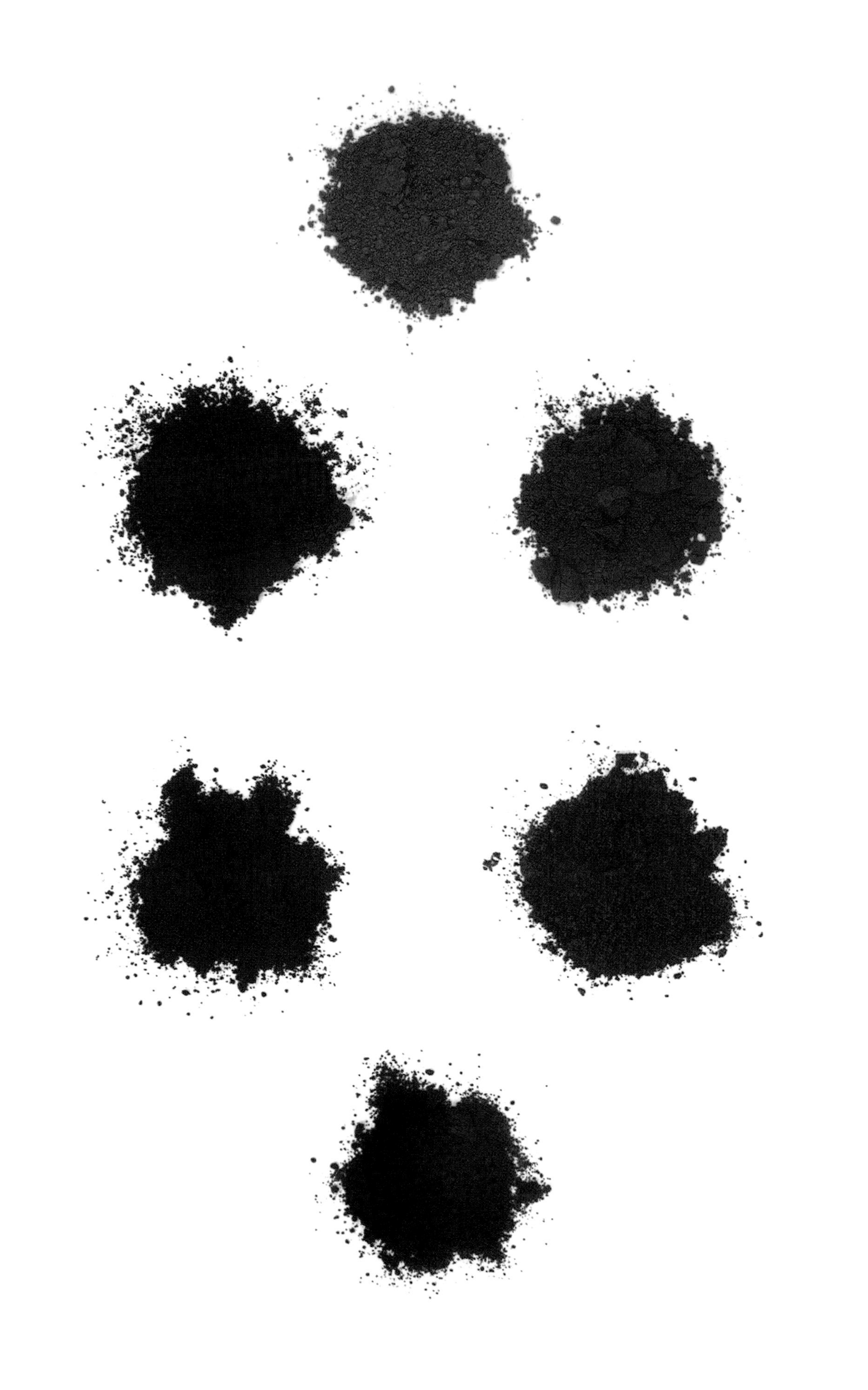

№ 6 ‖ Restoring Color

THE RESTORER, unlike an artist who concentrates on creating colors, focuses on matching existing colors on a surface that's already been restored and is ready for inpainting. Color matching involves duplicating not only the original colors but also their aged patina and any finishes covering them. To some degree, all color matching is a process of trial and error, but this chapter will help you minimize the trial and reduce the errors. Although color matching can be done by experimentation alone, understanding the basics of color theory will reduce the time spent, materials used, and frustration you experience, and will usually produce a better color match.

Because the first step in restoring an object's color is to find the original color that needs to be matched—not always as easy as it sounds!—we'll begin the chapter there. Next we'll turn to the basics of color and color theory, and then conclude with practical information about mixing colors and inpainting. Don't be surprised if, after working with this chapter, some of your long-held beliefs about color are slightly changed—ours certainly were years ago.

These mounds of powder, ground from inorganic minerals are yellow ochre, raw sienna, burnt sienna, raw umber, burnt umber, and black.

Photo © Randy Asplund

UNCOVERING ORIGINAL COLORS

**BUILDING A TOOLKIT:
TOOLS FOR UNCOVERING COLOR**

- → Cotton Swabs
- → Cheesecloth Squares
- → Pure Soap
- → Water
- → Sandpaper, #120 and #220 grit open-coat
- → Wet/dry silicone carbide papers, #400, 600, and 800
- → Wooden implements, like tongue depressors, cut square across the end
- → Single-edge razor blades
- → X-ACTO tools
- → Safety goggles
- → Magnifying tool

Over time many changes occur to surfaces, whether or not they're covered with a coat of paint or another finish. Dust and dirt accumulate; colors fade; and what were once clear finish coats often turn brittle, dark, amber, or opaque. If original color is not immediately visible on your object after looking at it under sunlight, color-balanced incandescent light, and magnification (try a hand-held magnifying glass, head magnifier, or close-up camera lens), turn to one or more of the following procedures on the object's surface, starting with the simplest strategy (listed first below) and working up to the more complex: removing mounts to find color, then cleaning, abrading, and scraping the surface.

Removing Mounts

A good place to look for original color is in areas that have been protected and therefore not exposed to the elements that change colors over time. One such protected area is under mounts (whether utilitarian, like the mount over the keyhole in the fall-front in photo A below, or purely decorative). These mounts are rarely, if ever, removed for dusting, cleaning, or polishing; and in the case of the fall-front on an eighteenth-century English secretary (B), the mounts (shown in place at photo A and removed at C) had covered both the light-yellow base-coat color and the more colorful flowers. (Note the similarity of the exposed shape in photo D and the mount in photo C). The dark areas inside the exposed shape and around its outer contours resulted from accumulations of dirt and dried polish.

When removing a mount, use the correct type and size of screwdriver, so you won't strip the screw's head or threads. Be sure to mark the mount's position on the back with masking tape to ensure that you can return it to the original holes drilled for it (as shown in C).

Look for original color beneath mounts, like the one in photo D. It was taken off the fall-front of an eighteenth-century English secretary (B). The mount (shown in A before it was taken off) preserved the colors of the original paint beneath it (shown in D). This helped when mixing and matching paint for inpainting areas that we were restored elsewhere on the secretary.

Sometimes removing a mount reveals unexpected results. Beneath the mount on an early- to mid-eighteenth-century American highboy, for example, where every bit of paint had disappeared from the entire surface, almost pristine japanning, painted to simulate red and black tortoise shell, was found. Note the shape of the preserved japanning, which is exactly the same as the mount that protected it at right.

Removing a mount sometimes unveils a dramatic contrast between paint underneath and the exposed areas around it. Here, a mount protected red-and-black tortoise-shell japanning on an eighteenth-century American highboy.

Cleaning

There's a fine line between cleaning and overcleaning. Proceed slowly when cleaning an object's surface, and be careful not to use harsh chemicals or methods that will remove any color that the original artist may have applied. This is especially true for toning glazes (pigmented translucent coatings discussed later in this chapter) that can be destroyed by overly zealous cleaning.

CLEAN, BUT DON'T OVERCLEAN

Decisions about cleaning painted surfaces have plagued conservators for years, even during the twenty-year restoration of the Sistine Chapel (1979–99). While removing dirt; darkened, discolored topcoats; and overpainting that had accumulated on Michaelangelo's famous ceiling over the centuries, evaluations had to be made at every stage to determine, among other issues, whether there were any glazes that were original and, if so, how to clean but not overclean them. By examining your object carefully where the surface is in good condition, you'll be able to discern whether the color is translucent (indicating a glaze) or opaque (indicating allover, even color without depth) (see Determining Glaze-Coat Color(s) on page 128).

The surface of your object may be merely dirty, and luckily most dirt is water-soluble. So, for starters, after removing any mounts, dusting the surface with a soft-haired brush, and removing any loose debris, start cleaning with the mildest materials available: pure soap (the fewer ingredients, the purer the soap) and water. Gently rub cotton swabs with a little soap and water on an area about 1-inch square, changing the swabs as they get dirty and continuing until no more dirt appears on the cotton. Then dry the area gently with a cheesecloth square. If this process is successful, repeat it over the entire surface. If dirt still remains, move on, first, to abrading and then scraping (described in detail below) to clean the surface.

CANNED AIR AS A CLEANING TOOL

Another cleaning tool to use at the outset is compressed air in canisters, which is available in office-supply stores. These canisters shoot a spurt of air to blow away dust that may cover existing color next to moldings or in crevices. Even if you can't clean those areas, at least clearing away dust will enable you to find clues to the piece's original colors.

The painted surface of the mid-eighteenth-century English clock case at right, for example, had been covered with dirt and grime. When this photo was taken, the cove (inwardly curved) molding along the upper part of the image had been cleaned on the right, starting with cleaning out the dust alongside the molding with compressed air; the molding on the far left and the base still remained to be cleaned.

To find original color on a dusty or dirty object, first try compressed air and dusting with a soft brush, then use cotton swabs and mild soap, which can work wonders (see the upper right of this mid-eighteenth-century English clock case; the rest remained to be cleaned). The raw wood, thin molding across the top had been added by the client to replace one that had disappeared.

There's a wide assortment of abrading papers available. The higher the number on the back of the paper, the finer its grit per inch. The gray and green papers are used for wet/dry abrading.

Abrading

More time-consuming than cleaning or removing mounts, abrading involves rubbing a surface to wear away an outer coating. Abrading uncovers color that was overcoated with another substance like paint.

There are many materials that will abrade a surface, from sandpaper in various types and grits, to higher grades of wet/dry silicone carbide papers (which range from 300 to 1,500 grits), to pumice and rottenstone (see the photo at left). The key to the abrading process is to begin testing grits in an inconspicuous area on your piece. To find the least damaging grit that will effectively abrade the surface and remove the overpaint, start with a fine grit and work down to a coarser one. As you abrade further down on the piece, work back up to finer-grit sandpaper to avoid damaging the original surface. Then, when you get to the final overpaint on the surface, abrade with the wet/dry papers. Note that, since you're abrading the paint, not the wooden surface itself, you needn't worry about sanding in any particular direction since paint has no grain. The abrading process always calls for patience and care, but it can be done at intervals rather than all at once.

ABRADING AN ANTIQUE TOOLBOX

In the case of a toolbox from the hose carriage (which had originally belonged to the firefighting unit of the Steinway Piano Company) that we were restoring for a major museum exhibit, we were faced with a layer of brittle, tan overpaint that had been applied in 1902 over the box's original mid-nineteenth-century painted surface. To remove the overpaint you see in the photo at the top of the opposite page, we scraped off the brittle areas, then abraded the remaining overpaint with wet/dry papers, which proved the only way to remove this layer without damaging the painted surface beneath. We started abrading with #120 grit open-coat sandpaper, then moved to #220, and finally used #400 and #600 wet/dry silicone paper. We cut the papers into 1½-inch-square pieces and used medium pressure (hard pressure is tiring and wears the paper away faster).

For the next stage, we used the wet/dry paper wet. The water prevents the paper from scratching the surface and also makes abrading easier. (When using wet/dry paper wet, dip the small piece you've cut into a bowl of water, and use it straight out of the bowl. Do not wet it with your tongue, as some people do, if you want to stay healthy.)

We abraded small areas at a time, and wiped them off with a slightly damp square of cheesecloth to view the progress. Done carefully, this procedure is the safest way to protect the surface underneath, since you can view what you uncover as you work. We found the original colors and designs that had been overpainted; and it took countless hours to reveal the decoration on the rest of the hose carriage. (Starting on page 256, you'll find a detailed discussion and photos of the restoration of this antique hose carriage.) Abrading this surface took a great deal of time because the overpainted layers had bonded tightly to the original layer underneath.

We also used wet/dry papers to abrade away the blackened areas on the original green paint on a chair made by Samuel Gragg of Boston

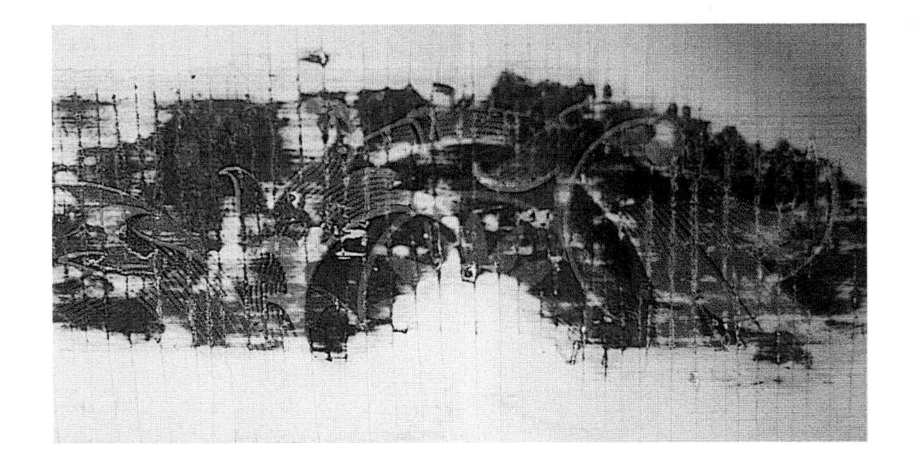

We abraded the surface of this nineteenth-century toolbox to remove the coating of overpaint, applied in 1902, which slowly unveiled amazing colors and designs beneath it in the original mid-nineteenth-century decoration.

On this American chair (c. 1808), the original green decorative paint had oxidized and turned black (far left). The darkened coating came off easily when abraded carefully with wet/dry paper, revealing the original leaf design underneath (left).

(c. 1808), which had oxidized from the sulphides in the air (see above photo left). With gentle abrading, enough darkened color came off for us to clearly identify Gragg's design on the chair and restore the original bronze-green color typical of the early nineteenth century (see above right).

Scraping

Time often damages finish coats, darkening them, making them brittle and discolored, and obscuring the original color(s) underneath. These finish coatings, now degraded, may have been original to the piece or added at a later date. The main method we used to remove such deteriorated and/or brittle coatings was scraping, which entails moving a hard or sharp edge along a surface to remove, or shave off, a coating.

Getting rid of deteriorated, brittle coats can be quite tedious, but revealing what's under them is well worth the effort. This is especially true when you realize that the aged coat you want to remove may have protected the original surface under it and kept it in good condition.

It's also interesting to note that in cases where you want to get back to an original surface that was painted over, dirt may actually be a help to you. An overcoating applied over an original layer that was not cleaned beforehand often chips off easily.

If the coating is brittle and has an edge that's sharp and well defined, it should respond well to scraping. This type of coating is usually composed of one of two substances: linseed-oil varnish that has oxidized into a darkened, almost opaque amber; or darkened shellac.

A tongue depressor, cut straight across to make a square edge, is a great scraping tool. Here, it was used to remove varnish that was so hard that two hands were required to exert enough pressure on the tool. Because old varnish and other coatings can be extremely brittle, it's a good idea to wear safety goggles when scraping off such finishes.

START MILD AND WORK UP

Start scraping with the mildest, least damaging tool you have: your fingernail. Then you can progress to wooden implements like an ice cream stick or tongue depressor, whose edge you'll need to cut square with a pair of sharp scissors (see left).

By exerting pressure on the tool, you will be able to "flick" off pieces of the unwanted coating. Use safety goggles when scraping since the chipped-off pieces can be very sharp.

A single-edged razor blade also makes a good sharp scraping tool. In below left, note how a razor blade is held almost parallel with the paint being removed. Experiment with other angles at which to hold the razor as you scrape, depending on how thick and/or easily removed the coating is.

X-ACTO knife blades are useful for chipping off ambered, brittle, linseed-oil varnish, as is being done below on the fall front of a japanned secretary (c. 1680). The procedures for completing the restoration of this secretary can be seen on page 32 in Chapter 2 (Unwarping the Panels on a Seventeenth-Century English Secretary) and on page 260 in Chapter 10 (Restoring Partially Visible Designs under Darkened Overcoats).

Above: A razor blade is a great scraping tool, but take real care when using this and other sharp scraping tools. Note, too, how the blade is held almost parallel to the surface to scrape it.

Right: X-ACTO knife blades work well, too, to chip away brittle, aged vanishes on japanned surfaces.

PAINT STRIPPERS VS. ABRADING AND SCRAPING

You may wonder why we didn't use commercially available chemical paint strippers instead of resorting to the slow procedures of abrading and scraping in our restorations. The answer is that we found that we had more control over the processes and materials described above. Using commercial strippers would increase the possibility of losing more of the original surface. Occasionally when working with heavily bonded areas of extremely thick paint on the objects we were restoring, we used mild, nontoxic strippers to "jump-start" the abrading process. These strippers worked more slowly than the readily available products with methyl chloride but were not as harmful to our health (see Resources on page 268 for suppliers of nontoxic materials).

UNDERSTANDING COLOR

In order to learn how to mix paints to match a color you need for restoring, it's important to first understand some of the basics of color, including how the eye sees color. So we'll start by looking at that, then turn to the three key elements of color (hue, value, and chroma), and finally examine earth colors, which are invaluable in mixing color for restoration.

How We See Color

Three things must be present for us to see color: A source of light, a surface, and a viewer. Without a source of light—whether the sun or a lamp, candle, or flashlight—there is no color.

IN THE ABSENCE OF LIGHT, THERE IS NO COLOR

Light itself is produced by electromagnetic waves, which make up a very small segment of the full electromagnetic spectrum (the entire range of wavelengths of electromagnetic radiation). The highest frequencies of electromagnetic waves include X-rays and ultraviolet light, while ultra-red and radio waves are at the lowest frequencies. In between is a narrow range of wavelengths of visible light, and each of these wavelengths has its own frequency. One frequency, for example, yields red light; and other individual frequencies produce yellow and blue lights as well as all the other intermediary colors we see.

So, first of all, seeing color requires light. Unlike music, in which sound is conveyed in waves whether anyone hears it or not, there is no color without light waves.

LIGHT NEEDS TO BE REFLECTED OFF A SURFACE

Second, seeing color requires a surface for the light to strike. And difficult as it may seem to grasp, even though we see different colors on the surfaces around us, the light hitting these surfaces is all the same. It's the molecular structure of each surface that light strikes that determines what color gets reflected back to us, with the remaining colors (light waves) getting absorbed into the surface itself.

FOR COLOR TO EXIST, OUR EYES MUST "RECORD" IT

Finally, seeing color requires a pair of eyes to record the phenomenon. When light hits a surface and reflects color back to us, that color is recorded on receptors in our eyes called *cones*, which enable us to see color, and *rods*, which allow us to see in very dim light (where there's very little color reflected back). Our brains synthesize this chemical message, which we then interpret as a specific color.

Elements of Color

In order to analyze a color and match it with paint, you need some way of distinguishing and measuring the various elements making up that color. The Munsell Color System, developed in 1905 by American painter Albert Munsell, is a very practical approach for measuring the three key elements of color—hue, value, and chroma—and will help you analyze the color you need to match on your restoration.

Hue is the family name for a color related to a specific wavelength of light reflected back to us from a surface (for example, red, yellow, or green). *Value* is the amount of light or dark in a hue (for example, navy blue vs. light blue). And *chroma* is the amount, or saturation, of pure, unadulterated pigment in a hue (for example, fire-engine red vs. brick red, which contains much less red pigment).

When you're mixing a color, changing even one of these three elements can drastically alter your mixture, leading you either closer to or farther from the color you want. As you read more about hue, value, and chroma below, refer to the Munsell System's Hue/Value/Chroma Chart below, which will help clarify the relationship of these three aspects of color.

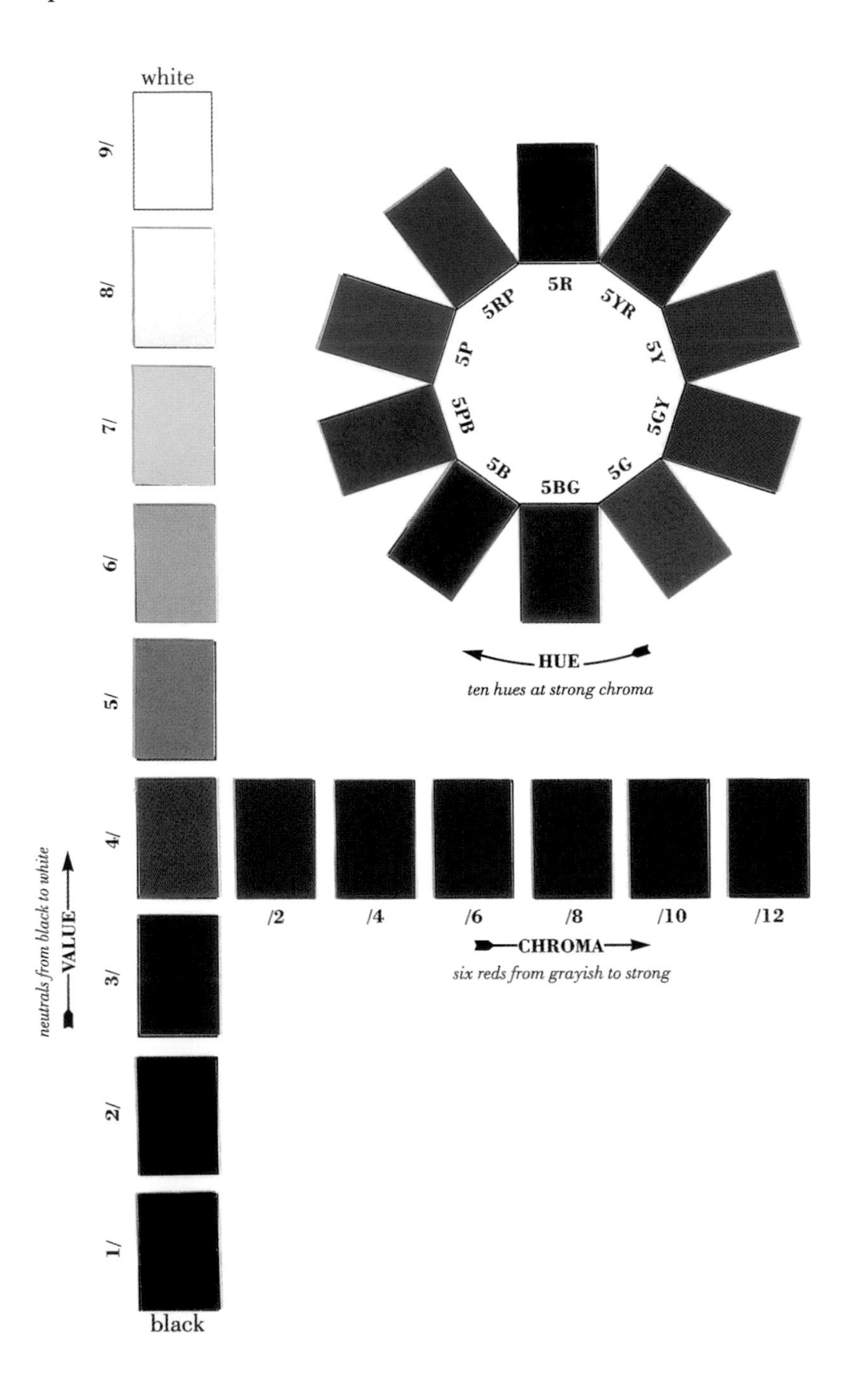

Hue is the color family, as seen in the ten chips arranged in the circle. Value is arranged in the vertical line, with the lightest at the top and the darkest at the bottom. Chroma can be seen as a horizontal line with the purest color at the far right.

Courtesy of Munsell Color Lab, a department of GretagMacbeth LLC, New Windsor, NY

HUE

The first "fact" many of us learned about color as children in school was that there are three primary hues—red, yellow, and blue—and that mixing two of these primaries together, one by one, creates orange, green, and purple. When these six colors are arranged in a circle as a traditional color wheel, red is opposite green, blue is opposite orange, and yellow is opposite purple. But the color wheel's arrangement of these six colors in equal amounts runs counter to the actual width of the wavelengths of these colors in the visible spectrum.

Munsell Color System

As you can see in the photo at right, the amounts of yellow and orange in the traditional six-color arrangement (the lower row) are far greater than their actual wavelengths (the upper spectrum). By contrast, the Munsell System has a hue distribution that's closer to the wavelengths of the visible spectrum (below); that is to say, it has fewer yellow and yellow-red hues and more hues in the blue range.

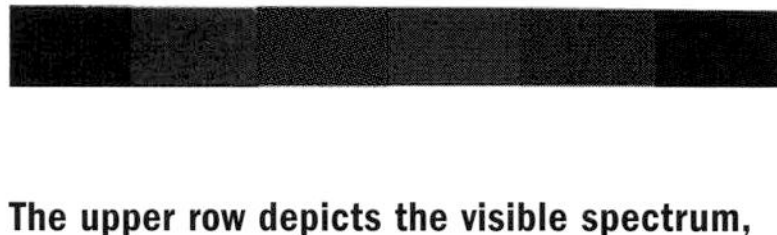

The upper row depicts the visible spectrum, and the lower row shows six equal colors on the traditional color wheel. Note how the smaller amounts of yellow and orange in the visible spectrum are unnaturally equalized on the traditional color wheel's distribution.

Photo courtesy of Nick Simone

Notice the large white circle in the Munsell Color System, with an arrangement of smaller circles at its perimeter representing the primary, secondary, and tertiary hues. To bring the printed hue information on the chart to life, we arranged each of the Munsell System's five sets of primary color charts and the intervening five sets of secondary color charts around the main circle. As you can see in the printed information at the edge of the white circle, the primary hues

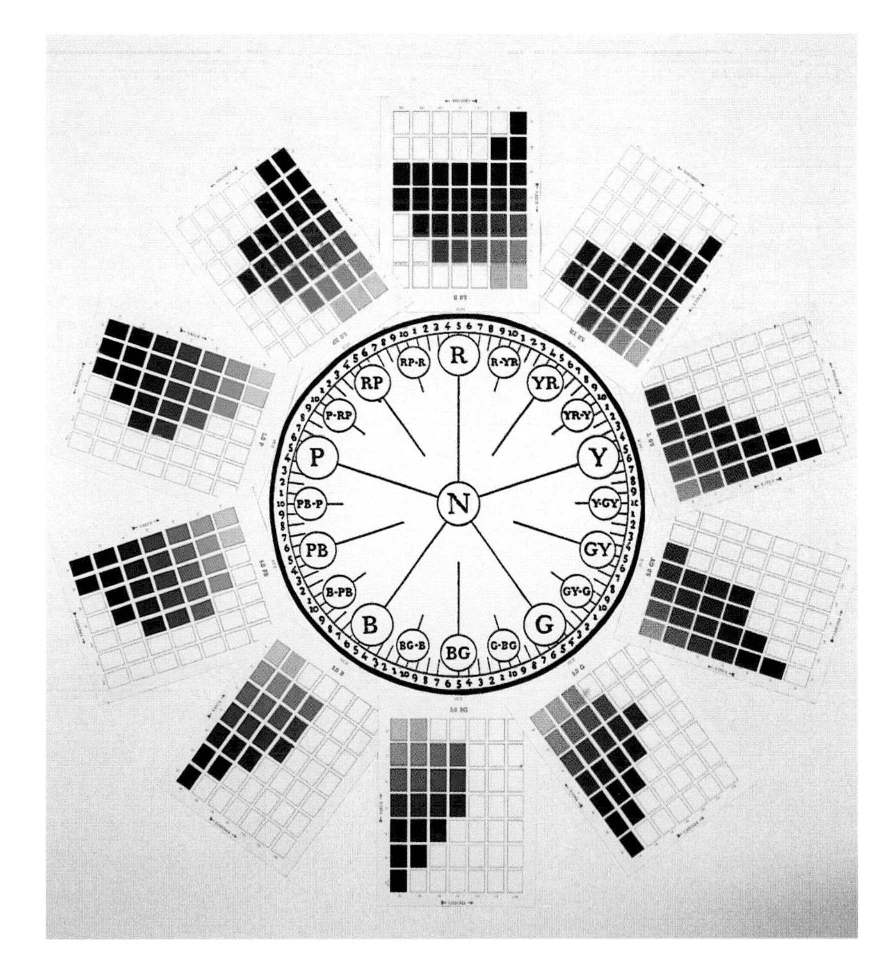

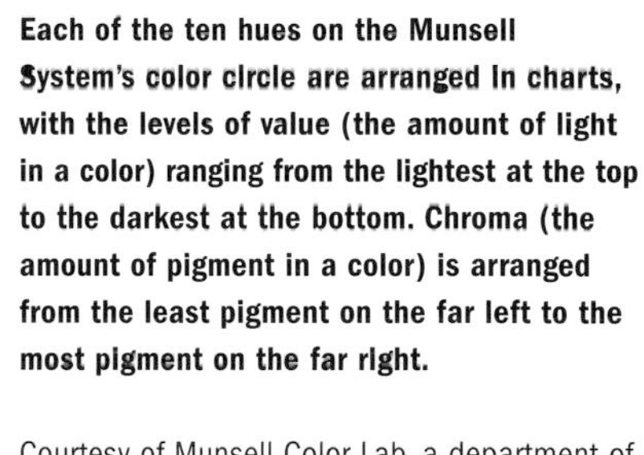

Each of the ten hues on the Munsell System's color circle are arranged in charts, with the levels of value (the amount of light in a color) ranging from the lightest at the top to the darkest at the bottom. Chroma (the amount of pigment in a color) is arranged from the least pigment on the far left to the most pigment on the far right.

Courtesy of Munsell Color Lab, a department of GretagMacbeth LLC, New Windsor, NY

are designated by a single letter: R (Red), Y (Yellow), G (Green), B (Blue), and P (Purple). They are separated by a secondary hue (designated by a double letter): YR (Yellow-Red), GY (Green-Yellow), BG (Blue-Green), PB (Purple-Blue), and RP (Red-Purple). Two tertiary hues are designated by triple letters.

Note, by the way, that purple is not a wavelength; it doesn't exist in the visible spectrum. In 1666, when Sir Isaac Newton used a prism to demonstrate that light was composed of different wavelengths (which were visible as different hues), there was no purple. He was the first to connect the red end of the visible spectrum with the violet, making a color circle, and thereby also creating a transition color: purple.

Color Temperature

In terms of learning to mix and match color, it's valuable to know about the perception referred to as "color temperature." Most hues have either a "cool" temperature (meaning the color contains some blue, which makes it look cool) or a "warm" temperature (meaning it contains some red, which makes it look warm). As you look around the Munsell System's color circle, notice that each hue is sandwiched with a warmer hue on one side and a cooler hue on the other side. For instance, G (green) has the warmer hue GY-G (Green-Yellow Green) on one side, and the cooler hue, G-BG (Green-Blue Green), on the other side. Therefore, for example, if you needed a cooler green for restoration, you would learn by looking at the color circle to put a touch of blue in the green you may have mixed already. You could also consult a color chart in your art supply store to choose a cool green that exists already in a paint tube.

As you become more knowledgeable about color temperature, you'll be able to focus in more quickly on the colors to mix that will match another color. Later in the chapter, we'll discuss color mixing and matching in greater detail, but, for now, just tuck away the concept of color temperature as something important to know about.

VALUE

Value refers to the amount of light on a surface. In each individual Munsell hue chart, value is indicated by a color's vertical position on the chart, which extends from very light at the highest row to very dark at the lowest row. The individual levels of value—the rows of each chart—correspond to the chips on the vertical scale at the far left of the chart on page 122, which is known as the neutral gray scale because it has no hue of its own. These chips have been assigned a Munsell number ranging from 9 (the highest, or lightest value) to 1 (the lowest, or darkest, value), which is calibrated with an internationally accepted scale of light-reflective values (LRVs). Therefore, the red chips in the horizontal row to the right of the chip in the vertical neutral gray scale all have the same amount of light (LRV) in them, as hard as that is to believe. This internationally recognized system allows the surface of every existing object to be measured for the light it contains, from a light-red sweater in a store window to your skin. (The light meter a photographer holds up to your face when you're sitting for a portrait, for example, measures the LRV of your skin to get a proper exposure of light for the photograph.)

Tints, Shades, and Tones

The addition of white and black to change value is often necessary. A *tint* is a lightened value of a color produced by adding white; a *shade* is a darkened value of a color made by adding black; and a *tone* is a color made by adding both white and black (that is, gray), regardless of whether the color produced is lighter or darker in value.

CHROMA

The third, and perhaps least understood, element of color is *chroma,* which refers to the purity of a hue, or the amount of pure pigment in it. In the Munsell System, chroma is measured on a horizontal scale (see the horizontal bar on page 122 and the individual hue charts at the bottom of page 123), starting with the far right chip, which has the most amount of pigment and moving to the far left chip, which has the least. Note that in the Munsell System's color circle the strongest chroma is always on the far right in each individual hue chart, but the horizontal row on which it appears (indicating its level of value) may differ. For example, on the Y (Yellow) chart the strongest chroma is on the top row, which happens also to be the lightest level of value, while, on the G (Green) chart, the strongest chroma is on the third row, or level of value. The reason for the differing positions on the levels of value is simple: The natural or synthetic sources of the pigments making up colors vary in their levels of value, or lightness.

To "Age" a Color

It's important when learning to mix paint to know how to reduce the strength of a color (that is, lower its chroma) so that you can create subtle, muted color variations of strong, vibrant colors (those with a higher chroma). This is especially important for restorers because the colors we often need to match on an object, which were possibly more vibrant and stronger in chroma when originally applied, have usually faded over time and must be given an "aged," grayer appearance (that is, one with a lower chroma).

To lower the chroma of a strong color, mix that color with its complement, or the hue opposite: That is to say, Red's complement is Blue-Green, Yellow's is Purple-Blue, and Blue's is Yellow-Red. In each case, the pair of complements supplies the missing hue, value, and chroma needed to balance, or complement, the other hue. To lower a color's chroma without changing its hue or value, choose a pair of complements that are on the same level of value, as shown, for example, on the top of page 126.

Looking at Lowering Chroma

To show you how this works, we mixed together the complementary colors at the top and bottom of the Munsell System's color circle, Red and Blue-Green, choosing the hues from the same level of value, the third row. As you can see on the jacket of our color video on page 126,

This Munsell chart shows how mixing a color (in this case, Purple-Blue) with its complement (Yellow) lowers the color's chroma and produces a grayed version of the color. Note how the purer, high-chroma hues at the ends of each row become grayer, low-chroma hues in the middle of the row. To keep the value of a hue constant when you're mixing a lower-chroma version of the hue, choose a complement that's positioned on the same horizontal line of value.

Courtesy of Munsell Color Lab, a department of GretagMacbeth LLC, New Windsor, NY

Right: Mixing red and its complement, blue-green, lowers the chroma, or pigment, of both hues, producing grayed-out versions of these colors in the center. As you can see, changing the proportions of red and blue-green in each block creates a wider assortment of in-between hues.

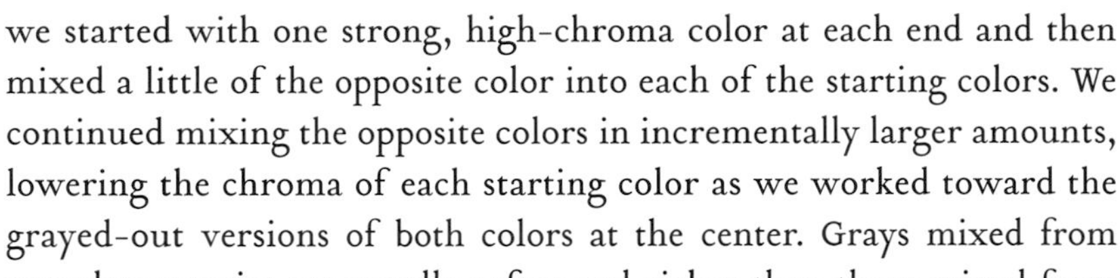

we started with one strong, high-chroma color at each end and then mixed a little of the opposite color into each of the starting colors. We continued mixing the opposite colors in incrementally larger amounts, lowering the chroma of each starting color as we worked toward the grayed-out versions of both colors at the center. Grays mixed from complementaries are usually softer and richer than those mixed from black and white. The spectrum above shows similar starting colors with even more mixed steps in-between and even lower chromas in the middle.

EARTH COLORS

Lowering chroma to create less intense hues can be done not only by mixing complements but also by using earth colors. These earth colors are inorganic pigments, derived from minerals, such as limonite, hematite, ochre, and manganese, which supply very useful hues for restoration.

The Most Common Earth Colors

In their raw form, earth colors are lighter in value than when they're calcined (burned), which turns them darker and richer in color. Six earth colors are the most commonly used in restoration: yellow ochre, a dull yellow; raw sienna, which is deeper and richer than yellow ochre; burnt sienna, a coppery hue; raw umber, which is a neutral, non-red

Earth colors are very useful for mixing colors for restoration. These colors include (from left) yellow ochre, raw sienna with burnt sienna below it; raw umber atop burnt umber, and black.

Photo © Randy Asplund

brown (whose name derives from the Latin word *ombre,* or "shadow"); burnt umber, which is a rich brown; and black (see the photo above of these earth colors).

Yellow ochre, raw sienna, burnt sienna, and burnt umber each combines with ultramarine blue (a purple-blue) in various proportions to create a range of lowered chromas and grays that are richer than the results produced by mixing this blue with the other two remaining earth colors, raw umber and black. Raw umber is a shadowy color with gray-green undertones, which is best used by itself or mixed with white to create an interesting range of lighter hues. Black lowers the value of any color in which it's mixed, but it also adds a touch of coolness (blue) as does white in a mixture. Aside from these earth colors in common usage, there's a full range of richer earth colors available from specialized suppliers, which might prove useful to you (see Resources on page 268).

BEFORE YOU CAN INPAINT

Before you can inpaint the surface you've restored or the cast you've integrated into a carving, you'll need to find the specific colors that need to be matched. If those colors are covered by dirt or by darkened, deteriorated coatings, refer to Uncovering Original Colors (starting on page 116) for various procedures to unveil those colors.

After uncovering original color, test it to see if all the overcoating has been removed from the surface by wiping it with a slightly damp piece of cheesecloth, which will show up any remaining coating. Be aware that, if you abrade or scrape a surface to uncover an original color, abrading or scraping will often make the surface colors appear dull. In addition, as paint ages and loses its vehicle (the liquid medium that carries the pigment), it also loses its reflective quality. Wiping the surface with a barely-dampened wad of cheesecloth will help the colors come alive for a few minutes and give you a preview of what the eventual

Top: To find the best match to the original glazed color on a lady's carriage we were restoring for a film, we mixed small amounts of various translucent glazes in plastic cups and then coated the test glazes over dried base coats of paint.

Above: After determining the right base-coat/glaze combination, we glazed the carriage, including the spokes on the wheels to enrich and deepen their base-coat color.

finished surface will look like. To remedy this loss of color and more accurately mirror the original artist's intent in terms of color, apply a clear coat of a thinned medium on an area that's dull (see A Bird's-Eye Look at Media on page 139 in Chapter 7 and also see the photos at the top of page 131.

Once you've found or uncovered the original color on your object, place the piece under a good light—sunlight, color-balanced incandescent light, or fluorescent light—and begin exploring to hone in more closely on the color(s) that you need to match. If you mixed colorants into filler paste when repairing a surface (see Coloring Filler Paste on pages 77 to 78 in Chapter 4) or when making casts (see Making a Cast on pages 104 to 107 in Chapter 5), you're already on your way to developing color-matching skills.

If the color you need to match is readily apparent but somewhat opaque, refer to Mixing and Matching Colors on the opposite page. But if the color you need to match looks as if it has depth, with what seems to be a thin, colored film coating over another color underneath, you're probably dealing with a surface that was glazed. Read on.

Determining Glaze-Coat Color(s)

A glaze is a sheer, translucent pigmented coat that changes the opaque color it covers. If your original surface was glazed, you'll need to match two colors in order to duplicate that surface: the opaque color under the glaze and the glaze color itself. To do this, prepare a number of base-coated surfaces on which to test the glaze color you're considering. This was what we did to match glaze for an antique lady's phaeton (carriage) that we were restoring for a motion picture (top left). We kept very complete records of our color testing to allow us to develop the correct color relationship between the base coat and glaze. Become familiar with each element of the pair you've created in your tests to be able to recognize the combinations of base-coat color and overglaze that create the different visual effects.

USUALLY A DARK GLAZE COVERS A LIGHT BASE

These panels show the varying effects of two different base- and glaze-coat combinations: At left, a dark glaze covers a light base coat, producing a warm effect; and on the right, a light glaze covers a dark base coat, yielding an icy effect. The rectangular block in each section shows the base-coat color, and the opaque areas at the top indicate the glaze coats before they were thinned down to the sheer covering below.

You'll find that most glazed surfaces are a combination of a darker glaze coated over a lighter base coat, which produces a rich, clear, warm effect, as shown at left in the photo at left. Once in a while you'll find the opposite glaze combination, a lighter glaze over a darker base coat, as shown at right in the same photo, which produces an icy, cool look. Both panels were developed using the same two colors in reverse: pink and red. The small rectangular blocks display the base-coat color of each panel under the glaze, and the opaque colors along the top of the image show the glaze colors before they were thinned out along the lower half of each panel.

Sometimes the base coat under the glaze isn't easy to discern. A base coat may be visible where a glaze has worn through; or, because glazes don't always spread evenly, the base coat may be exposed at one point or another on the surface, as you can see in the top photo on the opposite page. Use a foam-tipped applicator (sold in hardware and paint stores) to apply a totally smooth glaze without brush marks.

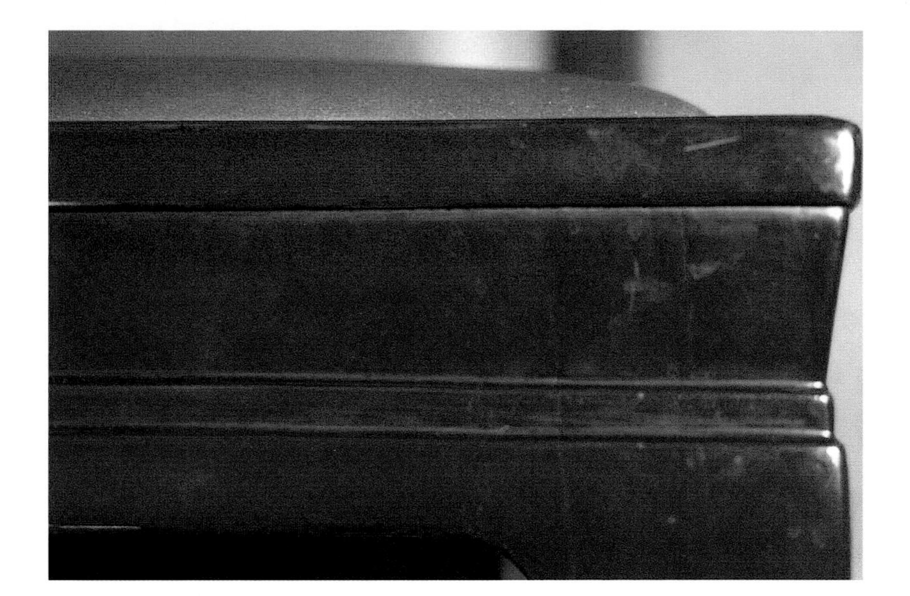

A glaze coating tends to spread unevenly and where it's sheer, it often reveals the base coat. On this Art Deco chair, the original, darker, burnt sienna-like glaze reveals portions of the lighter raw-sienna base coat.

A foam-tipped brush is good for applying glaze because it doesn't leave brush marks and holds a lot of glaze, which can be spread out in a sheer coating when applying.

MIXING AND MATCHING COLORS

Working with color is a joyful, lifelong process of learning that's filled with surprises. There are innumerable books on every aspect of color, but you'll learn the most about mixing color by doing your own experiments and keeping accurate records of them. If this is your first attempt at mixing and matching colors, don't be discouraged if the process takes longer than you expect. As you get more experienced at mixing and matching colors, the procedure will become less intimidating and take less time.

Color-Mixing Basics

The goal in mixing color is to produce the color you're trying to match as quickly and painlessly as possible. The best way to do this is to work with small amounts of paint on a nonabsorbent surface that allows the paints to be mixed and remain on that surface rather than being absorbed into it. We suggest using ¼-inch brushes to mix paint and painting small samples of color, which wastes far less paint than working with wide brushes and large samples. And, of course, we urge you to keep careful written and visual records of the formulas with measurements for each color used, along with a painted sample of the color itself. Below are some guidelines for experimenting with mixing and matching colors, followed by a set of specific steps for mixing colors.

TIPS FOR COLOR MIXING

The guidelines below will help you start experimenting with mixing and matching colors:

Paint Mixing Is Subtractive Mixing

Every time you add one paint to another, you're subtracting light (and remember that without light, there is no color). Therefore, the fewer colors you mix together, the clearer and less muddy your results will be. If you want a "muddy" (lower-chroma) color, mix it with the correct complements (see pages 125 to 126).

Every Color Has a Visual Temperature

To choose the most useful color to start your color mixing, keep in mind that every color has a temperature (see Hue on page 123). Colors with red in them are considered "warm," and those with blue in them are considered "cool." So, if you need to match a cool red, for example, start mixing with a red hue that contains some blue in it rather than yellow.

Test Color Matches Without Intervening Spaces

A color may look warm until you put an even warmer color next to it, which, in turn, makes the first color look cooler. If there's an intervening space between your test color and the original color, that space will affect the comparison. Therefore, place your test color directly adjacent to the color you're trying to match, without any intervening space between the two. This is the most accurate way to match a mixed color to an original color.

Color Is Not Seen in a Vacuum

Other colors usually surround a given color, influencing how that color is seen and making it hard to match. Therefore, to visually isolate the color you want to match from its surroundings, cut an opening, or frame (in whatever size needed), in white paper, through which to view the target color. Then place this "mask" directly over the color you're trying to match. Follow the guidelines above by placing your test color directly next to the color showing in the mask.

Start Mixing with a High-Chroma Color

Because it's easier to lower chroma than to raise it, start mixing with a high-chroma version of your target color and then lower it (see Chroma on page 125). If you must increase chroma strength, add pure saturated pigments.

Add Dark Colors Carefully to a Mixture

Because dark colors are powerful, add them carefully and gradually to a mixture. If you add too much of a dark color, you may need a much greater quantity of a light color to reduce the darkened effect.

Water-Based Paints Get Dull as They Dry

Water-based paints (except acrylics) get dull as they dry out because they lose the reflectivity that water provides. Try to match your test color to the original color while the paint is still wet. When the test color is dry, coat it with thinned, clear medium to approximate the original color (see A Bird's-Eye Look at Media on page 139 in Chapter 7).

The photos at right illustrate this point: The dull, grayish stripes in the top right photo indicate where gouache (which matched the rest of the surface when wet) had been inpainted and then dried. The photo on the bottom right shows the same area after being coated with a clear medium but before having toning glaze added to the inpainted areas to match the darker areas shown.

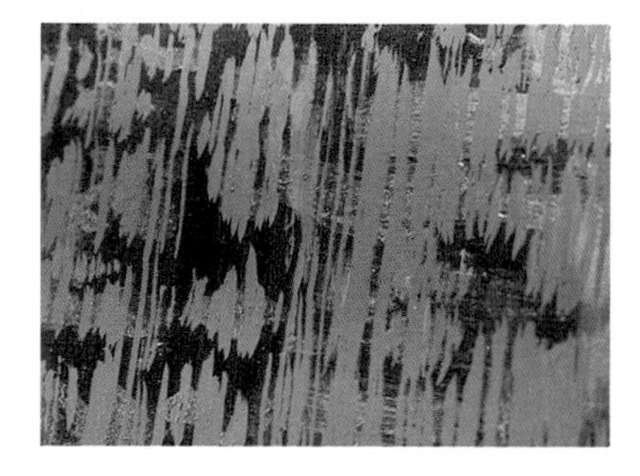

When inpainting, be aware that newly mixed paint that matches original paint when wet (as the bluish-gray gouaches stripes did), may look quite different when dry (top). But coating the dried restored areas with a clear medium before adding a toning glaze dramatically changes the look of the surface (above).

Poor Vision Detracts from Accurate Color Mixing

Be sure to wear your eyeglasses (if you need them), or use a magnifier.

Don't Mix More than Three Colors Together

If, after mixing three different colors to produce your target color, you're not satisfied with the results, toss out the paper plate or palette you're mixing on, and start working on a fresh mixing surface. Adding more paint to a wrong color only produces even more wrong color.

Steps in Color Mixing

Color mixing and matching can be time-consuming. In order to get the results you want, be sure to have enough time available to devote to the process. And, as always, keep careful records of what you're mixing, particularly as you get close to the color you're trying to match. To get the best results in color mixing, follow the steps on pages 132 to 133:

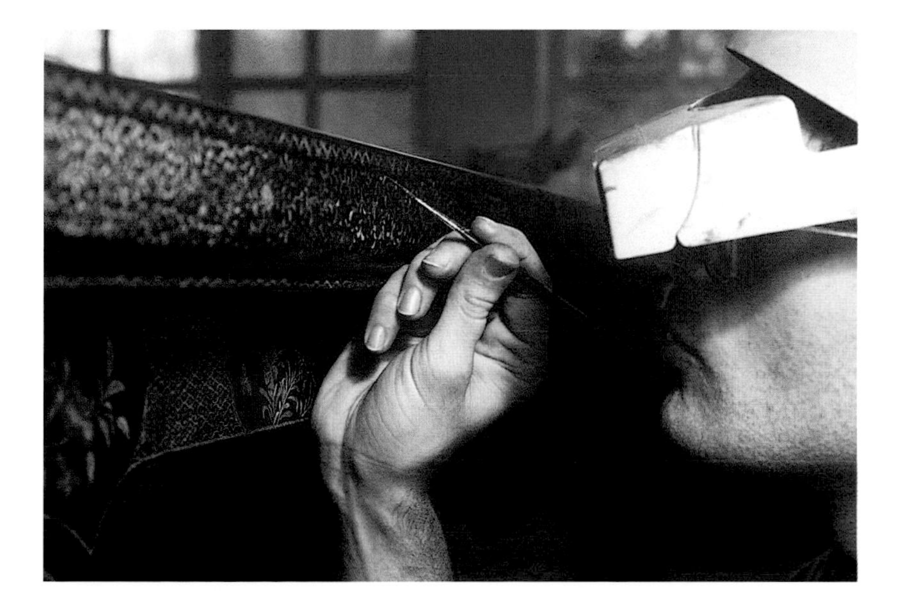

For some inpainting and other restoration tasks, you may find it helpful to use a head-band magnifier.

BUILDING A TOOLKIT: COLOR-MIXING TOOLS

- → The Munsell Student Set (for color reference; see Resources on page 268)
- → A set of measuring spoons
- → Cheesecloth squares
- → Palette knives
- → Note pad and pencil/pen
- → Container of water
- → 5-ounce plastic or coated paper cups
- → Film canisters or plastic/glass jars (for storing mixed paints)
- → Nonabsorbent paper plates or paper palettes (for mixing)
- → Supply of inexpensive, 1/4-inch and 1/2-inch soft-bristle brushes
- → Water-based pigments (gouache, casein, and water-based acrylics. Do not mix acrylics from different manufacturers: Their formulas may not be compatible). Note: Water-based color concentrates and powdered pigments, as well as compatible binders, are available for those wishing to mix their own gouache or acrylic paints (see the list in Resources on page 268).

STEP 1: ANALYZE TARGET COLOR

Analyze your target color, making notes about its hue, value, and chroma, which will help you focus in on the best choice of colors to start mixing with.

STEP 2: START MIXING COLOR

Begin mixing with the color closest to that you're trying to match, using a high-chroma version of your target color.

STEP 3: ADJUST MIXTURE AS NEEDED

If you want to lower the chroma of the color you're starting with, choose either the color's complement or an earth color to mix with it. (And keep in mind that the color(s) surrounding the target color you're trying to match influence how the color looks, like the photo on the opposite page.)

STEP 4: MAKE FURTHER ADJUSTMENTS

Add one or two other colors to your starting color, and/or white or black. Be careful when adding white or black since both add a touch of blue to a mixture.

If doing this doesn't produce a color near your target color, toss out the paper plate or palette that you were mixing on and start over. Record any components of your mixture that seemed to have been heading in the right direction, and clean all your brushes and wipe them dry.

STEP 5: IF YOUR MIXTURE IS WRONG

If you're starting again to mix your target color, remember that the mixing process can take a lot of time and may be frustrating, but don't be impatient. When you think you've arrived at your target color, let your sample dry, then coat it with a finish-coat medium that matches that on the surrounding areas (see Choosing a Finish on page 184 in Chapter 8).

STEP 6: ASSESS COLOR MATCH

Once you're satisfied with the color match and finish coat, stand up as you compare your mixed paint with the original in order to get a better view of your match.

STEP 7: REMIX A SUCCESSFUL COLOR, TAKING NOTES

If you're still happy with the results, backtrack and remix the color, taking and recording very careful measurements of each component of the mixture. Use your smallest paint-color measurement as one unit (you can work in units as small as a ⅛ teaspoon), and multiply your recorded measurements for the mixture to produce the larger quantity needed for your restoration.

STEP 8: STORE AND IDENTIFY MIXTURE

Scoop the paint into a container, dab a little paint on the cover and container to identify it, cap it tightly, and record your formula for the mixture, giving it the same number on the container as in your records.

Note that the same burnt sienna color looks slightly different each time the surrounding color is changed, an observation about color first noted by M. E. Chevreul, director of dyes in the early 1800s for the Gobelins tapestry works in France.

STEP 9: IF ADDITIONAL SURFACE EFFECTS ARE NEEDED

If you need to match more than color with the surrounding area—for example, if you need to age the surface with "dust"—see For an Aged, Dusty Patina Without Wear starting on page 223 in Chapter 9. And if you need to create the colors and layers required for restoring woods, see Chapter 7 on graining.

INPAINTING

The culmination of any surface restoration or cast installation is inpainting, which, as its name suggests, involves painting in missing areas to match the surrounding original paint. And more than any other factor, if the color of your inpainting is off, it will call attention to the restored area, even if your preparation was flawless.

There's usually enough evidence on your object to give you clues to the style or pattern of inpainting, so look carefully. Your goal is to have the viewer's eye move smoothly over your restoration without noticing any difference between your work and the original piece.

Before inpainting any area, think of the layers you might have to add to reproduce a correct match of color, design, and texture with the object's original surface and the height these layers may add (you don't want your restoration to bulge above the surrounding areas). Simple inpainting, with one color and a cover-coat, adds very little depth to the surface; and you probably won't have to reduce your restored area at all. But if you're going to add many layers—for instance, a base-coat color, several graining layers with isolating layers between them, a toning layer, and possibly texture—you'll have to reduce the level of the surface to be repaired before even beginning to inpaint your base-coat layer, so that the extra layers can be accommodated. You'll get some idea of what might be needed from the sample surfaces you make before inpainting your object (see Step 1 on the next page).

BUILDING A TOOLKIT: INPAINTING TOOLS

- → Premixed, matching paint
- → Containers for holding paint
- → Head magnifier (if needed)
- → Fine script-liner brushes
- → Wide, soft-bristle brushes
- → Toothbrushes (for visual textures)
- → Foam Brushes (for applying glazes)
- → Water
- → Paint thinner (if using paint thinner-soluble media)
- → Small cheesecloth squares
- → #400 grit wet/dry silicone carbide paper
- → Finish-coat media (see A Bird's-Eye Look at Media on page 139 in Chapter 7 and Chapter 8).

To reduce the surface, sand it with abrasive paper, erring on the side of reducing it a little too much rather than not enough. You can always build it up again with an extra layer in-between, or an extra layer or two of a final coating (see Chapter 8).

Steps for Inpainting

Before inpainting, prepare sample surfaces that are as close as possible to that of your original surface; and, on a very practical note, put your paint in containers that you can handle easily. Then follow the steps below:

STEP 1: PRACTICE, PRACTICE, PRACTICE!

Practice inpainting the one or more layers of inpainting required (for instance, several for restoring graining or adding texture) on the prepared surfaces you made. Use the appropriate brush: script-liners or other fine brushes for thin lines of color, broader brushes for wide swaths of colored media that are diluted enough to flow without brush marks, and foam brushes for applying glazes.

STEP 2: START INPAINTING WHERE IT WON'T BE SEEN

After practicing, begin inpainting in an obscure place on the object. Start with a small area since your painting technique is likely to improve as you continue.

STEP 3: DRYING IS KEY

Let each application of color dry before adding a new application.

STEP 4: ASSESS AND ADJUST INPAINTING AS NEEDED

View the inpainting you're doing from various angles and distances to discover possible problems with the paint color, and make any color adjustments that may be necessary.

STEP 5: APPLY FINISH COATS

Apply your tested finish coats after the completed inpainting has dried. If you're not satisfied at any stage of inpainting, wipe off the paint without a second thought and begin anew. As we say at the end of our seven videos on marbling, graining, glazing, and color (see Resources on page 268): "It's only paint"; so don't hesitate to wipe it off, and start over.

We hope the phrase " it's only paint" relaxes you while you're mixing paint. The process is completely reversible, and if you use the small amounts of paint that we recommend, relatively little time and materials are consumed.

The more colors you collect and study, the more you will hone your color discrimination and your ability to analyze the colors you'll need to match.

IMPROVING YOUR COLOR-MIXING AND -MATCHING SKILLS

Over the years, we've found it very valuable—and so have our students—to start and keep a file of colors cut from magazines and other printed matter. They'll provide sources for color comparisons to help train your eye to discern nuances among hues, values, and chromas.

When you come across an interesting color, don't cut out the object containing the color, just an area of the color itself, so you can focus on the color alone. It's surprising, for example, at how different a skin color looks when isolated from the printed face you found it on. The swatch of color is a reality all its own and becomes an object to study and to compare to many other cut-out colors.

Because of the nature of color printing with pixels (tiny dots of color), graded images like sunsets, and special effects will provide you with ideas for base coat and glaze colors. Be aware, though, that acquiring colors for a file can become very addictive: There's always one more color to collect.

№ 7 ‖ Graining for Restoration

GRAINING refers to painting surfaces to simulate the grain patterns of wood realistically or to render them purely decoratively at a larger-than-life scale. Also referred to as "painted wood" (but not "painted graining," which is redundant), graining has decorated plain surfaces with wood-like patterns since Egyptian times. In its heyday in nineteenth-century America, it was used both in realistic scale to ornament high-style urban furniture and in exaggerated scale to decorate country-painted furniture.

Nowadays when restoring an antique (or even modern) object of real wood, it's often out of the question to find a piece of solid wood or veneer to match the original wood. Given the number of mismatched veneers we've seen over the years on restored antiques, this has been a problem for a long time. To remedy this, graining offers a practical and welcome solution both to that problem and to restoring previously grained antiques that have been damaged.

By whisking through media while it's still wet with a stiff-bristled brush, it's easy to simulate a "woody" appearance.

All graining, whether for restoring real woods or previously grained surfaces, aims to match the innate characteristics of wood—its color, figure (grain pattern), pore markings (if there are any), and allover tone—and involves painting a series of layers for each of these characteristics that, when viewed together as a unit, simulates real wood. Successful graining requires determining not only the media, tools, and colors to be used but also the sequence in which the layers of paint and other media should be applied.

LAYERS IN GRAINING

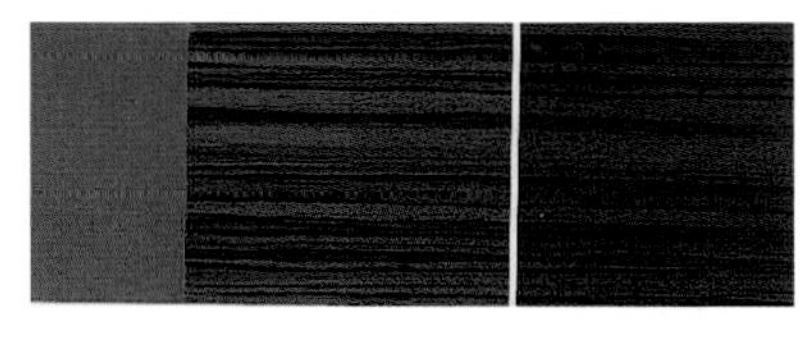

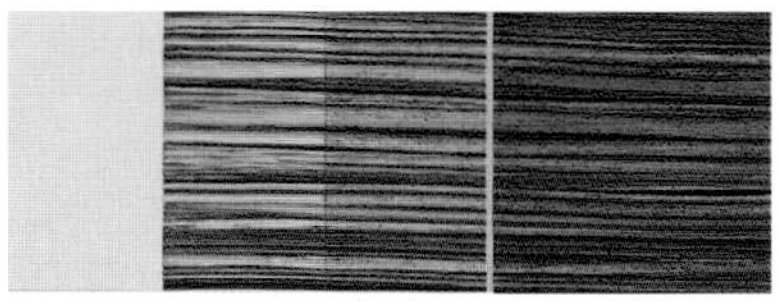

These samples, a rendering of macassar ebony, a warm-toned wood (top), and zebrawood, a cool-toned wood (bottom), show the four layers required for graining: (from left) a base coat, figure, wood pores, and toning.

Photo courtesy of Nick Simone

In contrast to creating many other painted surfaces, grain patterns are among the easiest of all natural substances to simulate in paint. When graining for restoration, even for very small areas, you'll typically need to simulate all four of the layers mentioned above that make up a wood's surface—its color, figure (grain pattern), pore structure (if there is one), and overall tone—though sometimes restoring a particular object successfully may call for applying only three or even fewer of these layers.

Whatever the number of layers required, the layers are applied in the order shown at left top and bottom, in which each layer is represented by a rectangle covering all the layers below it: The first layer, the base coat (at far left in each of the two photos), consists of a total covering coat of opaque paint that matches the lightest color of the wood's surface. The second layer is composed of thin grain lines of opaque paint that cover the base coat and duplicate the wood's figure, or pattern. The third layer covers the figure and base coats and duplicates the wood's pore structure if it has pores. The fourth layer (at far right in each photo) is a glaze (a translucent film of color, which serves as a toning layer that unifies and transforms the previously applied layers). Together, these four separately applied layers appear as a unit when finished, simulating the real wood surrounding the surface being grained.

The Concept of Layering

Because graining involves layering coats of paint and other media (see A Bird's-Eye Look at Media on the opposite page) it's important to understand how the solvents of various media interact. In fact, understanding the interaction of solvents for the media that you're working with is so important that we developed what we call the Concept of Layering (see The Concept of Layering on page 140). This concept outlines which of the many types of media can be layered over each other without causing problems and, conversely, those that will need a *barrier coat* (also called a "protective" or "isolating" coat) between them.

The Concept of Layering was very important when we were restoring, but it's even more important today because of the many ongoing changes in media. Some changes occur because of new developments in technology; others result from new legislation that prohibits the sale of substances harmful to the environment. Be aware, too, that product formulas can change (often without notification on the label) and that-

A BIRD'S-EYE LOOK AT MEDIA

When referring to painting materials, *medium* (or the plural *media*) refers to the liquid binding material that holds together pigment particles in paint and glaze formulas. In the case of paints and glazes, the liquid, which is also called a *vehicle*, binds together the pigments that add color and body to the mixture and holds them in suspension. (Because pigments don't dissolve, however, paints always need to be stirred.) In addition to pigments, a vehicle can also carry other ingredients making up a particular paint or glaze formula, such as binders, thinners, solvents and driers.

Solvent vs. Medium

A *solvent* is the term given to any fluid used in a formula to dilute or thin it, or used by itself to remove or dissolve another material. Solvents are available as separate fluids (the separate solvents we used mostly were water, denatured alcohol, and mineral spirits—the best grade of paint thinner), or mixed in already by a manufacturer as part of a product. Product labels for paint materials indicate the solvent needed by stating which solvent to use for thinning the product and cleaning brushes that have been used. Knowing the solvent for your restoration materials will allow you to change the viscosity to suit your needs: for instance, to achieve the right consistency to paint a smooth base-coat you may want to thin your paint with more solvent. Below, you'll find media and their solvents.

Media and Their Solvents

Knowledge of media and their solvents is important for the Concept of Layering, and for cleaning brushes and tools (use the solvent specified on the media label). The following lists group media by their solubility. Media of the same solubility can be combined with one another, while media of different solubilities can be interlayered.

Water

- → Acrylic paints (while liquid)
- → Casein paints
- → Gouache paints
- → Watercolors
- → Finish coats (check label)
- → Powdered pigments (check label)
- → Glue size (rabbit-skin)
- → Gilding sizes

Denatured Alcohol

Denatured alcohol was created in the U.S. during Prohibition, when substances were added to alcohol to render it poisonous for public consumption. Still toxic to drink, this so-called "denatured" alcohol is a mild solvent that's very effective.

- → Acrylic paints (become alcohol-solvent when dry)
- → Shellac (both clear and de-waxed, that is, with the natural wax content removed, which makes it less opaque)
- → Alcohol-soluble aniline powders
- → Powdered pigments (check label)

Mineral Spirits and Paint Thinner

- → Artists' oil tube colors
- → Japan paints
- → Stains (check label)
- → Finish coats (check label)
- → Linseed oil (boiled)
- → Asphaltum and asphaltum mixtures
- → Powdered pigments (check label)
- → Waxes
- → Gilding sizes
- → Naphtha

Lacquer Thinner and Acetone

- → Commercial lacquer (brush and spray)

different manufacturing plants of the same company may produce your favorite product differently. Hence, just because a product you've used works well for you, don't assume that another batch of the same product will continue to do so.

MAKE NUMEROUS TEST SAMPLES

For these reasons, we urge you to prepare many sample surfaces on which to test your layers. Try to apply the layers in as near as possible to the actual circumstances in which you'll work—excessive heat and humidity or freezing cold (we'll long remember working on a motion-picture set in Kalispell, Montana, in bone-chilling cold, trying to gold-leaf a lady's phaeton (carriage) while a propane tank spewed out debris along with heat).

Whatever your working circumstances, try to test your media as far ahead as possible before actually needing them in your restoration. You'll find that some media reactions happen immediately, while others take longer. Becoming familiar with media and the Concept of Layering as well as doing as much testing as possible will prove extremely helpful as you restore.

THE CONCEPT OF LAYERING

We developed the Concept of Layering to alert restorers to the troublesome reactions that might occur between layers while they're applying them. In a nutshell, there are two key points in the Concept of Layering.

Key Points to Remember

1. No two adjoining layers of media should have the same solvent. If they do, both layers may interact and ruin any inpainting. To prevent this from occurring, choose media for adjacent layers that are thinned by different solvents.
For example:

- → *Base coat:* Japan paint (mineral spirits-based)
- → *Figure layer:* Gouache (water-based)
- → *Pore layer* (if needed): Japan paint (mineral spirits-based)
- → *Toning layer:* Aniline dyes in shellac (alcohol-based)

2. If you want media thinned by the same solvents in adjacent layers, apply a clear, thin coat of a different solvent between the two layers. We refer to this coat as an *interlayer,* or an *isolating, barrier,* or *protective coat.* Keep any or all of these terms in mind when layering your media, to remind you of the importance of separating them.

Using an Interlayer

If you choose the option of an interlayer, you'll need to add one or more layers of the interlayer to the three or four needed to match the wood you're restoring with graining, depending on how many same-solvent media you use in adjacent layers. Here's a possible scenario of just this situation:

- → Base coat: Gouache (water-based)
- → *Isolating coat:* Shellac wash coat (alcohol-based)
- → *Figure layer:* Gouache (water-based)
- → *Isolating coat:* Shellac wash coat (alcohol-based)
- → *Pore layer* (if needed): Gouache (water-based)
- → *Toning layer:* Commercial stain or artist's oil pigments (both mineral spirits-based) OR aniline dyes in shellac (alcohol-based)

CREATING THE BASE-COAT COLOR: LAYER 1

The color of a wood surface, like any surface, has visual temperature, meaning that it looks either cool or warm, as you can see in the cool wood-veneer chips on the left in the photo at the top of the opposite page and the warm wood-veneer chips on the right (see page 124 in Chapter 6 for a discussion of color temperature). Therefore it's helpful to approach mixing and matching colors for restoring graining by first separating woods into warm and cool palettes. Cool-toned woods—those with a blue cast—include, among others, nut woods (pecan, walnut, butternut, and chestnut); fruitwoods (like apple and pear); and zebrawood. Warm-toned woods—those with a red or yellow-red cast—include cherry, some maples, mahogany, rosewood, macassar ebony, and most other tropical woods.

You'll find most of the warm and cool paint colors you'll need for graining in the orange hue known in the Munsell Color System as YR (Yellow-Red) and seen on the Munsell Student Color Chart 5YR at the bottom of the opposite page (see also page 123 in Chapter 6 for a discussion of the Munsell Color System). Note how similar the two vertical rows on the left of this chart are to the cool wood-veneer chips on the left in the top photo of the opposite page, and how much the remaining four vertical rows on the chart resemble the warm wood-veneer chips on the right. Bear in mind that to find warm wood colors for graining, you'll need to look on the center and right of the 5YR chart; while, for cool wood colors, you'll want to refer to the left of the 5YR chart.

These real-wood veneer chips show a range of temperatures that wood can display, from cool-toned woods on the bottom to warm-toned woods on the top.

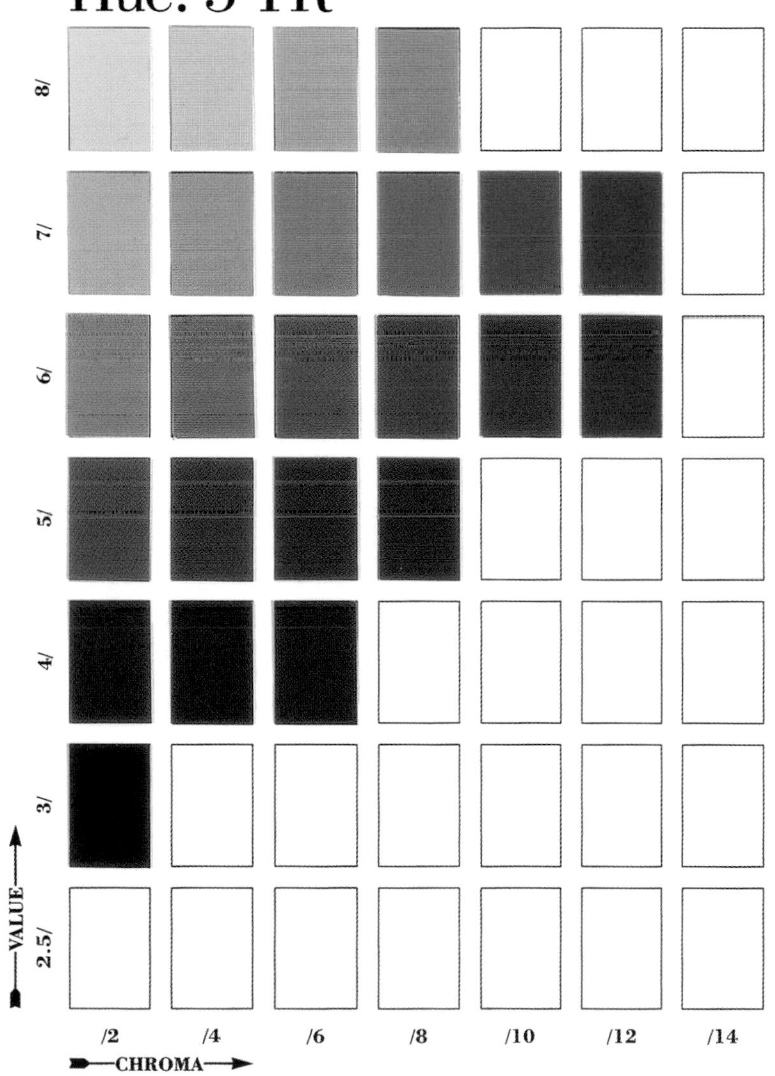

The chips in this Munsell color chart for yellow-red (YR) are arranged with the weakest, least pure, yellow-red colors on the left (those closest to cool real-wood colors) and the strongest, purest chips of this mixture on the right (those closest to warm real-wood colors).

Courtesy of Munsell Color Lab, a department of GretagMacbeth LLC, New Windsor, NY

Top and above: The base-coat color on this nineteenth-century long-case clock, grained in larger-than-life scale mahogany, was common in country-painted, warm woods.

Determining the Base-Coat Color

Choose your base coat color according to the visual warmth or coolness of the wood that you're restoring (see photos on page 138). To determine this base-coat color, first examine the real or grained wood surrounding the damaged area under magnification, sunlight, or incandescent light (but not florescent light unless it's color-balanced). Look for the color that underlies all the other wood colors: it's often the color with the lightest value. On a previously grained surface, you'll often find this color in one or more damaged areas on the grained surface.

For example, in the case of a nineteenth-century, country-grained, long-case clock we restored, shown at top left, the base coat was easy to see on the case's lower left side, where the lost graining exposed the base-coat color (bottom left). This base-coat color looks very similar to the color chip at far right in the top row of the Munsell 5YR chart on the bottom of page 141 and is therefore a warm base-coat color.

A range of pigments called *earth colors* is very useful for graining, and the most commonly used are yellow ochre, raw sienna, burnt sienna, raw umber, and burnt umber, or any combination of them (see the photo below). Lighter earth colors make good base coats (see page 126 in Chapter 6 for a general discussion of earth colors).

WHEN THE BASE COAT IS WRONG

If the base-coat color is wrong, your subsequent layers will also be wrong. For example, the color match for another repair shown at the top of the opposite page was too yellow in relation to the color of the real wood surrounding the restored area, which contained more red. Fortunately, a base-coat color that's wrong will probably leap out at you immediately, whether while it's still wet or after it has dried and been coated with a clear, isolating coat (see The Concept of Layering on page 140). You can then remove the coat with its solvent and cotton swabs, and dry the surface before mixing and applying a new base coat. If the color you've mixed is wrong, don't try to add more color to correct it. Instead, when your mixture is "off," we strongly urge you to start again from scratch.

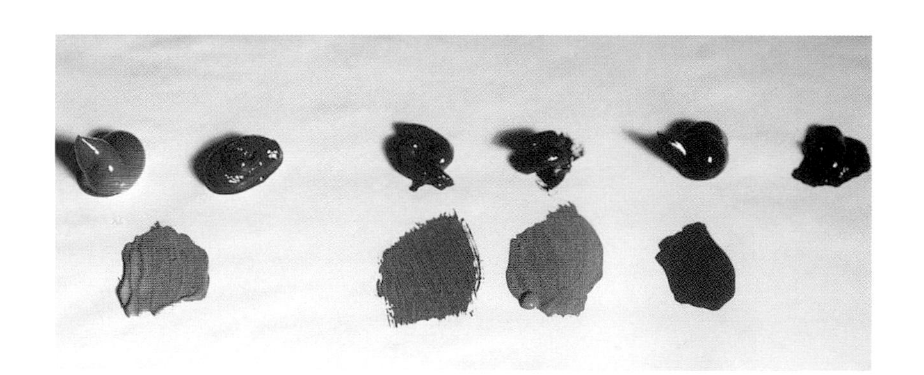

Right: Earth colors include (starting at the top row, from left) yellow ochre, raw sienna, raw umber, burnt umber, burnt sienna, and black. The bottom row shows the results when white was added (from left) to a mixture of yellow ochre and raw sienna; raw umber; burnt umber; and burnt sienna (which then turns toward pink).

Steps to a Successful Base Coat

Creating a successful base coat involves a few simple steps. Because getting the color right affects all the subsequent layers and the eventual success of the graining, be patient as you work through the steps below:

Matching base-coat colors is important. Otherwise, a repair will stand out, as shown above.

STEP 1: VISUALLY ANALYZE WOOD

Analyze the real or grained wood you're restoring to discover the lightest color that underlies all the other colors in the wood's surface. The lightest color will be the base-coat color that you're trying to match.

STEP 2: DETERMINE BASE-COAT COLOR'S TEMPERATURE

Decide whether the base-coat color is in a warm or cool palette. See the list of warm/cool woods given on page 140.

STEP 3: MIX PAINT, ADJUSTING MIXTURE'S COLOR TEMPERATURE

Mix your paints, referring to our discussion on page 126 in Chapter 6 of high-chroma colors (those with more pure pigment) and low-chroma colors (those with the color's complement mixed in). Because the complement of Munsell color YR is blue, adding blue to a YR mixture will make it look more like the cooler colors on the left side of the 5YR chart.

WHEN A BASE COAT IS ALL YOU NEED

Occasionally simulating a particular wood requires only applying a base-coat layer because that wood has no noticeable figure, pores, or toning. Such was the case with the wheel back chair shown at right which depicts one of a set of six late-eighteenth-century English chairs grained to simulate satinwood, a popular wood of the period. Because this pale wood has almost no visible markings, we needed only to restore the surface and then apply a base-coat color and a little toning before inpainting the decorative motifs.

Very little toning was needed over the light base coat to simulate satinwood in this wheel back chair.

COLORING FILLER MATERIAL

If you need to fill a damaged area that will be grained, mix modeling-paste filler material with gouache pigments, as described on page 77 in Chapter 4. This procedure saves a painting step; but, more importantly, the filler paste is composed of solid color throughout and can be sanded without having to be repainted every time it's abraded to make it smooth. Mixing the pigment and filler is a simple process, for which you really need only a palette knife and a palette (you can even use the plastic lid of a medium-size container as a palette).

RESTORING FIGURES IN WOOD: LAYER 2

BASIC GRAINING SPEAK

Ground	The surface on which you paint
Charge	Load a brush with a medium
Off-load	Eliminate excess paint or medium from a brush or tool
Render	Paint
Whisk	Elongate wet medium with a stiff-bristled brush

The term *figure* refers to the pattern of a tree's growth rings, which show up as the grain lines we see on a cut piece of wood. The dark grain lines that give each figure its unique pattern result from the summer growth, which is slower and denser than the spring growth, which produces the light-colored areas between the dark grain lines. Where a cut is made on a tree determines the appearance of the figure revealed.

Fortunately for restorers of graining, there's only a limited number of cutting options for trees and resulting figures; and the figure you'll be called upon most often to restore is straight grain, or the figure revealed when wood is cut quarter-sawn. More rarely you'll need to restore heart-grain (often called *V-grain*), which shows when wood is cut plain-sawn.

Quarter-sawn wood produces straight grain.

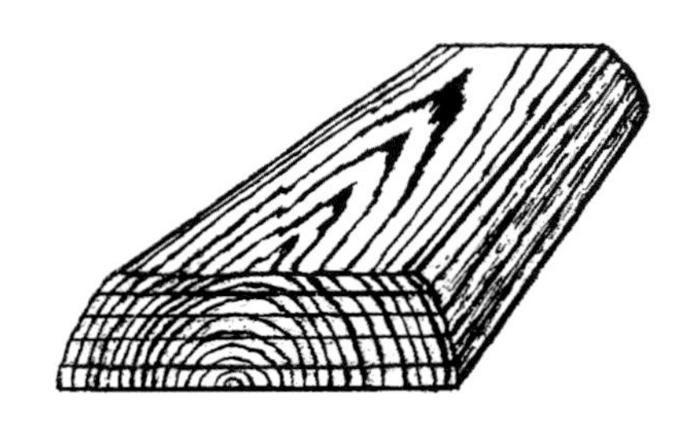

Plain-sawn wood reveals only one heart-grain, or V-grain, to a log.

Tree Cuts Producing Figures

Wood that's *quarter-sawn* is cut from a log that's been divided lengthwise into quarters, with each quarter then cut into boards (see illustration top left). Quarter-sawn wood displays straight grain down its entire length, in the same variations of light and dark as the tree's annual growth rings (which are really concentric columns that run down the length of the entire tree). The end grain of quarter-sawn boards appears as short, straight parallel lines. Because quarter-sawn wood is the strongest cut, it's used where strength is required in a structure. Therefore, when you're graining, render the figure of straight grain if the area you're graining is one where strength would be needed (see Grain Direction on page 150).

Wood that's *plain-sawn* is cut lengthwise down the tree trunk, in parallel cuts across the entire log from one end to the other. This cut exposes the figure most often illustrated when a piece of wood is depicted—heart-grain, or V-grain. Because plain-sawn wood is weaker than quarter-sawn wood except at the very center where the V-grain appears, it's not used where strength is needed in a structure.

There's another type of figure that you may need to restore, *crotch grain,* which occurs where a tree trunk begins to fork into two equal limbs. However, because the media and techniques that we have innovated for restoring this figure are vastly different from those for duplicating straight grain and heart-grain, you'll find these restoration techniques discussed later in the chapter on page 158.

Inpainting Figures

Although there's a limited number of figures in wood, grain lines can vary considerably in width, color, the distance between them, and whether they have pronounced wood fibers (see page 146). In order for your graining restoration to blend in obtrusively, you'll need to examine the appearance of existing grain lines as well as the path they follow. Pay particular attention to the grain lines on the top, bottom, and sides of the area being restored. Your goal is to connect these lines so that they continue their flow, seemingly uninterrupted, across the wood's surface.

APPLYING MEDIA

Before applying any media to a surface you're restoring, make sure that the surface has the same tactile quality—whether smooth or textured—as the areas surrounding it (see Chapter 4 to learn how to produce the surface needed). In addition to working on an appropriately prepared surface, successful graining also involves pairing a combination of specific brushes or tools with media whose consistency (degree of viscosity) is correct for the brush or tool being used.

Your choice of media for any painting technique depends on whether you'll apply the media on a surface and leave it (for example, when inpainting a defined grain line), or manipulate or remove the wet paint with a tool (for instance, to simulate some wood textures). We refer to the first method as the *applied method* and the second as the *removal method.*

Applied Method

In the applied method, dilute the media just enough to flow from the brush but not so much that you can't paint specific grain lines. The advantages of this method are that you have complete control over where to place your lines; you can apply lines at will; and, since applied lines are usually rendered individually, you can remove any lines you don't like. The main disadvantage of this method is that you must have skill with a brush.

Removal Method

In the removal method, media must stay workable long enough to manipulate it with tools but be thick enough to hold the imprint of any tool dragged through it. The advantages of this method are that complicated color and pattern renderings are possible and quick to do. The main disadvantages are that you must work quickly before the medium dries and that you'll need to remove the entire area of rendering if you're unhappy with even a small part of it.

When trying to analyze a painted surface to restore part of it, look for these clues to determine whether the paint has been applied or "removed" since you'll want to duplicate the method when graining: Applied paint is usually one color along the length of a line with rather defined edges. Removed paint changes in opacity and color because of the varying pressure exerted during the removal process: Heavy pressure removes more paint than light pressure, creating translucence and revealing more of the underlying surface's color.

BUILDING A TOOLKIT: GRAINING TOOLS

In graining, a wide variety of brushes is used, with bristles that are either natural (ranging from soft hairs like sable to stiff bristles like hog bristle) or synthetic. Some of these brushes, like the long-haired script-liner, are used for small-scale, freehand rendering (the most common for restoration), while larger brushes, like the flogger, are used for big architectural restorations.

→ Script-liner brushes, # 1–6, and stiff-bristle brushes, 1/2 inch and 1 inch
→ Foam brushes (1/2-inch and 1-inch wide)
→ Heel, or rocker, tool (for simulating V-grain)
→ Cheesecloth squares
→ Check roller (for simulating wood pores)
→ Cotton swabs
→ Painters' tape(s)
→ Tracing paper, pencils, and an eraser.

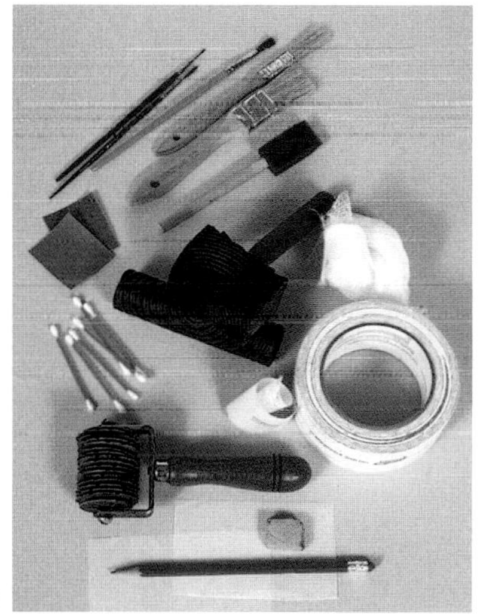

Photo courtesy of Connie Hougardy

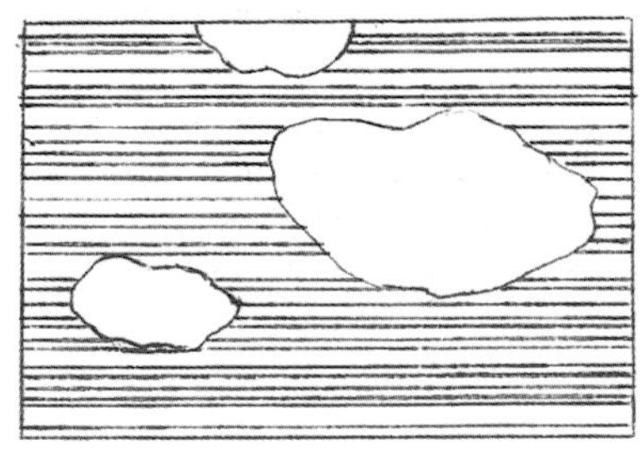
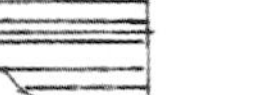

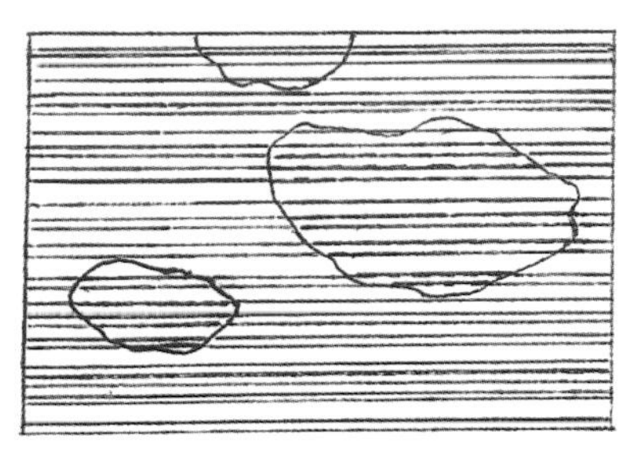

The goal in graining to restore straight grain is simply to connect the grain lines from one end of the missing area to the other.

INPAINTING STRAIGHT GRAIN

Straight grain is the easiest of all figures to inpaint if you're careful to reconnect the grain lines that belong together. Noticing whether these lines are thin or thick will help you rejoin them correctly.

Follow the steps below for inpainting straight grain. You'll also find it helpful to look at the illustrations at left to digest visually the concept of what you'll be doing.

STEP 1: STUDY AREA TO BE INPAINTED

Analyze the grain lines in the area surrounding that to be restored, noting their width, color, distance between them, and the look of their wood fibers.

STEP 2: TRACE AREA'S SHAPE AND GRAIN LINES

Using the illustration at the top left as a guide, trace both the outline of the shape to be restored on your object and the grain lines surrounding that area. Make several copies of the tracing to use as worksheets.

STEP 3: RECONNECT MISSING GRAIN LINES ON TRACING PAPER

Use a pencil on your tracing to reconnect the grain lines interrupted by the damaged area, rendering the lines as similar to the straight-grain figure in the surrounding wood as you can, and running the pencil lines parallel to the lengthwise grain lines in the undamaged wood, as in the illustration at bottom left.

STEP 4: TRANSFER GRAIN LINES TO MISSING AREA

When you're satisfied with your pencil rendering, trace the lines from your reconstructed tracing on the area needing it. (You can use transfer paper, commonly available in art-supply stores, to do this; or, alternatively, you can blacken the back of the tracing paper with a soft-leaded pencil, then press hard on the lines on the front of the paper to transfer them).

STEP 5: MIX PAINTS FOR INPAINTING

Mix paint(s) to match the existing grain lines and assemble the brush(es) you'll need: one or more sizes of script-liner brushes, depending on whether the grain lines in your piece vary in width.

You can hold the long-haired script-liner brush (useful for applying lines and doing touch-ups) like a pen using your little finger to steady your hand for better control.

STEP 6: INPAINT TRANSFERRED GRAIN LINES

After charging a script-liner brush with paint and off-loading the excess on newspaper, paint over the transferred lines (see bottom left) Remove any grain lines that you're not pleased with, using cotton swabs and/or cheesecloth squares. These grain lines are the basis for the success of your restoration, and it's well worth redoing them to get them integrated nicely with the existing grain lines.

STEP 7: LET DRY AND ERASE PENCIL LINES

When the painted grain lines are thoroughly dry, erase any pencil lines still visible.

INPAINTING HEART-GRAIN

Just like straight-grain lines, which can vary in width and color (indicating, for example, more rain one season than the previous one), plain-sawn heart-grain lines have the same variations in width and color. But because of the different way in which the log is cut, plain-sawn heart-grain lines duplicate the same width and color on both sides of the V. Knowing about the symmetry of heart-grain lines on each side of the V enables grainers to look at the existing grain lines and duplicate them where necessary.

Unlike most straight-grain lines, many heart-grain lines have pronounced, clearly defined wood fibers running down their length. Visually akin to elongated whiskers, these long fibers are quite apparent in the photo at top right of a piece of real American oak, both on the V-end of the heart-grain and on the grain on either side of it. Follow the steps below for inpainting heart-grain. Also look at the illustrations at bottom right to grasp the visual concept of what you'll be doing.

Notice both the V-tip of the heart-grain figure in this detail of real red American oak and how the wood's fibers all run in the same direction.

STEPS 1: STUDY AREA TO BE INPAINTED

Analyze the color, width, and distance between the grain lines.

STEP 2: TRACE AREA'S SHAPE AND GRAIN LINES

Using the illustrations at the right as a guide, trace both the outline of the shape to be restored and the grain lines surrounding that area. Make several copies of the tracing to use as worksheets.

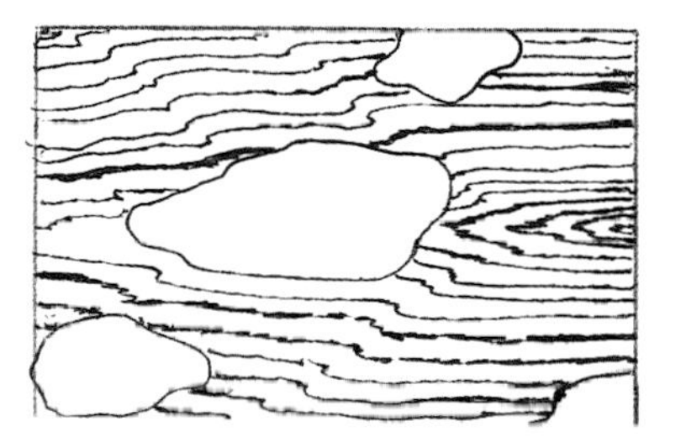

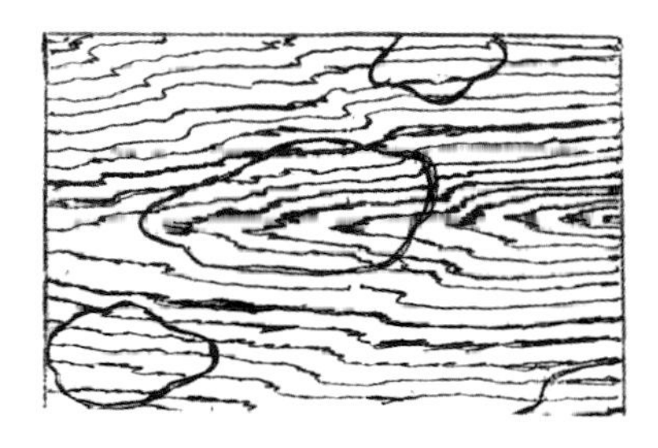

In the case of heart-grain, the idea is to continue the existing grain pattern into the missing or damaged area, simulating it as much as possible by mimicking both sides of each heart-grain.

STEP 3: RECONNECT MISSING GRAIN LINES ON TRACING PAPER

Use a pencil to draw lines that look similar to the existing lines. Erase and redo the drawn lines until you're satisfied with them. (In our book *Professional Painted Finishes* [see Resources on page 268], there's an in-depth analysis of heart-grain figures that you might find helpful. Remember, however, that analyzing the heart-grain of your particular wood is always crucial for the success of your restoration.)

STEP 4: TRANSFER GRAIN LINES TO MISSING AREA

Trace the lines from your pencil rendering on the area being restored (you'll find information about how to do this in Step 4 in the instructions on inpainting straight grain on the opposite page).

STEP 5: MIX PAINTS FOR INPAINTING

Mix paint(s) to match the existing grain lines and gather up a script-liner brush and a ½-inch stiff-bristled brush.

STEP 6: INPAINT TRANSFERRED GRAIN LINES

Charge your script-liner brush with paint, and off-load the excess paint on a newspaper. Then paint over the grain lines, working with only one V-grain at a time.

STEP 7: LET DRY AND ERASE PENCIL LINES

Let the painted grain lines dry thoroughly, and then erase any pencil lines that are still visible.

STEP 8: IF YOU'RE SIMULATING WOOD FIBERS

Simulated wood fibers are rendered while grain lines are still wet. If the wood surrounding the area you're restoring has no visible wood fibers, follow only Steps 1 to 7 on page 147 for inpainting heart-grain. If you're inpainting wood fibers, follow Steps 1 to 6 and then elongate the grain lines as follows:

While the paint is still wet, use a ½-inch stiff-bristled brush to whisk the grain lines in the direction of the length of the wood being duplicated. Whisking, which also thins out media, should be done in only one direction to remain true to the patterns of heart-grain. If the ½-inch brush is too wide for your restoration, turn it on edge so that only about ⅛-inch of the stiff bristles elongate the tip and sides of your heart grains. Continue rendering the rest of the grain lines, whisking each one as necessary.

As you can see in the photo below (showing ½-inch and 1-inch stiff-bristled brushes as well as a script-liner brush resting on a plastic-lid palette), the tip of the heart-grain in the upper part of image has already been whisked away from the V, while the brush at the bottom edge is in the process of whisking through the wet media. The thicker, jerky grain line on the right has not yet been whisked.

Note how similar the whisked (lightly brushed and softened) end of this painted heart-grain is to the same area of the real wood shown in the bottom photo.

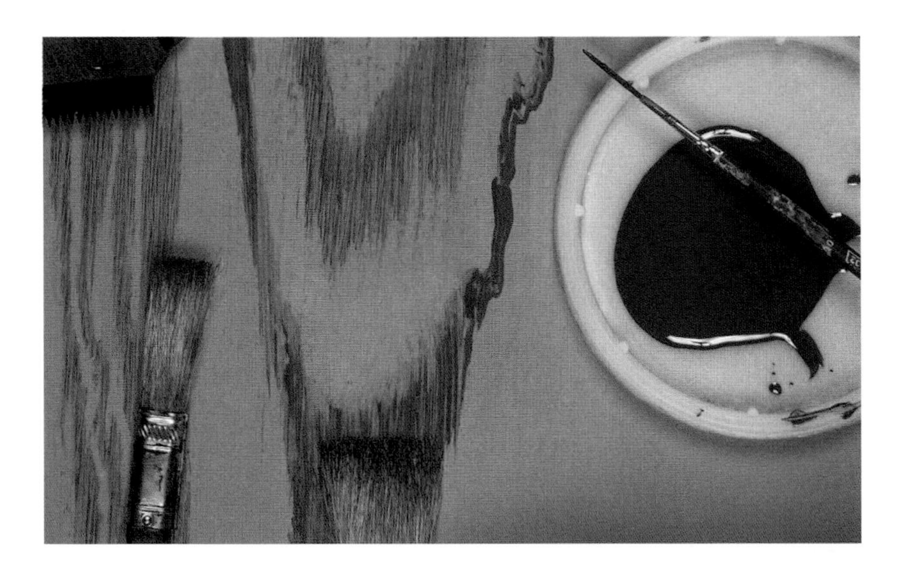

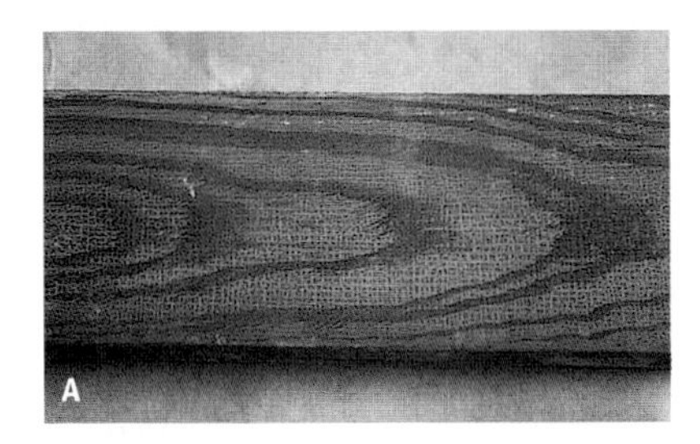

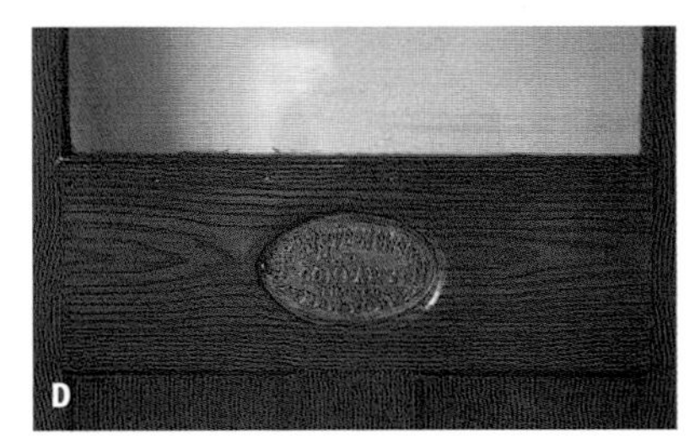

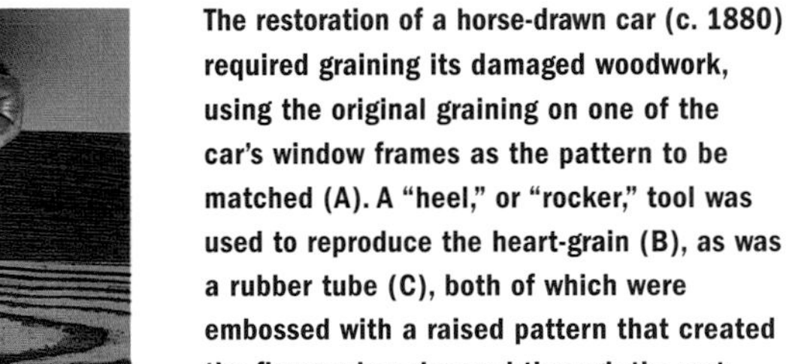

The restoration of a horse-drawn car (c. 1880) required graining its damaged woodwork, using the original graining on one of the car's window frames as the pattern to be matched (A). A "heel," or "rocker," tool was used to reproduce the heart-grain (B), as was a rubber tube (C), both of which were embossed with a raised pattern that created the figure when dragged through the wet medium. The restored door with its heart-grain rail was an exact replica of the remaining original door (D). Photo E is the restored car.

Restoring Heart-Grain with a Commercial Tool

A commission that we received from a museum to reproduce the heart-grained, wooden window frames and doors of an American, horse-drawn car (c. 1880) above was an example of the use of the V-grain center of plain-sawn wood (the strongest section of that wood). Following the restorers' mantra "Replace what you find," we restored the heart-grain figure. This American horse-drawn car required using a commercial graining tool to duplicate the original heart-grain, shown in photo A, for one of the window frames. Note the whisking that simulated wood fibers in the original graining.

The prototype for the tool in use today dates back to the mid-1800s, even before the original graining on this horse-drawn car was done. This tool was one of many mechanical means developed to produce wood grains quickly, if not always skillfully, to answer the enormous demand for graining in the mid and late nineteenth century.

The contemporary rubber-tipped tool that produces a heart-grain figure is called a "heel," or "rocker." It's a solid, quarter-circle, wooden wedge with dimensional rubber covering on the curved portion. This covering is embossed with a raised pattern of half-circles to produce the heart-grain when the tool is manipulated in wet paint along the same length of graining with the two steps that follow:

STEP 1: APPLY PAINT TO SURFACE

Paint a swath of medium on the surface to be grained, hold the tool by its handle, and then place the edge of the tool on the wet paint.

STEP 2: DRAG TOOL THROUGH PAINT

Drag the tool through the paint; and as it's being pulled along the surface, turn the tool slowly upward and downward to create the heart-grain pattern. (Note that the variation in the patterns in photo B on page 149 was due to the upward and downward movement of the tool, which is shown in the lower row, and the speed with which the tool was turned, which was faster in the upper row.)

We also used a second tool on the car's woodwork to create a heart-grain figure: a rubber tube embossed with the same raised pattern of half-circles as on the heel (both this tube and the heel are available in many paint stores and from sources found in Resources on page 268). To use the tube, insert the index finger of each hand in the opening at both ends of the tube. Then pull the tube through the wet paint, while turning it downward to render the heart-grain figure, as was being done when photo C on page 149 was snapped.

After using both the rocker and the tube to mimic the grain of the original nineteenth-century graining, we whisked the ends of the heart-grain with a stiff-bristled brush to simulate the wood fibers, as was done on the original. You can see the completed heart-grain figure produced on one of the car's doors in photo D and the completely restored car in photo E on page 149.

GRAIN DIRECTION

Grain direction is the path the figure takes on each separate piece of wood. When restoring a real-wood object, maintain the direction of the grain. When restoring a previously grained surface, follow the originally painted grain, even if that simulated grain pattern runs counter to how the correct grain would have run. Even when the area you're restoring is small, continue any grain clearly visible on the original into the area you're graining.

Our restoration of a pair of rosewood-grained Baltimore card tables (c. 1835) involved following existing grain direction on small areas. Although painted imitation of rosewood was popular in England and America in the early to mid nineteenth century, the grained furnishings made in Baltimore (of rosewood grained over real mahogany) were among the most sophisticated. The photo at below left shows some of the paint losses on the table's surface, which have been restored in the photo below right (see also page 79 in Chapter 4 to see the colored filling done on this table). The bottom photo displays the completely restored table, on which all the rosewood graining duplicated straight graining.

This rosewood-grained Baltimore card table (c. 1835) readily revealed the straight-grain direction of its damaged surface (far left). The left and bottom photos show the restored straight graining.

When Grain Direction Isn't Obvious

Sometimes the grain direction of real wood isn't obvious, especially if the object has been covered with paint that obscures the grain. This was the case with eight 2-inch-thick, mid-nineteenth-century doors that had been coated with a white primer on which we were to reproduce the regional graining for a historic house. We grained the doors correctly, following the dictate that joined construction requires using straight grain wherever strength is needed—on door and chair stiles (the long, side pieces of wood), rails (the horizontal pieces on doors and furniture), horizontally along the lengths of moldings, and vertically on recessed panels. The top left photo on page 152 shows one of the doors being grained horizontally on a rail and an already grained rail. Also pictured on this door are grained recessed panels of regional crotch-figure graining along with lengths of moldings surrounding them.

Right: After the door's coffered panels and moldings were grained, we worked next on graining the rails (the cross pieces above and below the panels), rendering them correctly with the straight grain running horizontally.

Far right: Made of the real curly (tiger) maple, this eighteenth-century American chest of drawers displays the wood's distinctive figure, which appears to run perpendicular to the length of the wood's straight grain.

Straight grain is also required for legs, tabletops, drawer fronts, splats (the vertical pieces on chair backs), and slats (the horizontal pieces on chair backs). Be careful about graining real woods like curly (tiger) maple, whose figure is deceptive: It appears perpendicular to the straight of grain running down it length (see photo at top right).

Changes in Grain Direction

When wooden objects are constructed of more than one piece of wood, the members meet at a joint, where the grain direction of each member is different, as in the illustration at left. In order to grain a member needing restoration that abuts a joint, tape off the neighboring member at the joint line (see Tapes and Taping on page 153). You can tape off several areas at once as long as they don't abut each other. For instance, in the illustration at left, note the two vertical left and right members that you could grain at one time. Then, once you've grained, protected, and dried these members, you can remove the tapes and grain the adjacent members. For graining members that abut joint lines, follow these steps:

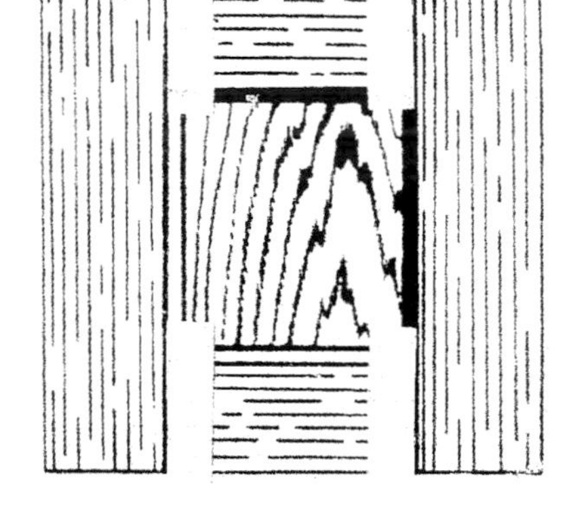

Any two nonadjacent members can be grained, toned, and protected at the same time by using tape to cover adjacent members (above). After the protective coat has dried, you can remove the tape and grain the other set of members.

STEP 1: TAPE NEIGHBORING MEMBER(S)

To isolate a member to be grained, tape off its neighboring member(s).

STEP 2: APPLY GRAINING LAYERS

Apply each graining layer, allowing it to dry and then protecting it before applying the next layer. Protect the final layer as well. If necessary, review the Concept of Layering on page 140, to determine which layers may need to be protected with an isolation, or barrier, coat.

STEP 3: REMOVE TAPE

When all the layers have been protected, remove the tape from the neighboring member(s).

STEP 4: LET LAYER DRY BEFORE GRAINING NEIGHBORING MEMBER(S)

If the neighboring member needs graining, don't tape the member just completed and protected: Taping too soon before the last layer has completely cured may ruin your restoration. Merely wipe away any medium that happens to "wander" over on the protected member.

TAPES AND TAPING

There's a wide variety of tapes available that are helpful in graining to create crisp joint lines between connecting wooden members by taping off one member of a joint from another. Choose a tape based on its ability to release easily without leaving any residue for the time frame in which you need it. We'll long remember a commission in which we had taped a design on glass doors that were 13 linear feet long and 6 feet high, not realizing that the sun would bake the tape for the week that it took us to render the design, making the tape impossible to remove. With a representative from the tape company and three of us releasing over 100 feet of tape loosened by vacuum cleaner exhausts and hair dryers, we finally finished a very time-consuming job. This lesson taught us to use long-release tape. By the way, if you're having trouble releasing a bit of tape, lift one corner of it, and exhale slowly under the lifted portion. As you peel the tape off, keep repeating this maneuver.

Types of Tape

Painters' tape, commonly available from paint and hardware suppliers, marks off a straight edge at joints well. Also, it has much less tack than masking tape, allowing it to release easily and leave no residue.

There are several types of specialty tapes available, including *quick-release tapes*, which won't damage delicate painted surfaces and that release safely and easily, and *long-release tapes,* which have an adhesive formulated to remain on a surface for up to seven days without damaging it or leaving a residue. You'll also find tapes from auto-suppliers that range from ⅛ inch wide to greater widths; and in art and drafting-supply stores, you'll find chart and map tapes that are thin and flexible, allowing them to be formed into curves.

Applying and Removing Tape

When applying tape, press the gummed edge down carefully using your fingernails, a plastic burnisher, or the flat side of a credit card. Note that after protecting a layer on a grained surface—half of a joint, for instance—you won't have to tape over it when graining the other half of the joint. Merely wipe away any unwanted medium from the protected half.

Remove tape from the surface as soon as possible. Pull it away from the surface at an oblique angle (30 degrees or less, even almost parallel to the still-adhered tape), using moderate pressure and speed. Paint seepage can be treated by rubbing the surface with the correct solvent on a cotton swab after the newly grained surface has been protected (although the best treatment is prevention, that is, by laying the tape carefully in the beginning).

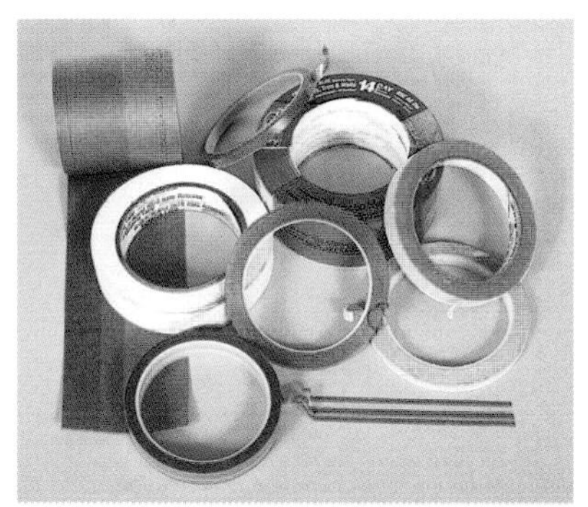

Photo courtesy of Connie Hougardy

Cross-Banded Grain Direction

Cross-banding is composed of short-pieces of straight-grain veneers laminated over solid wood. When these cross-banded pieces are applied as a border, the corners are joined with a miter joint; and the grain direction on each member of the joint will be different, producing a visually distinctive joint, as shown on the right.

For restoring cross-banded borders, whether in full or in part, it's helpful to make templates of the width and length of each side of the border, noting the grain direction on each member, as seen in photo A on page 154. If you mark the width of the border with ⅛-inch tape, the tape can also serve to preserve the base coat and mimic what's called *stringing*, or a fine inlay of a lighter wood, in this case, on a student's graining project (see photo on top of page 154).

A cross-banded border produces mitered corners that are far more visually distinctive than those of a straight-grain border.

In this photo, a student is removing tape to reveal the base coat and the fine line of simulated stringing (a fine inlay of lighter wood).

STEPS FOR CREATING CROSS-BANDING

When restoring or rendering cross-banding, tape off and paint opposite borders at the same time. The cross-banding process is a simple one that just requires methodically following the steps below:

STEP 1: TAPE OFF NEIGHBORING MEMBER(S)

To isolate a border to be cross-banded, tape off its neighboring borders at each end of the diagonal miters.

STEP 2: PAINT CROSS-BANDING

If you're inpainting straight grain to restore an area, match the graining layers to duplicate the existing cross-banding. If you're creating the cross-banding from scratch, determine the colors and grain lines you want the wood to have (review the photos on page 138 to get started).

Next, apply all the graining layers, allowing each to dry and protecting it before applying the next layer. Protect the last layer as well (review the Concept of Layering on page 140 to determine which layers may need to be protected with an isolation coat).

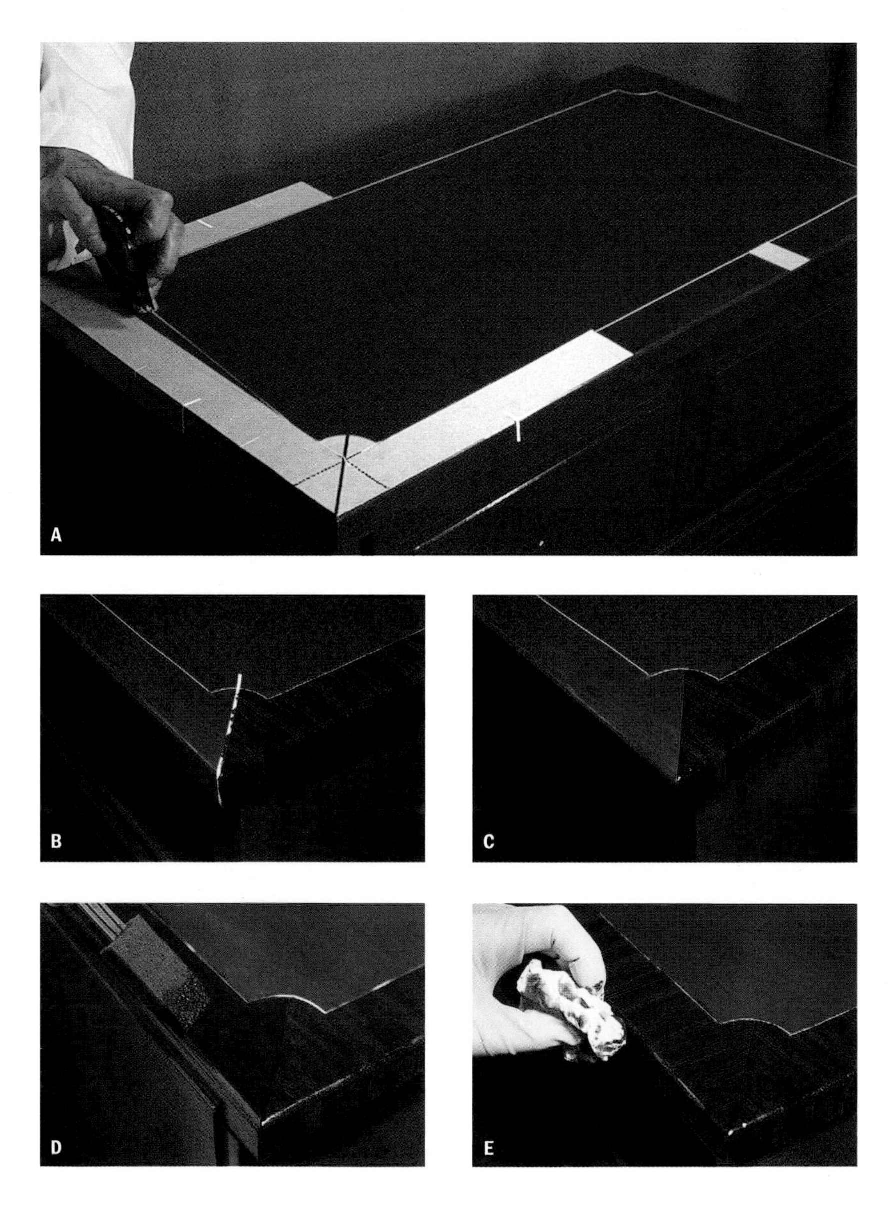

Using several templates, one of our students applied tape to mark the width of the border for this graining, then used 1/8-inch tape to mark the border's edge and left it in place while graining (A). By covering half the border's corner at a time (B), she was able to grain each side's border and half of the corner (C). After graining the adjacent borders (D), she produced in the end a simulated miter joint (E) in ribbon-stripe mahogany.

STEP 3: REMOVE TAPE

When all the layers have been protected, remove the tape from the neighboring members (photo C on the opposite page). The tape at the diagonal miter was removed after the cross-banding had dried and been protected.

STEP 4: CROSS-BANDING NEIGHBORING BORDERS

Apply medium (as is being done in photo D on the opposite page) adjacent to the already protected cross-banding (on the right in the photo), where any medium that had gotten on it has been wiped off. In photo E on the opposite page, cross-banding is being rendered, which will be protected after drying.

The formula for the medium used in these demonstration photos, Marglaze, can be found in the Rendering Crotch Figures on page 159. To render cross-banding of more defined grain lines, as in the bottom illustration on page 153, refer to the instructions on applying straight grain on page 146.

CREATING PORES IN WOOD: LAYER 3

Pores represent the cross-section of the cells running lengthwise down most hardwoods (that is, deciduous trees that lose their leaves in the fall). Softwoods (evergreens that retain their leaves all year long) do not have pores.

The pores in hardwoods appear either as rather small, uniform markings throughout the length of a piece of wood or as larger, defined lines that run down the length of the wood. According to the size of the area to be restored, both kinds of pores can be rendered with individual strokes (for very small areas) or with the techniques outlined below—spattering/whisking, "tapping" into wet paint, or using a check roller—for larger areas.

Spattering-and-Whisking Technique

One way to simulate evenly distributed, small pores is to spatter-and-whisk. The steps for this technique are outlined below:

STEP 1: LOAD PAINT ON TOOTHBRUSH AND SPATTER PAINT

Wearing gloves, dip a toothbrush in a dark brown color of paint, like burnt umber; off-load the excess paint; and, aiming the brush in the desired direction, run your index finger over the bristles to spatter the paint.

STEP 2: WHISK PAINT

While the spatters are still wet, whisk them, using a stiff-bristled brush to elongate them and turn them into "pores" running in the same direction as the pores in the surrounding areas (photo at right).

Rendering wood pores involves spattering and then whisking the spatters to create pores (above).

Tapping Technique

To produce allover pore structure under grain lines, or just to create a "woody" appearance in the small area you're restoring, follow the steps below:

STEP 1: APPLY THIN LAYER OF DILUTED PAINT

Apply a thin layer of diluted paint (that matches the color of the surrounding pores) to the area being grained, in the same lengthwise direction as the visible pores or in the lengthwise direction of the general "woodiness."

STEP 2: TAP BRUSH TO CREATE PORES

If possible, turn the object you're restoring to position the area being restored nearest you. Starting at that near end, do the following: Place the front ¼-inch of a stiff-bristled brush in the wet medium, and tap the tip of the brush lightly up and down, constantly moving away from yourself, in small increments, along the same lengthwise direction of the surrounding pores. If the brush is too wide, turn it on edge and use this narrower width.

For large-scale restorations, the same tapping technique to create woodiness can be done using a long-bristled brush called a *flogger*. The double-exposure photo below shows the position to use the flogger (as well as the ½-inch, stiff-bristled brush described above in Step 2).

This double exposure shows the up-and-down strokes of the flogger being used to simulate small pores and "woodiness."

Using a Check Roller for Large Areas of Pores

On small areas of restoration, longer, defined pores can be inpainted by hand with a script-liner brush; but for larger areas requiring such pores, there's a tool to use that produces them: a check roller, seen in the top photo on the opposite page. The check roller is composed of notched metal disks separated by washers, strung on a metal rod, which "print" paint on the surface as the tool is rolled along. Since a check roller has no bristles to accept a medium, it must be loaded with paint (we used a medium-laden foam brush) as it's being rolled. You'll need both hands

The check roller is useful for duplicating long pores on straight grain.

to manipulate the tool: one to hold it and the other to hold the media-laden brush against the metal disks as you roll the tool.

Running the check-roller along newspaper to off-load excess paint before applying it to the grained surface prevents the tool from producing lines of paint that are too thick. A light whisking of the painted lines softens them and gives them a more natural, wood-fiber appearance.

In addition to the brushes and tools shown here, keep your antenna up to find others that will permit you to do something special in graining. You'll doubtless find interesting candidates if you keep your eyes open.

CREATING TONING: LAYER 4

Toning your graining produces magical effects: It unifies the rendering, pulling the other layers together and lowering the contrast between the base coat and the figures. It also turns flat, lifeless color into rich wood colors with shading and depth. Toning techniques can even provide an extra quality that some woods have, called "crossfire," which is discussed in depth on pages 195 to 204 in our first book, *Professional Painted Finishes* (see Further Reading on page 270).

The toning layer is really a glaze, or pigmented translucent film through which the other layers are visible. Any medium that can be thinned down with a solvent to create a translucent film can be used for toning (page 128 in Chapter 6 provides additional information on glazes, and see also information on solvents in A Bird's-Eye Look at Media on page 139).

Tips for Choosing and Applying Glazes

Below are some tips for choosing and applying glazes:

→ Commercial stains, available in both mineral spirit- and water-based solutions, are valuable for toning. They can be thinned with the proper solvent (listed on the label) to a sheer translucency that will allow your graining layers to turn into "wood" effortlessly.

→ Making many charts of stains over warm and cool base coats is both a good exercise in toning and a valuable resource for selecting base-coat, figure, and toning combinations.

To make such charts, block off 4-inch squares with ⅛-inch tape on several nonabsorbent surfaces (such as the oak-tag stock sold in most stationary stores for making posters). Paint several rows of the squares light and medium values of both warm and cool base coats. Then coat the dried base coats with mahogany (warm) and walnut (cool) stains, using our charts below as a guide. Then dilute the stain to the sheerness of a glaze to coat the other bands on the squares, leaving a band of untouched base coat in the middle of each square. Keep notes on the various combinations of base-coat colors and stain for future reference.

Right: Base-coated squares toned with diluted stains can serve as a reference for realistic base-coat and toning combinations. We made these charts by first ruling off the poster boards into squares and then painting the squares with different base-coat colors, which we coated with various stains, ranging from full-strength at one end (vertically along one end) to diluted (horizontally across the squares), with an uncoated section of base-coat color showing in between.

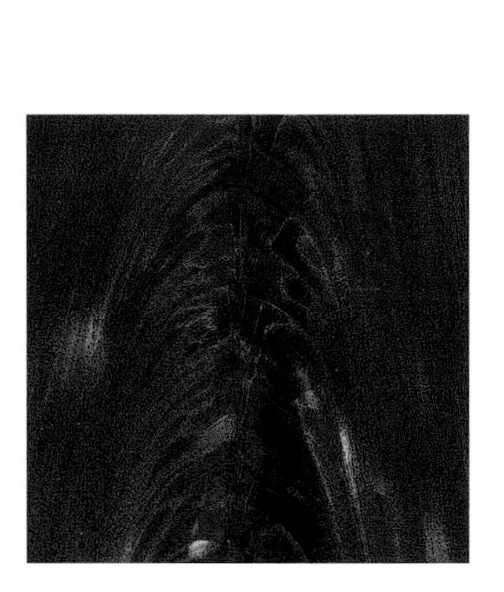

Above: A sample of a real crotch figure, where a tree begins to fork on its interior into two equal limbs.

THE CROTCH FIGURE

The *crotch figure* is revealed when a cut is made vertically through the center of the tree where a crotch (the area between two large, forking limbs) has formed. This figure, called a crotch, or feather, figure, develops within the trunk of the main tree when the forking limbs merge before each becomes a separate limb. This merging creates an inter-grown and twisted figure composed of an entire range of light to dark, warm browns. Since crotch figures have no internal strength, they're used as veneers, usually installed upside down—giving the illusion of a human rib cage.

Crotch-figure graining, mainly simulating mahogany, played an important part in the history of graining through the early- to mid-nineteenth century in America. Realistic renderings of mahogany's unique figure and rich, warm brown palette enriched moldings, paneling, and doors in the homes of the affluent during this period (see photo at right). Nineteenth-century country-painted versions of the crotch figure on objects are easily recognizable as having been inspired by the real crotch figure and are nowadays collectors' items.

A real crotch figures provided inspiration for realistic crotch-figure graining.

Rendering Crotch Figures

We developed a medium for rendering the realistic crotch figure for the reproduction graining we did in historic houses. That medium produces both rich, dark browns and thinner glazes, which cover the base coat, to mirror the figure's distinctive color characteristics. We named this medium "Marglaze" after—you guessed it—Marx's glaze.

WORKING WITH MARGLAZE MEDIUM

Marglaze medium is composed of:

- → 8 parts mahogany penetrating stain (mineral-spirits-soluble)
- → 7 parts high-gloss finish (mineral-spirits-soluble)
- → 5 parts asphaltum (mineral-spirits-soluble; see page 220)

In addition, a real crotch figure gave inspiration for stylized country graining.

We used this medium over opaque, satin-finish base-coat colors of either pink, terra cotta, or tan, depending on the client's choice. When thoroughly dry, the renderings were isolated with shellac, than coated with wax.

The rendering technique we innovated combined a little bit of applying media with a great deal of removing, or wiping off, some of it. Our tools of choice were a 1-inch foam brush for applying the medium and pieces of crumpled facial tissue for removing it.

When graining a crotch figure on a horizontal surface, we suggest standing up, so that the painting movement you'll need can emanate from your shoulder to your hand. You can use the other hand for balance. To grain a crotch figure, follow the steps below:

STEP 1: LOAD BRUSH WITH MEDIUM

Dip the first ½ inch of a 1-inch foam brush into the Marglaze medium, which you should stir frequently.

STEP 2: APPLY MEDIUM IN WIDELY SPACED ARCS

Apply the loaded brush to the surface in widely spaced arc patterns, with the high point of the arc in the appropriate center of your panel. The strokes should go outward and downward alternately on each side (see top of next page, in which the beginning strokes of a book-matched, double-crotch figure are being demonstrated). These initial arc strokes will give your arm and hand the movement you'll need to create the rest of the crotch figure.

Rendering a mirror-image crotch figure begins with the first step of painting double arcs (this was the first sample in a demonstration for book-matching crotch figures).

STEP 3: FILL IN AREAS IN-BETWEEN ARCS

After creating these guidelines for the crotch-figure pattern, continue filling in the areas between the ribs of the original strokes. These new strokes will be slightly lighter in color than the initial strokes because the foam brush will now hold less medium. If you need to re-load the foam brush, dip only the first 1/4 inch into the Marglaze. This captures only small amounts of medium, which will translate into a paler color when applied, in contrast to the guideline strokes.

STEP 4: LIGHTLY WIPE OUT MEDIUM APPLIED

Loosely crumple up a piece of facial tissue so that it forms numerous protrusions to wipe away media. Start lightly wiping out the results of steps 1 and 2, wiping with a slight "hook" in the approximate center and continuing to wipe out the "ribs" to either side. Alternate your wipe-out strokes, first on one side of the center then on the other side, being careful to apply asymmetrical strokes. Vary your pressure to reveal different lighter and darker amounts of the base coat, just as the growth pattern would appear in real mahogany, as in photo below.

Studying real crotch figures is valuable when simulating them, here being done by removing applied paint while still wet with a crumpled facial tissue.

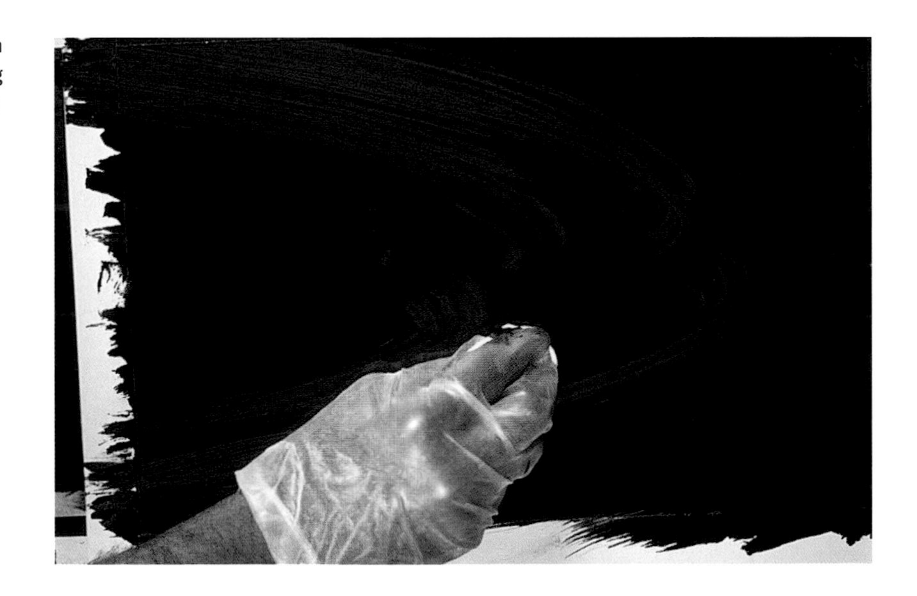

Rendering Architectural Elements

Traditionally, real crotch-figure mahogany veneers were installed sideways on dado panels (the lower, horizontal panels in a paneled space), which is simulated in the photo at right. When rendering reproduction architectural graining for interiors, follow the same sequence of steps described previously of taping off adjacent members abutting a joint and then graining, protecting, and curing one member before repeating the steps on the neighboring members. For example, the photo below right shows a panel that was divided in half to render book-matched graining (a traditional treatment for wide panels). The right half of the panel is being grained after the graining on the left half was applied, dried, protected, and cured. Notice the many members on the paneling that were taped off before graining the adjacent members.

Rendering the crotch figure sideways simulates the traditional placement of real crotch-figure mahogany veneers on dado panels.

CREATING MIRROR-IMAGE GRAINING

When dealing with veneers on architectural elements and furniture with a strong figure, like the crotch figure, measure the midpoint to create mirror-image graining, or what's called a "book-matched figure," on either side of the center. This will maintain a balanced appearance and simulate the architectural veneering of real woods. The light, horizontal, base-coated area to the right of the figure being rendered in the photo below (the sideways crotch figure on the left of the panel) will receive a reverse image of the crotch figure being applied. Instructions for graining members that abut joint-lines, such as for book-matched figures, can be found on page 152 earlier in this chapter.

GRAINING HISTORIC DOORS

Historic doors require several separate sequences of taping off adjacent members and graining because of the many joints and moldings involved on each side. Don't try to hurry the process: Working with these doors is time-consuming but well worth the effort for the final results. After removing the keyhole lock, knob, and escutcheon plates on the doors, preserve any evidence of the type of wood revealed by covering this exposed wood with tape before proceeding with the graining.

Above: Restoring this 14-feet-high, 40-feet-long salon involved recreating nineteenth-century crotch-graining on numerous book-matched graining on panels, doors, and other architectural elements in the room.

Left: Reversing the crotch figure at midpoint on a surface recreates traditional veneering.

Before graining eight mid-nineteenth-century doors, we taped areas of the original wood that had been under hardware and never painted (the light circles with the dark center, which were the original placements for the hardware) to preserve and document them.

When you've completed the graining, remove the tape to reveal the preserved original wood, illustrated in the photo at left, which can be examined at any time by again removing the hardware that was replaced.

Graining both sides of a door can be accomplished more quickly and easily than you might think if you screw two pieces of wood on each end of the door. These added pieces make turning easier (with one person on each end) and allow the underside of the door to dry while the upper side is being grained (see the photo below).

Doors can also be grained while they're still attached to their hinges, as was done with the door in the top photo on the opposite page, which was grained at the same time that the paneling and balustrade were grained. When graining surfaces with a slick finish coat (in which the finish coat and stained wood under it had to be treated before applying the light tan base coat), abrade the surface with #80–120 grit sandpaper; then use a tack cloth to eliminate residue. A detail of this large space in the bottom photo on the opposie page exhibits the mahogany graining on every architectural surface.

When graining a door, screwing pieces of wood on each end makes the door easier to turn to work on the other side and also protect the newly grained surface by raising it off the work surface.

You'll find additional information about graining in our first book, *Professional Painted Finishes: A Guide to the Art and Business of Decorative Painting*, as well as in our two videos on graining, all of which are listed in Further Reading on page 270. We hope this chapter has raised your awareness and awakened your eye, so that now when you look at objects with wood surfaces, you'll ask yourself, "Is it real, or is it grained?"

Doors can also be grained while still attached to their hinges, which is being done in the left photo. In this case, because the door had a slick finish coat, we abraded the surface before graining with #80-120 grit sandpaper, and then used a tack cloth to eliminate residue. The photo below shows some of the completed graining in the salon, recreating solid and veneered mahogany on all the architectural elements in the room.

Nº 8 ‖ Restoring Veneers and Finishes

ALL WOODEN OBJECTS whose surfaces have not been obscured by paint reveal the wood's color and figure. These elements are seen through one or more clear layers, called *finish coats*, which were applied to the wood to bring out its beauty and also protect it from damage. But, if a finish's uppermost layer becomes damaged, its lower layers and even the wood itself will often deteriorate. This is true, also, when finishes over other surfaces—like paint or gilding—are damaged and problems then occur in the lower layers.

The most common problems to which finish coats are subject include damage of all kinds like white rings, lifting, alligatoring, and darkening that obscures the wood, paint, or gilding underneath. As well, wood veneers—thin slices of wood laminated to a surface—can lift, blister, and detach. This chapter offers solutions to all these problems.

Because, as its name implies, a finish coat is the last coating to be put on a surface, it cannot be applied until problems with the surface and color have been solved and the veneer repairs completed.

The image at top left exhibits one of the stages in our restoration of a seventeenth-century oyster marquetry cabinet on stand, which has been placed horizontally here. The bottom image displays a detail of the top of a chest of the same period. The two oyster marquetry designs are exactly the same.

RESTORING VENEERS

BUILDING A TOOLKIT: VENEER-REPAIR TOOLS

Professionals specializing in replacing entire surfaces of veneers use a wide variety of tools and materials. For the damages on the veneered objects that we've restored, the following supplies (which are listed in the order of their use) have been more than adequate:

Veneer-Removal Tools

- → Household iron
- → Brown paper bag
- → Wooden block
- → Palette knife

Glue-Removal Tools

- → X-ACTO knife blade
- → Warm vinegar
- → #120 and #220 grit open-coat sandpaper
- → Tack cloth

Glue-Application Tools

- → Cheesecloth squares
- → Palette knife
- → Glue brush
- → Glue injector
- → Yellow glue
- → Tape
- → Clamps (various sizes)
- → Hide glue (either glue granules or liquid hide glue)
- → Heating unit
- → Pot and stirrer

The detached piece of veneer on this contemporary chest of drawers was a perfect fit because the repair was made before the piece could shrink or warp.

Veneers are thin slices of wood used as a face on, or an inlay into, another surface. They can decorate in ways solid wood cannot, rendering a utilitarian surface more aesthetically pleasing, whether as a one-piece covering or an assembly of separate pieces in pictorial or geometric patterns.

Veneers have been used for centuries, dating back to the ancient Egyptians, who decorated the surfaces of caskets and furnishings with geometric veneering. Later, in Gothic times, artisan monks became the "masters of intarsia" (inlaying veneers into solid wood), with which they decorated churches throughout northern Italy. From the eighteenth century on, veneering enriched furnishings worldwide.

Veneers vary in thickness, depending on the technology of the method used to cut them. Antique veneers often measure a relatively thick 1/8 inch, compared to their modern counterparts, which range in thickness from 1/28 inch to 1/32 inch.

Our experience with restoring veneers has been primarily in replacing missing or damaged veneers, rather than replacing entire surfaces.

The general instructions in the box on the opposite page are the simplest, most basic repair procedures for many damaged veneers, regardless of the problem. Additions or changes to these procedures that are needed for repairing specific veneer problems will be addressed as we discuss each problem in turn. As well, cleaning surfaces of dirt and grime after repairing veneer and also choosing appropriate protective finish coats are covered later in this chapter.

Replacing Missing Veneers

Replacing missing pieces of veneer involves only one more step than the basic directions for veneer repair on page 167. Before you can re-adhere the missing piece or glue in new veneer if you've lost the detached piece, you must tightly glue down the edges of the veneers surrounding the missing section(s).

If you still have the missing piece of veneer and it broke off only a short time before, the repair is relatively simple, since the detached piece will not have had time to shrink or warp and should fit exactly. Such was the case with the damaged base on the small, contemporary chest of drawers at left. Some of the underlying wood had broken off when the section of veneer detached, but the repair was successfully made after tightly gluing down the edges of the surrounding veneer and then following Basic Steps for Adhering Veneers at the top of page 167.

Straight-grain veneer detaches most often on cross-banded borders (cross-banding is made of short lengths of straight-grain veneers that, when joined together, appear to be a striped border; see page 153 in Chapter 7 for detailed information about cross-banding). Careless dusting with cloths whose threads catch the corners of the individual pieces of veneer can often lift and detach sections of veneer, which frequently get lost.

BASIC STEPS FOR ADHERING VENEERS

Below are the basic steps for adhering damaged veneers with original or replaced veneers.

Step 1: Remove Hardware
Unscrew any hardware and mounts, and mark the location of each on tape applied to the back of the hardware or mount to insure accurate replacement.

Step 2: Remove Old Glue
Eliminate all old, dried glue from any original veneer and the substrate to which it will be re-attached, with warm vinegar, sandpaper, and an X-ACTO knife blade (see Cleaning Off Old Glue on page 44 in Chapter 3 for detailed instructions). The telltale signs of prior gluing are any shiny patches on the back of the veneer and on the substrate, or, if hide glue was used, small, brown globs of dried glue.

Step 3: Adhere Veneer
Glue original or new veneer by applying yellow glue or hide glue with a brush and/or a glue injector to both the back of the veneer and the surface where it will be replaced (see top photo below).

Step 4: Apply Pressure to Glue Bond
Apply pressure to affix the veneer, using tape or a caul and clamps (see Repairing Tent Cleavage on Asian Lacquers, starting on page 86 in Chapter 4, for detailed instructions).

Step 5: Clean Excess Glue
Clean off any glue that has seeped out of the repair, using a cheesecloth square dampened slightly with warm vinegar, and then dry the surface (see bottom photo).

Step 6: Let Glue Dry
After the glue has cured thoroughly, remove all tape or clamps and cauls.

After scraping off the old glue from the underside of the veneer and substrate of this late-nineteenth-century art nouveau table whose veneer had lifted, we injected yellow glue to re-adhere the veneer, clamped the repair, and cleaned the excess glue.

Straight-grain walnut veneer (the light sheet atop the table) provided a good match for the missing piece on the edge of this eighteenth-century table, as shown by the color of the wet-test on the veneer.

On this contemporary, triangular table, masking tape provided the necessary pressure to insure a good glue bond for replaced pieces of missing veneer.

Replacing missing veneers on cross-banding is usually relatively easy. You can buy veneers to supply the missing wood from many sources, which offer both ordinary and exotic varieties of veneer (see Resources on page 268). In the case of an eighteenth-century tabletop (see the detail photo at left), the piece of veneer missing on the lower right corner of the cross-banding was walnut, a commonly available veneer. After cutting a replacement piece of veneer (the small rectangle sitting atop the paper protecting the edge of the sheet of veneer) and gluing it in place, we used tape to secure it and apply pressure while the glue dried, just as we did on another table at bottom left. (For information on coloring veneers, see Restoring Wood Color on page 176, and for information on finishing veneers, see Traditional Finishes on page 181, Choosing a Finish on page 184, and Applying Finishes on page 187.)

Repairing Parquetry with Hide Glue

Parquetry refers to small pieces of straight-grain veneers arranged into geometric patterns and overlaid as a single unit on an object. You'll find a traditional example of parquetry in the detail shot at bottom left and the restored small eighteenth-century French table at bottom right.

The general steps for veneer repair outlined in Basic Steps for Repairing Veneers on page 167 work equally well for repairing parquetry, using hide glue (instead of yellow glue), as was done in the original veneering. Follow Steps 1 and 2 to remove and mark the mounts (as shown in the photo top left on page 169 of the French table mentioned above), and then clean the old glue off the substrate and parquetry pieces, as was the next step in the photo at top right on page 169.

To prepare and apply hide glue, follow the label directions on the product you're using. Apply hide glue while it's hot but not boiling, using a stiff-bristled brush of the appropriate size: 1/4 inch for small applications and up to 1 inch for large applications. Finally, apply pressure, clean off the excess glue, and allow the glue to dry, as described in Steps 4 to 6 in Basic Steps for Adhering Veneers on page 167.

The parquetry design in the center of the apron of this eighteenth-century French table was impressively combined with thin cross-banding and straight-grain veneers set on the diagonal around the parquetry at right. The restored table is pictured at far right.

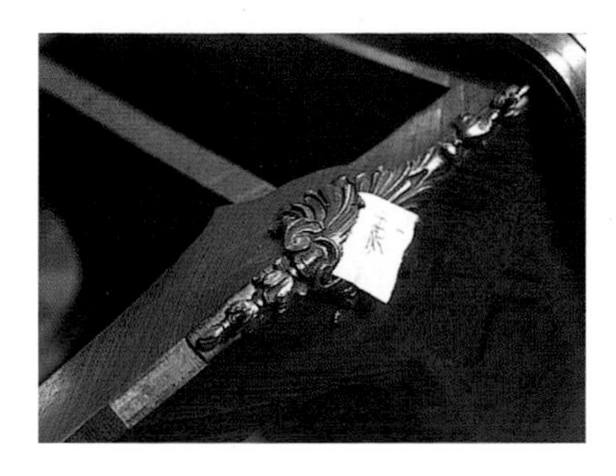

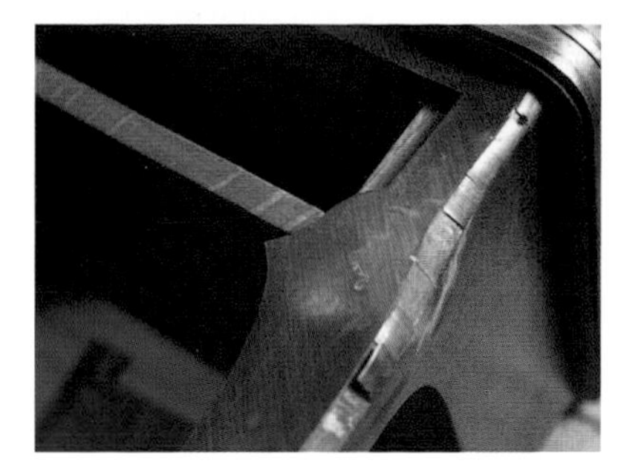

Masking tape with the notation "FR" ("front right") marks the bronze mount in the far left photo. The left photo shows the substrate before it was cleaned of old glue.

Repairing Oyster Marquetry

Oyster marquetry is composed of pieces cut from smaller branches of trees with a distinctive end-grain figure (like olive, kingwood, and walnut), assembled in unique patterns and overlaid as a single unit on another structure. This type of marquetry was used in past centuries primarily for drawer fronts and cabinet doors, like those on the restored seventeenth-century English cabinet on stand below.

On this piece, the shrinkage of the carcass on which the veneers had been laid caused the pieces of oyster-marquetry veneer to split apart along the entire length of the long, vertical joints, which had opened. The photo below right shows a detail of one of these vertical splits.

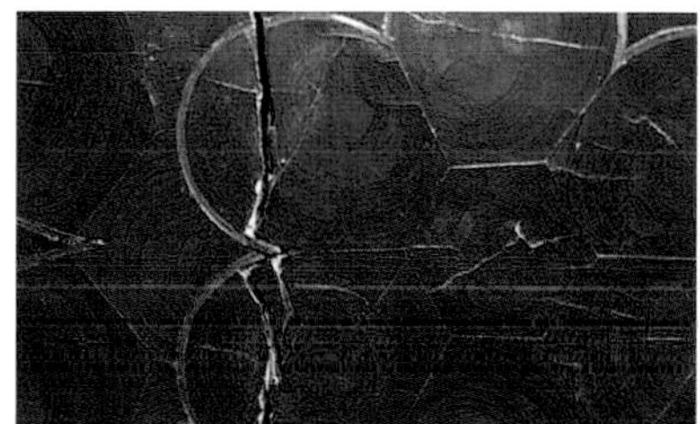

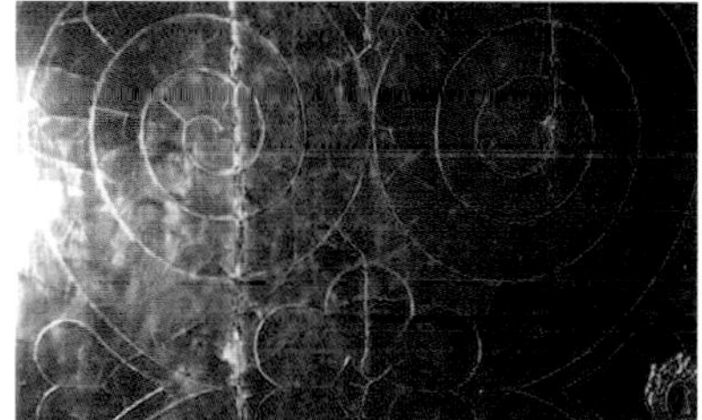

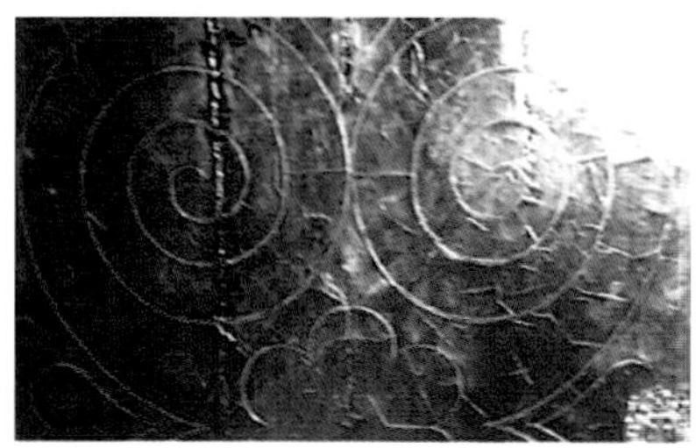

The intricate oyster marquetry on this seventeenth-century English cabinet on stand was badly fractured in a jagged configuration (top photo). Because the split was too narrow to inset pieces of veneer, we mixed raw sienna gouache paint into filler paste to fill the gap (center photo), and then grained the repair (bottom photo). At left is the restored cabinet.

Because the gap in these vertical splits was too narrow, it wasn't possible to insert veneers, nor could we close the opened joints of the carcass under the veneered doors. Therefore, to restore the door, we filled the long opening with surface-repair materials, then grained the filled areas (see center and bottom photos on page 169, and refer to page 76 in Chapter 4 for guidelines on filling materials and processes and to Chapter 7 for information on graining).

Repairing Blisters in Veneers

A blister develops in veneer when the glue fails in an area, which then delaminates. Such was the case with a small eighteenth-century English veneered table with painted decoration that developed a blister under one of the painted veneered sides.

To repair a blister, a slit must be made in it, glue injected, and pressure applied to set the glue bond. But it's important that all slits be made along the veneer's grain lines, not across them. Accordingly, in the eighteenth-century table, we made slits in the blister along several vertical grain lines and inserted glue with a spatula and a glue syringe. We placed a caul over the bulge, and clamped it in position. As described in Repairing Tent Cleavage on Asian Lacquers beginning on page 86 in Chapter 4, we next removed the clamp and caul, wiped excess glue off from every surface, replaced the caul and clamp again, and then tightened the clamp until the glue cured. The result of these procedures: the blister disappeared.

When the glue failed in the center of the painted, veneered apron of this eighteenth-century English table above, a horizontal blister developed. To repair the blister, vertical slits were cut into it, glue injected, and the repair clamped. Pictured at right is a pair of tables of the same period.

Right photo © Christie's Images Ltd. 2006

STEPS TO RE-ADHERING HIDE GLUE

Step 1: Use Brown Paper and an Iron to Apply Heat
Place a large sheet of heavy paper (an opened-out brown paper bag, for instance) over the veneer and slowly glide a regular household iron, set to a medium temperature over the paper. Be patient, the heat will slowly soften and re-liquefy the hide glue. As the heat reactivates the hide glue, you'll sense the blister or lifted veneer softening and settling down. If the veneer isn't reacting, turn the heat setting on the iron a tad higher.

Step 2: Replace Paper and Iron with Clamps and Pressure
Remove the iron and brown paper and replace them quickly with a rigid block of wood (or a cold slab of metal, as was used in the past) and clamps.

Step 3: Let Glue Dry
Allow the glue to cure thoroughly. This process can be repeated if necessary.

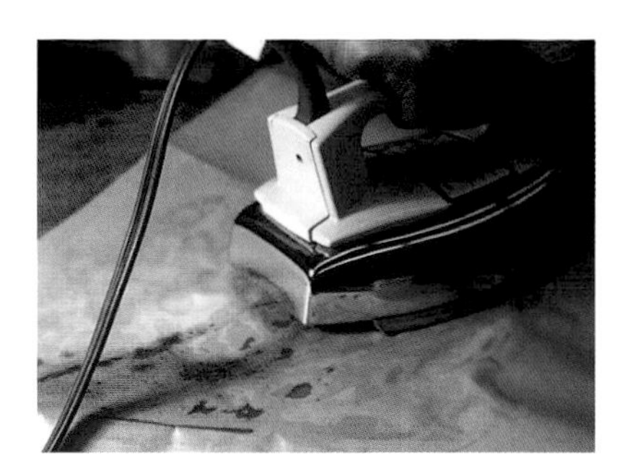

RE-ADHERING HIDE GLUE

There's another way to repair blisters in veneer—and also lifted veneers—if the original adhesive for the veneer was hide glue: The hide glue can be heated to re-liquefy it, which will, in turn, re-adhere the glue. However, if the veneer has painted surface decoration, as did the eighteenth-century table, this approach cannot be used since the heat might damage the decoration. For unpainted, blistered, or lifted veneer, the steps for this method of re-adhering the hide glue are above.

Removing Veneer

There may be times when you don't want to restore a veneered surface but instead want to remove it or to replace it entirely. This might be the case, for example, if matching veneers are unavailable, you don't wish to grain the missing areas, or if you want to make use of a piece's solid, older construction under the veneer. Such was the case with the chest of drawers at right, found in an auction sale, whose solid construction and marble top made it a good candidate for removing veneers.

Using the steps below, it should not be difficult to remove damaged veneer adhered with hide glue (which is what was used on most older pieces). After taking off the veneer, you can apply new veneer or paint the entire surface decoratively.

When veneers are badly damaged, as they were on the chest of drawers found at auction (above), they can be easily removed. Use heat to liquefy old hide glue and then a palette knife to remove the broken pieces.

STEP 1: APPLY HEAT TO VENEER

Place a large sheet of heavy paper (an opened-out brown paper bag works well) over the veneer and slowly glide a regular household iron over it (see Step 1 in Steps to Re-Adhering Hide Glue above for additional information).

STEP 2: GENTLY PRY OFF VENEER

When the glue has re-liquefied, slip a palette knife between the veneer and substrate, and gently and slowly pry off the veneer, as seen in the top photo on page 172. You may have to repeat the heating process in Step 1 more than once.

After removing the pieces of veneer with a palette knife (top), a student painted a design on the surface after cleaning it thoroughly (bottom).

STEP 3: TO SAVE REMOVED VENEER

If you want to save the removed veneer (particularly when you have an interesting veneer like that in the photo on page 171, and would like to use it on another object, clean off all old glue from the back of the veneer, as described in Step 2 on page 167. Then sandwich the veneer between two flat boards, clamped tightly, and/or place the veneer under heavy weights until you're ready to reuse it. In the case of a tall stand, a student decided against reapplying veneer, cut the stand off its base, and painted an original design on the previously veneered surfaces before installing it onto a new base (shown at left top and bottom).

RESTORING WOOD SURFACES

Any wood surface has at least one finish coat, since uncoated wood collects dust, dirt, and grime in its cells, which are almost impossible to remove. Usually, in fact, there's more than a single-layer finish coat; and, for this reason, the first step in restoring a wood surface is to analyze its layers.

Analyzing a Wood Surface

The topmost layer could be a wax finish coat, which, if all the layers beneath it are in good condition, may only require removing and replacing with a new coat (see Wax Finishes on page 183 later in this chapter for instructions on doing this). Under the wax layer—or instead of it—may be one or several layers of varnish and/or shellac. Old varnish is hard, brittle, often darkened and opaque, and hard to repair; and it's therefore usually removed and replaced. Shellac is softer and can be susceptible to white rings and "bloom" (cloudiness), but it's easier to remove and replace than varnish (see Removing White Rings and Bloom on page 173).

Under one or more of the above layers is the wood itself. If it's damaged, refer to Chapter 4 or Chapter 7, depending, respectively, on whether the damage requires restoring the surface or rendering graining. Lastly, look at the color of the wood to see if it's what you want and if it's in good condition. Once you've assessed the wood and its finish coats, you can begin to restore its surface, starting with the topmost finish coat.

Finish Coat Problems

Because finish coats sit on the surfaces of wood, paint and gilding—instead of being incorporated into their cell structure—they're subject to all kinds of damage, including, among other things, white rings and bloom, lifting, and what's called *alligatoring*.

WHITE RINGS AND BLOOM

White rings and bloom develop when shellac or synthetic lacquer surfaces are exposed to liquor, perfume, and other alcohol- or lacquer-thinner-based liquids (see bottom left, page 173). If the white rings are confined to a small area, remove them following the directions in Removing White Rings and Bloom on page 173. If white rings cover a much larger area, remove the entire finish.

REMOVING WHITE RINGS AND BLOOM

Shellac and contemporary lacquer-thinned finishes are susceptible to developing white rings from perfume, liquor, and other alcohol- or lacquer-thinner-based liquids. Shellac predates contemporary lacquer and is probably the finish coat an older object would have.

Abrading Is Usually the Answer
Since white rings and bloom occur only in the upper levels of a shellac finish, abrading usually eliminates them. Recipes for rubbing them away have a long history, and all include mild abrasives (like cigar ashes, toothpaste, and rottenstone, for instance) and a liquid (water, and possibly light oil). We prefer mixing rottenstone and water into a paste to rub over the area with a cloth (cheesecloth works well and has a mild abrasive action of its own) and #600 wet/dry silicone carbide paper, if needed.

It may be time-consuming to rub through the finish enough to eliminate the white rings and cloudiness. Be very careful not to develop a dip or depression where the white ring exists by making sure to work in an area wider than the rings and bloom.

Alternatively, Remove the Entire Shellac Finish
If you have no success after rubbing for a while, you may want to remove the entire shellac finish using denatured alcohol. Test a small area using alcohol on a cotton swab. An old finish will probably need several applications of alcohol. If the test proves successful, remove the whole surface, as we had to do for the American papier-mâché tray from the 1840s in the photo at right. On pages 246 to 247, you can see the surface that was under the cloudy finish, painted to simulate burl and stenciled with gold powder.

Our client was quite surprised to discover that this was a painted burl—she had bought it as a painted tortoise shell.

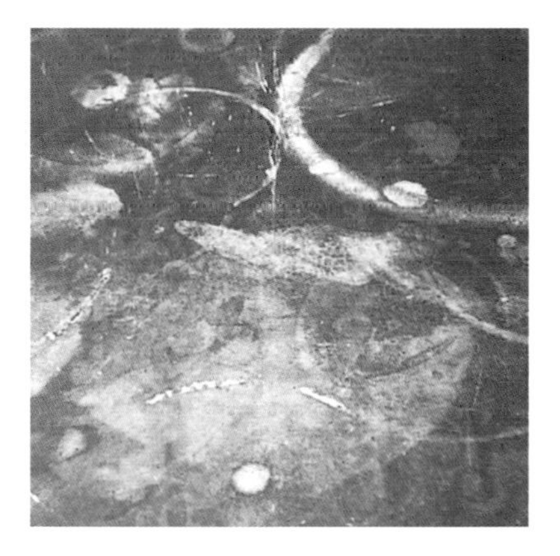

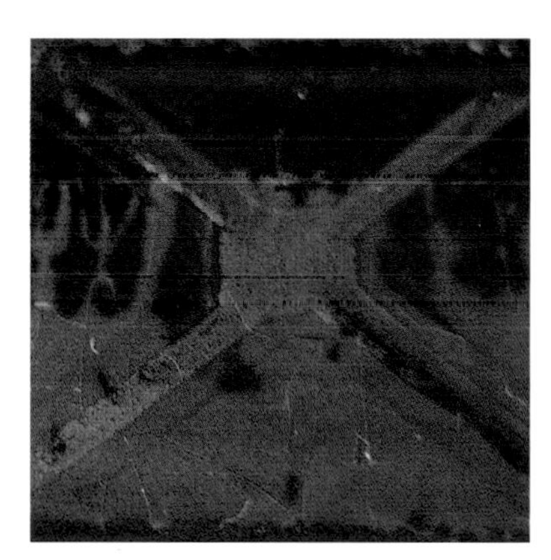

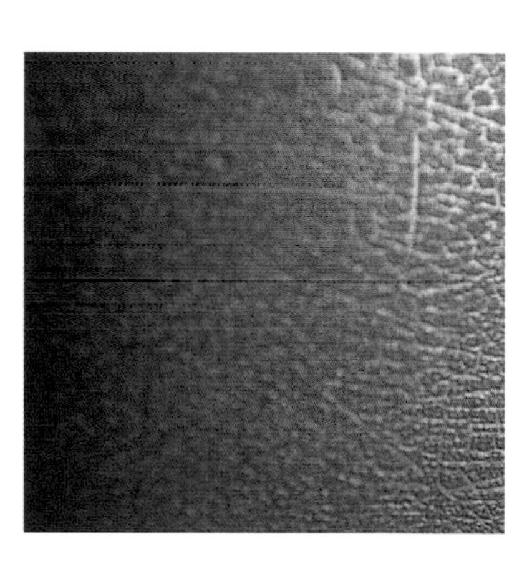

Common finish-coat problems include, from left, white rings and bloom (cloudiness), lifted coats, and alligatoring, or extensive cracking.

LIFTED COATS

A coat lifts when a contemporary synthetic finish fails to bond with a prior coat, as the photo above center illustrates. Always remove lifted coatings along with any coat that may be over it before reapplying new finish coats.

ALLIGATORING

A surface alligators, or cracks extensively, when a finish coat is applied before the prior layer has dried, which happened in the photo above right. To remedy this, remove and reapply new finish coats.

BUILDING A TOOLKIT: FINISH-REMOVAL TOOLS

Below are listed the different agents you will need to remove finishes.

Removal Agents Solvents:

→ Denatured alcohol
→ Mineral spirits
→ Naphtha
→ Lacquer thinner
→ Acetone
→ Choice of commercial strippers

Removal Supplies

→ Newspapers
→ Stiff-bristled brushes
→ Putty scrapers with rounded edges
→ #00 and 000 steel wool
→ #120 and #220 grit open-coat sandpaper
→ Tack cloth
→ Cheesecloth squares
→ Cotton swabs
→ Bags for disposal

Safety Supplies

→ Gloves
→ Safety goggles
→ Apron/smock
→ Mask or respirator (if necessary)
→ Fan

Removing Finish Coats

For restoring wood—in addition to removing damaged finish coats—you'll also need to remove finishes if you want to change the type of finish coat, restore the wood itself, or change the wood's color. Any finish coat left on the wood's surface will prevent it from absorbing the necessary materials (like bleach or stain) required for these procedures. Of course, if you have any inkling that there's an original finish under later coatings, you need to get the finish analyzed before beginning to remove even the later layers.

The many advances made in the conservation of surfaces in recent years include the development of sophisticated instruments for analyzing not only the number of layers added over the original but also their identity and how to remove them. Current thinking prefers, if possible, leaving one or two clear layers over the original one (see Resources on page 268 for sources of coatings analysis).

There are many ways to remove surface finishes, some more toxic than others or more abusive to the wood. The most common removal methods involve solvents and commercial removers (often called *strippers*). If you must use a remover, we suggest using nontoxic strippers, which are kinder to you and the environment (see Resources). Abrading and scraping are also helpful removal techniques under certain circumstances (see pages 118 to 119 for more information on these methods).

BEFORE REMOVING FINISHES

There are a few preparations to do before removing any finish coats:

STEP 1: REMOVE AND MARK HARDWARE

Take off and mark for replacement all handles, drawer pulls, and hinges. Plug up drilled screw holes with bits of rolled newspaper.

STEP 2: MAKE JOINERY AND SURFACE REPAIRS

Complete all joinery and surface repairs before removing surface finishes, so that none of the material being removed seeps into open joints or other openings.

STEP 3: PREPARE SAFE WORK AREA

Make sure to have proper ventilation in your work area as well as safety goggles, gloves, a cover-up to protect your clothes, a mask (a respirator, if necessary), and coverings for your worktable and floor.

STEP 4: PREPARE SUPPLIES

Follow label directions carefully to prepare each product that you're using. Also observe the label's directions for methods of application, timing for the product, removal of sludge (the thick mass of material lifted off by a solvent or stripper), clean-up, and any additional processes.

REMOVING FINISHES WITH SOLVENTS

Because the original finish coat may have had additional coats applied over the years, there may be several layers to remove, each requiring a different solvent. For instance, wax, which is likely to be the uppermost layer, needs to be removed with naphtha or mineral spirits. A shellac layer requires denatured alcohol as a solvent, and a commercial lacquer layer (not Asian lacquer) should be dissolved with lacquer thinner or acetone. To remove these various finishes, proceed methodically as outlined in Steps for Removing Finishes with Solvents below.

STEPS FOR REMOVING FINISHES WITH SOLVENTS

Follow these steps to remove finishes with solvents.

Step 1: Assemble Solvents
Assemble the various solvents listed in the toolkit on page 174.

Step 2: Remove Possible Wax Coat
In as inconspicuous a spot as possible, test if there's a wax topcoat by trying to dissolve it with naphtha and/or mineral spirits. Wipe the surface with a cotton swab and a little solvent, and see if there's any residue on the swab. If there is, the solvent has lifted the wax; and you can repeat the process over the entire surface, using cheesecloth squares. Continue until you've completely removed the wax from the desired area. This may be all that's needed if the layers under the grimy wax are in good condition. Then see page 183 for instructions on applying a new coat of wax on a surface.

Step 3: Remove Possible Shellac Layer
To dissolve a possible shellac layer, repeat step 2 using denatured alcohol instead of naptha. If you successfully remove shellac in your test area, dissolve the entire shellac surface. If not, move on to lacquer thinner or acetone to test whether the finish is synthetic lacquer.

Step 4: If Necessary, Use Commercial Remover
If none of the above solvents removes the top finish coat, the finish is probably hardened varnish. In that case, you'll need to remove it with a commercial product (see the guidelines below).

To Remove Finishes with Commercial Products

Remove old varnishes, especially those composed of hardened linseed oil, with commercial removers, but avoid commercial products containing methyl chloride, a hazardous chemical. There are less toxic strippers that take longer, and there's an entire system that peels away finishes and isn't toxic at all (see Resources).

After following the steps in Before Removing Finishes on the previous page, apply the commercial remover according to its label directions. As finish coats soften, remove them with round-edged putty scrapers and/or steel wool. Clean off the putty scraper on newspaper as you work, and keep unrolling the steel wool to expose a fresh surface. When the steel wool becomes saturated, throw it away.

Sanding After Removing Finishes

Before applying new finish coats, remove any remaining residue, which would prevent subsequent materials from being absorbed into the wood cells: Hand-sand the surface, first, with #120 grit open-coat sandpaper and, then, with #220 grit open-coat sandpaper wrapped over a felt or wood block. Be sure to sand with the wood's grain. If you're

Scratches from an electric sander must be removed to prevent spoiling finish work on the surface.

using a mechanical sander, hand-sand afterward to remove any scratches left by the sander (see the photo at left).

After sanding, use a tack cloth to eliminate any residue: Unfold the tack cloth completely, then crumple it into a loose ball. Wiping with the grain, wipe the surface firmly enough to pick up the dust but not so hard as to deposit any tacky substance on it. Store the tack cloth in a covered jar.

RESTORING WOOD COLOR

Coloring wood entails one or more procedures to get the results you want. After removing all coats on the wood surface, which will enable the wood to absorb materials, you'll be able to bleach the wood, fill its pores, color it, and even give it a different type of finish that sinks into the pores rather than just sits on the surface. Not every wood will react in the same way to these procedures, but testing on the same kind of wood that you want to treat will give you an idea of what to expect.

Bleaching Wood

After wood has been bleached, it can be stained to have a color temperature different than normal. The test on these two boards produced an uncharacteristically cool-toned mahogany (on top) and warm-toned walnut (on bottom).

Bleaching removes undesirable infiltrates from wood (like rust and minerals in water that have turned the wood black), and it also can lighten the top layer of the wood's natural and stained colors. Once you've bleached the wood, you can stain it again and even change its color temperature (see Coloring with Stains on page 178). For example, after bleaching warm-toned woods, like mahogany and cherry, you can stain them with a cool color, like walnut or chestnut; or, conversely, you can stain a cool-toned walnut or chestnut to warm up its color. In the case of the two solid-wood boards shown in photo at left—the upper one originally was a warm-colored mahogany and the lower one a cool-colored walnut—our tests showed that each board could, in fact, be stained to resemble the other wood.

There are many kinds of bleach that you can use, ranging from mild household bleach to a much stronger, two-part commercial bleach system. In every case, follow label directions very carefully. Exercise caution when working with all bleaches, but especially with two-part commercial bleaches because the dust raised while sanding dried bleach is toxic; therefore, we suggest wearing a mask.

As consultants to architects of an historic house, we used A&B, a two-part bleach, to find out how light the oak to be used to restore the house could be bleached. The wood had to be lightened considerably, so that, in turn, it could be given an aged, gray patina, which the oak's original color would have precluded. As you can see in the photos at the top of page 177, the wood bleached as light as was possible.

Filling Open Pores

When coloring wood, take into account its pore structure. In some woods (oak, for instance), the pores are quite noticeable and require being filled before or after staining with commercial products called

These oak boards are being bleached to lighten them in preparation to give them an aged, gray color, which wouldn't have been possible with the original dark tan color of the wood.

"paste fillers." (In other woods, maple, for example, the much smaller or unnoticeable pores don't require filling.) Note that these paste fillers are not to be confused with the filler material used to repair damaged surfaces in Chapter 4.

Fillers are useful for producing a smooth, unbroken surface appearance before you apply a new finish coat. (Eighteenth-century furniture designer Thomas Sheraton used brick dust and water or oil to fill wood pores and polish the surface at the same time.) Your filler can match the color of the wood, or it can create an interesting effect by contrasting in color, as, for example, in the close-up detail at right. Alternatively, you can fill pores by applying our oil-resin finish, whose directions are in Steps for Working with Oil-Resin Finish on page 180.

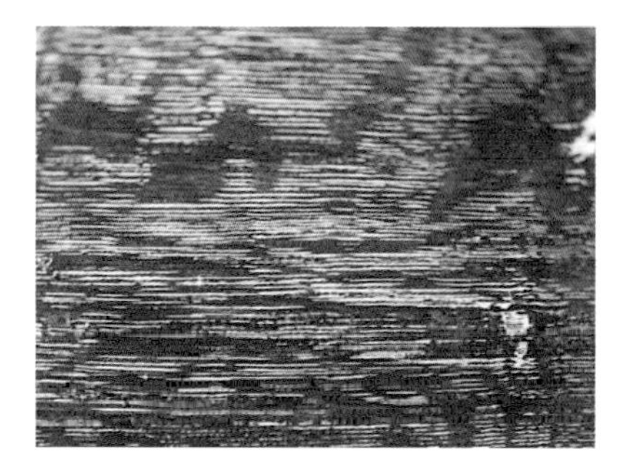

You can match filler paste to color of the wood pores you're filling or create a striking contrast by making the paste another color, as a student did on this detail of a country oak table. A matte finish was applied to protect it.

STEPS FOR FILLING WOOD PORES

Follow the steps below to fill the wood's pores and prepare the surface for coloring:

STEP 1: THIN AND APPLY PASTE FILLER

Thin the paste filler to brushing consistency (follow label directions), apply it, and let it set (again, according to directions) until it loses its wet, shiny appearance.

STEP 2: SCRUB SURFACE TO FORCE FILLER INTO PORES

Make a pad of a coarse cloth, like burlap, and scrub the surface in a circular motion to force the filler into the pores.

STEP 3: WIPE SURFACE AND LET DRY

Finish the process by wiping the surface with a clean cloth along the grain. Allow the filler to dry for at least 24 hours before coloring the wood.

Coloring Wood

After you've filled the wood's pores, if required, the wood is ready to accept one or more of the many available coloring agents. Wood can be colored with any pigmented substance—paint, dye, glaze, shoe polish, or anything else—that can be absorbed into the wood's cells. In fact, any

BUILDING A TOOLKIT: STAINING TOOLS

You will need the following materials for staining:

→ #120 grit and #220 grit open-coat sandpaper
→ Tack cloth
→ Denatured alcohol
→ Cheesecloth squares
→ Test pieces of wood
→ Soft cloths (2)
→ Bristle brush
→ Shellac wash coat (5 parts alcohol, 1 part clear shellac)
→ Stain/coloring agents
→ Solvents for stains

material can be absorbed into wood if it's diluted enough; or, if it's too thick to be absorbed completely, it can be applied, then wiped off before drying and still serve to color the wood. The most familiar colorants are commercial stains available in paint, hardware, and home-improvement stores, which come in a wide range of wood colors and consistencies (and companies are always adding new stain products to their line). Whatever product you select, be sure to follow the directions on its label.

COLORING WITH STAINS

Stains have many uses. They lend color to woods that are normally colorless, bring out a wood's figure and grain, and can change a wood's color temperature (see Creating the Base-Coat Color: Layer 1 on page 140) after bleaching.

Generally speaking, there are two basic types of stains: those made from dyes that penetrate (absorb) into wood quickly and those made from pigments that absorb into wood more slowly. Slower-penetrating stains, like pigmented oil stains, give you more time to wipe them off and hence more control over the staining process than fast-penetrating stains.

When applying a pigmented stain (see Steps for Applying Stains below), don't spread it on so thickly that an opaque film (more like a paint coat) is left on the wood's surface instead of penetrating into the wood. Instead, apply the stain according to label directions and always along

STEPS FOR APPLYING STAINS

Follow the steps below to apply a stain.

Step 1: Remove and Mark Hardware
Remove all hardware, including handles and hinges, and mark them for correct replacement. Mask hinges that remain in place.

Step 2: Sand Any Surface Scratches
Look for and remove scratches left from sanding, using, first, #120-grit open-coat sandpaper, then #220 grit open-coat sandpaper, making sure in both cases to sand along the grain.

Step 3: Remove Sanding Dust
Remove dust left from sanding with a tack cloth.

Step 4: Wipe Surface with Denatured Alcohol
Wipe the surface with denatured alcohol to remove any additional residue to ensure a clean surface for even staining.

Step 5: Apply Wash Coat on End Grain
If your object has an area of exposed end-grain, such as the thin end on a solid tabletop, apply a thin wash-coat of shellac (see Shellac on page 181) to the end grain to prevent it from absorbing stain too deeply and turning darker than the other surfaces.

Step 6: Test Stain
Test the stain on similar wood or on the underside or another inconspicuous spot on your object. Remember that fast-absorbing dye stains give you little time to control the depth of color. Let the test stain dry, and then apply the finish that you plan to use (see Options for Finishes on page 185).

Step 7: Apply Stain
When you're satisfied with the results of your test stain and finish coat, apply the stain with a soft cloth or bristle brush on the least conspicuous areas of your object first and finally, say, in the case of a table, on the tabletop.

Step 8: Wipe Stain Off
Slow-absorbing oil stains can be left on until they produce the desired depth of color; then you should wipe off all excess stain that hasn't been absorbed into the wood. Do not leave any wet stain on the surface.

the grain as well as on an entire section at once. Don't stop the application in the middle of a piece of wood.

The most difficult aspect of staining is trying to match the stain color to the real wood surrounding a repair, as, for example, matching an area where you've bleached out a black ring with the surrounding tabletop. In such cases, either use a slow-penetrating stain, which will enable you to control the color, or bleach the entire surface after removing the finish coat to get an even coat when you stain the surface.

COLORING WITH AN OIL-RESIN FINISH

A second way to color wood is with an oil-resin finish that penetrates the wood. On older pieces, this method produces rich, deep color; on more contemporary objects, the color ranges from medium-dark to deep tones.

We taught this method to our students, and one of them used it to change the color and surface finish on her late-nineteenth-century American Renaissance Revival chair at top left photo below. (If she had chosen to retain the original color and finish of this period, she would

On a student's nineteenth-century American chair at top left that badly needed attention, our oil-resin finish provided a rich, deep color on the stripped piece (bottom left). By contrast, the same finish applied to a contemporary piece (above) turned a lighter color.

FORMULA FOR OIL-RESIN FINISH

The formula we used is a variation on what's sometimes called a *gunstock finish*. This finish penetrates the wood and fills up the pores completely, and enhances not only the wood's color but also its "hand" (the feel of the wood surface). Since the finish penetrates the wood, not just sits on its surface, it cannot be damaged. There are prepared products available that will produce similar results (consult your local hardware or paint-supply store). Our formula below should be prepared several days ahead of using it and stored in a tightly covered jar:

- → 1 part boiled linseed oil
- → 2 parts fast-drying varnish (mineral-spirits-soluble)
- → 3 parts mineral spirits

Cautionary Note: Because linseed oil rags can ignite through spontaneous combustion, store them in metal containers. Wet them thoroughly with water and wring them out before discarding in the trash.

have instead used the cleaning method outlined in Caring for Furniture on page 188.) After completing all the preparatory steps of joinery, surface repair, and removing the old finish, the student applied our oil-resin formula (see Formula for Oil-Resin Finish at left), using the Steps for Working with Oil-Resin Finish below. The wood was so dry that it absorbed the mixture immediately and turned the chair a rich, deep brown (bottom of page 179). Woods that aren't as old and dry turn a more medium color (top right photo, page 179). Be sure to mix the formula for the oil-resin finish several days ahead of using it.

STEPS FOR WORKING WITH OIL-RESIN FINISH

Follow the steps below to apply an oil-resin finish:

Step 1: "Wet-Test" Small Area
Using a miniscule amount of water, wet-test an inconspicuous spot on your object. This will show what color the wood will become when a finish, but no stain, is applied. If your object has several kinds of wood, test each one.

Step 2: Apply Oil-Resin Formula
Stir the oil-resin mixture and apply it with a brush or rag, making sure all surfaces and crevices are saturated. If the object is large or has many turnings and moldings, cover only those surfaces that you can comfortably work with at one time.

Step 3: Apply Additional Coats, as Needed
Let the mixture soak in, applying more to areas drinking it up more quickly (within 15 minutes). Do this until the surface will absorb no more and shows no "dry" spots. This should take about an hour total.

Step 4: Wipe Off Mixture
Using cheesecloth, rub off any remaining mixture, rubbing with the grain of the wood. Be careful to rub off every trace of oil mixture since any left on the wood will become tacky and gummy. If the surface is at all tacky, wipe it clean with a cloth and a very little paint thinner.

Step 5: If Color Needs Darkening
If the wet test produces a lighter color than you'd like, apply the oil-resin mixture in its clear form to the wood and wipe it off. Apply an artist's oil tube color, usually burnt umber, to a cloth, and rub it into the wood with firm pressure along the grain. Wipe off all excess with a clean cheesecloth square, making sure no paint remains on the surface. This process is very useful for uniting different woods in one object to make them appear to be the same wood.

If you want to deepen color further, allow the first application to dry, rub more color in, again wiping off the excess paint. If your piece requires so much pigment that the wood looks masked, use a commercial stain instead.

Step 6: Rub Surface with Steel Wool
Let the surface dry overnight (or longer, depending on the weather), then rub it with fine steel wool (#000 or #0000); use a tack cloth, and repeat the process. Do this several more times until the surface is smooth and even, and no glints of steel wool can be seen.

Step 7: Apply Finish "Dressing"
Apply the oil-resin mixture with a cloth to a small area along the grain. Rub it with a small pad of flannel or leather (an old leather glove worn on the hand is best—though it may need a lubricant of equal parts of paint thinner and linseed oil for smoother rubbing). Repeat this process on the entire surface until it's dry, smooth, and lustrous.

A Danish-type flat finish can be produced by using less oil and more paint thinner in the oil-resin mixture to thin it. Alternately, these flat finishes are available ready-made in hardware stores and home-improvement centers. Use only one coat, touching up dry spots where they appear. Also apply the mixture to the underside of the object to prevent warping.

TRADITIONAL FINISHES

Experts believe that very few original finishes now exist on antiques. Over the years since the original finishes were put on these objects, it's likely that numerous other materials may also have been applied over them. Analytical laboratories can help you determine the components of your specific finish and suggest treatment strategies to uncover the original finish (see Resources on page 268). And, unless meticulous records of provenance (prior ownership) and care are available, you probably may assume that the finish on your object is not original.

Another reason that few original finishes exist nowadays is that, up until the mid-nineteenth century, craftsmen created their own formulas for both stains and finishes from natural resins and oils, which they guarded closely and which are largely unknown today. What is known, though, is that the interactions between layers often caused problems. For instance, some bright stain colors made with acids not only faded over time, giving us the mellow colors we see now, but also caused the finishes over the stains to deteriorate. Although we may not know exact formulas for stains and finishes, the roster of earlier finishes generally included varnish, shellac, oil, and wax, each of which we'll discuss in turn.

BUILDING A TOOLKIT: FINISHING TOOLS

Below are the finishing materials you will need:

Finish-Coat Supplies

- → Varnish
- → Mineral spirits or water-soluble finish
- → Container of warm water
- → Shellac, or shellac flakes
- → Alcohol
- → Stir sticks
- → Ox-hair brushes (chiseled)
- → Foam brush
- → "Bob" material (see page 198 in Chapter 9)

Polishing Supplies

- → #220 grit open-coat sandpaper
- → Tack cloth
- → #400 and #600 wet/dry silicone carbide paper, cut into 1 1/2-inch squares
- → Water
- → #0000 steel wool
- → Rottenstone
- → Lemon oil
- → Palette
- → Hard buffing cloth without a nap (men's suiting fabric is good)

Waxing Supplies

- → Wax
- → Cotton knit fabric

Varnishes

In past centuries, varnishes were made from natural resins tapped from living trees and from fossilized sap, like amber. It's suggested that the term "varnish" derives from *berenice,* the name of the African area from which the natural sandarac resin (once called berenice) was exported. In the past, varnish meant any coating, including shellac, that sat on the surface and produced a glossy finish. Today, varnish refers to resins mixed with drying oils; but, because of volatile-organic-compound (VOC) legislation, discussed on page 184 in Product Changes, nowadays fewer real varnishes are produced.

CONTEMPORARY VARNISHES

Finish coats have undergone changes in recent years. There used to be a whole group of finishes known as varnishes, but now there are very few, with those remaining mostly spar varnishes for heavy-duty use on boats and outdoor installations but rarely for furniture. In fact, very few products currently bear the term *varnish* on their label. Instead, these products are now known simply as "finishes" or "finish coats," meaning that they don't contain varnish and are mostly water-soluble materials.

Experiment with the finishes available now: Test these finishes with various combinations of both the layers you apply under and over them, checking carefully to discover any discoloration, lack of bonding, or other problem among the three layers.

Shellac

Used since the sixteenth century as a finish (and for centuries before that as both a medicine and a dye), shellac is derived from the deep red-brown, natural resin exuded by the lac insect (*Laccifer lacca*) as a scaly,

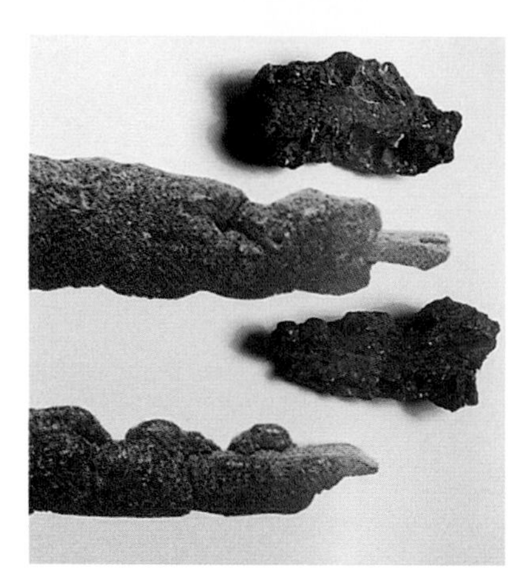

Right: Shellac comes from the natural, cocoon-like resin deposited by the lac insect on twigs in the Near East. On the right are two pieces of stick-lac removed from twigs.

Far right: The resin undergoes flaking and other processes to prepare it for use.

cocoon-like covering on twigs of acacia and soapberry trees in India, Thailand, and Myanmar (Burma) (see top left photo). After this resin is scraped off twigs, the best grade, called *seed-lac*, undergoes many processes, including flaking and bleaching, to produce a variety of colors of shellac from light (blond) to dark (button-lac). "De-waxed" shellac is the clearest shellac of all, having the natural wax content removed. All flakes are dissolved in alcohol in different proportions to produce shellac of varied strengths. For instance, five pounds of flakes dissolved in one gallon of alcohol yield a five-pound "cut," which is thicker shellac than a three-pound "cut," which has fewer shellac flakes, as illustrated in photo top right. For guidelines on using shellac, see the sidebar Tips for Using Shellac on page 183.

SHELLAC'S ADVANTAGES

The advantages of shellac over other finishes are many:

→ Shellac dries quickly, and therefore a surface can have many applications in a day.

→ When a three-pound cut of shellac is used, multiple coats can be rubbed down with steel wool and wax or with the fine-furniture finishing materials (see Options for Finishes on page 185).

→ Shellac can be diluted for a variety of purposes, for instance:

→ Reduced with an equal quantity of alcohol, it can be used as an interlayer between media requiring the same solvent (see The Concept of Layering on page 140 in Chapter 7).

→ Reduced to a "wash coat" (one part clear or de-waxed shellac to five parts alcohol), it can be applied as a sheer coat over dull surfaces to add "life" (light reflectivity).

→ As a wash coat, shellac can also be applied over the end grain of raw wood to prevent stain from absorbing too deeply in that area and darkening it too much.

TIPS FOR USING SHELLAC

- When purchasing shellac, look for an expiration date on the can that's as far as possible from your date of purchase to prevent drying problems, since old shellac takes longer to dry.
- Whether you purchase shellac or mix it from flakes, keep the container lid on the shellac closed tightly.
- Decant (pour) from the large container of shellac, the amount you might need into another container (you can always pour out more).
- If the shellac seems to drag, or be too thick, while you're applying it, add more alcohol a little bit at a time.
- Load the brush fully, and lay on long, parallel strokes along the grain of the wood. Don't backtrack over the wet surface.
- We've often used foam brushes to apply shellac. But, because some foam reacts to shellac by shedding, you'll need to try out different brands of brushes. You can apply sheer coats of shellac with a "bob" (see Preparing a "Bob" to Spread Size on page 198 in Chapter 9).

You must work quickly since shellac is so fast-drying.

French Polish

French polish, originally termed *friction polish* when it was developed in the late 1830s, is a labor-intensive finish of shellac applied with a pad and linseed oil. It's preferred for fine antiques for many reasons: It enhances wood's color and figure; allows new areas of French polish to be blended in easily; has a rich appearance; provides an excellent base for waxing; and, importantly, allows the shellac to be removed and replaced when damaged by water, heat, or alcohol.

Oil Finishes

In the past, oil finishes were mostly made of linseed oil, one of the natural resins from the seeds of the flax plant. Linseed-oil finishes were much in favor in the eighteenth century often with a final coating of beeswax, which may have slowed down the darkening of the linseed oil, a natural occurrence as linseed oil ages. Nowadays there are many commercial finishes termed *oil finish* on the label. Try them, following label directions carefully. In Coloring with an Oil-Resin Finish on page 179, you'll find our formula for oil-resin finish using linseed oil, along with directions for applying this finish. These oil-resin finishes soak into raw wood, darkening the color of the wood and also providing protection in wood's interior and its uppermost exterior surface. That is to say, there's no separate layer sitting on top of the wood to become damaged.

Wax Finishes

According to researchers, the preferred wax in the eighteenth century was beeswax. When mixed with turpentine and varnish, this beeswax mixture was sometimes rubbed into the wood and became a fine finish both to the eye and to the touch.

STEPS FOR APPLYING A WAX COAT

Follow the steps below to apply a wax coat:

Step 1: Cut Fabric and Make Wax Applicator

Cut an 8-inch to 10-inch square of cotton knit fabric. Depending on the amount of wax you'll need, put a lump of a good-quality paste wax (with a high carnauba wax content) in the center of the square. Pull up the square's corners, and fasten them with a rubber band.

Step 2: Rub on Wax

Rub the applicator along the surface you're waxing. Doing this will warm the wax, melting it enough to squeeze it through the knit fabric and deposit just the right amount.

Step 3: Buff Wax Coat

Follow label direction for buffing: Usually 15 to 20 minutes is enough time to allow the wax to cure. Buff with a clean piece of hard-surfaced fabric (like men's suiting fabric) along the grain. If you wish, apply another coat of wax in a week.

Wax applied directly on wood sinks into the wood's pores and grabs onto every bit of dust and dirt that land on it. For that reason—and because wax should be removed and replaced once or twice a year—wax is applied over other finishes, but no finish should ever be applied over wax. Wax is removed with mineral spirits or naphtha.

Our favorite method of applying wax, which solves the common problem of uneven applications and excess wax buildup in crevices and around moldings, is with a cotton knit fabric, like a T-shirt. You'll find the directions for this method in Steps for Applying a Wax Coat at left.

Product Changes

Most furniture commercially produced since the mid-twentieth century has a sprayed nitrocellulose, high-gloss finish, which was developed in France in the 1920s. Aerosol spray cans of nitrocellulose lacquer are available for consumer use (and must be used with proper ventilation) since the lacquer is hard to brush on smoothly. Many of our students have removed these high-gloss finishes in favor of the softer, nonreflective finish produced by our oil-resin formula given on page 180.

In recent years, federal environmental legislation to reduce volatile-organic-compound (VOC) in media—including oleoresins and gum turpentine—have caused changes in media nationwide. Therefore, familiar products that you may have been using are fast disappearing from store shelves. Nontraditional materials, like polyurethane, other catalyst finishes, and acrylics, have been developed to replace these other media. The interaction of these new materials with one another and with traditional finishes is problematic and should be tested. Be aware that product manufacturers often change formulas but not labels. Success with one can of a product doesn't necessarily mean it will be as successful the next time you use it. Experiment with any product, especially one that is new to you, before applying it to the object that you're restoring.

CHOOSING A FINISH

There is no one perfect finish coat. There are advantages and disadvantages to all finish coats. Before choosing any finish coat, think about the following: How much protection will your object's surface need to give good service, how will it feel to the hand (if the piece is going to be handled), how will it look (especially if the piece will be in raking light that may reveal its imperfections), and, most importantly, how will it relate to the layer it covers. For instance, you wouldn't want to put shellac over an alcohol-soluble layer (such as a patina on leaf that was alcohol-soluble) because the alcohol in the shellac finish would dissolve the existing patina. Likewise, you'll have to be careful about putting shellac over an acrylic layer, since dried acrylics are alcohol-soluble. For additional information on the issue of layering and finish coats, review The Concept of Layering on page 140.

Carefully read and compare label information on the various containers of finish-coat materials you're considering, including the solvent to be used to thin and clean up the finish, its degree of sheen (high gloss, medium, or low luster), drying time, coverage, temperature restrictions (meaning the temperatures at which to use and store the product), and any special instructions for the products' use. After you decide which finish option you want to select (see Options for Finishes below), try the finish on the similar sample surfaces that you've made or on odd pieces of wood.

Options for Finishes

After answering the questions posed above in Choosing a Finish, you have four possible options for finishing the surfaces of objects: (1) leaving a low- or semi-gloss finish "as is," meaning you do nothing else to it; (2) rubbing down a high-gloss finish with steel wool and wax; (3) producing a rich, fine-furniture finish; and, for wood only, (4) creating an oil-resin finish that penetrates the wood. The effects of each treatment and the differing amounts of effort each requires are described below.

LOW- OR SEMI-GLOSS FINISH LEFT "AS IS"

Leaving a surface as is—meaning with just a couple of unpolished coats of low-luster or semi-gloss finish—is suitable for an informal object that doesn't need much protection and will not be placed in strong, raking light.

If an object needs more protection, apply two coats of high-gloss finish (letting each one dry before applying the next coat), followed by a lower-luster finish coat; but don't polish any of these coats. High-gloss finishes offer better protection than low-luster finishes since materials like mica, silica, talc, and wax are added to lower-luster finishes to reduce sheen; but they also reduce strength.

HIGH-GLOSS FINISH RUBBED DOWN WITH STEEL WOOL AND WAX

Objects with several high-gloss finish coats that have been rubbed down with steel wool and wax feel better to the touch and look better under moderate (but not direct) lighting than when left in a high-gloss state. Unpolished high-gloss finishes are too harsh on both the eye and the hand. To create this finish, follow the steps below:

STEP 1: APPLY HIGH-GLOSS FINISH

Apply two coats of high-gloss finish, letting the first coat dry before applying the second coat and letting it dry, too.

STEP 2: RUB DOWN WAX WITH STEEL WOOL

Dip a pad of #0000 steel wool into a good-quality wax, and rub the surface parallel with the grain, using moderate pressure. Keep unraveling the pad of steel wool to expose fresh areas as the steel wool gets saturated with wax (rolling the used-up steel wool into its own pad at the other end). Rubbing reduces the sheen of the high-gloss finish but will not level the surface of all imperfections.

This very early-eighteenth-century English Queen Anne chair became even more handsome after an oil-resin finish brought out the figure of the walnut veneers and solid wood.

RICH, FINE-FURNITURE FINISH

This finish resembles the finish on fine antiques. It's quite labor-intensive but is well worth the effort, particularly for tabletops and other objects that will be handled and seen under varied lighting conditions. For directions on applying this finish, see Steps for a Fine-Furniture Finish on page 187.

OIL-RESIN FINISH

An oil-resin finish is totally different from other finishes. This finish is applicable on wood only, as it penetrates and fills the open pores and cells in the wood, producing a mellow, low-luster sheen that's impervious to heat, water, and alcohol (above). While it doesn't have the high sheen of some other finishes, it has a special beauty and richness of its own. It darkens raw wood and imparts a richness to both formal and informal objects. It's easier to apply than other finishes and can be renewed with little effort. Instructions can be found in Steps for Working with Oil-Resin Finish on page 180.

STEPS FOR A FINE-FURNITURE FINISH

Follow the steps below to apply a fine-furniture finish:

Step 1: Apply Multiple Coats of High-Gloss Finish
Apply four to six coats of a high-gloss finish, letting each one dry before applying the next. After applying the first two or three coats, sand the dried surface with #220 grit open-coat sandpaper, and use a tack cloth.

Step 2: Abrade with Wet/Dry Sandpaper
Place two separate, 1½-inch square pieces of #400-grit, wet/dry silicone-carbide sandpaper on top of one another, both with grit side down; and moisten the pair with water. Begin to abrade the surface with the sandpaper, using moderate pressure. Sand approximately 3-inch-square areas, rubbing with the grain if the surface is wood.

With a damp cheesecloth square, wipe the sanded areas, which, when dry, will reveal a dull gray surface (indicating that the gloss has been reduced and the surface is smoother). Complete sanding the entire surface, then repeat the process using #600-grit wet/dry silicone-carbide sandpaper.

Step 3: Polish with Rottenstone-Oil Paste
Mix rottenstone (start with 2 tablespoons for a small surface) and half as much water or linseed oil into a paste on a palette. Don an old leather glove to polish the surface with the mixture, bringing up a rich sheen and smooth hand. Then buff the surface with a tightly woven cloth (like a piece of men's suiting fabric).

APPLYING FINISHES

After choosing a finish option from those listed above (except for an oil-resin finish), consider the following concerns with regard to applying finishes. You'll find instructions on how to apply a finish on page 188.

→ If possible, apply finishes on dry, mild days in an environment that's as dust-free as possible.

→ Apply the finish on a level, horizontal surface to prevent "pooling" at a lower end. Shore up the lower end, if necessary.

→ Use good-quality, ox-hair brushes for applying finishes. Dip only half the bristles in the finish, gently squeezing out the excess against the inside of the container (dragging the brush against the rim can cause air bubbles to form in the finish).

→ Brush out any sags or drips in the finish that may have spilled over the edges of your object before they have a chance to set.

→ While working, keep some sort of "pick stick" handy to pick up dust particles before they become embedded in the finish. In the eighteenth century, a bit of rosin on the end of a stick was used. We've used any kind of a sticky substance, including a folded, sticky-side-out piece of tape.

→ Allow every coat to dry thoroughly (see label directions). Sand lightly with #220 grit open-coat sandpaper between coats to supply tooth, and wipe with a tack cloth before adding new coats.

After curing, the finish coat had to be abraded to remove the imprint of a moving-van quilt, which had been wrapped around the surface too early in the drying process.

STEPS FOR APPLYING A FINISH

Follow the steps below to apply a finish:

Step 1: Decant Small Amount of Finish

Pour enough finish from the original container to fill a third of an empty soup can, and replace the lid on the mother lode tightly. If using varnish, set the soup can in a pan of hot water away from any flame to warm the contents.

Step 2: Load Brush and Apply Finish

Load a brush half-way, gently squeezing out the excess on the inside of the soup can. Using light to medium pressure, bush on the finish along the grain with as few, long, parallel strokes as possible. If the brush's bristles bend, you're using too much pressure.

Step 3: Brush at Right Angles to Original Strokes

While the first coat is still workable, brush at right angles to the original strokes. Then, using only the bristles' tips and an almost-dry brush, end with strokes parallel to the first ones. Alternating directions thins the medium, enabling it to dry better and eliminating holidays. If using shellac, work quickly before it dries.

Step 4: Let Dry

Allow the finish to dry thoroughly (see the label). Continue with the steps of the treatment option you've chosen (see Options for Finishes on page 185). After completing the last step, allow the finish to cure for at least a week.
Any object set on the finish before then may indent or leave a textured impression on the surface (see above).

CARING FOR FURNITURE

Caring for furniture and other objects involves first preventing damage before it occurs by handling the object carefully: Pick a chair up under the seat (not by a crest rail or an arm), and lift it, instead of dragging it. Likewise, resist the temptation to move a table by pulling it along by the tabletop. Also, be careful when vacuuming not to bang into furniture feet and bases.

Careless dusting with a loose-weave cloth could easily catch and pull off these pieces of inlaid veneer.

Cleaning

If you have a piece that may have an original surface under later coatings, don't clean it until you have it analyzed (see Analyzing Objects for Restoration in Chapter 1) to determine the best cleaning strategy. Otherwise, there's no reason not to clean an object's surface of dirt and grime so that you can enjoy its beauty, hand, and possibly sentimental value.

DUSTING

Dusting is the least damaging way to clean and prolong the life of an object with intact finish coats. Be aware, however, that dust cloths can catch on edges and lift veneers, as might well happen with the veneers in the photo above. Also note that the quills and shafts on feather dusters can break and scratch a surface. Instead use one of the safest dusting implements: a slightly damp chamois cloth (available in auto supply stores), a hake brush (a full-bodied, white-haired Asian brush sold in art supply stores), or a short-handled, full-haired complexion brush (sold with beauty supplies). Do not, however, use dusting sprays of any kind.

REMOVING DIRT AND GRIME

Most accumulations on surfaces are a combination of dirt and dust mixed in with household air-borne elements that produce a grease-like film. Dozens of cleaning products and formulas exist, but the one we've had great success with—both to eliminate the accumulated film and to polish the surface—is simple: Dampen a household, soap-filled, steel-wool pad, and rub it with slight pressure along the grain, if it is wood, in a small area. Wipe the area clean and dry it with a paper towel or cloth; then feel the difference between that area and the neighboring, untreated one. (For information on eliminating white rings and bloom, see Removing White Rings and Bloom on page 173.)

Using the information in this chapter will protect and prolong the life of your furnishings for many years to come. We hope, as well, that exploring and mastering the restoration techniques we've described will bring you pleasure and a sense of pride in being the nurturing guardian of the objects that surround you.

Nº 9 ‖ Restoring Gilding

GILDING IS THE APPLICATION of very thin leaves of precious or common metal to a surface to lend it a luminous, reflective radiance. Dating back thousands of years to Africa and ancient Egypt and Greece, gilding has long been practiced in various cultures around the world, and is still done today. The best-known form of gilding is that applied on top of surfaces like wood, porcelain, leather, and metal. Less well known, but endowed with its own lengthy history, is gilding behind glass (also called reverse gilding or *verre églomisé*) and refers to leaf that's applied to the reverse side of glass. These two types of gilding share some of the same techniques, tools, and supplies, but the methods for working with them are distinct.

The first part of this chapter addresses the tools, materials, and techniques used for water and mordant gilding, as well as for matching gilded surfaces. The second part of the chapter explores the procedures for restoring gilding behind glass.

Water gilding a surface with real gold leaf and then using a burnishing tool gives the object the illusion of being solidified, molten gold, as seen in the already-burnished molding near the gilder.

Photo courtesy of Sydney Miller

GILDING ON A SURFACE

Adhering leaf to a surface can be done in two ways, each producing a different visual effect: The first method, called *water gilding*, is done with real gold leaf that's burnished (polished) to give the illusion that the entire object is made of solidified, molten gold.

The second approach is called *mordant gilding* (and is also known as *oil* or *size gilding*) because the leaf is attached with a size (technically termed a *siccatif*), which is a liquid used to adhere leaf (for a full discussion on sizes see page 196. Mordant gilding can be done with either real gold or with metal leaf. However, even when well done, it doesn't produce the solidified, molten appearance of water gilding.

Before addressing how to attach leaf to a surface, let's first look at the various kinds of leaf available for restoration. There are two basic types of leaf: precious leaf, which is real gold and silver leaf that comes in several forms, and metal leaf, which is made of metals like copper, zinc, and aluminum. Both kinds of leaf are available from specialized suppliers listed in the Resources on page 268.

For centuries, real gold leaf has been used in religious and secular art for luminous backgrounds and fine details. In fact, the numerous medieval recipes for imitating gold by coating tin with transparent yellow varnishes (called *auripetrum*) attests to gold leaf's popularity. For just as long, furniture and objects have been covered and decorated with real gold leaf.

Precious Leaf

Precious leaf can be composed of gold, palladium (a not-so-precious—or "noble," as is sometimes said—form of leaf), or silver. There are more than thirty varieties of real leaf available. The purest gold leaf contains 100 percent gold, and is designated as 24kt. "Kt" comes from the Arabic word *carat,* meaning "bean" or "seed," and is the abbreviation for karat, which is the unit used to measure gold's purity. When the gold content is reduced by alloying (mixing) it with other metals, like silver and copper, the gold changes color and name. Depending on its gold content, the gold alloy is known as French Pale (22kt), Lemon Gold (18kt), or White Gold (12kt, or only 35 percent gold). Pure silver leaf is all silver, and there are no less-pure varieties of silver leaf.

HOW GOLD LEAF IS MADE

Gold leaf is made by, first, melting gold, molding it into a bar, passing it between rollers to flatten it into a ribbon about 1⁄800 th of an inch thick, and then cutting the ribbon into 1-inch squares. After several separate beatings to make the leaf even thinner, the squares are eventually reduced to sheets that are so thin—about 1⁄250,000 th of an inch thick—that light shines through them. Finally, the sheets are cut into 3⅜-inch squares, packaged between rouged paper that has been treated with a reddish iron-oxide powder, which is used for polishing metal. The leaf is sold in books containing twenty-five leafs, and are referred to as "loose leaf."

Despite the fact that the karat content of a given alloy "category" of gold leaf stays constant from one manufacturer to another (meaning that all 22kt leaf has the same gold content, regardless of the company selling it), it may be surprising to discover that there are so many differences in how various brands of leaf behave and are packaged. Happily, however, with regard to the differing color tones of various brands, manufacturers assemble color charts of their leaf so restorers and artists can choose the color that best suits their needs. Regardless of brand, precious leaf can be used for both water and mordant gilding.

PATENT, OR TRANSFER, LEAF

Gold, silver, and palladium leaf are also available adhered to a backing. When in this form, it is called *patent leaf*, or transfer leaf. Patent leaf also comes in books containing twenty-five leafs as well as in rolls or ribbons of many different widths. Patent leaf is particularly useful when loose leaf cannot be used—for instance, on ceilings or for gilding outdoors, which is aptly termed *gilding in the wind*. Patent leaf can be used for mordant gilding but not for water gilding.

Since patent leaf is made in limited "colors," meaning that only several set amounts of alloy are used to produce the color variations for commercially available patent leaf, we had to make our own patent leaf for certain restorations to match colors of gold leaf. You may find it helpful to know how to do this, too, guided by the directions below.

Steps for Making Patent Leaf

To make your own patent leaf, gather a book of leaf, a brayer (a roller with a handle), and wax paper, and then follow the directions below:

STEP 1: EXPOSE LEAF OF GOLD IN BOOK

Open a book of leaf very slowly and gently to expose one leaf, as seen in the photo at right.

Pictured above is a book of leaf with one leaf exposed.

STEP 2: COVER LEAF WITH WAXED PAPER

Place a square of household waxed paper that is a little larger than a sheet of leaf carefully and slowly over the leaf.

STEP 3: BRAYER OVER WAXED PAPER

Using a brayer, photographed below left, roll it slowly over the leaf several times. Alternatively, rub the flat underside of your fingers lightly over the waxed paper to adhere the leaf as shown in the photo below right.

Place a square of wax paper over a sheet of leaf in the book, and roll the brayer over the wax paper to adhere it to the leaf, as pictured far left. Instead of using a brayer, you can also rub the wax paper with the flat of your fingers to adhere it to the leaf, illustrated at left.

STEP 4: TURN OVER WAXED PAPER

After adhering the leaf to the wax paper, turn the wax paper over to expose the leaf.

STEP 5: PROTECT LEAF WITH ROUGED PAPER

Until you're ready to use the patent leaf, protect it with the rouged paper that covered the loose leaf in the book of leaf.

POWDER GOLD OR SILVER LEAF

Precious leaf also comes in powder form, which has several uses in restoration, such as touching up gold or silver leafing, making ink for manuscript illumination, and duplicating decorative techniques of Japanese *maki-e*—which are techniques that involve sprinkling particles of leaf on prepared surfaces. Powders can be purchased from suppliers (see Resources on page 268), or, for economy's sake, you can make your own from precious leaf. Powder leaf may be used for mordant gilding but not for water gilding.

To Make Your Own Powder Leaf

Lightly tap a dry, soft-haired brush, which hasn't touched liquids, up and down on a sheet of gold leaf to pulverize it, as shown in photo A on the opposite page. The particles will become finer the longer you tap, eventually turning to dust. The gold powder will last indefinitely, and can be stored in a paper envelope.

To apply powdered leaf, push the pulverized leaf through a fine tea strainer that is held over the sized area you want to gild. Alternatively, you can sprinkle the pulverized leaf through a tool called a *tsu-tsu*, which is a hollow bamboo tube with mesh covering one end. They are available with meshes with variously sized openings.

To make your own tsu-tsu tube, tape a piece of nylon stocking over one end of a rolled-up paper tube. Photo B on opposite page shows powdered leaf being tapped through a hand-rolled paper tube over a sized area of an insect's wings. The powdered leaf that didn't adhere to the size was brushed away. Photo C on opposite page displays powder gold that was sprinkled on the wings of the butterflies and insects (in imitation of a Japanese sprinkled *maki-e* technique called *Nashiji*); burnished gold that was used on the bodies of the butterflies and insects; matte gold (gold leaf that hasn't been burnished) that was sprinkled on the solid portions of the wings; and shell gold (see below) that was used on the veins of the wings.

SHELL GOLD

Shell gold is made into round and rectangular tablets of powdered gold or silver that are formed with a water-soluble substance called *gum Arabic*. They are used for applying fine lines of gold or silver, and for touch-ups. To make your own shell gold, which, of course, is less expensive than buying it, you can mix your own powdered gold with gum arabic. You'll have to arrive at the proportions of powdered gold-to-gum arabic by a little trial and error, since there is no set formula. If too little powder is used, the results will be colorless and runny. If too much powder is used, the mix will look grainy and not flow well.

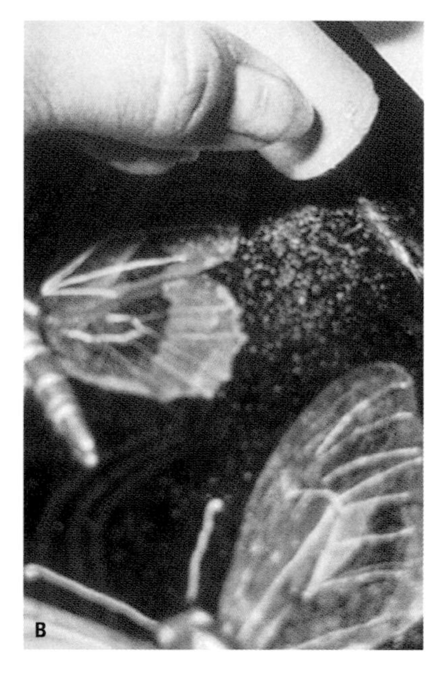

Use a soft-bristled brush to make your own powdered gold leaf, dabbing the brush into the sheet of leaf to break it into fine particles (A). In photo B, the powdered gold being tapped through a paper cardboard tube (as it's done with a *tsu-tsu* tube in the Japanese *Nashiji* technique) will adhere only to the sized area on the insect's wing, and the excess powder will be brushed away. The detail photo of a demonstration piece in photo C shows four different uses of leaf: powdered gold sprinkled on the "triangular" areas of the wings, burnished gold covering the butterflies' bodies, matte gold on the "solid" parts of the wings, and shell gold creating the veins in the wings. Photo D is the entire display of the butterflies.

Metal Leaf

The second basic kind of leaf is metal leaf. It has been used for centuries, especially when made of tin. Nowadays there are four different types of metal leaf in use: composition, aluminum, variegated, and copper leaf.

→ Composition leaf, also called Dutch metal, looks like a version of real gold leaf, but is made from various combinations of copper and zinc. Varying the proportions of this mixture produces several colors of composition leaf. Using 90 percent copper and 10 percent zinc yields the warmest, reddest color, while a mixture of 82 percent copper and 18 percent zinc creates a cooler, more "lemony" color.

→ Aluminum leaf—sometimes called *composition,* or *imitation,* silver—is 100 percent aluminum, and is shinier than silver. But, unlike silver, aluminum leaf will not tarnish.

→ Variegated leaf is composition leaf that has been heat-treated to produce brilliant red, blue, green, and black splashes of color.

→ Copper leaf is 100 percent copper, which produces the warmest, reddest color of all the metal leafs.

Composition, variegated, and copper leafs must be protected from tarnishing in the future. Conversely, these three types of leaf can be tarnished chemically to provide a wide variety of effects.

All four variations of metal leaf are made into 5½-inch square sheets and packaged in books of twenty-five leafs each. Metal leaf is too thick to be used for water gilding, but either loose metal leafs or patent metal leaf (made by the same method described in Patent, or Transfer, Leaf on page 193) can be used for mordant gilding. Stay current with new types of metal leaf that become available by requesting catalogs of gilding products from specialty suppliers (see Resources on page 268).

MORDANT GILDING

Practiced since ancient times, mordant gilding is less complicated than water gilding, so let's start with the simpler of the two techniques. As mentioned earlier, mordant gilding uses a size, or siccatif, to adhere either precious leaf or metal leaf to a surface. In past centuries gums from plant sources and glair, made from egg white, were used as sizes. Nowadays specialized gilders still use these sizes, but most gilders work with commercially prepared size products, which we'll look at next.

Sizes for Mordant Gilding

There are two types of liquid size used to adhere leaf in mordant gilding: (1) size soluble with paint thinner and (2) size soluble with water. Both are discussed below, as are the directions for applying them.

PAINT-THINNER-BASED SIZES

Getting the optimum brilliance from the leaf laid in mordant gilding with paint-thinner-based sizes relates to the "open time," or the time it takes for the size to come to "tack"—that is, be ready for leaf to be laid on it. The longer the size takes to come to tack, the more luminous the resulting leaf will be. And the longer it takes size to come to tack, the longer the "window of opportunity" in which to lay the leaf will be.

Correct tack is reached when (1) there's no pull on your knuckle when touched quickly to the size and (2) you can hear a slight "click" as you draw your knuckle away. The tack required for the most successful leafing is the very driest possible for precious leaf, and slightly less dry for metal leaf.

There are many paint-thinner-based sizes, which provide a wide range of open time and windows of opportunity for leafing. For instance, *quick size* (a generic term for any size that reaches tack quickly) reaches tack in one to three hours, and leafing must be done during a short period after the correct tack is reached. By comparison, slow size takes 12 hours to come to tack and allows from 12 to 18 hours thereafter in which to apply leaf. These time guidelines usually work well, but not always. For example, we well remember once leafing at 3 a.m., five hours later than planned. Bear in mind that temperature and humidity, among other factors, influence many materials used in gilding (as in many other restoration procedures).

WATER-BASED SIZES

Water-based sizes are used more with metal leaf than gold leaf, and for interior rather than exterior use, which means they're rarely used in restoration. Currently, many brands do not flow and level out as well as paint-thinner-soluble sizes. Therefore, the surface can show brush marks. To counter this, dilute the size with a bit of water for better leveling. Make sure you read the label for the correct proportions. Water-based sizes can be leafed as soon as they turn clear (they are milky white at the outset), which can happen in as little as 15 minutes. Their open time is long, from 24 to 30 hours or longer.

Prepare Surface Before Applying Size

Surfaces are leafed to simulate real metals. Badly prepared surfaces will greatly mar this illusion. Therefore, refer to Chapter 4 for guidelines on surface preparation that will produce a smooth, unblemished surface on which to gild.

Leaf must be laid on a nonabsorbent surface, whether flat or carved. If size is absorbed into a surface, it will not reach the correct degree of tack, and therefore won't allow the leaf to adhere. There are several options for producing a nonabsorbent surface for mordant gilding: (1) Use a specific paint-thinner-based gilding primer (see Resources on page 268); (2) apply any gloss paint that can be diluted to level out smoothly; or (3) coat the surface with shellac or varnish to provide a slick, unbroken expanse (see Traditional Finishes on page 181 in Chapter 8). The higher the surface's sheen, the more brilliant the leafing will be.

BUILDING A TOOLKIT: MORDANT-GILDING TOOLS

You will need the following tools for mordant gilding:

- → Stiff-bristled brush
- → Cotton wad
- → Piece of nylon stocking
- → Elastic band
- → Books of leaf
- → Single-edged razor blade
- → Talcum powder
- → Sterile cotton
- → Envelope(s)

A nontraditional way to match the lines of low-dimensional surface designs (*pastiglia*), is to etch the designs first with an X-ACTO knife, then apply white glue directly to the etched lines and let it dry before gilding the surface.

If you need to duplicate missing dimensional carvings before making the surface nonabsorbent, see Chapter 5 on mold-making and casting. In addition to duplicating mid- to high-level dimensional elements with molds and casts, there may be times when you need to reproduce low-level dimensional elements, like *pastiglia* (slightly raised elements under gilding), which is pictured on page 197. A nontraditional way to do this that we learned from a manuscript illuminator is to apply white glue directly from the nozzle of its squeezable plastic container—or through a cake-decorating tube—to match existing pastiglia that you trace and transfer to the surface where needed. Before doing this, etch cross-hatched lines in the appropriate area with the tip of an X-ACTO knife to provide some tooth to the surface to enable material added to it to bond tightly.

Preparing a "Bob" to Spread Size

A "bob," or soft cotton wad encased in a smooth, absorbent covering, is very useful for spreading and smoothing liquid material and absorbing any excess. It's particularly good for thinning paint-thinner-based size into a sheer layer after it's applied with a brush, so it comes to tack more quickly and allows the leaf to appear more brilliant.

To make a bob, you will need an 8- or 9-inch square of untextured silk, a wad of sterile cotton, and a small elastic band. Then proceed as follows:

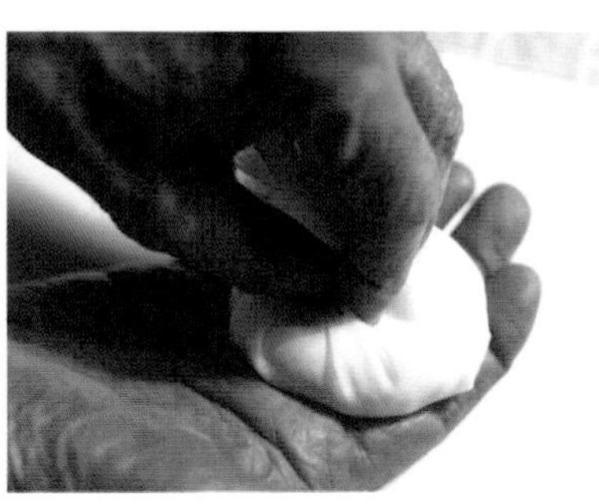

Make a bob to spread the size with a square of silk, a cotton wad, and a rubber band. After wrapping the bob with the rubber band, tap it sharply on your palm to flatten it.

STEP 1: PLACE COTTON IN SILK SQUARE

With the cotton in the center of the silk square, pull up the fabric's four corners.

STEP 2: TWIST AND SECURE WRAPPED WAD

Twist the silk-wrapped cotton wad making a tightly enclosed ball, and wrap an elastic band around it several times just above the ball.

STEP 3: FLATTEN WAD'S SHAPE

Flatten the ball shape by rapping it sharply against the palm of your hand while holding the end with the excess silk.

Applying Size

Paint-thinner-based size and water-based size differ not only in the time they take to reach tack but also in the window of opportunity for leafing. As well, they require different techniques for their application. Below are some tips for applying any type of size:

Whether you're working with paint-thinner-based or water-based size, here are some tips that you may find helpful for applying it:

→ Size (and later leaf) vertical objects from the bottom upwards.

→ For clean corners when leafing a box-shaped object, size opposite, not adjacent, sides. First lay and polish the leaf on opposite sides before applying size to the remaining un-leafed two sides.

Apply size to deep carvings in two stages (unless you're painting the base of the carving yellow ochre, in which case see Leafing Carvings on page 203). In stage 1, size the deepest points of the carvings nearly up to the top of the carvings with a stiff-bristled brush that doesn't have too much size on it (excess size will take too long to come to tack). In stage 2, size the tops of carvings only after leafing the depths of the carvings.

APPLYING PAINT-THINNER-BASED SIZE

Before applying paint-thinner-based size to a surface to be leafed, you need to "prep" the surface so any spots that miss getting sized will show up when you apply the size. Prep the surface in one of two ways: You can mix the size with yellow-ochre paint-thinner medium (note that colored size will take longer to come to tack, depending on how much paint is added). Alternatively, you can sprinkle ordinary talcum powder on the surface that will be sized and then blow off the excess powder from the work area. The dulled surface will show up any missed spots when you apply the shiny size. Next, apply the paint-thinner-based size, following the steps below:

STEP 1: APPLY THE SIZE WITH A BRUSH

Dip a stiff-bristled brush partially into the size, and apply it to the surface you're gilding, smoothing the size out as much as possible, particularly if there are crevices where the size will accumulate. Change directions several times as you apply the size to eliminate "holidays" (missed areas).

STEP 2: STROKE THE APPLIED SIZE WITH THE BOB

Follow immediately by stroking the applied size slowly and firmly with both the wide and narrow parts of the bob, as in the photo below.

After applying size to the surface to be gilded, spread it evenly with a bob, which will absorb the excess. The matte, talcum-powdered surface on the frame's left, which hasn't received size yet (which is what any "holiday," or area missing size, would look like) contrasts with the shiny sized area on the right.

TIPS FOR SUCCESSFUL LEAFING

Below are some tips for successfully leafing an object:

- → Approach the task of laying leaf with a calm, unhurried, patient attitude.
- → As much as possible, lay leaf in a draft-free environment.
- → While leafing, don't allow anything—fingers, brush, or cotton—to touch sized areas.
- → Keep all loose leaf far away from the sized areas. It leaf touches any sized area, it will stick to it permanently.
- → Use the tip of a toothpick to separate each edge of leaf from the rouged paper to make picking up the leaf easier.
- → When working on a vertical surface, lay loose leaf from the bottom upwards to prevent small pieces of leaf from falling into the sized areas below.

STEP 3: SET SIZED OBJECT ASIDE

Set the sized object aside in a dust-free environment to allow it to come to tack.

APPLYING WATER-BASED SIZE

Applying water-based size requires no preparation of the surface with colored size or powder. Just follow the steps below:

STEP 1: THIN SIZE

You can thin the size up to 20 percent with water, making it easier to spread and level out. Still, the size may be too thick to spread with a bob.

STEP 2: APPLY SIZE

Dip the tip of a foam brush or another brush into the size, and apply it to the surface as carefully as possible without going over any sized area again.

STEP 3: SET SIZED OBJECT ASIDE

Set the sized object aside in a dust-free environment. The size will turn milky and be ready to leaf (according to the label directions) in as little as 15 minutes. It will remain ready to leaf for many hours, possibly a day.

Laying Loose Leaf

Before you lay loose leaf, there are a couple of preparatory things to do:

1. In order to lift out the leaf from a book of metal leaf, cut the book's spine with a sharp, single-edged razor blade, working from the middle out to each end in separate strokes. To cut leaf narrower than full width, position the book with the spine at the top and, using a razor blade, cut the book vertically from the spine to the bottom edge. Don't use scissors to try to cut the book; they will mash the edges of the leaf.

2. Assemble envelopes or containers—a separate one for each type of leaf you're working with—to collect excess leaf that you'll remove after leafing. This excess leaf is called *skewings.*

3. Powder your fingertips using talcum powder to prevent leaf from sticking to them. Do the powdering away from any sized surface, and at the same time get rid of any excess.

STEPS FOR LAYING LOOSE LEAF

Despite the fact that metal leaf is comparatively thick compared to gold leaf, the method below for laying loose metal leaf on a sized surface gives you control of placing the leaf, and is good to use if you've never handled leaf.

There are two points to remember about laying any leaf: (1) any piece of leaf that lands on a sized surface is there to stay, whether or not you want it there, and (2) one piece of leaf will not stick to another piece of leaf. In other words, only one sheet of leaf will stick to a sized surface. Follow the steps on page 201 for laying loose and patent leaf:

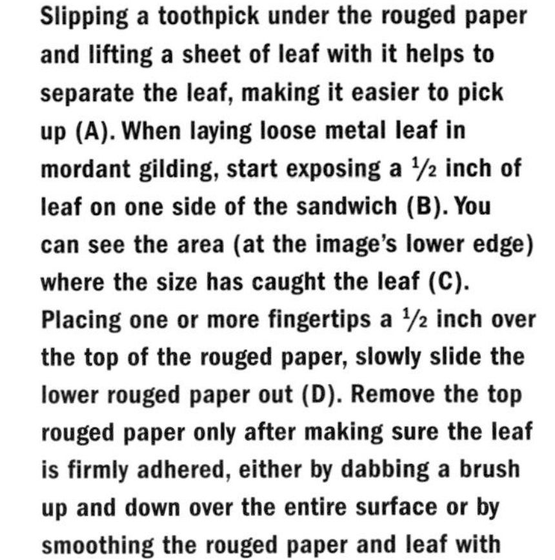

Slipping a toothpick under the rouged paper and lifting a sheet of leaf with it helps to separate the leaf, making it easier to pick up (A). When laying loose metal leaf in mordant gilding, start exposing a ½ inch of leaf on one side of the sandwich (B). You can see the area (at the image's lower edge) where the size has caught the leaf (C). Placing one or more fingertips a ½ inch over the top of the rouged paper, slowly slide the lower rouged paper out (D). Remove the top rouged paper only after making sure the leaf is firmly adhered, either by dabbing a brush up and down over the entire surface or by smoothing the rouged paper and leaf with the flat of your fingers (E).

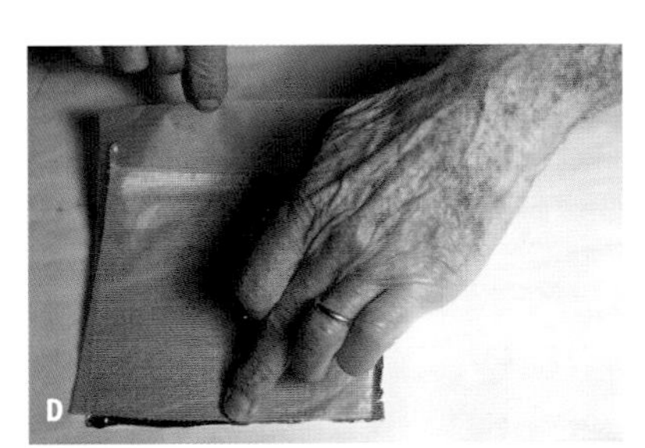

STEP 1: SEPARATE LEAF AND ROUGED PAPER WITH TOOTHPICK

Carefully slip the tip of a toothpick under a rouged paper below a sheet of leaf to make picking up the leaf easier (photo A above).

STEP 2: SANDWICH LEAF BETWEEN ROUGED PAPERS

If you're using composition, aluminum, variegated, or copper leaf, sandwich a sheet of leaf between two rouged papers, with the top rouged paper positioned ½ inch lower than the top of the leaf (see photo B above).

STEP 3: DETERMINE WHERE TO LAY LEAF

Holding the sandwich between your hands, turn it over, and decide where you want to lay the leaf. Remember that once any part of the exposed leaf touches the sized surface, the leaf cannot be moved.

STEP 4: LAY EXPOSED LEAF ON SIZED SURFACE

Tilting the back end of the sandwich (the one nearest you) up away from the sized surface, lay only the exposed ½ inch of leaf on the sized surface, as illustrated in photo C on page 201. Then remove the rouged paper now below the sheet of leaf, illustrated in photo D.

STEP 5: REMOVE TOP ROUGED PAPER

Before removing the top rouged paper, make sure the leaf is completely adhered to the size by dabbing a soft-haired brush over the entire rouged paper in an up-and-down motion. Alternatively, smooth the rouged paper and leaf with the flat of your fingers. When you're convinced that all the leaf is adhered to the surface, lift off the top rouged paper, as illustrated in photo E.

STEP 6: RELEASE LEAF FROM WAXED PAPER, IF USED

If you're using patent leaf, pick up the wax paper with the leaf attached, lay it on the surface (leaf facing down), and press gently to release the leaf. If all the leaf doesn't transfer, correct this by patching the missing area with the leaf remaining on the waxed paper, as in the photo below.

It's easy to cut patent leaf into small sections that can be used to patch holidays, or missing areas of leaf.

STEP 7: TO LEAF MULTI-SHEET AREAS

For leafing surfaces larger than one sheet, size the whole area. Lay the first sheet of leaf as instructed above. Place the second sheet of leaf a ½ inch over the side edge of the already-adhered sheet of leaf, still keeping the sandwich tilted up in the air as above. Don't lay the exposed ½ inch on the sized surface before making sure that the top edge of the sandwich is aligned with the already-laid leaf, as seen in Step 4. While the leaf sandwich is still tilted up, slide the bottom rouged paper away from the side edge so that ¼ inch of leaf is exposed along the side edge. As you lower the sandwich, slide the bottom rouged paper toward you, allowing the now exposed leaf to adhere to the side overlap and the sized surface. Smooth the top sheet of rouged paper and leaf as before, so the leaf adheres securely to the surface, paying particular attention to

The surface is leafed with overlapping leaves of aluminum. Any excess leaf will be carefully removed later in the process.

pressing the leaf firmly along the line where the edge of the lower leaf ends. This ensures that there will not be any gap between the lines of leafing. Repeat this overlapping procedure until all the leaf is laid and there's an unattached ¼-inch flap of leaf all around the leafed squares, as shown above.

REPAIRING HOLIDAYS

If you discover holidays immediately after leafing a surface, repair them at once with the leaf taken from the book of leaf or from a piece of loose leaf. Make sure when repairing holidays that the same side of the leaf is laid upward as that on the leaf already laid, since some brands of leaf differ slightly from top side to underside.

In order to get the new leaf to adhere to the exposed size of a holiday that may be almost dry, take a deep breath and exhale slowly and deliberately from your mouth onto the areas missing leaf to reactivate the size. If you patch with leaf immediately, you may not have to add size to the missed area. If the size in the area is already dry and must be reapplied, use as dry a brush as possible, and don't leaf too soon after sizing. Err on the side of waiting too long (at least as long as after the initial sizing) rather than leafing too soon.

LEAFING CARVINGS

When leafing carvings with deep depressions above eye-level, you may want to follow what eighteenth-century gilders did: Paint yellow ochre in the depths of the carvings. The omission of leaf in these depressions saved time, labor, and expensive leaf. Of course, if the object you're restoring has yellow-ochre paint in the carving's depressions, don't apply size or leaf; instead conform to the original by restoring the yellow-ochre color where it's necessary.

If you want to leaf the depths of your carvings, do this in two steps:

STEP 1: APPLY TWO SHEETS OF LEAF ON CARVED DEPTHS

After the depths of the carvings have reached the right tack, push a minimum of two loose leaves and skewings into these depths with a

Above left: On large surfaces, it's very helpful to vacuum away excess leaf from the depths of carvings.

Above right: When leafing crevices in a deeply carved surface, use a stiff-bristled brush to push the leaf into the recesses (note that you can touch the metal leaf if you've lightly powdered your fingertips).

stiff-bristled brush and cotton swabs, making sure to press and smooth the leaf in place. You'll need several sheets of leaf when leafing carvings because, as one leaf splits, the one behind it will fill in the gap where the size has been exposed (see right photo above). When the size is dry, use a stiff-bristled brush or a vacuum cleaner to remove all excess leaf from the depths of the carvings. Put the loose excess leaf in the proper envelopes you prepared earlier and toss out the vacuumed leaf.

STEP 2: SIZE AND LEAF TOPS OF CARVINGS
Size and leaf the tops of the carvings, whether their depths are covered with leaf or yellow-ochre paint.

Removing Excess Leaf and Polishing the Leaf

Surfaces that have had sheets of leaf laid with a ¼-inch overlap require special handling. Follow the steps below:

STEP 1: FIRMLY PRESS OVERLAPPED EDGES
Before removing excess leaf from overlapped areas, lightly flip the ¼-inch excess, unattached flap of the leaf halfway (but not all the way) back onto the join. Press straight down on the folded excess leaf with your powdered index fingers, and release the pressure before repeating this step slowly all along the join. Carefully pressing the leaf this way ensures that any exposed sliver of size between the joined sheets will "grab" the leaf you're pressing over it. Continue this process slowly until you're finished. Don't remove the excess leaf at this time.

STEP 2: SMOOTH EXCESS LEAF IN SAME DIRECTION
Gently smooth the excess remaining leaf in the same direction of the excess "flap." Don't push the flap back from the overlapped join, which might cause a fine line of the surface underneath to show between the leaves.

STEP 3: REMOVE EXCESS LEAF

Next, remove as much excess leaf as possible, using a soft-haired brush and balls of sterile cotton. Use both gently at first, then press a little more firmly to remove excess leaf. Put this excess leaf in an envelope to prevent it from attaching to exposed size, which will also make clean-up easier.

Keep turning and replacing the cotton balls to reduce scratches from specks of leaf that may be on the cotton. If this process exposes holidays, try not to touch the exposed size, which will cause it to lose its tack. To fix holidays, follow the instructions on page 203 for repairing holidays.

STEP 4: POLISH SURFACE

After the excess leaf is removed, use fresh, sterile cotton to polish the surface of the leaf. Keep rotating and changing the cotton so that bits of leaf caught on the cotton will not scratch the newly laid leaf. While polishing the leaf, you'll probably notice what may look like wrinkles running in many directions. In fact, these wrinkles are lines of excess leaf that didn't get adhered. Use cotton balls to press down firmly along any wrinkles in the leaf, varying the direction according to that of each individual wrinkle.

Your leafed surface is now ready to receive a patina to match the original surface of your restored piece. See Patination for Leaf on page 216 to choose the most suitable media and techniques to blend your restoration in with the original surface of your object.

WATER GILDING

Water gilding is the traditional form of the art that creates the most valued, enduring, and elegant gilding. Although more complicated than mordant gilding, a water-gilded surface of gold leaf appears to be solidified, molten gold, with rich, deep color unmarked by any brassiness, as seen in the photo below.

This detail of a ceiling medallion shows the rich, solid-gold appearance produced by water gilding.

BUILDING A TOOLKIT: WATER GILDING SUPPLIES AND TOOLS

You will need the following tools to water gild an object:

Surface-Preparation Supplies:

→ Rabbit-skin glue granules
→ Tap and distilled water
→ White glue
→ Metal strainer, and nylon hosiery or other fine mesh strainer
→ Gilder's whiting (natural calcium carbonate chalk)
→ Stiff-bristled brush
→ Cheesecloth
→ White silicone carbide wet/dry paper
→ Bole paste
→ Horsehair cloth
→ Burnisher (agate or hematite)

Gilding Supplies and Tools:

→ Book(s) of gold leaf
→ Gilder's cushion (suede-covered pad, also known as a "klinker," that holds leaf firmly and may have a paper cuff to lessen drafts that might disturb loose leaf)
→ Gilder's knife (a knife sharp enough to score and cut leaf into smaller pieces but not sharp enough to cut the gilder's cushion)
→ Gilder's mop (full, soft-haired brush to apply gilder's liquid on the object being gilded, reactivating the rabbit-skin glue in the bole)
→ Gilder's tip (usually made of squirrel hairs, this brush picks up gold leaf from the gilder's cushion)
→ Isopropyl alcohol
→ Burnisher

There are probably as many different formulas for the mixtures of materials used in water gilding as there are gilders—and each gilder believes his or her formula is the best. With that said, the basic materials for preparing a flawless surface for water gilding are the same as gilders have used for centuries: rabbit-skin glue, gesso (pronounced *JE-so*), bole (pronounced *bowl*), and gilder's liquor, all of which are explained in detail below.

Before You Water Gild

As we mentioned, there are three preliminary steps you will need to perform before water gilding. You will have to apply layers of rabbit-skin glue, gesso, and bole (see Resources for suppliers of the ingredients) first in order to prepare the surface for water gilding. The rabbit-skin glue completely seals the wood to prevent shrinkage and expansion, and enables the gesso, a paste-like material that prepares a surface to accept the leaf, to bond well to the wood. Finally, bole is a clay substance that is applied over the gesso to provide the right "cushion" for the leaf. There are many formulas for mixing the rabbit-skin glue, gesso, and bole, but the basic ones are outlined on the next page. We suggest you make parallel samples of each stage to test various formulas.

RABBIT-SKIN GLUE

It would probably take years to experiment with all the different formulas for rabbit-skin glue that are mentioned in various gilding sources, which sometimes range from 1 part rabbit-skin-glue granules to 7 (or up to 15) parts water, with adjustments for seasonal temperature and humidity.

The glue part of these formulas is usually expressed in grams weighed on a gram scale. To convert grams to ounces, multiply the number of grams by .035. For example, 30 grams x .035 equals 1.05 ounces, or a little over an ounce (an ounce is equivalent to two tablespoons). Below, you'll find a basic formula for rabbit-skin glue.

BASIC FORMULA FOR RABBIT-SKIN GLUE

Below are the directions for making a basic formula for rabbit-skin glue:

Step 1: Soak Rabbit-Skin Granules
Soak 30 grams of rabbit-skin glue granules in 8 ounces (1 cup) of water for three to four hours in a heat-proof container (glass is fine) to soften the granules so they become gelatinous and swell in volume (top photo at right).

Step 2: Stir Mixture over Low Heat
Stir over low heat in a double-boiler until all the glue has dissolved (bottom photo at right).

Step 3: Remove from Heat
Remove the double-boiler from the heat, and add 8 ounces (1 cup) of boiling water. Then let it cool a bit. The resulting mixture will be thick and jelly-like, and will develop mold if not used soon after mixing or not refrigerated

Step 4: Apply Glue and Let Dry
While the glue is still hot, use a stiff-bristled brush to coat every surface of raw wood front, back, and rabbet (the recess into which glass is installed in a frame) to seal the wood and prevent it from warping. Let the glue dry overnight.

GESSO

Gesso has traditionally been used to cover flat or carved wood with uniform coats that envelop the wood, smooth it, and provide a solid base for gilding. The formulas for mixing gesso vary with individual gilders, but all of them have several things in common: They're composed,

Gesso that drips like heavy cream from the brush is just the correct consistency.

among other ingredients, of some sort of animal glue and whiting (calcium-carbonate chalk); and they're never boiled, which leads to poor bonding (see Basic Formula for Gesso below).

The relationship of glue stock to whiting is an important factor in making gesso. Glue makes gesso hard, while whiting provides body, bulk, and softness. As you work with gesso, you may need to increase either the glue or whiting to produce gesso that's hard enough to burnish, but not so hard that it won't sand well. Over time, we—and our fellow gilders—have used additives to gesso like white glue, linseed oil, kaolin powder, garlic cloves, sugar, and denatured alcohol to get just the right gesso for environmental conditions. Don't be afraid to experiment—experimenting goes with the territory of being a gilder. To begin with, aim for the consistency of heavy cream.

All the gesso applications should be done at one time to bond the layers together. You'll need six to ten coats to be able to sand and still have a good "cushion" under the leaf. The gesso must be kept warm (body temperature, sometimes called "blood warm"), but it must never boil, which will ruin its strength. As you're working, you'll need to add water as the gesso thickens to maintain a good spreading consistency without brush marks, and to prevent the mixture from becoming too thick. The extra water won't spoil the gesso, but will, instead, evaporate during drying.

BASIC FORMULA FOR GESSO

Below are the directions for making a basic formula for gesso:

Step 1: Combine Glue Stock and Whiting
Combine the remaining rabbit-skin glue stock left after you coated the wood surface in Step 4 on page 207 (which will be less than 8 ounces and still warm) with 12 ounces (1 ½ cups) of whiting (finely ground natural chalk, which is calcium carbonate).

Step 2: Stir with Stiff-Bristled Brush
Using a stiff-bristled brush, stir the mixture slowly (to prevent air bubbles, which create pinholes in the gesso), breaking up any lumps of whiting against the side of the container, shown below.

Step 3: Strain Mixture
Strain the mixture twice through a fine strainer (available from paint stores), or cut a piece of a fine mesh stocking and secure it over a wide-mouthed jar with an elastic band.

Step 4: Clean Brush
Clean the brush with water.

Step 5: Allow Gesso to Cool
Allow the gesso to cool naturally for 15 to 20 minutes.

Step 6: Discard Any Skin That Forms
If a skin forms on top with air bubbles, scoop it out and discard it.

Step 7: Refrigerate Gesso
Refrigerate the gesso until ready to use it. It will become solid and must be warmed to liquefy it for use. When you're ready to apply gesso, plan to do all the coats in one day.

Directions for Applying and Smoothing Gesso

Use the steps below to apply and smooth the gesso:

STEP 1: WARM GESSO

Warm the solidified gesso in a double-boiler to body temperature.

STEP 2: APPLY FIRST COAT OF GESSO

Apply the first coat of gesso with a stiff-bristled brush in an up and down (stippling) motion over the surface, being sure to push the brush into all the depressions, as shown below. This first coat should be textured, to act as "tooth" for the next coats.

STEP 3: APPLY SECOND COAT OF GESSO

The next coat can be applied with an ox-hair or another flexible brush, when the tops of carvings are white (indicating that the first coat of gesso has dried) and while the depressions are still gray (moist). The idea is to have the coats bond to each other. Use long, flowing strokes on flat areas, as shown below, and take excess gesso out of depressions with the edge of a dry, stiff-bristled brush.

STEP 4: APPLY FOUR OR MORE COATS

Add four or more coats of gesso that should be thin enough to coat the surface without any brush strokes. Add water as necessary to the gesso in the container to assure a smooth flow. If you see pinholes in the gesso, push some gesso into them with your fingertips and allow the filled pinholes to dry.

STEP 5: ADJUST SURFACE LAYER OF GESSO

If you notice really built-up areas on edges and corners as you're working, stop and try to trim them level with the surface while they can still be trimmed easily: Use a single-edge razor blade or an X-ACTO blade held horizontally and parallel with the surface, working carefully and slowly. As you add subsequent layers of gesso, each one will take a little longer to dry.

STEP 6: LET GESSO DRY COMPLETELY

The gesso must be completely dry on all areas—corners, edges, carvings, and flats—before any sanding and shaping can be done. This should take at least 24 hours, or maybe longer.

STEP 7: SAND GESSO

When the gesso is thoroughly dry, sand it with #220 grit, white silicone-carbide wet/dry paper (or regular #220 grit open-coat sandpaper). Wipe the surface with a *very* slightly damp cheesecloth. Smooth further with damp cheesecloth wrapped around your index finger and later a piece of horsehair cloth, until the gesso looks and feels like porcelain.

When the gesso is dry, first sand with wet/dry paper (A). Smooth with a damp cloth wrapped around your fingers (B). Finally, using a horsehair cloth, wipe away any dried gesso residue (C).

Photos on pages 209 and 210 courtesy of Sydney Miller

CARVED GESSO

When coating gesso on carved surfaces, it's important not to apply too many layers because they can obscure the crispness of the original relief and distort its carver's intent. To reshape indistinct gessoed carvings, restorers use specially shaped tools (which carve on the pull stroke) in a process called "re-cutting."

By contrast, fine eighteenth-century French frames often contained less precise woodcarvings, over which an unusual number of coats of gesso were applied to give master gesso carvers an amply gessoed surface on which to carve sculptural forms and textures (for example, diaper patterns, called *Quadrillages*). Their art, brought to an unsurpassed level in the 1700s, is called *réparure* (literally "re-ornamentation"), at which the master of the art, the *répareur,* excelled.

Carving Gesso

After building up a dimensional form stroke by stroke with gesso, it can also be "carved" by abrading it with white silicone-carbide paper, horsehair cloth, cheesecloth, small, stiff stencil brushes, and so on. See the detail photo at top right for an in-process example of carved gesso. This corner of a flat, wooden frame, on which we were building up a dimensional gesso swan to match three other corners we'd made, shows several things: The roughness of newly laid gesso brush strokes (on the feathers), the porcelain-like quality of smoothed gesso (on the neck), and the depth gesso can have (see the lower portion of the split miter). Unfortunately, this frame sustained such abuse that the *intelaggio* (the fabric over the miter) could not perform its function. For a completed example of similarly applied and carved gesso, see the bodies of the butterflies and insects on page 195.

Compo, a Kindred Substance

Another type of dimensional ornament very popular in the late eighteenth and nineteenth centuries was made of a material called "compo" (short for *composition*), whose chief ingredients were whiting, resins, and linseed oil. Compo was pressed into molds to form all sorts of casts that were attached to furniture with glue or small pins. Noted English architect Robert Adam made particular use of compo affixed to wire to create intricate pendants and tracery to ornament mirrors and other wall furniture in England in the 1770s. He introduced the French term *Carton-Pierre* for compo.

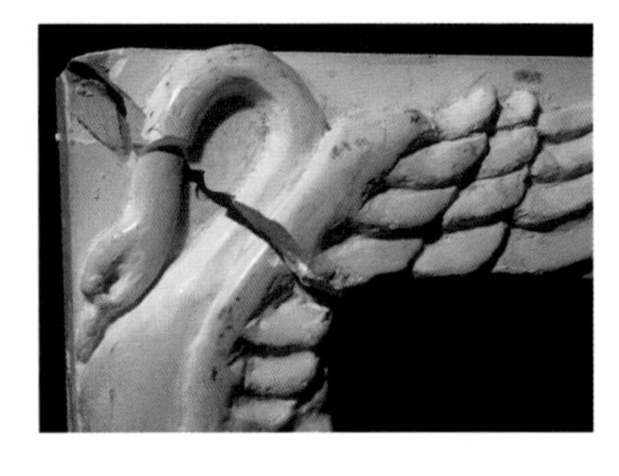

This detail of a damaged corner with a built-up gesso swan shows the depth to which gesso can be layered and then carved.

BOLE

After the gesso has been sanded and has a smooth, flawless appearance, it needs to be covered with a clay substance called *bole,* also known as gilder's clay. One of bole's main characteristics is that it's soft and can be burnished (polished) to a high sheen, while still providing the right support for the gold leaf, just as it has since medieval times.

Along with other tools you will need to work with bole, The photo at the top of page 212 shows the two forms in which bole is available: (1) a cone, which must be ground for use, and (2) an already ground paste, which is easy to use and which is available in the traditional colors—red, yellow ochre, and black—and also in many newer clay colors in grays and blues (which are used under silver and white gold). Traditionally, two different colors of bole are added to carvings: yellow-ochre bole for the lower areas, which will not get burnished and remain matte, and red bole for the higher carvings that will get burnished.

Also shown in the photo are two burnishing tools used to polish bole. Usually made of agate, burnishing tools are currently available in many shapes: A thin, pencil-tipped burnisher is shown at the bottom of the image, and above it is a 100-year-old burnisher, resting on a porcelain-like

Pictured at right are the tools you will need to prepare an extremely smooth surface for gilding. Bole comes in two forms: (1) a paste, and (2) a cone, which can be ground into a paste. Other tools include various burnishers, such as a hematite stone (3), and a contemporary pencil-tipped burnisher (4). Above the pencil-tipped burnisher in the photo is a 100-year-old burnisher (5). A water-gilded, burnished clamshell is also pictured (6).

piece of gesso. Polished stones such as hematite (shown above) can also be used to burnish bole. The high sheen that can be achieved by polishing the bole can be seen on the rail on the far right of an American Empire sofa (c. 1845) in the detail photo at bottom left. The restored sofa is shown in the bottom right photo.

When restoring a surface, try to match the bole color as closely as you can to the color of the original bole. To get the desired color, you can mix two or more bole-paste colors. (By the way, the color of the bole under the damaged leafing that you're restoring may indicate where the object came from: Various red-clay boles, for example, can be seen on many European antiques—from coral bole on many eighteenth-century German frames to almost wine-red bole on eighteenth-century Russian frames. Yellow-ochre clay bole was popular on Italian antiques.)

Above, burnishing the bole produces a high sheen and prepares it for water gilding. At right is the restored, water-gilded, and reupholstered sofa.

Steps for Using Paste Bole

Apply bole with a flexible ox-hair brush in a pourable consistency, like heavy cream, using the steps below. If you can see brush strokes as you apply the bole, thin it out with a little water.

STEP 1: MIX PASTE WITH RABBIT-SKIN GLUE

Mix the paste with rabbit-skin glue in equal proportions, mixing and working with the yellow bole first and then the red bole.

STEP 2: APPLY COATS OF YELLOW-OCHRE BOLE

Apply three or four coats of the yellow-ochre bole paste to the entire surface, letting each dry (for 5 minutes or so) before applying the next one, and then letting all the coats dry.

STEP 3: APPLY RED BOLE COATS

Repeat the process above with one or two coats of a red-clay mixture on the high areas of carvings, edges, and tips of moldings, letting the coats dry about 5 minutes between applications.

STEP 4: POLISH DRIED RED-BOLE SURFACE

Rub the dried red bole with a horsehair cloth to polish the surface, and, if you want, bring up a higher sheen by softly rubbing the surface with the side of a burnisher.

Steps in Water Gilding

After applying the rabbit-glue, gesso, and bole layers, we are now ready to water gild. The first step is to prepare what's called *gilder's liquor,* the liquid that reactivates the rabbit-skin glue in the bole and allows the leaf to adhere to the bole. To make gilder's liquor, mix three parts water to one part isopropyl alcohol, or grain alcohol. Cautionary Note: Do not use methyl alcohol; it is toxic. Tilt the object to be leafed upward, to allow the gilder's liquid to flow evenly from the top to the bottom. Then follow the steps below for laying the leaf:

STEP 1: RUB VASELINE ON BACK OF HAND

Place a very small smear of petroleum jelly (Vaseline) on the back of the hand that won't hold the gilder's tip, and rub it in thoroughly until there's barely any more on the surface of your hand, or give a light coat of lip balm.

STEP 2: REMOVE SINGLE SHEET OF LEAF FROM BOOK

Remove a single sheet of leaf from a book of leaf by opening the book to expose one sheet of leaf and flipping the book over quickly onto the gilder's pad, so the exposed sheet of leaf sticks to the suede on the gilder's pad. Roll the rest of the upended book away from the leaf on the pad, or pull the book away from the pad very slowly. If the leaf isn't lying flat on the pad, exhale quickly with a sharp, short breath on the center of the leaf to flatten it.

STEP 3: CUT SHEET INTO THIRDS

Because cut pieces of leaf are easier to handle and less wasteful than working with a whole sheet of leaf, cut the sheet of leaf in thirds as follows: Place one edge of the gilder's knife on one-third of the leaf and draw it slowly, with even pressure, across the leaf and onto the pad before picking up the knife (if you lift the knife up while it's still on the leaf, the leaf will stick to it). Repeat the process to make the second cut and for the other sheets that you'll need to continue leafing as you need them.

STEP 4: PICK UP HINT OF VASELINE ON GILDER'S TIP

Holding the cardboard end of the gilder's tip parallel to the back of the hand with the Vaseline on it, whisk the hairs of the gilder's tip across the Vaseline or lip balm, picking up a bare minimum.

After laying a single sheet of leaf on the gilder's pad (see directions in Step 2), hold the gilder's tip parallel to the pad to pick up 1/2 inch of the sheet of leaf.

STEP 5: LIFT LEAF FROM PAD WITH GILDER'S TIP

Still holding the tip parallel to the back of your hand, lay the underside of the tip's hairs on the end of the leaf on the pad, and lift the leaf away from the pad, still parallel to it. Because it's such a narrow piece of leaf (a little more than 1 inch), it will not flutter in the air.

STEP 6: LOAD MOP WITH GILDER'S LIQUOR

Holding the gilder's tip and the leaf in one hand, put the gilder's mop into the container with gilder's liquor, and gather up a full load of the liquor to "flood" the area to be leafed (about 3 inches, or the width of the leaf on the tip).

STEP 7: FLOOD AREA TO BE LEAFED WITH LIQUOR AND LAY LEAF

Flood the area you want to leaf with gilder's liquor, and immediately lay the leaf on it, as shown below (the liquor turns the wet bole brown). As you become more experienced, you'll develop a rhythm of flooding the surface and laying the leaf. Repeat flooding the area and laying the leaf, overlapping each leaf 3/8-inch to 1/2-inch over the previous one. Keep the mop in the liquor in between use.

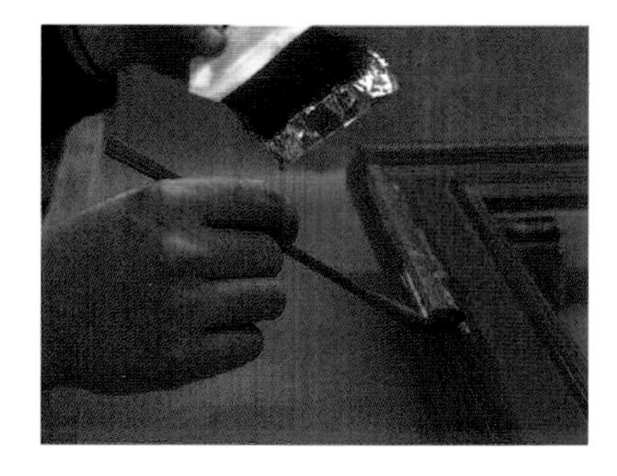

Above: With the piece to be gilded supported on an incline, apply the gilder's liquor with the gilder's mop, starting at the topmost point to be gilded so the liquor can run downhill.

Right: Lay the leaf with a quick in-and-out motion to allow it to "grab" onto the bole (the red substance on the carvings; note also the yellow ochre bole in the depths of the carvings).

Gently rub sterile cotton in a circular motion to remove excess leaf.

STEP 8: PUSH DOWN BRIDGES IN LAID LEAF

When you've completed laying five or six pieces of leaf, pause to address what may become a problem later: With the other, dry end of the gilder's mop (or with another small brush), lightly push down any "bridged" areas of leaf. These are places where leaf has "tented" over a crevice instead of conforming to the depression. Touch the brush to your skin before performing this operation—if the brush isn't totally dry, wait until it is to perform this operation.

STEP 9: REPEAT STEPS 6, 7, AND 8 AS NEEDED

Repeat Steps 6 through 8 until you've completed leafing the entire area.

STEP 10: LET GILDING DRY THOROUGHLY

Allow the gilding to dry thoroughly—even overnight, if necessary—before removing excess gold leaf. When you're ready to remove the excess leaf, tilt the object (if possible) over a clean cardboard box or container (which cannot be plastic since leaf will stick to plastic), and gently sweep the leaf into it with sterile cotton or a dry brush. As you're doing this, gold "dust" may fill up any tiny "faults" (missed areas of leaf), or you can size these missed areas later with a touch of gilder's liquor and then lay the missing leaf.

STEP 11: BURNISH AFTER LEAF IS THOROUGHLY DRY

Allow all leaf to dry thoroughly before burnishing, which is explained in detail below.

BURNISHING LEAF

Burnishing polishes a leafed surface to a high sheen. Use burnishing tools on their sides, not on their tips, taking short strokes to meld the leaf to the bole, but don't scratch the leaf, which can happen if you use too much pressure or a rough burnisher. To keep your burnisher from becoming

Burnish the laid leaf a small area at a time, using short stokes. Here, an agate burnisher is being held with both hands for more control of the burnishing process. The already-burnished area is on the right.

Photos on pages 214 and 215 courtesy of Sydney Miller

rough, cover it with soft flannel between uses. First, try burnishing on your parallel sample, which we suggested making earlier, or an inconspicuous area on your object first to practice your stroke.

Burnish the high points of gilded carving with circular movements and short strokes; then you can use slightly longer strokes on these same areas (as see in the photo on page 215). Leave the lower areas of the carved surface matte—that is to say, don't burnish them. When burnishing a flat surface, use the same strategy of starting with short strokes and then lengthening the strokes. However, avoid using any circular strokes on a flat surface.

ALTERNATE METHOD FOR WATER GILDING

As you can see, the steps involved in water gilding are very time-consuming. Therefore, it's not surprising that a unique gilding system has been developed that uses many of the same materials and techniques we explained in the previous pages about water gilding, but eliminates the tedious mixing of the many formulas. This system, originally sold as a packaged product and now sold as individual components (see Resources on page 268 for suppliers of these products), is one that we used with graduate students when we were college adjunct professors. The system not only enables you to produce burnished gold, but also offers a worthwhile, less-intimidating introduction to the materials and techniques involved in water gilding than the traditional method.

PATINATION FOR LEAF

The word patina refers to any film, coloring, or incrustation that has developed gradually over time on a surface due to long use and exposure to the environment. Patinas on leaf run the gamut from fly specks and a little film of dirt here and there to thickly caked material that covers almost the entire leafed surface.

Recreating or matching patinas on leaf—a process called *patination*—involves using media that produce an unlimited range of effects, from translucent to incrusted. The following media and techniques are merely an introduction to the myriad possibilities for aging a surface. When restoring or matching an object's patina, experiment and test on prepared and leafed sample surfaces that duplicate the original surface as closely as possible. Keep careful, complete records of all techniques and layers used on each test, so you'll be able to duplicate later those you deem suitable.

To increase your knowledge of patinas, look at as many different kinds of aged surfaces as possible on objects in museums, antique shops, and auction houses. Train your eye to distinguish between authentic patinas and fake ones (among other things, repetitive patterns of wear and incorrect patinas on leaf—such as tarnish on what purports to be real gold—can indicate fakes). Also note that wear, aging, surface appearance, and texture develop from various causes, including certain chemical and environmental reactions. Bear in mind that even experts can be deceived, as has occasionally proven the case when contemporary wood and pigment analysis cast a different light on a prior assessment.

While the information below has been written primarily for working with leafed surfaces, much of it can also be used, or adapted, for restoring painted or plain surfaces. Always keep in mind that any recognizable pattern, tool, or brushwork from your restoration processes will spoil your effort to create natural, aged-looking patinas that blend with their surrounding surfaces.

BUILDING A TOOLKIT: PATINATION MEDIA, TOOLS, AND SUUPLIES

Below you will find the materials you need to for patination:

Water-based media

→ Casein paint
→ Gouache paints
→ Acrylic paints

Paint-thinner-based media

→ Artist's oil tube paints
→ Asphaltum (brownish-black substance derived from petroleum that produces a range of rich, light-to-dark, semi-transparent films)
→ Wax
→ Varnish

Alcohol-based media

→ Shellac
→ Alcohol-soluble aniline dye powders

Other tools and supplies

→ Soft-haired and stiff-bristled brushes
→ Marine sponges
→ Chamois
→ Cheesecloth squares
→ Abrasive papers
→ Steel wool
→ Masking tape
→ Single-edged razor blades
→ Rottenstone
→ Powdered pigments
→ Whiting (natural calcium-carbonate chalk)

Patinas on Gold Leaf

Antique objects gilded with gold leaf have usually been subjected to two main abuses: (1) accumulations of substances (like candle smoke, incorrect cleaning materials, careless waxing, and fly specks); and (2) the loss of gold (and possibly bole and gesso down to wood) due to wear and abrasion. (We'll discuss how to duplicate both types of patinas later in this chapter.)

The detail in the photo bottom left of a neoclassical, late-eighteenth-century English sideboard is a good example of a surface marred by accretions. Note the dirt, dried polish, and grime around the gilded area that once held a scallop shell and now holds only a few globs of dried brown hide glue.

The detail at far left from an eighteenth-century English sideboard shows sideboard accretions around mint-condition gilding from which a gilded scallop-shell ornament had disappeared. At left, the detail shows the loss of leaf, red bole, and gesso from the surface of an early-eighteenth-century mirror frame.

The detail at bottom right on page 217 of an early-eighteenth-century gilded frame shows the second type of common patina, wear and abuse. This can be caused by very slight abrasion or, as in this example, by more extensive damage that wears all the way through the leaf, bole, and gesso, exposing the original wood carving in several places.

Choosing Media for Patination

Before you can choose media to duplicate original patinas on an object you're restoring, you must first analyze the surface. You need to determine whether you'll be working on the leaf as it exists in an undamaged state (meaning the object didn't get any abuse, only accretions) or you need to match the age of the surface (the leaf and possibly the undercoats, down to the initial wood structure) by physically damaging them. Several aging possibilities are presented further in Simulating Age and Wear on page 223.

Over the years we've used media with three solvents—water, mineral spirits, and alcohol—to produce the visual and textural patinas we were trying to match. When you must match original patinas using various media, be aware of the possible adverse reaction that the solvent in one layer may have on a previous or future layer; and refer to The Concept of Layering on page 140 in Chapter 7 to become familiar with the rules of layering media. The information that follows will help you choose media for matching patinas on leaf or other surfaces.

WATER-BASED MEDIA

Water-based media can be mixed with any other water-soluble medium, for instance, watercolor, casein, gouache, and acrylic paints. However, be aware of two facts about acrylic media: (1) different brands may contain formulated ingredients that aren't compatible with other water-based media (you'll need to experiment to determine this); and (2) acrylic paints are water-soluble only when wet. When they dry, water-based media can be layered over them.

When applying a water-based layer on leaf, you may need to break the surface tension (a surface's resistance to accepting media) to enable the medium to adhere to the surface. To do this, apply the media to be used (or whiting, the calcium carbonate chalk used in gilding preparations) which serves as a mild abrasive), scrub it into the surface with a brush or a wad of cheesecloth, and wipe it off thoroughly. The action of scrubbing the media or whiting into the surface will change it from slick to matte.

ALCOHOL-BASED MEDIA

The alcohol-based medium used for creating patinas is shellac (see Shellac on page 181 in Chapter 8 for detailed information about shellac). Dissolving alcohol-based aniline dye powders in alcohol and then adding shellac to this mixture produces a particularly translucent patinating liquid, whether for subtle, light patinas or rich, dark ones in which more aniline-dye powders have been dissolved.

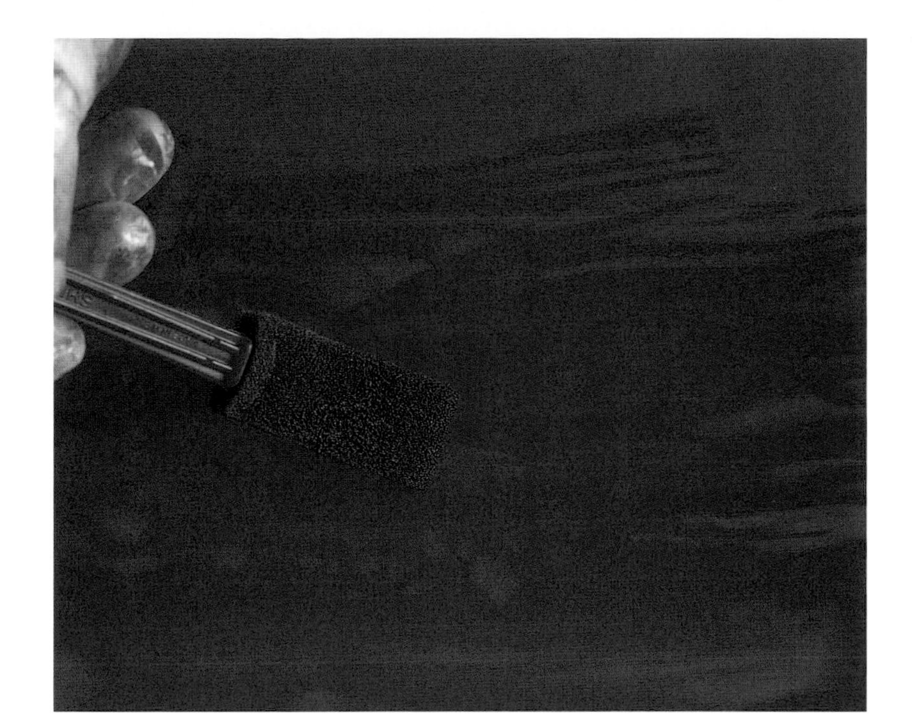

When first applied water-based media often *cisses* (separates into circular openings revealing the base coat below), as shown at left. Whiting sprinkled on the surface and rubbed into the wet media (below) breaks the surface tension causing the cissing.

Dyes vs. Pigments

Dyes differ from pigments in that dyes dissolve completely in a liquid, while pigments (no matter how finely ground) do not. As a result, a mixture made with pigments are never as clear as one made with dyes. Be careful when purchasing aniline dyes (coal-tar products) to specify alcohol-based, since there are dye powders available that use other solvents (see Resources on page 268 for suppliers).

With regard to mixing shellac with an aniline dye power, a good rule is to remember that the aniline dye powders are powerful, and a little goes a long way. For a very light patina, start by dissolving ¼ teaspoon of aniline powder, scooped out, not poured, in 16 ounces of alcohol; then combine that mixture with 16 ounces of shellac. Next try experimenting with different proportions for your shellac mixture, and see what kinds of results you get.

There are many colors of aniline dyes, but those named for woods are especially useful for creating subtle but rich patinas for restoration. To give a warm tone to gold, composition leaf, and copper leaf, choose mahogany, cherry, or rosewood aniline powder; and mix the dye with orange shellac. Oak, walnut, pecan, or chestnut anilines mixed with clear shellac produce cooler colors that are good over silver and aluminum leaf. Add black or burnt umber aniline to darken the mixtures as desired.

Mixing Aniline Dyes

Follow the manufacturer's instructions on the label for mixing an aniline dye. Before opening the dye package or envelope, place it in a larger container so that if any powder finds its way out of the package, at least it will keep the finely ground powder from dispersing all over. Don't pour the powder out, but instead scoop it out gently into another container (a jar that can be covered later and that you won't use again for anything else).

CAUTIONARY NOTE: Since the powders are carcinogenic, you may want to wear a dust mask and be extra careful not to breathe in either the dry powders or let the mixtures get on our skin.

MINERAL-SPIRITS- AND PAINT-THINNER-BASED MEDIA

Because mineral spirits is a higher-quality solvent than paint thinner, we used it for most mixing purposes and reserved paint thinner for cleaning brushes and tools used for applying the paint-thinner-based media. There are many media that are mineral-spirits based, including artist's oil tube colors, varnishes, asphaltum, and wax.

Tips for Working with Mineral-Spirits- and Paint-Thinner-Based Media

Use the following tips when working with mineral-spirits- and paint-thinner-based media:

→ Artist's oil tube colors, when thinned, are very useful, particularly the transparent colors like alizarin crimson and Prussian blue.

→ Clear varnishes mixed with artist's oil tube colors create glazes that are very helpful, although not as sheer as aniline-dye solutions.

→ Asphaltum is a petroleum-based coal substance that has been used since ancient Egyptian times. When mixed with any, or all, mineral spirits, varnish, and/or naphtha (sold as V.M. & P. naphtha—which stands for Varnish Makers and Painters naphtha—and is used as turpentine), it becomes translucent in varying degrees.

→ Wax can be used to dab (also called *pounce*) on a surface before dusting with rottenstone and/or powdered pigments. It can also be mixed with dry powdered pigments and dabbed or brushed on. As well, it can be mixed with any other mineral-spirits-soluble medium to create coarser, thicker-textured effects. Because of its thick nature, no other finish can bond over it except for rottenstone and dry powdered pigments that are sprinkled on. Therefore, wax is the last substance to be applied in creating a patina.

Choosing Brushes and Tools for Patination

Before choosing a brush or tool for patination, think about how that brush or tool will help create the appearance or texture you want. Brushes, which come in many forms, as illustrated below, and tools can be used either to apply or remove media; and each process produces very different-looking results. For example, applying paint with a brush stroke leaves a line or swath in the applied medium. Removing paint with the same brush leaves a thin or thick channel, depending on the brush's width, in the wet medium. Similarly, whether the medium on the surface is wet or dry affects the outcome of any brush or tool technique differently.

Both soft- and stiff-bristle brushes are used for patination. Soft brushes, like the sampling shown at left (along with a foam brush at far right) are used for applying and smoothing media. Brushes with springy bristles, like those shown below, allow media to be manipulated by dragging, pouncing, and splattering.

Also, be aware that brushes and tools can be manipulated in endless ways. They can be dragged, twirled, or rolled; used to spatter, whisk, blend, fuse, or print; worked with wet or dry, handled flat or on edge; and used as is, or cut, torn, notched, crumpled, pleated, or wadded. Each variation in technique will produce different results. Yet while there's enormous variation possible with brushes, tools, and techniques, there's one simple, overarching guideline for any decisions about tools and techniques: Be sure not to produce a pattern that can be identified as coming from a particular brush, tool, or technique.

DIRECTIONS FOR POUNCING

To pounce, start by pouring a small amount of medium on a plastic-lid palette or piece of wax or freezer paper. Load the tip of a stiff-bristled brush held vertically, and off-load the excess medium on a newspaper. Still holding the brush vertically, move over the surface to be patinated. Repeatedly dab it lightly and lift it to apply medium to the surface. Repeat the process, moving around the surface and avoiding creating a row of dabs. The goal is to apply paint without any apparent pattern.

In this detail of a test done before applying asphaltum on a gilded art deco panel, naphtha was spattered on the wet asphaltum-painted test surface to open up areas of the asphaltum to show gold leaf beneath.

DIRECTIONS FOR SPATTERING

Spattering medium will apply paint to the surface. Spattering solvent on a surface on which a previously applied medium is still wet will open up the medium at each point the solvent touches, revealing the coat underneath, as in the photo at left. This effect is called *cissing*.

To spatter, first deposit a small amount of media or solvent on a palette. Then sparingly load a short, stiff-bristled brush (a toothbrush, or cut-off brush) with media, and off-load the excess. Aim the brush at a specific area, and use your index finger to flick the brush's bristles slowly, moving continually in one direction across the bristles. The effect of the spattering is determined by the amount of medium or solvent on your brush, the distance you hold the brush from the surface, and the manner in which you "flick."

For an alternate method of spattering with either medium or solvent, load a stiff-bristled brush, hold it over the surface to be spattered, and rap it sharply on a stick or another brush handle. This will deposit medium or solvent on the surface below the brush. Just as with the other method, after loading the brush, off-load excess medium on newspaper before spattering. The disadvantage of this method is that it usually delivers coarser spatters and gives you little or no control over the spattering.

USING OTHER NATURAL MATERIALS FOR PATINATION

In addition to brush bristles and hairs, tools made from natural materials, such as chamois and a wide variety of marine sponges, can be used to create visual textures that are useful in patination. There are three cautions with regard to using these tools:

1. They must be wet with water and wrung out before using them.
2. When you're finished, clean these tools thoroughly with the solvent of the medium you're using. Then rinse them with water and wring them out again to keep them soft and re-useable.

3. If you find yourself repeating a visual pattern (for instance, applying or removing a medium in a row of repetitive dabs), wipe it off, and start over. The aim is to create a patina with the random patterns nature would produce.

Simulating Age and Wear

Antique surfaces indicate signs of their age by showing faded color, accumulations of dust and dirt, wear on protuberances, and unpatterned disintegration of surface coatings and leaf. The older you want your surface to look, the more leaf, gesso, and bole should be exposed, particularly on edges and other flat surfaces that would typically get highly worn. Think where your object would "wear," based on its design, function, and the circumstances in which it might have been used. In other words, a very fine object would no doubt have been cared for over the years and show less hard wear and abuse than a more modest object.

TIPS FOR MATCHING PATINAS

The following tips may help you match more closely the existing patinas on an object. Experiment with these tips on sample surfaces.

→ To simulate a little wear on protuberances and other areas that would naturally receive wear (like the sides of an object that gets handled or on the bottom of an object that rests on another surface), rub the leaf through to the bole color, using #000 steel wool, or fabric and alcohol, or both. When doing this, be careful not to create a pattern as you rub.

→ For even more wear, hold a single-edged razor blade perpendicular to the surface and scrape off very small increments of surface coatings. Again, remember not to create patterns as you scrape.

→ To duplicate a particularly random pattern of wear or abuse on gold leaf, place a strip of masking tape on a newly laid area of leaf. To produce the appearance of considerable fragmentation of the leaf, rip the tape off immediately. For a less-fragmented effect, let the tape remain on longer. Time your experiments so you'll know which time frame produces which effect.

Starting Points for Patinas

The possibilities for developing patinas are almost endless, and the following processes are suggested starting points for your own experiments with patination.

FOR AN AGED, DUSTY PATINA WITHOUT WEAR

Pounce suitable media over the surface. Repeat the pouncing process to darken edges, crevices of moldings, and the depths of carvings. For even more aging, set the object on newspaper or in a box, pounce wax over the surface with a small, stiff-bristled brush, and then pile rottenstone (pulverized limestone) on the object.

In creating the patina on this small capital, we used a small, stiff-bristled brush to pounce an aniline mixture that would reach the depths of the carving, shown in photo A. To further age the patina, we pounced it with wax. Then coated it with rottenstone (pulverized limestone) to produce a dusty appearance in the depths of the carvings, as seen in B. The capital's restored patina was intended to have a rather formal look, as in C, similar to the detail of the authentic patina on a carved frame in D.

A

B

C

D

An authentic excavated Chinese bronze sculpture, shown in photo A, provided inspiration for creating the verdigris patina on a late nineteenth-century garden sculpture at D. To create the patina, the student started by laying composition leaf, illustrated in B, and then added a layer of aniline dye powder mixed with alcohol and shellac to deepen the tone (shown at C). The final restored piece is pictured in D.

A

B

C

D

Leave the rottenstone on a minimum of 30 minutes. Longer contact with the rottenstone will create a dustier effect. Repeat the processes on the other sides of the object. Then dump off the excess rottenstone and buff the object perpendicular to the surface with crumpled newspaper to expose highlights of leaf on carvings. In this process, the newsprint will deposit a bit of ink to slightly "dirty" the surface, as well. The finished effect (shown in photo C at the top of the opposite page) simulates the authentic patina (shown in D).

FOR A VERDIGRIS PATINA

An excavated Chinese bronze rhinoceros, shown in photo A at middle of the opposite page, was the inspiration for simulating a verdigris patina on the sculpture a student found in his garden. He began by leafing with composition leaf and then pouncing the leaf with aniline powder in alcohol and shellac for depth of tone. Next, he mixed white casein paint with a cool blue-green, red, and raw umber to create a gray-green mixture that he applied to the aniline-leafed surface. Just as it dried, he buffed it with crumpled newspaper to reveal glints of leaf. Then he pounced a light coat of wax over the surface, into which he sprinkled a few red and blue, dry powdered pigments to suggest iron and cobalt in the bronze. The result of his efforts is shown in photo D.

VERDIGRIS OR VERTE ANTIQUE

Verdigris (from Old French meaning the "green of Greece" and pronounced *VER-de-gree)* is the gray-green patina that develops on bronze when it undergoes chemical changes and effloresces. You've seen verdigris on many antique objects, outdoor sculptures, and, of course, the Statue of Liberty. The mid-eighteenth-century excavations at Herculaneum (the city buried along with Pompeii in A.D. 79) unearthed many objects with a verdigris patina, prompting a trend in the decorative arts (especially in the late 1700s and early 1800s) to duplicate this gray-green color on metal and painted surfaces. For an example of real verdigris, see the Shang Dynasty vessel (c. 1400 B.C.) made of bronze (an alloy of copper and tin) at top right, which had once been covered with gold leaf/foil.

Verte Antique (Antique Green)

A dark-green variation of verdigris, known as *Verte antique* (meaning "antique green"), a term adopted later in the nineteenth century and used today, was even more popular worldwide than verdigris in the early to mid nineteenth century. Gilders and decorative artists used various techniques to produce Antique Green, often using bronzing powders and faux patinating techniques that combined gilder's materials and faux-painting such as marbling. A detail of an American window bench (c. 1810) that we restored shows Antique Green on the eagle's body and verdigris on its feathers at bottom right.

Although gold leaf does not tarnish or undergo chemical changes—meaning it never acquires verdigris—this patina can be produced chemically on nonprecious leaf containing copper: copper leaf, composition leaf, and variegated leaf. There are innumerable formulas for producing chemical reactions on metal leaf (many found in the Society of Gilders' journal, *Gilder's Tip* (see Resources on page 268), and those available from chemical suppliers. There are also already formulated products that produce chemical changes (see Resources).

OPTIONS FOR RESTORING GILDED OBJECTS

When restoring a gilded object, there are two possible approaches, depending on the state of the damaged object. When a large area of the object's gilded surface and patina still exist, you can match and unify the object's patina after restoring the missing gilding. Alternatively, when almost all the original gilded surfaces and patinas have been lost, you can restore the surfaces to simulate the appearance the original object when made, before being subjected to aging or abuse.

Matching an Existing Patina

In the case of a French Régence framed mirror (c. 1715), details of which are shown below, we found the object in the basement of our client's home where we were to work on it. Analysis of the frame, which the client did not want removed from the mirror, revealed missing carvings, along with random abrasions through all layers of gold leaf, gesso, and red bole, down to the walnut carving.

In addition to the gilding losses, there were missing elements that had to be molded and cast. After these missing elements were molded and cast (see page 96 in Chapter 5 for information on the frame's repair), we applied gesso and bole wherever required. Because little burnishing was apparent under the heavy patina, the client didn't want us to do water gilding. Therefore, we mordant-gilded the frame with slow size and 22kt gold leaf after installing the casts and applying gesso and bole.

Then, after much testing on sample surfaces, we decided to use several methods to approximate the different wear patterns on the original surface. We began with several of the patination techniques discussed on page 223 to simulate the wear and abuse on the frame. Then, to duplicate the abrasions on the frame, we used several grades of

The detail at right of a French Régence mirror frame (c. 1715) shows the original loss of leaf, bole, and gesso, which the masking-tape method of fragmenting leaf and other methods described earlier duplicated exactly. The detail photo at far right displays the surface after we had molded and cast the missing elements, and replaced gesso and bole before gilding. After mordant gilding the mirror frame, we matched the patina in the final piece at bottom far right to simulate the original, which showed considerable wear and abuse.

Our restoration of the eighteenth-century Italian giltwood side table (c. 1735) at top left began with "shopping" broken-off parts in a client's shopping bag to find elements missing from this table. We discovered several missing pieces (atop the table awaiting restoration), but not the right arm for the corner satyr, which we had to mold and cast to replace. Before attaching the arm, we painted areas needing gilding with a layer of yellow-ochre bole (shown in photo at top right). Then we finished the gilding and completed the restoration (shown in bottom photo; the restored arm is on the right corner).

abrasive papers, steel wool, and files, with varying pressure to blend in with the existing, adjacent worn areas. We also used the masking-tape technique (see page 223) on freshly gilded areas, which, when ripped off, brought random flecks of leaf with it.

The final tone and texture of the aged surface was simulated with rottenstone. It was used over a pounced-on wax base and then buffed off with newspaper. At opposite page, below right, is the restored frame.

Replacing Original Gold Leaf

When a gilded object has been coated completely with an irreversible material and no patina remains, the options are twofold: (1) Research similar objects of the period and use their appearance as a guide to simulating an aged patina after leafing the object (in essence, producing a "fake"); or (2) gild the object and have it appear as a new object that came from the shop. In the case of an Italian giltwood side table (c. 1735) that we were asked to restore, the client and curator of the collection opted for the second approach to the restoration, and we agreed.

This restoration began with the client leading us to a massive table in a long corridor. Handing us a Tiffany shopping bag filled to the brim with gilded pieces broken off from many objects, the client asked, "What can you do with this hunk of junk?", referring to the Italian side table (c. 1735) before us. The photo at top left above shows the table's condition before treatment. We had already started work on the broken-off volute foot on the tabletop, shown along with the other appropriate missing pieces that we had unearthed from the bag.

The surface under the dirt and grime looked strange, and our client explained that it had been coated with bronze radiator paint in the 1920s. We made many attempts to remove the paint, but our efforts were causing more damage than already existed because of the fragile nature of the brittle layers. Therefore, before we could re-gild the table, the structure had to be repaired, delaminated layers re-adhered, and missing elements duplicated (including the missing right arm of the satyr on the corner, which we molded and cast to repair). Finally, we rejoined the broken-off pieces of heads, wings, and tails to their respective owners and made all the surfaces level with the areas surrounding them.

After coating yellow-ochre bole on those areas needing it, as shown in the top right photo on page 227, and attaching the arm on the satyr on the right end of the table, we gilded the table (bottom photo).

REVERSE GILDING

Gilding behind glass is a less-common technique than surface gilding, and goes by a variety of names: reverse-glass gilding, reverse gilding, glass-gilding, etched gold leaf behind glass, and *verre églomisé* (named for the eighteenth-century Parisian framer Jean-Baptiset Glomy, who popularized the process of gilding behind glass for his glass picture mounts). Reverse gilding refers to the process of applying gold and silver leaf behind glass, allowing the leaf, when seen through the front of the glass, to reflect a constantly shifting play of light. When paint is used as well, it's known by the German term *Hinterglasmalerei,* meaning "painting behind glass."

Reverse gilding dates back to ancient Rome, and over the centuries was put to exquisite use in many countries in both secular and religious works. It flourished as a cottage industry in many northern European countries, especially in the winter months. In early-nineteenth-century America, reverse gilding was very popular, especially in cities with sophisticated patronage like Philadelphia and Baltimore, and was used for embellishing the glass on clocks, pictures, and glass panels on furniture; see, for example, a lady's writing desk on the opposite page.

The process of reverse gilding is quite simple and involves only a few steps, described very generally below:

1. Gold leaf is laid on the back of a piece of glass according to a planned design.

2. The leaf is then etched through to the glass, opening a fine channel wherever the lines of the design are to appear.

3. A colored coating (most often black) is put over the gold leaf on the back of the glass, which allows the etched design to show through on the front of the glass.

Reverse-gilded and -painted panels inset into furniture, as on this early-nineteenth-century Baltimore lady's cabinet and writing desk, were popular with sophisticated patrons.

Learning the Basics with a Practice Project

Before attempting any restoration of reverse gilding, we recommend that you become familiar with the basic techniques involved by doing a small project from start to finish. We suggest working on a small frame, about 3 inches by 5 inches, which should be readily available in local stores.

Regular glass is fine to use for reverse gilding, but, if you decide to do more reverse gilding, you'll find that old glass is even better, because its irregularities accentuate the shifting qualities of the light reflected by the gilding. You can often find old glass in framed pictures at flea markets, in attics, and so on.

STAND AND LIGHT SOURCE

For reverse gilding, you'll need a stand to hold the glass upright. You'll also need a light source behind the glass to throw light on the areas of the glass to be gilded.

BUILDING A TOOLKIT: REVERSE GILDING TOOLS AND SUPPLIES

You will need the following tools for reverse gilding:

Preparation Tools and Supplies

- → Scissors
- → Measuring cup
- → Water
- → Glass jar
- → Double-boiler
- → Heating unit with temperature control
- → Glass to be restored
- → Bar of abrasive soap, such as Bon Ami
- → Alcohol
- → Tissue paper
- → Pencil and pen
- → Tracing paper
- → Masking tape
- → Transfer paper/carbon paper
- → Grease pencil/marker for glass

Gilding Tools and Supplies

- → Block or stand
- → Book(s) of gold leaf
- → Gelatin sheets or #00 gelatin capsules
- → Soft-haired brushes, 1/4 inch to 1/2 inch
- → Vaseline
- → Gilder's tip
- → Gilder's cushion
- → Gilder's knife
- → Light source
- → Etching tools
- → Sterile cotton
- → Cotton swabs

Backing-Up Supplies

- → Brush for backing paint
- → Tweezer (for restoration)
- → Japan paint (mineral-spirits-soluble, opaque paint) for backing
- → Mineral spirits (to dilute Japan paint)

A plastic cookbook holder makes a great stand to hold a small piece for reverse gilding and can accommodate a light behind it to illuminate your work.

Place the glass to be leafed in an upright, or nearly vertical, position so that the excess size can run down the glass after you apply it. To do this, you can lean the glass up against a block of wood or against a clear-plastic cookbook stand (as we did in the picture above). We've also used other setups, including constructing special frames to hold the glass totally vertical and, for a pair of two-foot-tall glass secretary doors, cutting out the center from the top of a tilting drafting table (you'll see this restoration later in this chapter).

SIZE FOR REVERSE GILDING

As explained earlier in the Mordant Gilding section starting on page 196, size is the substance that bonds leaf to a surface. The size used in reverse gilding differs from that used in surface gilding in that it must be completely clear and leave no residue or barrier between the leaf and the glass. Gelatin answers those requirements.

Size 00 gelatin capsules (the kind your pharmacist uses) were routinely used for years but now seem to be somewhat difficult to find. Hence, sheets of gelatin available from suppliers of gilding materials, as well as from suppliers to the bakery trade, are the currently preferred product. These sheets are scored in a pattern of 80 diamonds, which can be cut apart easily with scissors. Two of these diamonds dissolved in 8 ounces of water make enough size to adhere gold leaf to glass for a large project (for a small project, use one diamond of gelatin for 4 ounces of water). Since water varies in hardness from place to place, however, experiment with other proportions of gelatin to water, if necessary. (If the mix has too much gelatin, the size will be cloudy. If it doesn't have enough gelatin, the gold will not bond to the glass.)

While you're leafing, keep the size warm by pouring it into a glass jar and setting the jar in a pot of hot water on your heating unit. Be sure to turn the control on the heating unit to a low temperature so that the size does not come to a boil, which could make the leaf cloudy.

The bamboo skewer that a student is using here to etch through the gold leaf had its tip sharpened on sandpaper to shape a sharp point.

TOOLS FOR ETCHING THE GOLD LEAF

You can use any tools for etching that have a point to make a channel through the gold leaf laid on the back of the glass. Possible tools include sharpened bamboo skewers, illustrated above, X-ACTO knife blades, scribers, and even sewing and knitting needles.

Steps Before You Start Leafing

Before laying leaf, you should have some idea of what you want to accomplish, which will determine where to lay your leaf. For instance, on the 3-inch-by-5-inch piece of glass that our students practiced on, they made diverse choices, two of which you can see in the photo below. On the glass on the right, the border as well as the center motif required leaf. The glass on the left required leaf only on its wide border.

These two in-progress, reverse gilding projects by students display different approaches to a gilding design: The one on the left uses a small amount of etching on a relatively large gilded field; that on the right opts for a heavily etched, rather narrow border.

PREPARATORY STEPS BEFORE LEAFING

To prepare for actually laying the leaf, follow the steps below:

STEP 1: TRACE DESIGN ON TRACING PAPER

Finalize your design, and trace it on thin tracing paper with a pencil.

STEP 2: MARK DESIGN'S OUTLINE ON FRONT OF GLASS

Place the design under your glass, and trace it on the front of the glass with a marking pen, grease pencil, or other non-water-soluble writing implement. This step establishes a boundary within which you'll place your leaf.

STEP 3: CLEAN BACK OF GLASS

Clean the back of your glass by making a paste of a little water and a mild abrasive soap, wiping on the paste and allowing it to dry. Then wipe off the paste with crumpled tissue paper and clean off any residue with more crumpled tissue paper and denatured alcohol. Do not use spray window cleaners or rub anything on the glass that will leave a hint of liquid or lint.

REVERSE GILDING STEPS

Reverse gilding uses the same tools for applying the leaf as shown in the box on page 197 for water gilding: gold leaf, a gilder's cushion, gilder's knife, and gilder's tip. However, this is where the similarity ends, because a different size is required and the leaf is laid in a different way.

Applying Size to the Glass

Use a soft-haired brush to apply the size to the back of the glass. If you're right-handed, start applying the size in the upper left corner; if you're left-handed, start in the upper right corner. Apply a swath of gelatin size several inches wide and long. Your 3-inch-by-5-inch glass may need only two applications of size.

The size will run down the glass (which is why you start the application at the top of the glass). If you use the outline you inked on the front of the glass as your boundary for sizing and laying leaf, you won't waste leaf where it isn't needed.

Steps for Laying Leaf Behind Glass

The first step is to take the leaf off the gilder's cushion with the gilder's tip. Use the water gilding directions in Steps 1 to 5 on pages 213 to 214 for doing this. Then follow the steps below:

STEP 1: USE A SWEEPING MOTION TO LAY LEAF

After taking the leaf off the cushion with the gilder's tip, use a sweeping motion to lay the leaf on the glass. It's important to use a smooth, unbroken movement to pick up the leaf from the gilder's cushion. Sweep it up toward the glass; bring it close to (but not touching it) the glass; and allow the leaf to "jump" onto the glass. When you're using the gilder's tip for any leafing, especially leafing behind glass, make sure to keep the tip's hairs dry. If the tip's hairs touch the size on the glass, the tip will have had to be dried completely before using it again to pick up leaf. (Remember, this is a practice project, so you can easily wipe off your 3-inch-by-5-inch glass and redo any of the steps as many times as you need.)

STEP 2: APPLY MORE SIZE TO LAY MORE LEAF

Brush on more size just before laying the next sheet of leaf. Repeat the steps for laying leaf, overlapping each sheet 1/4 inch over the one previously laid.

STEP 3: DRY GLASS IN VERTICAL POSITION

After leafing the glass, leave it in the vertical position, so that the size can dry; or, place it leafed side up under a lamp until the applied leaf is completely dry.

ANOTHER METHOD FOR LAYING LEAF: OUT OF THE BOOK

Another method of laying leaf (for both reverse gilding and surface gilding) involves what's called "gilding out of the book," or using a gilder's tip to take leaf directly from a book of leaf. We're including this technique because many gilders have told us that they've never seen it done. Below are the steps for laying leaf out of the book:

STEP 1: PLACE CARDBOARD AT BACK OF BOOK OF LEAF

Slip a piece of heavy cardboard, cut to the size of the book of leaf, in the back of the book.

STEP 2: SCORE LEAF IN HALF

Roll back the leaf and rouged paper with one hand, and score the leaf with the gilder's knife to allow the gilder's tip to pull off the leaf on the scored line. Alternately, open the book of leaf and fold the first rouged paper down in half, so that its top half covers the bottom half. Run your sharpest fingernail, or a bamboo skewer, just above the fold to score the leaf without touching the rest of it with your fingertip, as shown below left.

Far left: To lay leaf out of the book, slip a piece of heavy mat-board in the back of the book, and, holding the leaf and rouged paper with one hand, score the leaf with your fingernail, before using the tip.

Left: After very lightly brushing the gilder's tip in the Vaseline on the back of your hand, place the tip on the leaf's top edge to lift it out of the book.

Photo courtesy of Sydney Miller

STEP 3: RUB VASELINE ON WRIST

Rub a little bit of Vaseline, which now comes in lip-balm form in a handy tube, on your wrist or back of your hand, and brush the gilder's tip very lightly over the Vaseline. Then place the underside of the gilder's tip on the leaf and lift the leaf away from the book, illustrated bottom right on page 233. Once the leaf is firmly attached to the tip, you can swoop it up, as explained in Step 1 of Steps for Laying Leaf Behind Glass.

Steps for Polishing the Leaf

After all the size has dried and the leaf is solidly adhered, you can begin to polish the leaf. Follow the steps below:

STEP 1: REMOVE EXCESS LEAF AND POLISH LAID LEAF

Use a soft wad of sterile cotton to remove the excess leaf and polish the laid leaf. Do this very gently, turning the cotton as you work to prevent bits of leaf that get stuck to the cotton from scratching the next area of leaf that you polish.

STEP 2: CHECK FOR HOLIDAYS

After removing all the excess leaf, check the gilded surface for any holidays (missed areas of leaf—see page 203).

STEP 3: FILL HOLIDAYS

To fill a holiday, use the tip of a fine brush to apply gelatin and size and then a dry brush to apply the leaf. If you have a lot of holidays, you may want to leaf the entire surface again. If you do double-leaf, note that etching through the leaf later will be a bit more difficult.

STEP 4: REMOVE EXCESS LEAF AND POLISH LEAF

When you've finished all the leafing and removed the excess leaf, polish the leaf with fresh cotton, using a little stronger pressure.

After polishing the leaf on the back of the glass, you're ready to transfer your design and begin etching it. Once you've etched the design, you need to cover it with a non-water-soluble coating (a process called "backing up the design") to preserve it. When that coating has dried, you'll remove all the gold that wasn't backed up.

Steps for Transferring the Design

To prepare for transferring the design, gather the supplies below:

→ The design you want to transfer to the glass
→ Tracing paper
→ Transfer paper (a form of carbon paper, available in art-supply stores; white, red, or black is easier to see than gray and yellow) or carbon paper
→ Pen and pencil
→ Clear tape

After gathering the supplies listed above, follow with the steps on the next page to transfer your design:

STEP 1: MAKE TRANSFER SANDWICH

Make a "sandwich" for transferring the design by first putting the leafed glass on the bottom, with the leafed surface facing up. Place the transfer paper on the leafed surface, with the transfer side touching the leaf. Position your design on top of the transfer paper. If your design contains words or numbers, turn the tracing over, so it's backward on the back of the glass to ensure that it will read correctly from the front of the glass (see photo at right).

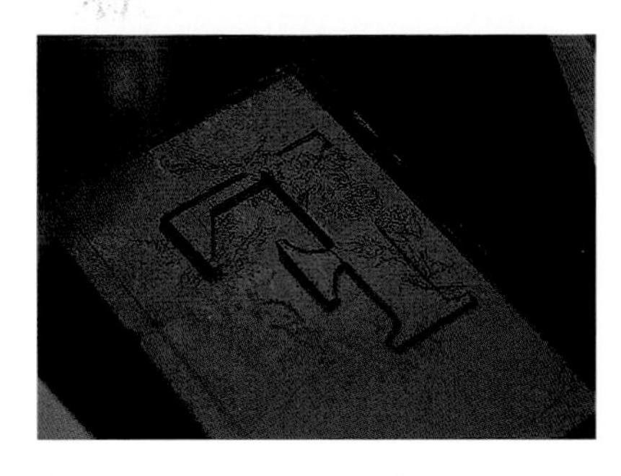

If your design contains words, flip it over so the words will be right-reading in the finished piece after you've transferred your design to the glass for etching.

STEP 2: TAPE SANDWICH TOGETHER

Tape the glass, transfer paper, and tracing together to prevent movement while you transfer the design.

STEP 3: TRACE OVER DESIGN LINES

Trace over your pencil lines with a pen, pressing down hard to make sure the lines of your design have been completely transferred to the glass by the transfer or carbon paper.

Steps for Etching and Backing up Your Leaf

Each tool used for etching the traced design creates a different-width channel in the leaf. Bamboo skewers are particularly useful, because they can be sharpened on a piece of #220 grit open-coat sandpaper to produce points of various widths.

While etching your lines, slip a piece of paper under your work that's the color you want your etched lines to be (the color you'll use for backing). As you etch the traced lines, the colored paper showing through the channels will give you a clear idea of how the finished design will look. For etching very fine details, you may want to work under magnification.

You can use various tools to etch your design into the leaf. Holding the tool (here a bamboo skewer being sharpened on a piece of #220 grit sandpaper) at an even lower angle than shown will produce an even sharper point.

To see how your lines will look viewed from the front, etch them, slipping paper of the proposed backing color beneath the glass. Etched lines look thinner over a black backing (the traditional color) than a white one (A). The black backing paint on these student pieces is drying in D. After the backing paint has dried and locked in the etched-leaf design, as shown in B, you need to remove all the excess leaf, using slightly damp cotton swabs or any scraper that will remove the extra leaf. Photo C shows the back of the glass before the remaining gold leaf on the glass was scraped off.

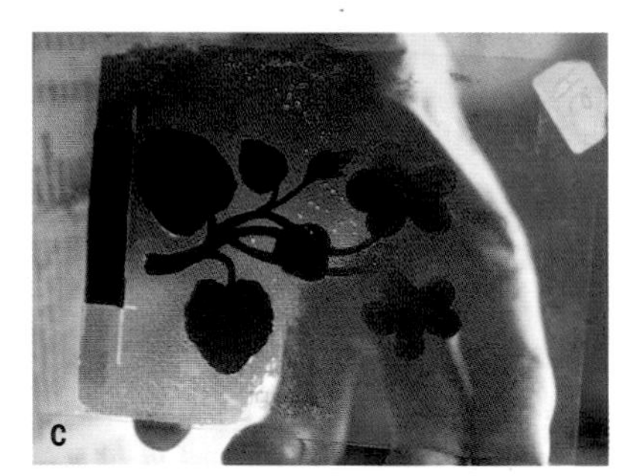

The images above show the various stages of the etching process and the backing up of the gold leaf. Note in photo A the difference in etched lines showing through the glass. Those over black backing paper appear narrower than those over the white newspaper the student was working over. Black is the color most often used in reverse gilding. Therefore, we suggest you etch over a piece of paper of the same color backing that you plan to use. Unless you plan to back up your gold with white paint—unusual, but which we have seen done on several old glasses—using a white surface under the glass provides a distorted idea of the width of the etched lines, which will always appear disproportionately wide over a white backing.

After finishing all your etching, the next step is to "back up" every bit of gold leaf that you want to appear on the front of your glass. This means you will need to brush on non-water-based black, or another color of paint, over the gold leaf and the etched lines you want to save.

Design Options for Un-Leafed Area

While the back-up paint is drying, you can think about the different design options for the area of the glass that hasn't been leafed. For the following three possibilities, you'll have to clean off all the remaining gold leaf (we'll cover that shortly).

After leafing, backing up, and etching your design areas, you can either leave the un-leafed areas blank or paint them black (the traditional color) or another color like the lively red in this student piece.

1. The first option is to leave the un-leafed portions of the glass totally clear, as in the students' work at bottom on page 231.

2. Option two is to paint the rest of the glass black or another color, like red at right.

3. The third option is to resize the glass and lay silver or another leaf around the gold leafed design.

Removing Unwanted Gold Leaf

When the back-up paint is thoroughly dry (so that it has locked in the desired gold leafed shapes and etched lines), you must remove the unprotected leaf from the back of the glass. Slightly damp with water small balls of sterile cotton, cotton swabs, bamboo skewers, or any tool that will get rid of even the most minute speck of gold leaf. We even used head magnifiers to check that all the bits of leaf were eliminated. Gold leaf held by gelatin size is very tenacious, so you'll probably have to spend more effort than you might expect to clean off every bit of leaf.

If you see specks of gold locked in by the paint you've applied, just scrape off the paint and the specks with a cotton swab or a bamboo skewer, and then repaint the area. This can be done while the paint is wet or after it has dried.

RESTORING REVERSE GILDING

In addition to the basic procedures outlined in the practice project, there are other steps involved in restoring reverse gilding when you undertake a real project. You need to document the piece's condition before beginning treatment, remove any detached fragments, decide what must be replaced, reconstruct the original design, integrate new gold leaf into existing gold leaf, etch new leaf, and mix and apply paints to match existing colors. The procedures are outlined below:

Documenting the Existing Condition

Documenting the existing condition of the reverse gilding before treatment accomplishes two tasks: (1) it records what remains of the original gilding, etching, and painting (if any), and (2) it provides the starting point from which to reconstruct the composition. The two best ways to document the original condition of reverse gilding are photography and tracing.

DOCUMENTING WITH PHOTOGRAPHY

Unlike documenting surface gilding with photographs, documenting reverse gilding requires photographing both the front and back of the glass. To do this, you'll need to photograph the glass, both lying flat on a surface and positioned vertically on a stand that is lit from behind. As well, in both cases, you'll also need to change the photographic lighting in order to shoot it at several different angles to capture elements of the piece's condition that may otherwise elude the camera. Photos A and B below show examples of both kinds of such documentation of an American lyre clock (c. 1835).

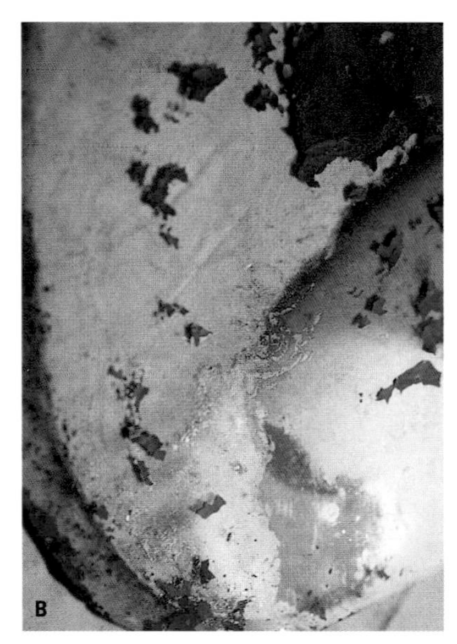

With the usual light setup, photographing the back of this lyre-shaped clock glass shows no gold leaf left from the original design (A). By photographing the piece with raking light held at various angles, however, small "ghost" segments of the gilded design become visible (B).

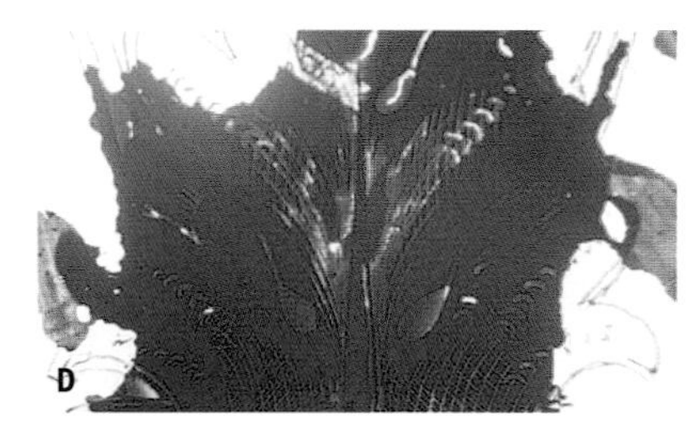

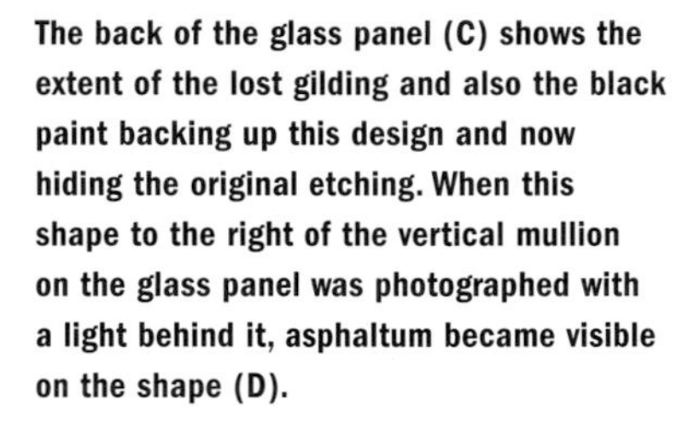

The back of the glass panel (C) shows the extent of the lost gilding and also the black paint backing up this design and now hiding the original etching. When this shape to the right of the vertical mullion on the glass panel was photographed with a light behind it, asphaltum became visible on the shape (D).

Photo A shows very little evidence of the missing design on the back of the glass when the lights were in the usual position (at an angle of 45 or more degrees) on either side. But when the lights were placed at a 30-degree oblique angle to the glass in photo B, "ghosts" of gold leaf appeared, attesting to the tenacious nature of gold leaf over gelatin on glass. By moving the lights, we captured dozens of "ghosts."

In the case of an American secretary (c. 1800), the reverse-gilded back of one of a pair of cabinet doors was first photographed on a flat surface, with the lights on either side, as shown in photo C. Then, photographing the door set upright, with the light source behind it, revealed the translucent backing coat of asphaltum seen through the etched areas (photo D), a use of asphaltum that we would have otherwise not known about. Photo D is a detail of the first shape to the right of the middle vertical mullion (the wooden tracery in glazed doors of secretaries and bookcases) in photo C.

DOCUMENTING BY TRACING

Drawing on the front, ungilded side of a reverse-gilded glass with a grease pencil records what still exists of the remaining gold leaf, etching, and fragments of color. Tracing these lines on onion-skin tracing paper or clear transparent mylar provides both a permanent record of the condition before treatment and also a basis for reconstructing the missing design. Below shows the original condition of one of the four 5-inch-by-2½-inch inset glass panels, all in similar condition, from the secretary's glass doors. The tracing we made from this panel, shown below right, is in the middle of two of the other traced panels.

Above left: One of the inset, reverse-gilded glass panels on a nineteenth-century American secretary shows the extensive losses in the design.

Above right: Pictured are three of the four condition before treatment tracings from the panels. The lowest tracing already had some of the design reconstructed.

You may have recognized the top panel—it's the tracing of the front of the glass of the right panel shown in photo C on the opposite page. We had already begun to reconstruct the motif of the gothic arches in the lowest panel in above right.

Steps for Restoring Reverse Gilding After Documentation

After documenting the piece's existing condition, determine the order of the procedures for its restoration. First, you'll need to eliminate anything that's not, or cannot be, attached to the glass. This will reveal what's missing and must be replaced. If the design is a repetitive motif, you'll probably be able to assemble different parts of the motif to construct one that's complete. Next you'll precisely establish the placement of the gold leaf and etching, and then execute the gilding and etching. Finally, you'll need to mix, match, and in-paint color; and, last, back up the completed work, which we'll discuss in a moment.

STEP 1: ELIMINATE DETACHED PAINT

Carefully remove cupped and brittle paint with tweezers. Fragments, like those in the photo on top of page 240, cannot be made flexible again and re-attached to the glass, but it's important to save as many as of these fragments as possible in a container with a lid rather than an envelope since they may be useful for matching colors when mixing

Remove any remaining brittle paint with tweezers and save it in case you need to match its color for restoration.

paint. Make sure to leave in place any paint that's tightly adhered to the glass. Although it's unusual for any bits of gold leaf to be loose, if they are, gently remove them too.

STEP 2: RECONSTRUCT DESIGN

Make several copies of the tracing you did (documenting the original design on the glass) to try out possible solutions for completing the missing parts of the design. If the design is composed of repetitive motifs, you can probably trace a portion of one motif to fill in the same missing section of other motifs. That's what we did to derive the stylized-acanthus-leaf motif and the painted gothic arches that echoed the gothic tracery of the mullions on the secretary doors (if you need a help reconstructing design, refer to Reconstructing Repetitive Designs in Chapter 10 on page 246).

STEP 3: MARK DESIGN ON FRONT OF GLASS

Wipe off the grease pencil from the front of the glass that you used to trace existing gold leaf and etching. Based on your reconstructed design, use the grease pencil or ink to replace the outlines of the missing design on the front of the glass, freehand, as in below.

To start the reconstruction, draw on the front of the glass freehand with a pen and ink to complete the lines and shapes you discover on undamaged parts of the same design.

STEP 4: REPLACE MISSING GOLD LEAF

Place your glass on the stand with the light source behind it, so the inked outlines for the gold leaf on the front of the glass are visible through the gold leaf and act as boundaries (they'll guide you when laying leaf). Apply the leaf slightly beyond the lines for the procedures outlined in the practice project on page 229, lay and polish the gold leaf.

STEP 5: ETCH LINES

Before etching the lines in the gold leaf, test the width of the lines made by your etching tools on the gold leaf outside the boundaries of the leafed shapes. Use a tool that matches the lines' width in the piece's original etching, which you'll need to view from the front of the glass. After testing, eliminate the excess leaf outside of the inked boundaries, as in photo at right (the piece is set against a flat white ground, which shows the shadows cast from the photographic lights).

When the glass is upright on a stand with a light behind it, it's easy to see the inked lines on the front of the glass when viewing them from the back of the glass through the newly laid leaf because the leaf is so sheer. But it may be difficult to continue the original etched lines onto the newly laid leaf because the original backing of the existing gilded shapes and lines will have obscured the original etching shown in photo C on page 238. To make the process of connecting and continuing the etched line easier, position the glass so its front faces you. Then reach around behind the glass, and make a tiny scratch in the leaf where you think the scratch will start to continue the original line. The light shining through the tiny scratch from the back will show you the line's location. More often than not, your scratching will be slightly misaligned, but it will enable you to reposition a new line nearby and match its width to the original line. Repeat this process to etch all the lines; then re-leaf the areas with the initial tiny scratches. The photo at middle right shows the back of one of the small panels after it had been etched. The original etched and backed lines from the front have been extended and are seen here as white (even though when backed with black, they will appear as narrow as the lines on the front).

Looking through the front of the glass you can see that the excess leaf has been removed from around the inked outlines before etching.

Seen from the back of the glass, the white lines at the bottom and top of the acanthus leaves and within the arches appear the same width. But this is an optical illusion because these lines will appear the same width as the etched lines on the front after they're backed with black.

STEP 6: BACK UP PIECE; THEN REMOVE EXCESS LEAF

Refer to the steps in the practice project to back up the leaf and etched lines, and then, after the backing has thoroughly dried, to remove the excess leaf. Finally, you'll need to mix colors, if needed, for restoring any reverse painting.

Mixing Colors for Reverse Painting

Matching color for reverse painting differs from the regular process of matching color in that once a color is painted behind glass, the underside of the applied paint is what's seen from the front of the glass, and there's no way to adjust it. Therefore, if the color doesn't match, the paint has to be removed.

To mix opaque, solid colors for inpainting, you can usually find clues for these colors in many places scattered around the glass you're restoring (see center photo on page 240). If all else fails, find the needed color by looking at the glass's edge protected by the rabbet (the recess into which glass is installed in a frame), here the grey-blue color at the top of the photo at right.

If you can't find the color that needs to be matched on a reverse-gilded glass, look at the edge of the piece where the color has been protected by the rabbet, or recessed area under the frame into which the glass is installed. Here that color appears along the top edge of the glass.

STEPS FOR MIXING COLORS FOR REVERSE PAINTING

Follow the steps below to mix colors for reverse painting:

STEP 1: BEGIN MIXING TEST COLORS

Follow the color-mixing Steps 1 to 8 in Chapter 6 on pages 131 to 133, to begin the process for matching colors for reverse painting. Keep records of the colors and proportions of each that you use in your mixture.

STEP 2: APPLY TEST PAINT AND LET DRY

When you think you have a match, place a dab of this color on the back of the glass adjacent to the color you're matching, with no intervening space between the two colors. Then allow the paint to air-dry. (Don't use a hair dryer to dry the paint since it may disturb the fragile, original paint.)

STEP 3: ASSESS TEST COLOR(S)

View the test color from the front of the glass. (We always viewed under magnification). If the color matches the original, mix more than you need, and store it in a film canister or other container.

STEP 4: ADJUST COLOR, IF NECESSARY

If the match isn't correct, carefully remove it with firm pressure on a cotton swab or by scraping delicately with an X-ACTO knife blade (try not to remove any original paint). Continue with the mixing-and-matching processes until the match is correct. Be patient; this may take more time than you expect.

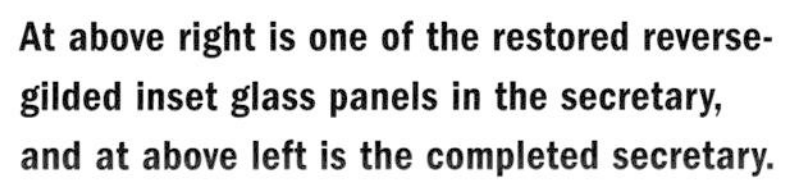

At above right is one of the restored reverse-gilded inset glass panels in the secretary, and at above left is the completed secretary.

STEP 5: INPAINT THE SURFACE

After mixing the correct colors, which is easier on one-color panels like the one pictured above, inpaint where required. The photo above shows one of the completed panels. The photo above left shows the four restored panels installed in the upper glass doors.

To inpaint a multi-colored scene, reverse the normal order of painting a surface. First, paint the colors that you would ordinarily paint last (like dark colors and accents). For example, paint blush color on a cheek before painting the face's flesh color. Then paint backgrounds last. Photo A on the opposite page shows how the reverse-painted scene for a banjo clock looked when we began restoring it. After

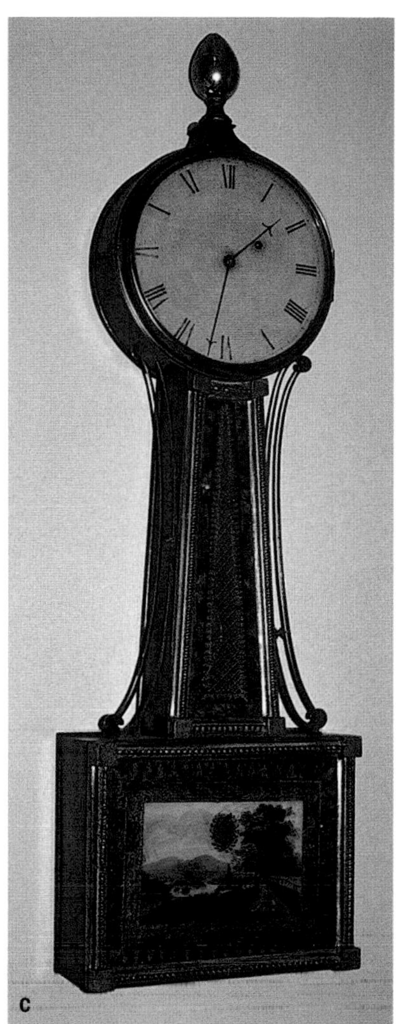

applying the darkest lines first, we painted the colors behind the dark lines (B). Photo C shows the clock with its restored glass.

Laying leaf, whether precious or common, and the myriad possibilities for period and contemporary applications is so uniquely satisfying that it can become a life-long addiction. The Society of Gilders, an international association, welcomes all those who are, or wish to be, involved with any aspect of the gilding arts.

When restoring a painted piece with several colors, inpaint the darkest colors first, then apply the lightest colors—just the opposite of how you would normally paint a scene. In photo A, the reverse painting on a nineteenth-century banjo clock shows the missing areas on the damaged piece. Photo B shows the restored piece, and photo C is the complete, restored clock.

№ 10 ‖ Reconstructing Surface Design

In addition to restoring countless gilded carvings and solid and veneered wood surfaces during our career, we also specialized in restoring ornamented surfaces. In particular, we worked extensively with surfaces decorated with Asian lacquer, japanning, and painted designs with both repetitive and free-form motifs.

Restoring a surface design as closely as possible to the original artisan's intent requires uncovering design clues and investigating and analyzing every bit of evidence you can find about the surface design on your object. In short, you'll need to develop the skills of a detective to solve what may, at first, seem like a design mystery. And keep in mind that you don't need to be an artist to restore a design. In fact, reconstructing a design developed by someone else is quite different from creating original art.

The design on the spokes of one of the wheels of a hose carriage that belonged to the Steinway Piano Company's fire-fighters was reconstructed after analyzing many clues.

RECONSTRUCTING REPETITIVE DESIGNS

BUILDING A TOOLKIT: DESIGN RECONSTRUCTION SUPPLIES

- → Tracing paper
- → Pencil and pen
- → Tape (safe-release)
- → Transfer paper (black and white)
- → Paper for templates
- → Ruler
- → 1/8-inch tape (optional)
- → X-ACTO knife
- → #120 and #220 grit open-coat sandpaper

The actual procedures for reconstructing designs differ from one restoration to the next, but the damaged, designed surfaces fall into two broad categories: (1) those with a layer of paint applied over an earlier surface, obscuring it, which must be removed to restore the original surface, and (2) those with enough remaining clues about the original surface design to enable restoring it. Since the second of the two groups offers the more visible and more readily accessible design information, we'll start there; then we'll move to the more complex process of uncovering and restoring partially or fully hidden designs. And because, in our experience, repetitive designs are far more plentiful in the decorative arts and more easily restored than free-form, nonrepetitive designs, we'll begin by looking at restoring repetitive designs.

The ornamentation on artifacts throughout the ages suggests that their makers had a natural instinct for creating balanced, symmetrical designs with repetitive motifs. Such motifs are among the easiest design restoration problems to solve. What's missing from one motif is likely to be found in a neighboring one; and even if the neighboring motif is itself damaged, the damage will probably be located in a different area from that on the first motif.

Tracing and Transferring Repetitive Design Units

Follow the steps below when you need to replace a missing part of a repetitive design. The object illustrating these steps is an American papier-mâché tray (c. 1848), which had four repetitive stenciled motifs on its rim and bed. After removing the white rings and cloudiness from the tray (shown in Removing White Rings and Bloom on page 173 in Chapter 8), we proceeded to reconstruct the stenciled design that had worn off.

STEPS TO RECONSTRUCT PARTIALLY MISSING REPETITIVE DESIGNS

Follow the steps below to reconstruct a partially missing repetitive design:

To trace an undamaged motif, first tape tracing paper over the motif, using strips of tracing paper under the tape to protect the surface and "extend" the tape to the back or underside of the object, where it can be secured with more tape.

STEP 1: ANCHOR TRACING PAPER OVER UNDAMAGED MOTIF

Find an undamaged repetitive motif on your object to copy; then anchor onion-skin tracing paper over it with special-release tape (see Resources on page 268), testing the tape in an inconspicuous spot on the object to see if it damages the surface. If it does—or just as a preventative measure—slip a narrow strip of tracing paper under the tape as was done on the tray's rim in the photo on the opposite page to "extend" the tape around to the back or underside of the object, where you can affix these extensions with additional tape without damaging the surface.

STEP 2: TRACE NEEDED AREA OF MOTIF

Using a hard pencil, trace the part of the motif you need, along with the lines that surround it.

STEP 3: PLACE TRACED DESIGN OVER DAMAGED AREA

After completing the tracing of the undamaged motif, align the tracing paper over the area with losses, again slipping strips of tracing paper under the masking tape, as described above, to prevent damaging the surface.

After tracing the design with a pencil and positioning it over the needed area, slip the transfer paper beneath the tracing paper and press a pen firmly over the traced lines to transfer the design to the surface.

In this photo, the white transfer lines show areas where the motif will be gilded.

STEP 4: RETRACE DESIGN OVER TRANSFER PAPER

Slip transfer paper under the tracing paper and retrace your initial pencil lines using a pen (don't try to use clear mylar film as tracing paper since it's too rigid for this pencil/pen procedure). If a pencil line remains uncovered by ink, it means the line has not yet been been transferred to the object.

STEP 5: REMOVE TAPES AND TRANSFER AND TRACING PAPERS

Detach all tapes holding the tracing paper in place and remove the tracing and transfer papers. The bottom photo on page 247 shows the reconstructed part of the design, which later was gilded to match the existing stenciling. See page 173 in Chapter 8 for more information about this tray.

Finding a Duplicate Repetitive Design to Trace

If the motif you need for reconstructing an object isn't as obvious as that on the papier-mâché tray, you may have to look carefully to find one with the area you need to duplicate. For instance, in the case of an American window bench pictured below (c. 1810), a section of the left

This nineteenth-century American window bench had lost both mahogany-toned glaze and stenciling (A). It took a while to find a motif elsewhere on the bench to copy for the repair, but, in the end, the right half of the mirror-image stenciled design on the front torus molding offered up what was needed (B). Photo C shows the transferred outline of the neoclassical stenciling, and photo D displays the inpainted design that was etched through to the mahogany glaze. At E is the restored bench.

side of the torus (half-round) molding was missing most of its stenciled design, as you can clearly see in photo A on the opposite page. While examining the symmetrical design on the long, center section of the torus molding on the front, which connected the eagle carvings on each end, we realized that the right half of the design's mirror image would be exactly what was needed to integrate with the few fragments of remaining stenciling on the left front molding, as seen in photo B.

After following the tracing and transferring procedures outlined in Steps 1 to 5 on pages 247 to 248, we completed the outline that included the existing stenciling shown in C on the opposite page. Photo D shows the restored stenciling after etching through to the mahogany glaze, and photo E displays the restored left front corner of the window bench.

Reconstructing Designs with Templates

The previous examples have involved reconstructing motifs on flat or slightly rounded surfaces. By contrast, in the example below, you'll find a solution for reconstructing motifs on a round, three-dimensional surface.

The finials on the feet of this nineteenth-century, rosewood-grained, Baltimore card table, one of a pair, were severely abraded and chipped (A). To repair the graining, we applied a first layer of colored filler (B) and then grained over the colored filler (C).
To recreate the lobbed motif on the finals, we made paper templates, which we placed atop each final (D). Rubber bands held the paper template in place on the finial (E), so we could trace its outline (F). We matched the existing crackle paint on the finals by scratching through the inpainting with the tip of a needle (G). Photo H is one of the restored tables.

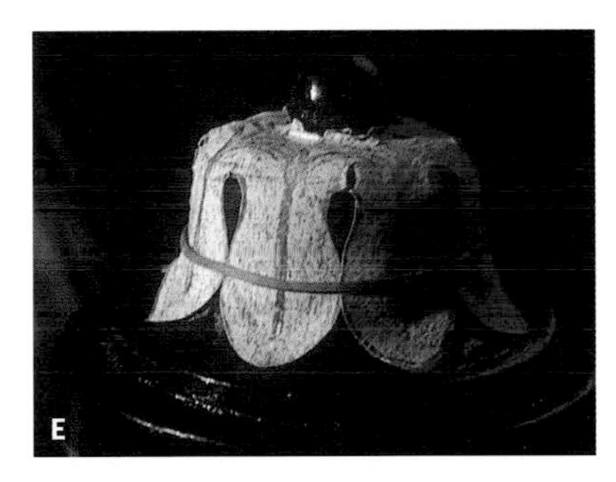

In restoring a pair of Baltimore rosewood-grained card tables (c. 1845), one of our challenges was to develop a motif that would encircle the small, round finials (vertical decorative endings on a structure) on the tables' feet. Only fragments of the original motifs remained on each finial, as photo A on page 249 shows. In B, you'll find a close-up view of one of the finials showing motif fragments and the orange-colored filler that we used to repair the surface before graining it as rosewood. Photo C shows the way all the finials were grained before reconstructing the motif.

We first traced any elements of the design remaining on each of the eight finials, and then assembled the tracings to develop a completed motif. Next, we fashioned the completed motif into a template, pictured in D and placed it over existing fragments on each of the eight finials, one by one, securing the tracing with an elastic band. Tracing the templates produced a complete, correct motif.

After inpainting the finials, we matched the existing aged crackle on the surface. To mimic the crackle pattern of minute surface cracks on coatings that result from wood's contraction and expansion over the years, we inserted the eye-end of a needle into a cork and then scratched the inpainting with the needle's tip. When the restoration was completed, the finials, which are shown in H mirrored with paint the metal mounts we later saw on a similarly styled Baltimore card table from the same period.

RESTORING FREE-FORM DESIGNS

A free-form design (for our purposes in this chapter) is a design with no repetitive elements of any kind. Given this definition, a mirror-image design (such as that in photo B on page 248) cannot be considered free-form, since after tracing half of a mirror-image design, the tracing can be turned over and the missing areas on the other half of the design can be reconstructed. Because free-form designs lack repetitive motifs—and hence sources from which to derive missing elements of a given motif—they are more difficult to restore than repetitive designs. Nonetheless, free-form designs can be analyzed in terms of what they're missing and therefore what needs to be restored. We'll look first at restoring the least complicated type of free-form design: one on a small area. Then we'll look at restoring the most difficult kind of free-form design: large, missing areas of a design that must be integrated seamlessly into an overall existing design. And, finally, we'll look at restoring a design by researching period ornament.

Restoring Small Areas of Missing Design

The easiest free-form designs to restore are those with obvious gaps in the flow of their lines. Restoring such designs usually requires just reconnecting two points where a line appears to be missing. Regardless of how many such missing lines a design may have, this reconstruction problem is easy to solve if you focus on just one missing line at a time.

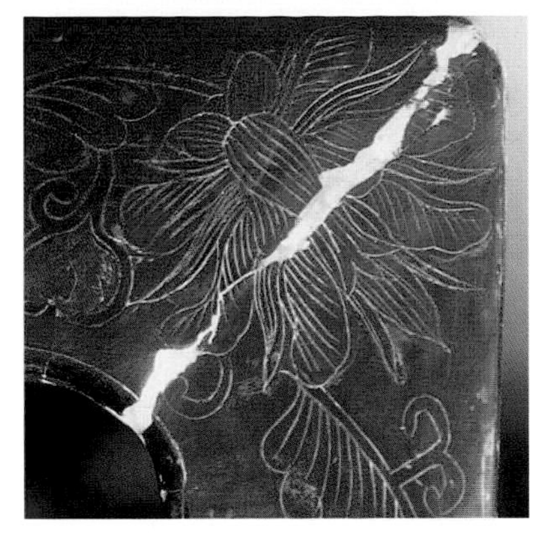

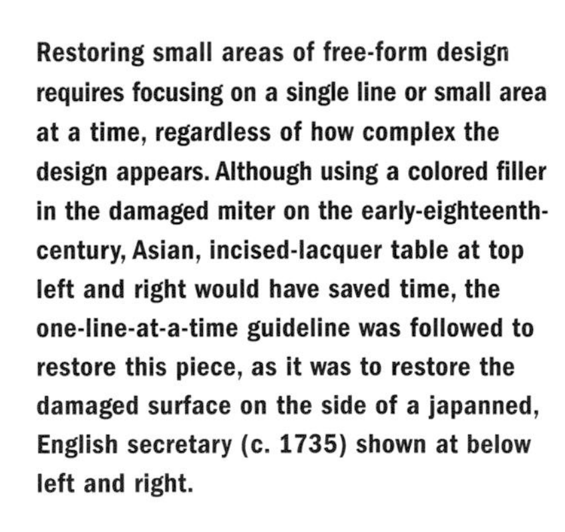

Restoring small areas of free-form design requires focusing on a single line or small area at a time, regardless of how complex the design appears. Although using a colored filler in the damaged miter on the early-eighteenth-century, Asian, incised-lacquer table at top left and right would have saved time, the one-line-at-a-time guideline was followed to restore this piece, as it was to restore the damaged surface on the side of a japanned, English secretary (c. 1735) shown at below left and right.

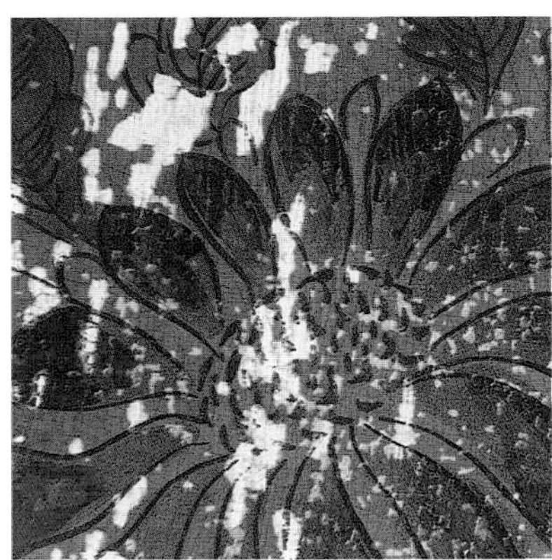

For instance, it wasn't difficult to close the design gap in the damaged miter joint in the eighteenth-century Chinese lacquer table at top left. Concentrating on only one line at a time, we connected each line separately, as you can see in the partially completed design restoration in the photo at top right. (See also the discussion of the rest of this table's restoration in the section Restoring Large Areas of Missing Design on page 252).

Similarly, in the damaged free-form design on the side panel of a japanned English secretary (c. 1735), shown in detail at top left, we focused our attention on each individual line in the restoration. And even though there were numerous lines that required connecting, each individual void was simple to fill in. At top right is a view of the completed, inpainted design restoration.

Again, connecting one line at a time proved the guiding principle for the restoration of the badly abraded surface on this bracket foot of the japanned English secretary.

In the case of a damaged bracket foot on the same japanned English secretary, a detail of which is shown on the bottom left of page 251, even though the design looked quite intricate, the same working principle applied: Stay focused on one line at a time. By isolating each missing line in turn, we successfully restored the floral design (bottom right). See also the photos on page 116 in Chapter 6 for the fully restored secretary.

Restoring Large Areas of Missing Design

One of the most challenging design restorations of our entire career involved replacing an area approximately 6-inch square on a Chinese, incised-lacquer long table from the early eighteenth century. The damaged area of the table is shown at left. The steps below are those that we used for this restoration and will provide you with a starting point for replacing any large, missing areas of a design.

The missing 6-inch-square area of incised lacquer on this eighteenth-century Chinese long table provided a real challenge to restore. The steps for reconstructing this and any large missing design area are detailed at right.

STEPS FOR REPLACING LARGE MISSING DESIGN

Follow these steps to replace a large piece of a missing design:

STEP 1: TRACE AREA SURROUNDING MISSING SECTION
Carefully trace the damaged outline and all the existing design, especially where each line and shape abuts the open, missing area. Make several copies of the tracing to enable you to do "tests" for filling in the missing design.

STEP 2: DUPLICATE SURFACE TEXTURE
Before turning to restoring the missing design itself, be sure to duplicate the texture of the surface on which the design will be replaced. We later applied colored filler (see Coloring Filler Paste on page 77 in Chapter 4) after giving it the ridged appearance of the surrounding original surface.

STEP 3: STUDY OVERALL DESIGN SCHEME
Analyze the entire surface in detail to get an understanding of the design scheme. Does the design display naturalistic, curvilinear shapes and flowing lines, or are its shapes and lines more stylized and less realistic? Then examine the area of loss, paying particular attention to the parts of the design missing from each element bordering the void.

STEP 4: FILL IN MISSING AREAS ON TRACING
Begin filling in the missing area on one of your tracings by extending lines and shapes from the damaged edges into the missing parts of the design. This will create a "border" around the entire perimeter of the missing area that moves inwards into the missing area, reducing its size.

STEP 5: FINISH TRACING
Continue the process in Step 4 of extending the border until the missing area is completely filled.

STEP 6: STUDY TRACING
Put your restored tracing away for a while so that you can look at it later with a fresh eye to find any areas that are out of place or are not in the spirit or style of the original design. Make any changes necessary.

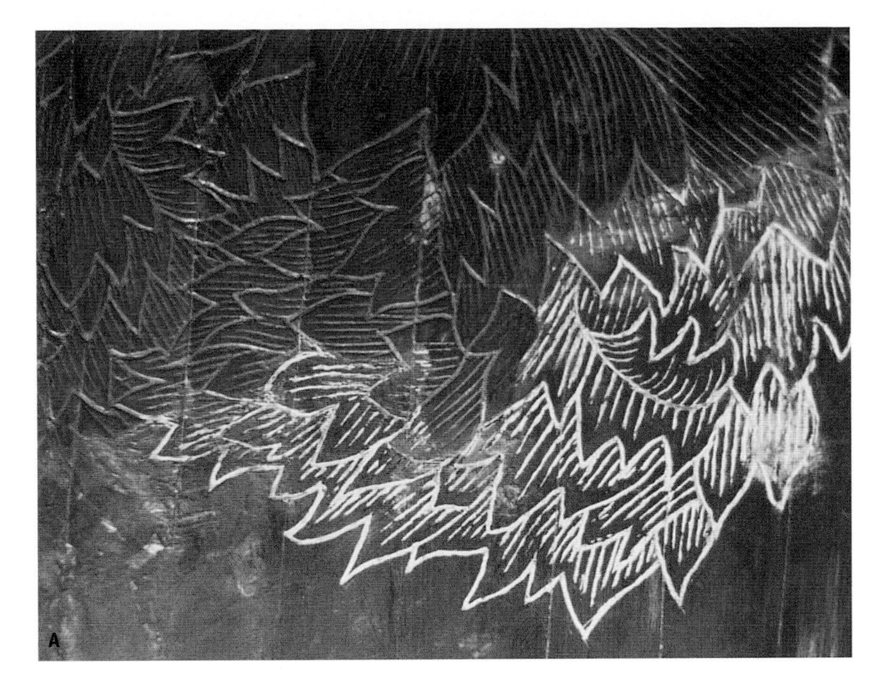

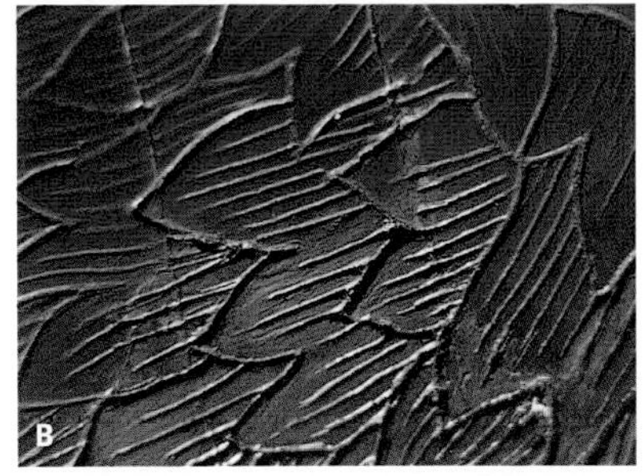

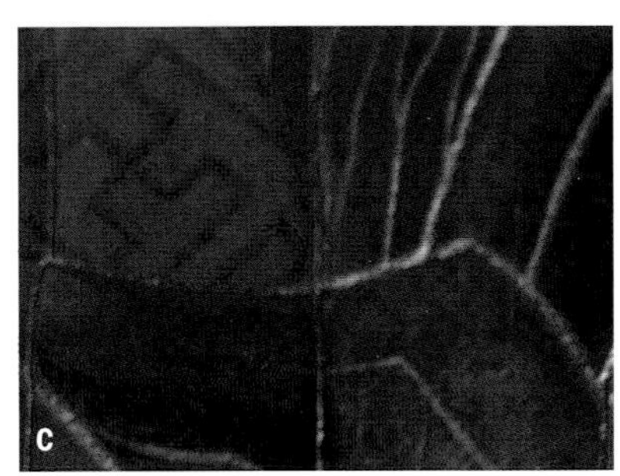

After mixing and applying colored filler to the missing area, we etched the design into the filler with an X-ACTO blade (A). In the detail of this incised area (B), the brown coloring is the undercoat before inpainting the red lacquer color, using the color palette of the tabletop, shown in a detail at C.

STEP 7: TRANSFER DESIGN

When you're satisfied with your revised tracing, transfer the design to the surface where it belongs, using the same process as described in Steps 3 to 5 in Tracing and Transferring Repetitive Design Units on pages 246 to 248.

Since the tabletop we were restoring was covered with incised lacquer, after we had transferred our design, we etched the extended design into the colored filler with the tip of an X-ACTO knife blade, seen in photo A above. The etched lines uncovered the white ground under the lacquer.

At photo B above is a close-up detail of the upper right corner after it was incised. The light brown area indicates the color we inpainted in the newly etched area to conform to the same color we found under the existing red lacquer next to it. We followed the color palette found all over the tabletop, a detail of which is shown in photo C above.

As our incising and coloring continued, the missing area began to resemble the surrounding surfaces. We applied color in layers to duplicate the way color had originally been handled on the piece. The completed area of restoration (photo B) appears on page 254, as well as the completed restoration of the tabletop (photo C).

Research to Reconstruct a Design

When large areas of a design are missing and there aren't any design clues on surrounding areas, you may be able to find the information needed to reconstruct it by researching the design period in which the piece was made. There's an enormous amount of material available for almost every conceivable period of design and style worldwide, and doing research—and using tracings, enlargements, photocopies, and computer-generated aids to get what you need from your research—will help you solve period design problems and confirm that your decisions are correct.

D

Before applying the final colors, most of the newly transferred design has been etched over the underlying colors of each part of the reconstructed design (A). Photo B is a detail of the completed restoration, which is shown in C. For a better perspective, photo D is a similar table from the same period at auction.

Photo D © Christie's Images Ltd. 2006

The four grained English Regency armchairs (c. 1820) that we were once asked to restore provide a case in point. In addition to restoring the gilding and graining, we had to reconstruct the vignettes on the chairs' crest rails. The crest rail pictured at A on the opposite page, one of the four in similar condition, offered us what you see to work with—almost nothing—but nonetheless enough to get us started. Unfortunately, all that remained of the original work was a suggestion of a tree, a wing, and two heads, one of which is shown at B on the opposite page and whose brushwork we duplicated in our later restoration.

Our research into the period offered up many designs featuring chubby *putti* (naked babies), depicted in all sorts of activities. The classic design at C on the opposite page was the inspiration for one of the chairs (each crest rail was restored with a different image). Photo D on the opposite page shows the beginning of our replacement. We included a lyre, a much-used element of early-nineteenth-century design vocabulary. Photo E on opposite page shows the restored crest rail.

When the damaged design is all but non-existent, as it was on the crest rail of this early-nineteenth-century English Regency armchair (A), one of a set of four, search for any existing clues you can find, like the 1/2-inch cherub heads we found in B. Then research the period to find other design information and clues, like the cherub etching typical of the period that we found. Using the etching at C and incorporating a lyre, a common instrument of the period, we began to build our replacement design (D), which is shown completed at E. Photo F is the entire restored chair.

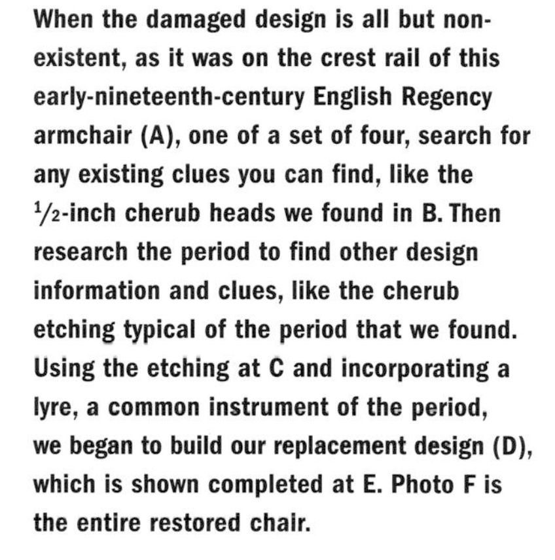

BEFORE RESTORING OVERPAINTED DESIGNS

Generally speaking, original surfaces were usually overpainted at some later date for one of several reasons: an object's new owner might simply want a change; he or she might decide that, as long as damaged surfaces and designs had to be restored, they might as well be painted in what had then become a more current fashion; or the owner might decide that the original design was too costly to restore as it was.

General Steps in Restoring Overpainted Designs

Whatever the reason for the overpainting, restoring overpainted original designs involves the following steps: *design discovery* (finding indications of the original design); *design retrieval* (uncovering existing design clues); and *design reconstruction and restoration* (recreating the design scheme as close as possible to the original). But before you can begin restoring overpainted surfaces, you'll need to address several key questions:

1. Has the original surface, in fact, been overpainted?
2. If so, should you try to remove this overpainting to expose the original surface?
3. What kind of skills and time will be required to remove the overpainting?

The decision about whether to remove overpainting depends on if you're restoring the object for yourself (and whether you have unlimited time, patience, and developing skills) or for a client. If it's for a client, he or she must decide about the extra time, and therefore, additional cost required to remove the overpainting.

RESTORING PARTIALLY VISIBLE, OVERPAINTED DESIGNS

An original design on a damaged object that's had paint or a finish coat later applied over it may still be partially visible or not visible at all. In each case, deciding whether to remove the overpainted or overcoated surface is the first step in restoring the design. If you do decide to remove the surface, you'll need to determine next what time, skills, and procedures will be involved. In general, the process for restoring any original overpainted design will involve finding indications of that original design, uncovering existing design clues, and reconstructing the design as closely as possible to the original (see also Before Restoring Overpainted Designs on page 255). If you (or your client) decide not to remove the overpainted or -coated surface, follow the Restoring Surfaces instructions on pages 76 to 77 in Chapter 4.

A Case in Point: An Antique Hose Carriage

In the case of an antique hose carriage used by the firemen of the Steinway Piano Company in New York City we mentioned in Chapter 1, pictured below, that we were to restore for a museum exhibition called "The Art of the Conservator," the entire carriage was covered with drab tan paint and some ornament and striping, all dating from 1902. However, in examining the carriage's surface, we found that wherever the overpainted surface had chipped off or been abraded over the years, the original designs were partially visible, as seen in photo below left.

Having established that the entire original surface had been overpainted, we needed to determine with our museum client whether we would remove the overpainting and restore the original layer or simply restore the overpainting. While the museum was delighted with our photographic documentation revealing a prior layer and excited by the

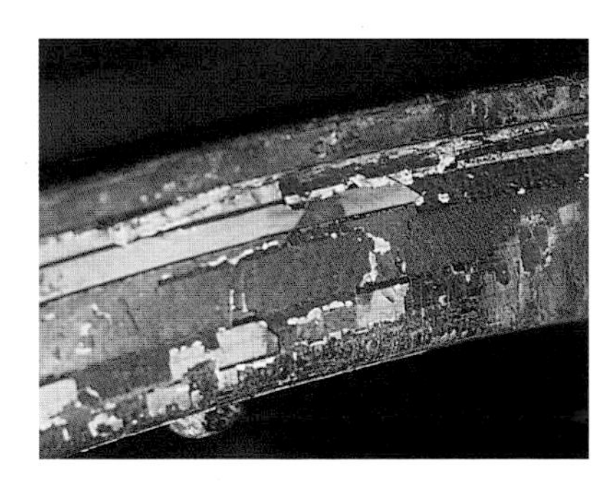

The chipped-off areas of the 1902 overpaint on this fire-fighting hose carriage (right) revealed a prior deep-blue layer with gold leaf banding and red striping (above).

Photo at right courtesy of Strong National Museum of Play, Rochester, New York

possibility of restoring the earlier decoration, the budget for the restoration had been agreed upon, and no more funding was available. Nonetheless, because the museum could send all the carriage's removable parts (except its steel skeleton) back to our studio to be worked on there, saving us numerous time-consuming trips into the city, we decided to undertake the more extensive restoration of the original surfaces. This experience shows that even though a fee may not be commensurate with the actual time you spend on a restoration, sometimes doing what you're passionate about (in this case, restoring the hose carriage) may lead to another restoration. Little did we know that having the restored carriage in the exhibition would, in fact, lead to restoring another carriage, this time for a major motion picture.

PROCESS—AND DISCOVERIES

We began removing the top coat on the steel frame, using the scraping and abrading methods described on pages 118 to 120 in Chapter 6, where you'll also find a discussion of the restoration of the carriage's toolbox. The photo below left displays the condition of the entire frame. The overpaint to be chipped off mirrored exactly the striping and gold-leafed banding of the original layer below. This discovery enabled us to restore the entire spidery steel frame with the correct, earlier design scheme found under the overpaint (photo below right).

Our next discovery was almost exactly the opposite of the first: Similar elements in a structure overpainted with the same design motif may not necessarily bear the identical motifs underneath. In fact, all four large wheels had been overpainted with the same motif adjacent to the wheel hub, which is visible in photo B on page 258. As we chipped off the overpaint on the front wheels, we found the overpainted design duplicated in the layer exposed underneath (photo C). Yet, when we began to remove the same overpainted design on the first of the two back wheels, you can imagine our surprise at finding a totally different

When restoring a damaged overpainted surface, the overpainting may mimic the original surface beneath it, as it did in the case of the steel carriage frame at left.

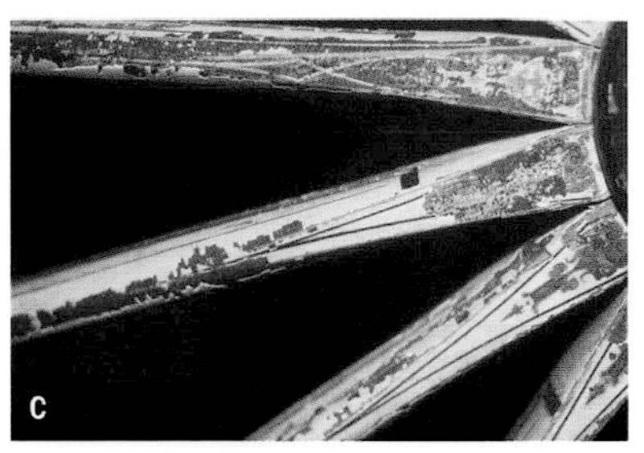

All the design clues were present to guide us in our restoration of this hose carriage, with the final restoration shown at A. The 1902 overpainting mimicked the original motif that it covered, which we could see in the exposed areas (B). As we chipped the overpaint on the front wheels, the overpainted design was duplicated in the layer underneath (C). We found a different motif under the 1902 overpaint (D). At E is the newly exposed motif after restoration. Later, we discovered a mid-nineteenth-century catalog of carriage designs that displayed the two motifs as decal on leaf, which had taken us weeks to laboriously hand paint (F).

Photo A courtesy of Strong National Museum of Play, Rochester, New York

motif emerge on the layer beneath. Photo D shows the new design that we exposed, and photo E displays the same design restored, which decorated both rear wheels of the carriage.

It had taken long hours to put clues together for the designs; and after days of reconstructing the motifs and meticulously inpainting them, we had another surprise: We discovered the two spoke motifs in a period catalog of designs for carriages (photo F) when we were researching prototypes for a lady's carriage for a motion picture on which we later worked. But the ultimate surprise was that the spoke motifs were decals on gold leaf, which cost $1.75 for one hundred. It amused us to find these decals in the catalog and to think that we had hand-painted what originally had been printed mechanically. Nonetheless, we were pleased that our reconstructions so closely matched the original decals.

In the end, the hose carriage had been restored as it was in the mid nineteenth century, pictured in A above: a handsomely decorated piece of equipment used only for parades and musters (competitions), and our restoration brought to life the previously hidden design schemes.

TIPS FOR PAINTING STRIPES

Follow the tips below to successfully paint stripes:

Measure the width of stripes and bands with a ruler, making a mark every few inches. Connect the marks with a ruler (for a straight stripe) or freehand (for a curved stripe or band). When you have a stripe or band along an edge, you can steady your hand by placing one finger on the edge of where you want your stripe to be, and moving a pencil along the entire length, without altering the established position of the pencil or your hand, as we did for the striping on the frame of the hose carriage below.

Make use of design aids from art- and drafting-supply stores for measuring, taping, and creating curved segments and shapes, as shown bottom left. Tapes come in various widths and forms, including configurations that enable you to paint several stripes at once. Below right shows one such striping tape on the far right. See also page 153 in Chapter 7 for hints on using tapes.

To create striped designs, many crisp angles are often needed. For a sharp-angled cut on tape, hold a single-edged razor blade at the appropriate angle against the tape where you want your cut to be, and tear the tape up against the razor blade, as is beginning to be done in photo below to create the striping on the spokes of the carriage wheels discussed on page 258.

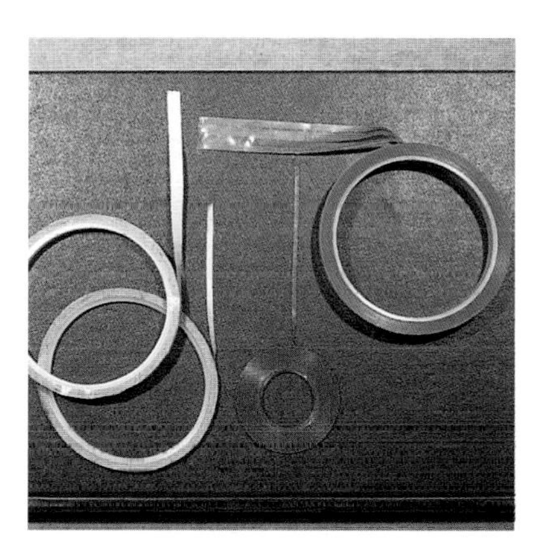

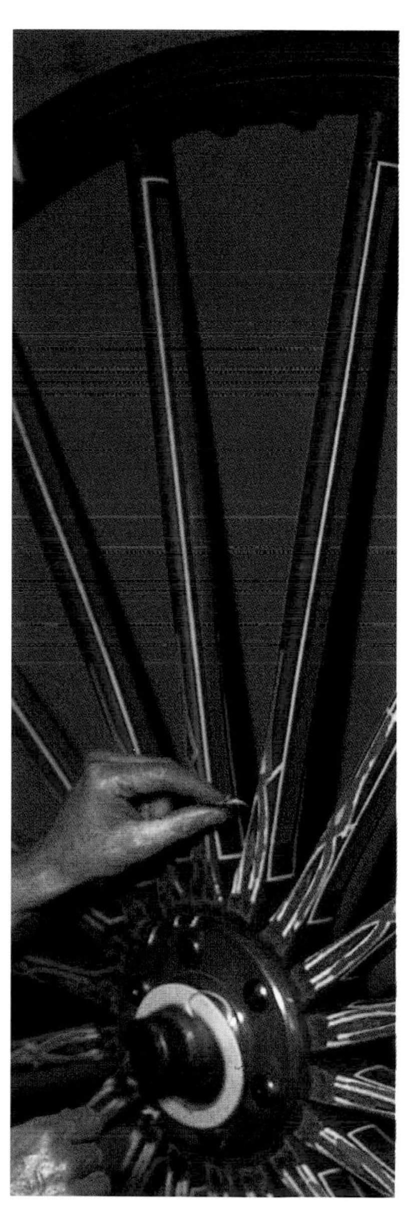

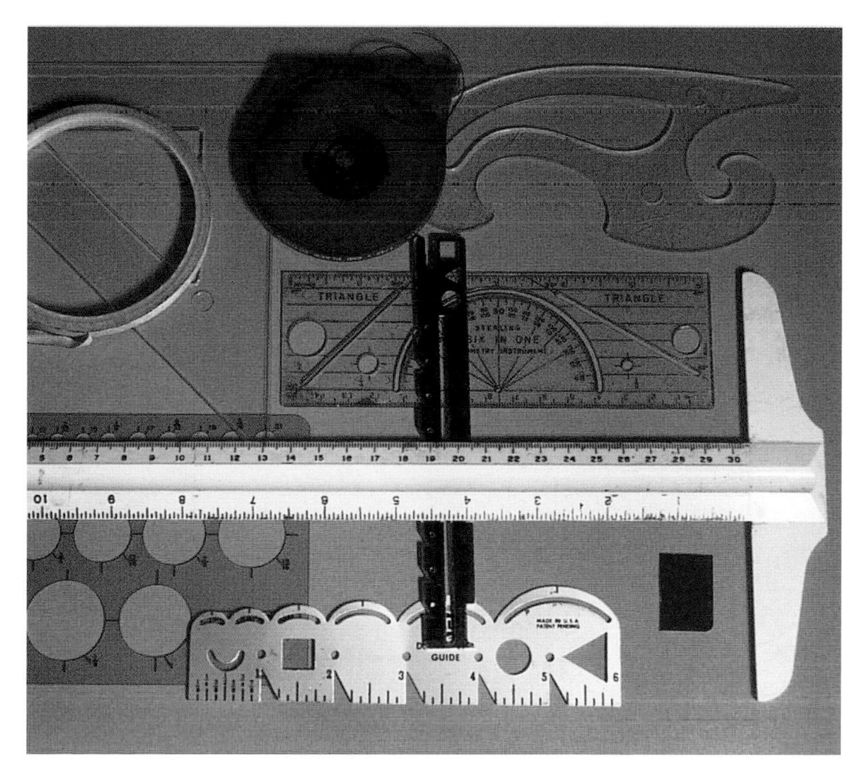

RESTORING PARTIALLY VISIBLE DESIGNS UNDER DARKENED OVERCOATS

Overcoats, in this case, refer to finish coats that once were clear but that have darkened over time, producing the second type of design restoration you may encounter: overcoated designs that are now only partially visible. You can remove these finish coats with the same scraping and abrading methods described in Chapter 6 (starting on page 118) for uncovering color. In contrast to painted coatings, whose pigment bonds more tightly to the surfaces they cover, darkened coatings often help protect the design surface under them from damage; and they usually chip off easily.

In the case of a walnut-veneered and japanned English fall-front secretary (c. 1680) below, it was difficult to tell what the darkened finish on it was covering. But once we had lowered the fall-front, we found the original, mint-condition japanning on the drawers.

When finish coats age, they often darken and obscure the original surface design beneath them. Yet they can also protect that original surface, as they did with the seventeenth-century secretary at right, and can often be easily chipped off. When the secretary's damaged, badly warped fall-front was lowered, a japanned set of drawers in perfect condition was revealed, providing inspiration for uncovering the japanned designs on the front of the fall-front as well as on the entire secretary.

Because design restoration cannot begin until all the structural and surface problems on an object have been addressed, we first had to unwarp the secretary's central panels. But before the unwarping could begin, we had to remove the veneer from the front of the panels. Also see page 32 in Chapter 2 for more information about this project.

In the case of this seventeenth-century English secretary, the fall-front had to have its veneers removed before it could be unwarped.

Removing the Veneer

Removing the veneer should have been relatively straightforward, but this process was complicated by the fact that the veneer was covered with japanning. This meant that we could not remove the veneers the way we usually did, with heat (see the Removing Veneer section on page 171 in Chapter 8), for fear of damaging the japanning. Instead, we used steam, diluted vinegar, and palette knives to work the veneer off the warped panels. At right shows some of the many pieces of veneer that we removed from the two panels, as well as the newspaper we adhered to the back of some of the veneers to provide another gluing surface (a technique that ensures a stronger glue bond, which we learned from Ina's English grandfather). The unwarping of these panels is detailed starting on page 32 in Chapter 2.

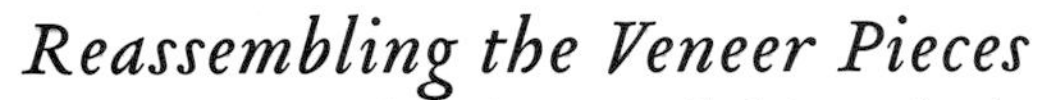

Reassembling the Veneer Pieces

Once unwarped and reinstalled into the back of the fall-front below left, the front of the panels provided the "bed" on which the veneer pieces would be adhered. Trying to determine where each veneer piece went was very confusing since the design was so obscured. Assembling the veneer pieces was akin to working on a jigsaw puzzle, putting the pieces together by shape rather than by design (below right).

Bottom left shows a close-up detail of the center of the assembled veneer pieces before they were adhered with yellow glue, which we knew would soften them enough to relax and flatten them. At bottom right, you can see this same area after gluing and clamping.

At far left is pictured the back of the bed on which the veneer pieces would be adhered. Then, removed veneer pieces were repositioned like a jigsaw puzzle on the front (left).

The pieces were glued with yellow glue (far left), which relaxed them, so they could be clamped and then dried. At left is the same area after it was glued and clamped.

Scraping the darkened finish coating off the secretary's fall-front surface (right) yielded original japanning beneath, as did the same treatment for one of the drawers (far right).

Once the surface was stabilized, we scraped off all the darkened finish to reveal the japanned design (top left). The lower drawers responded well to scraping, as you can see in top right, showing the partially unveiled right half of the top drawer.

We restored the upper and lower sections of the secretary incorporating all the existing japanning (below). In the end, the results were well worth our effort, and the client was pleased to have a restored, late-seventeenth-century japanned secretary in his collection.

Here are the restored fall-front (right) and lower drawers (far right).

Restoring Partially Visible, Overpainted, Inlaid Designs

Another type of overpainted design you may encounter is one in which a design must be restored based on the placement of existing inlays. For instance, in documenting one of a pair of mid-nineteenth-century, Chinese, inlaid-lacquer cabinets, we discovered mother-of-pearl inlays on the cabinet door adjacent to rather crude overpainting on both the door and cabinet frame (below). These inlays were encircled with what

Partially visible, overpainted, in-laid designs present another restoration challenge: On the corner of a mid-nineteenth-century Chinese cabinet (one of a pair), several overpainted areas hid the inlays on the upper part.

DIAPER PATTERNS

Diaper pattern was originally the term for an allover pattern of small, repeated, geometric shapes based on square, rectangular, or diagonal grids (often with identical motifs repeated within each individual unit). Although there's a long history of these patterns used in mosaics and stone work that dates back centuries, the diaper patterns familiar to most of us are those on Chinese decorative objects.

Origin of the Term

The term's origin is shrouded in mystery, with varying accounts put forth. One is that the patterns on the Asian silks imported into the Belgian city of Ypres in the sixteenth century were copied on fabrics woven there, which were known in French as *d'Ypres* ("from Ypres") but incorrectly pronounced in English as *DIE-a-pur,* which, in turn, evolved into the pronunciation of the English word *diaper.*

Another possible derivation of the term comes from the English word *diaper* itself, denoting a white cloth of linen (used in that sense by Shakespeare in *The Taming of the Shrew*). Other sources connect the word "diaper" with the small, repetitive, geometric patterns woven in the white fabric first used in what we know today as a diaper.

Whatever the origin of the term, diaper patterns became so much a part of Western design vocabulary from the mid seventeenth century onward that these patterns appeared on all types of objects, with the repetitive diapers encased within a shaped border, as, for instance in top right, a detail of the damaged drawer front of a japanned English secretary (c. 1735) and bottom right, a detail of the restored drawer front, with its diaper pattern reconstructed.

are known as *diaper patterns,* a motif seen on many Chinese objects (see Diaper Patterns above). Because the fee for replacing real mother-of-pearl inlays would have been prohibitive, our client requested that we remove all overpainting from the cabinets and inpaint both the missing diaper pattern and the inlays.

We began the process of uncovering the inlays on the corner of the frame by abrading the overpaint with #120 and #220 grit open-coat sandpaper, followed by #400 and #600 wet/dry silicone carbide paper, used wet, which exposed inlays around which we could reconstruct the diaper pattern (right). We followed the same process for the upper segment on the cabinet door, which, surprisingly, revealed no inlays. But because we were going to extend the existing diaper pattern into the area to be restored on the door, we weren't concerned.

Abrading the frame revealed the inlays, around which the diaper pattern could be reconstructed.

Reconstructing a Diaper Pattern

After analyzing the original diaper pattern on the cabinet door, we realized that it was based on a square grid. Therefore, to reconstruct this pattern, we first drew a vertical and horizontal grid based on the original diaper pattern on the door at top right on page 264. Then we drew a grid on which to practice this diaper pattern, which wasn't difficult to reproduce. At top left on page 264 shows the curved units placed in each space in the right-angle grid and how, together, they create the pattern known as the *coin pattern.* The crossed grid in the

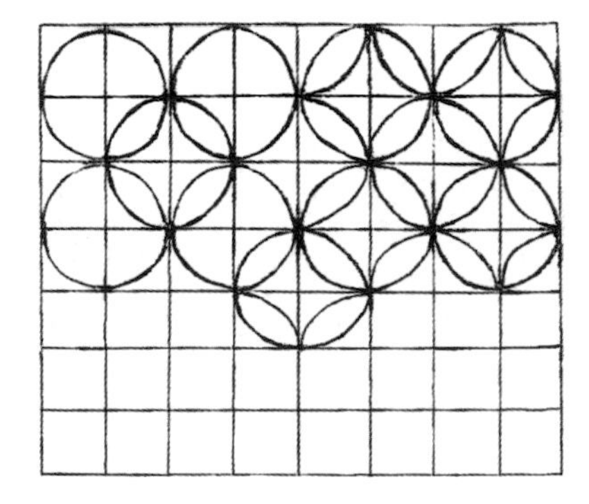

To reconstruct the missing areas of the diaper pattern on the cabinet, we first penciled in the vertical lines of a grid on the filled, smoothed surface (right). Next we added horizontal lines to complete the grid and finally pencil in the curved elements of the pattern in each grid square, as in the sample diaper pattern above.

center of each coin (which we marked with a dot on the cabinets) helped locate the positioning for the small, horizontal and vertical, interior motifs. Of course, if the diaper pattern you're restoring has a diagonal repeat (as in photos on page 263) start recreating it by drawing a diagonal grid.

Once the grid was in place, the process of duplicating the pattern was fairly mechanical since the grid issued from the existing diaper pattern (photo A below). Although you need to try to keep your pattern evenly spaced, be alert to the fact that if the original pattern is askew, you must not try to improve upon it. We used a brush and paint to create the diaper pattern but realized later that it would have been a great deal easier and more efficient to use a special pen that could be filled with paint (see Resources on page 268) because when the brushed and painted lines dried, many of them had to be thinned down with an X-ACTO knife blade.

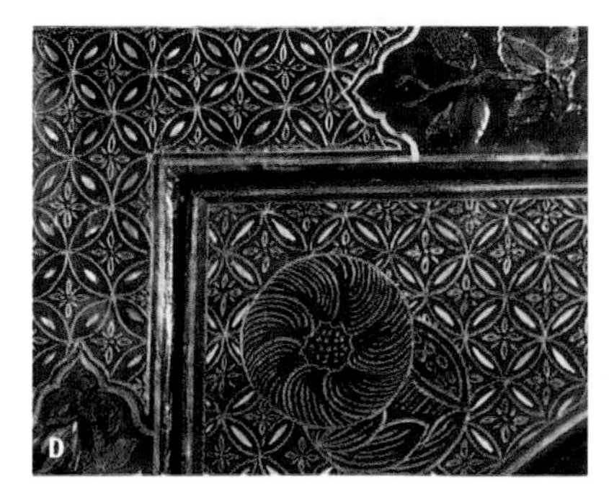

With the grid in place, we painted in one unit of the coin pattern in each grid square (A). Then we repeated the procedures on all the damaged surfaces on both cabinets, as, for example, on the corner of the second cabinet (B), to remove the overpaint and expose the mother-of-pearl inlays, which dictated the placement of the diaper pattern (C). Finally, we inpainted the missing inlays (D). At E are the pair of restored cabinets.

Repeating the same procedures (removing overpaint to expose the inlays, drawing a grid, and adding the coin pattern), we restored the other overpainted areas on both the cabinets as well (B, C, and D on the opposite page). Photo D displays both restored cabinets.

RESTORING INLAYS

Certain restorations may be able to be restored by actually inlaying materials (as similar as possible to the original) into the surface of an object instead of inpainting them. When you're restoring a damaged surface that's being filled and brought up to level with a colored filler (as described in Filling Surface Depressions and Abrasions on page 76 in Chapter 4), embed inlays, such as cut pieces of mother-of-pearl into the not-yet-cured surface so that they become an integral part of the surface, not, as with paint, on top of the filler. (Refer to Resources on page 268 for sources for mother-of-pearl.

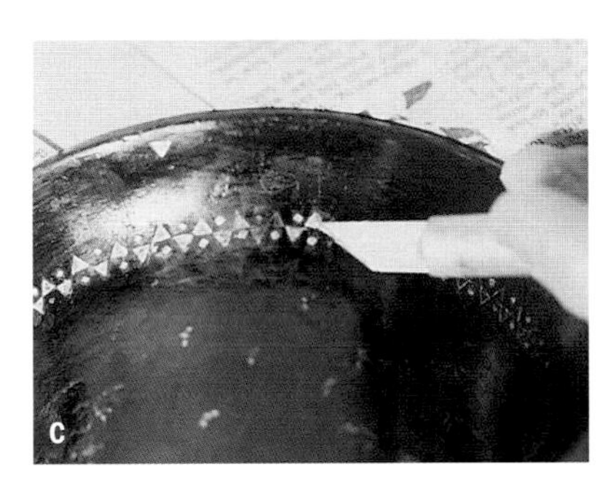

We began the restoration of this late-eighteenth-century, Chinese, lacquer-on-ceramic, mother-of-pearl and shell-inlaid vase by first cutting pieces of matching shell to size with an X-ACTO knife (A). Then we colored filler paste black and filled and smoothed the damaged surface (B) before setting the cut shells in the still-wet filler paste, using the X-ACTO knife blade to correctly position each shell (C).

RESTORING AN INVISIBLE OVERPAINTED DESIGN

The last category of overpainted designs that you might encounter is one that's invisible—that is, one on which the overpainting effectively obscures the original design altogether. In the case of a very early-eighteenth-century Chinese scholar's table, we had been photographing the beetle infestation tunneling in the foot of one of the shell-and-metal-encrusted legs when we photographed the tabletop as a matter of course. Had we not done so, the designs that were under the black painted tabletop would still remain hidden. Whether it was the position of our photographic lights or the angle from which we shot our images (or a combination of both), our photographs revealed many not-quite-distinct shapes on the top of the table that our eyes apparently couldn't see (photo C on page 266).

During the design-retrieval phase, we scraped the surface to uncover the figures earlier hidden by black paint. Among other images that our scraping revealed, for example, was the figure seen in photo D.

After we had retrieved the scores of figures from under the black overpaint, we realized that they all had been made from many pieces of thin, inlaid shell, set into not-yet-hardened Asian lacquer. Oddly enough, most of the shells composing the flowered border were still there when we scraped the black paint off them (photo E). And, surprisingly, interspersed between each "flowered" segment were coin diaper patterns formed from minute pieces of metal, some of which we had to restore with an etching tool and, later, leaf (see the far left of photo F).

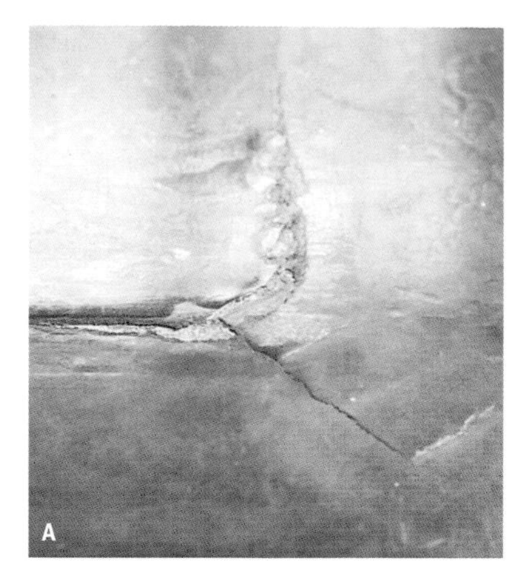

When working on the highly ornamented legs and base of this early-eighteenth-century Chinese scholar's table, we wondered why the top surface was black (photos A and B) while the rest of the table was covered with shell-and-metal inlays. Documenting the table with photography yielded a dim image of a figure on the top surface (C), which emerged more clearly once we had scraped off the black overpaint covering the top surface (D).

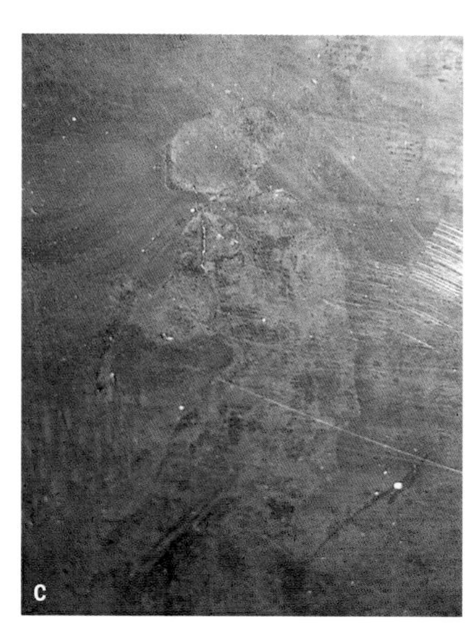

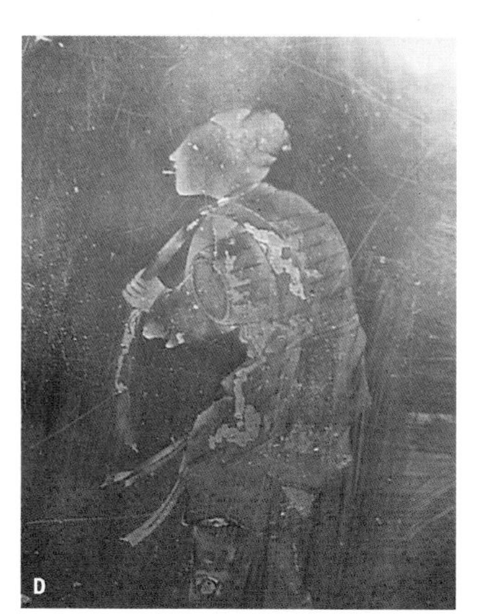

When we scraped off the table's overpainted border, we found intact most of its flowers and leaves, which had been made from the watermelon- and celadon-colored underside of the Burgos shell (E) and minute, inlaid metal, coin-diaper patterns, some of which needed restoration (see the far left of F).

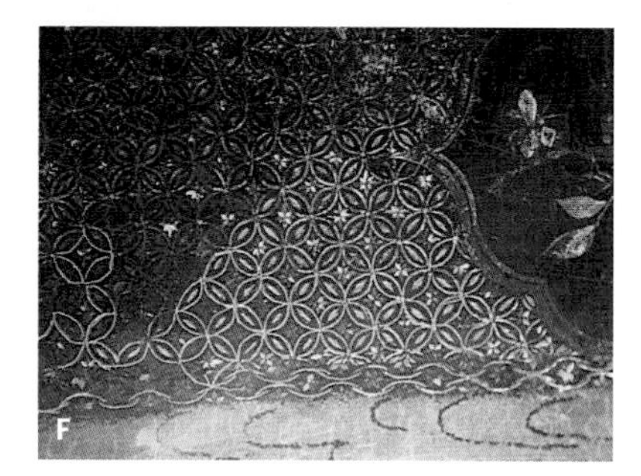

Substituting Leafing for Shell Inlays

It would have been impossible to duplicate the thousands of shells that were missing. With the approval of our client (who had previously requested that we remove the black paint even though she knew this would necessarily increase the time we spent and consequently our fee), we used gold and silver leaf (which is reversible) to fill in the depressions left by the missing shells. After leafing, we etched through the leaf to the black lacquer wherever there was an indication of a separate piece of shell (top of page 267), recreating the look of the original design.

We laid the gold and silver leaf on the tabletop and table's apron with mordant gilding after delicately applying slow size. The figure in the top photo on page 267, the least elaborate of scores of other figures, is in the middle area, above the lower border in the photo below left. The entire procession in the design is shown in the bottom photo.

An inscription in Chinese underneath the tabletop revealed that the table was made in the Manchu Dynasty, during the reign of Emperor Kangxi (so our Chinese sources stated) in the years between 1662 and 1722, during what's called the Kangxi period.

We hope that this chapter has helped you begin to think like a design detective and that, in the future, you'll look with a new, discerning eye at the damaged or obscured surface designs on objects in flea markets, tag sales, auction houses, and the back rooms of antique shops. And, if those objects are also plagued with squeaky joints or missing carvings, for example, we hope that you'll put to use the information in the preceding chapters to help resolve those problems. Finally, we hope this book helps you gain the confidence to undertake the procedures we've detailed for extending the functional and aesthetic life of the objects around you. In the process, you may discover skills that you never knew you possessed—which is exactly what happened to us.

Because of the vast number of missing shell inlays on this table, we restored the design by applying slow size, laying leaf, and then delicately etching it to mimic the missing inlaid designs, pictured below.

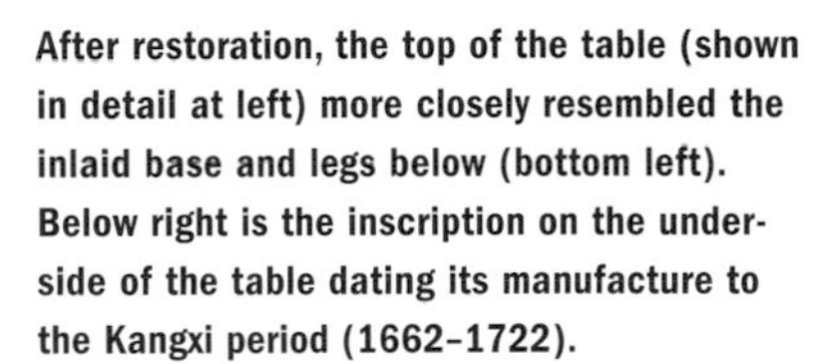

After restoration, the top of the table (shown in detail at left) more closely resembled the inlaid base and legs below (bottom left). Below right is the inscription on the underside of the table dating its manufacture to the Kangxi period (1662–1722).

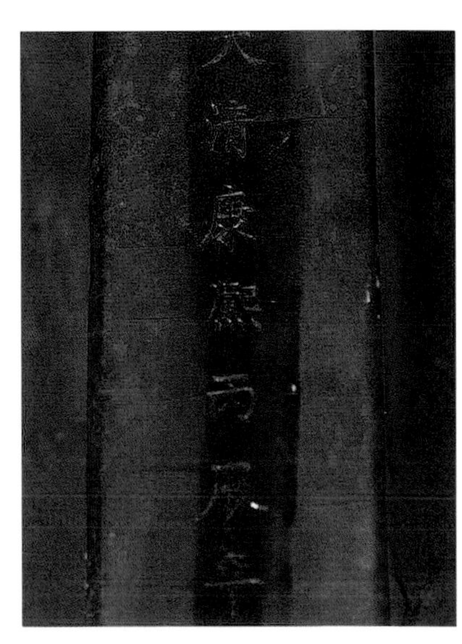

Resources

ACE HARDWARE
www.acehardware.com
(866) 290-5334
Joinery and Hardware Supplies

ADJUSTABLE CLAMP COMPANY-JORGENSEN
417 North Ashland Avenue, Chicago, IL 60622
www.ajustableclamp.com
Ph: (312) 666-0640 | Fax: (312) 666-2723
Clamps

ADVANCE EQUIPMENT MFG. CO.
4617-19 West Chicago Avenue, Chicago, IL 60651
www.advanceequipment.com
Graining Tools

AMERICAN INSTITUTE FOR CONSERVATION (AIC)
1717 K Street, N.W., Suite 301, Washington, D.C. 20006
www.aic.stanford.edu
info@aic-faic.org
(202) 452-9545
Conservation Information and Referrals

APPRAISERS ASSOCIATION OF AMERICA
386 Park Avenue South, 20th floor, New York, NY 10016
www.appraisersassociation.org
aaa@appraisersassoc.org
(212) 889-5404
Appraisal Information and Referrals

ATLAS MINERALS & CHEMICALS
1227 Valley Road
P.O. Box 38, Mertztown, PA 19539-0038
www.atlasmin.com
Ph: (800) 523-8269 | Fax: (610) 682-9200
Epoxy Putty

THE COMPLEAT SCULPTOR
90 Vandam Street, New York, NY 10013
www.sculp.com
(800) 9-SCULP or (212) 367-7561
Sculpture, Mold Making, and Casting Supplies

CONSERVATION MATERIALS, LTD.
1395 Greg Street Suite 110
P.O. Box 2884, Sparks, NV 69431
Ph: (800) 733-5283 or (702) 331-0582
Fax: (702) 331-0588
Conservation and Restoration Materials

DONALD DURHAM CO.
P.O. Box 804
Des Moines, IA 50304-0804
www.waterputty.com
(515) 243-0491
Rock Hard Water Putty

DUMOND CHEMICALS
1501 Broadway, New York, NY 10036
www.dumondchemicals.com
plaway@aol.com
Ph: (212) 869-6350 | Fax: (212) 764-5762
Peel-Away (Non-Toxic Strippers)

EASY LEAF
6001 Santa Monica Blvd., Los Angles, CA 90038-2610
www.NEI-Group.com
Ph: (323) 769-4800 | Fax: (877) 386-1489
Gilding Tools, Leaf, and Supplies

THE FINISHING SCHOOL
50 Carnation Ave., Bldg. 2, Floral Park, NY 11001
www.thefinishingschool.com
Ph: (516) 327-4850 | Fax: (516) 327-4853
Books: Professional Painted Finishes, and Furniture Restoration, Videos, CDs/DVDs, Classes, Supplies

FRANKLIN INTERNATIONAL
2020 Bruck Street, Columbus, OH 43207
www.titebond.com
(800) 669-4583 or (800) 347-GLUE
Titebond (Yellow) and Other Glues

FURNITURE RESTORATION STEP BY STEP
www.FurnitureRestorationStepbyStep.com
Marx@FurnitureRestorationStepbyStep.com
Books, Videos, and CD/DVDs by Ina Brosseau Marx and Allen Marx

GARRETT WADE
161 Avenue of the Americas, New York, NY 10013
www.Garrettwade.com
(800) 221-2942
Woodworking Tools

GRETAGMACBETH LLC
617 Little Britain Rd., New Windsor, NY 12553
www.GretagMacbethStore.com
(845) 565-7660
Munsell Student Set of Color Charts

THE HISTORICAL SOCIETY OF EARLY AMERICAN DECORATION
HSEAD, Inc. at the Farmers Museum
P.O. Box 30, Cooperstown, NY 13326-0030
www.hsead.org
(866) 304-7323
Historic Decorative Arts Information

INDUSTRIAL PLASTICS
309 Canal Street, New York, NY 10013
(212) 226-2010
Plastic Cauls

KREMER PIGMENTS
247 West 29 St., New York, NY 10001
www.kremer-pigmente.de/englisch/homee.htm
Ph: (212) 219-2394 | Fax: (212) 219-2395
Raw Materials for Conservators and Artists

LIBERTY ADVISORS INTERIORS
P.O.Box 531, West Stockbridge, MA 01266
liberty@vgernet.net
(800) 248-5239 or (413) 499-4534
Vermiculation Pens for Fine Lines

W. D. LOCKWOOD
81-83 Franklin St., New York, NY 10013
www.wdlockwood.com
(212) 966-4046 or (866) 293-8913
Aniline Dye Powders

T.J. RONAN PAINT CORP.
749 East 135 Street, Bronx, NY 10454
www.ronanpaints.com
(718) 292-1100
Japan Paints

SEPP LEAF PRODUCTS
381 Park Avenue South, New York, NY 10016
www.seppleaf.com
sales@seppleaf.com
Ph: (212) 683-2840 | Fax: (212) 725-0308
Gilding Tools, Leaf, Supplies, Mother-of-Pearl

SOCIETY OF GILDERS
www.societyofgilders.org
information@societyofgilders.org
(888) 991-7676
Gilding Organization—International

3M PRODUCT INFORMATION
Building 223-4S-01, 3M Center
St. Paul, MN 55144-1000
www.3M.com
(800) 364-3577
Safest Stripper and Tapes

WETZLER CLAMP CO.
P.O. Box 175, Mt. Bethel, PA 18343
(800) 451-1852 or (570) 897-7101
www.wetzler.com
Clamps

WOODCRAFT
560 Airport Industrial Park
P.O. Box 1686, Parkersburg, WV 26102-1686
www.woodcraft.com
Technical Advice: (800) 535-4486
Orders: (800) 225-1153
Veneers and Tools

Further Reading

Drayman-Weisser, Terry, ed. *Gilded Metals.* London: Archetype Publications, Ltd., 2000.

Aronson, Joseph. *The Encyclopedia of Furniture.* New York: Crown, 1948.

Ayres, James. *The Artist's Craft: A History of Tools, Techniques and Materials.* Oxford: Phaidon Press Limited, 1985.

Bigelow, Deborah, Elisabeth Cornu, Gregory J. Landrey, and Cornelis van Horne, eds. *Gilded Wood.* Madison, CT: Sound View Press, 1991.

Cennini, Cennino. *The Craftsman's Handbook.* New York: Dover Publications, 1978.

Crossman, Carl L. *The China Trade.* Princeton, NJ: The Pyne Press, 1972.

Dorge, Valerie and F. Carey Howlett, eds. *Painted Wood: History and Conservation.* Los Angeles: The Getty Conservation Institute, 1998.

Fleming, John and Hugh Honour. *Dictionary of Decorative Arts.* New York: Harper and Row, 1977

Gettens, Rutherford J. and George L. Stout. *Painting Materials: A Short Encyclopedia.* New York: Van Nostrand Reinhold, 1942.

Harley, R. D. *Artists' Pigments c. 1600–1835.* London: Butterworth Heinemann, 1970.

Harris, Cyril M., ed. *Dictionary of Architecture and Construction.* New York: McGraw-Hill, 1975.

Hoadley, R. Bruce. *Understanding Wood.* Newtown, CT: Taunton Press, 1980.

Hope, Augustine and Margaret Walch. *The Color Compendium.* New York: Van Nostrand Reinhold, 1989.

Lincoln, William. *The Art of and Practice of Marquetry.* New York: Constantine, 1971.

Marx, Ina Brosseau. *The Finishing School Presents Color with Ina Brosseau Marx.* Videocassette. Great Neck, NY: The Finishing School, 1993.

Marx, Ina Brosseau, Allen, and Robert. *Professional Painted Finishes.* New York: Watson-Guptill Publications, 1991.

Marx, Ina Brosseau, Allen, and Robert. *The Video Companion Series to Professional Painted Finishes.* 6 videocassettes. Floral Park, NY: The Finishing School, 1991.

Mason, Lark E. *Asian Art.* Suffolk, England: Antique Collectors Club Dist A/C, 2002.

Mayer, Franz Sales. *Handbook of Ornament.* New York: Dover Publications, 1957.

Munsell, Albert H. *A Color Notation: An Illustrated System Defining All Color and Their Relations by Measured Scales of Hue, Value and Chroma.* Baltimore: Munsell Color Company, 1988.

Plenderleith, H. J. and A. E. A. Werner. *The Conservation of Antiquities and Works of Art.* London: Oxford University Press, 1979.

Rivers, Shayne and Nick Umney. *Conservation of Furniture.* London: Butterworth Heinemann, 2003.

Trench, Lucy, ed. *Materials and Techniques in Decorative Arts: An Illustrated Dictionary.* Chicago: University of Chicago Press, 2000.

Turner, Jane M., ed. *The Dictionary of Art.* London: Reed Business Information, 1996.

Williams, C. A. S. *Outlines of Chinese Symbolism and Art Motives.* New York: Dover Publications, 1976.

Yonemura, Ann. *Japanese Lacquer.* Washington, DC: The Freer Gallery of Art, 1979.

Index